BUNNY**DROP** ²

yumi unita

STORY

Upon the death of his grandfather, Daikichi
Kawachi decides to adopt and raise his dearly
departed's illegitimate child, Rin. With the help
of friends and family, the determined Daikichi
struggles over the rough terrain of child-rearing,
which he quickly discovers is full of ups and downs.
In order to search out clues about Rin's mother,
Daikichi returns to his late grandfather's residence
at the end of the year, only to discover . . . !?

MAIN CHARACTERS

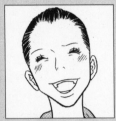

GOTOU-SAN
An energetic, enthusiastic working mother at Daikichi's workplace. A supportive confidante.

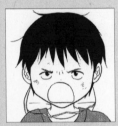

KOUKI & KOUKI'S MOM
Rin's friend from nursery school and his mother.

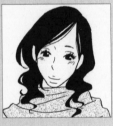

DAIKICHI KAWACHI
Thirty-year-old bachelor. Like a fish out of water around women and children.

RIN KAGA
A smart, responsible six-year-old. Technically Daikichi's aunt.

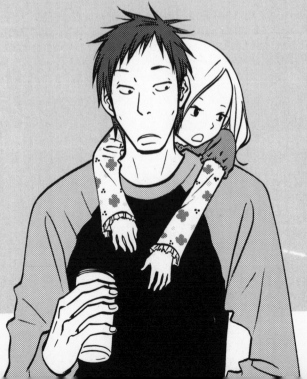

contents

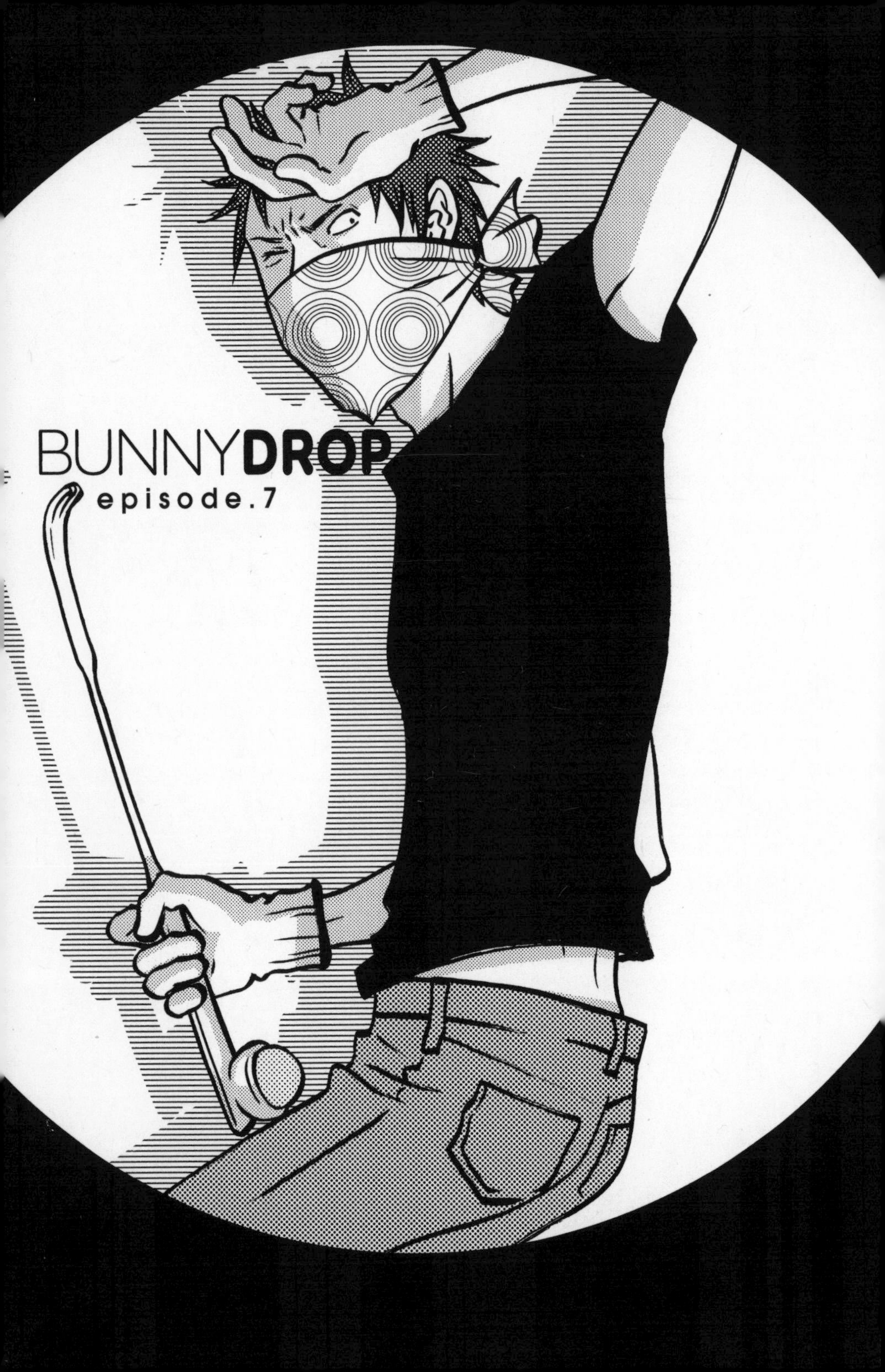
BUNNYDROP
episode.7

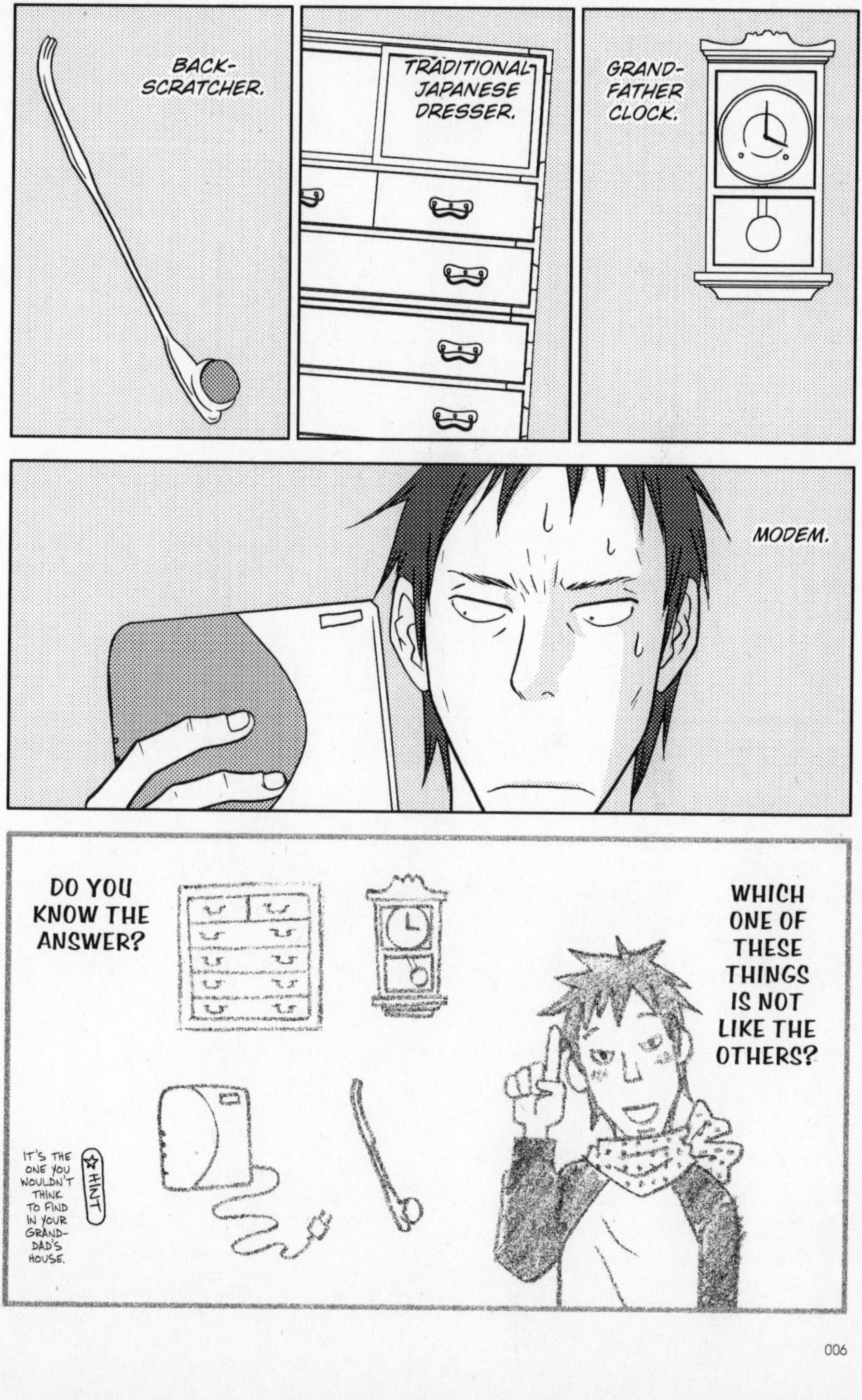
GRAND-
FATHER
CLOCK.
TRADITIONAL
JAPANESE
DRESSER.
BACK-
SCRATCHER.
MODEM.
WHICH ONE OF THESE THINGS IS NOT LIKE THE OTHERS?
DO YOU KNOW THE ANSWER?
☆HINT
IT'S THE ONE YOU WOULDN'T THINK TO FIND IN YOUR GRAND-DAD'S HOUSE.

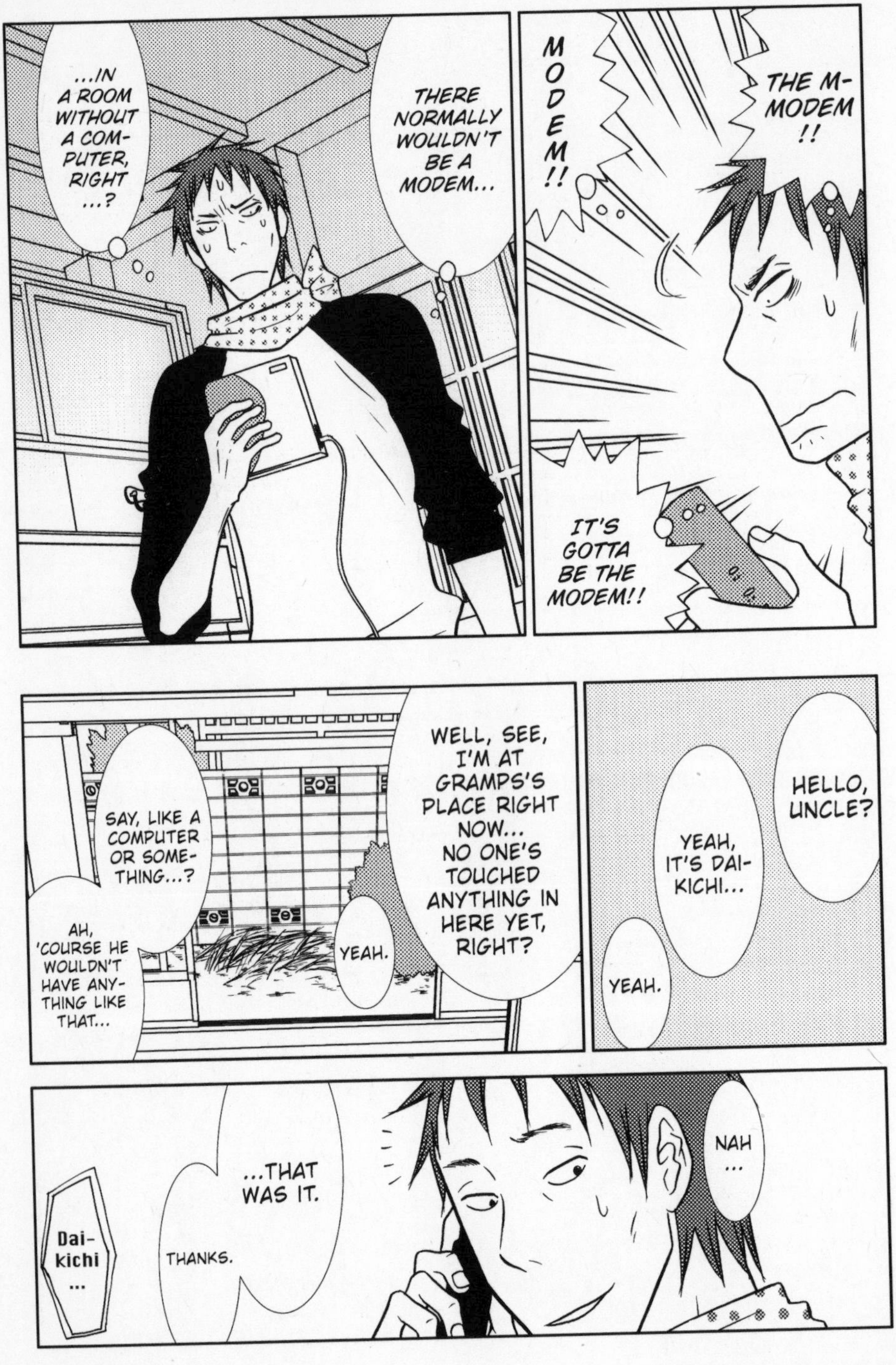
THE M-MODEM!!
MODEM!!
IT'S GOTTA BE THE MODEM!!
THERE NORMALLY WOULDN'T BE A MODEM...
...IN A ROOM WITHOUT A COMPUTER, RIGHT...?
HELLO, UNCLE?
YEAH, IT'S DAIKICHI...
YEAH.
WELL, SEE, I'M AT GRAMPS'S PLACE RIGHT NOW... NO ONE'S TOUCHED ANYTHING IN HERE YET, RIGHT?
YEAH.
SAY, LIKE A COMPUTER OR SOMETHING...?
AH, 'COURSE HE WOULDN'T HAVE ANYTHING LIKE THAT...
NAH...
...THAT WAS IT.
THANKS.
Daikichi...

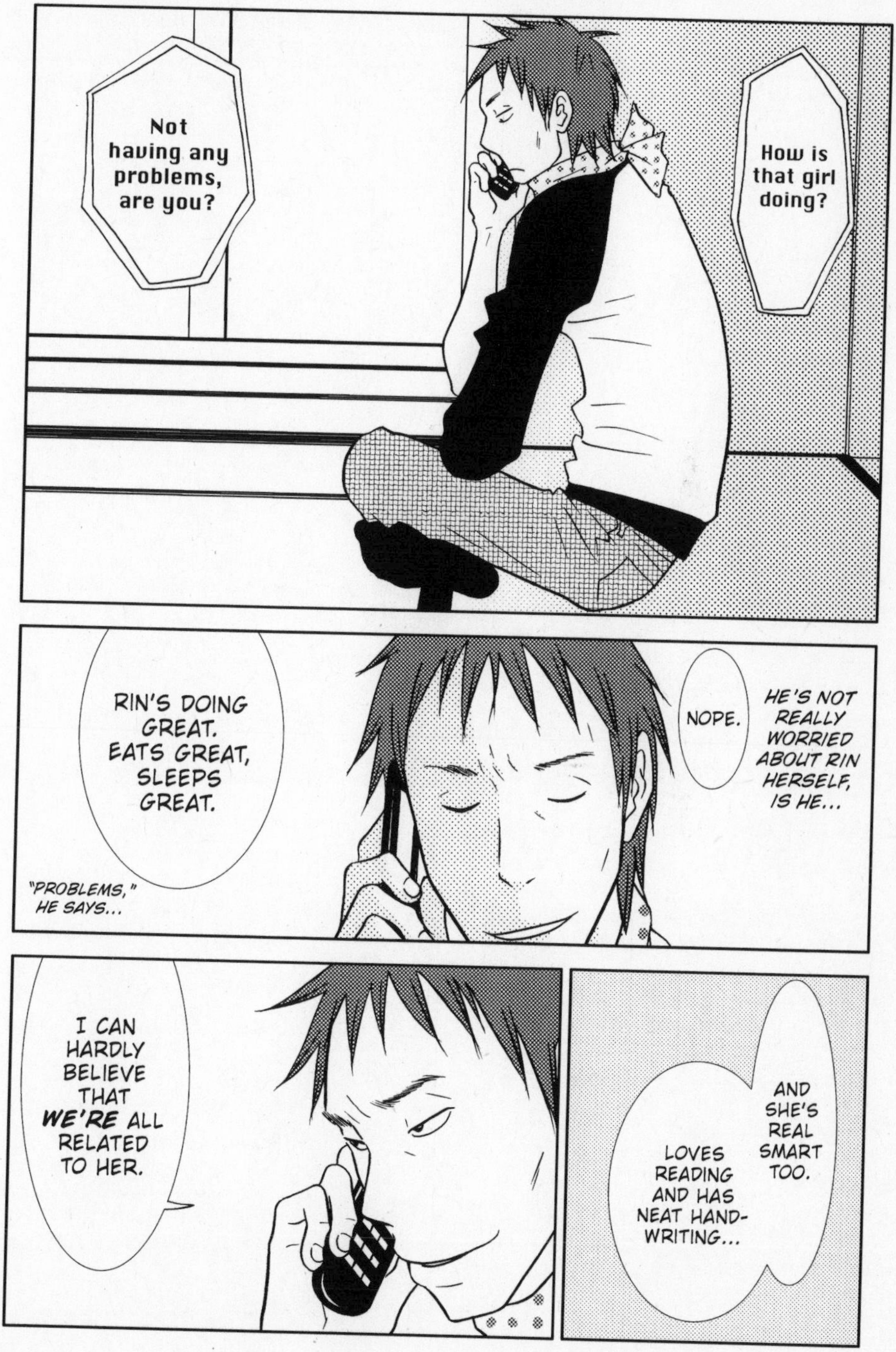
How is that girl doing?
Not having any problems, are you?
HE'S NOT REALLY WORRIED ABOUT RIN HERSELF, IS HE...
NOPE.
RIN'S DOING GREAT. EATS GREAT, SLEEPS GREAT.
"PROBLEMS," HE SAYS...
LOVES READING AND HAS NEAT HAND-WRITING... AND SHE'S REAL SMART TOO.
I CAN HARDLY BELIEVE THAT *WE'RE* ALL RELATED TO HER.

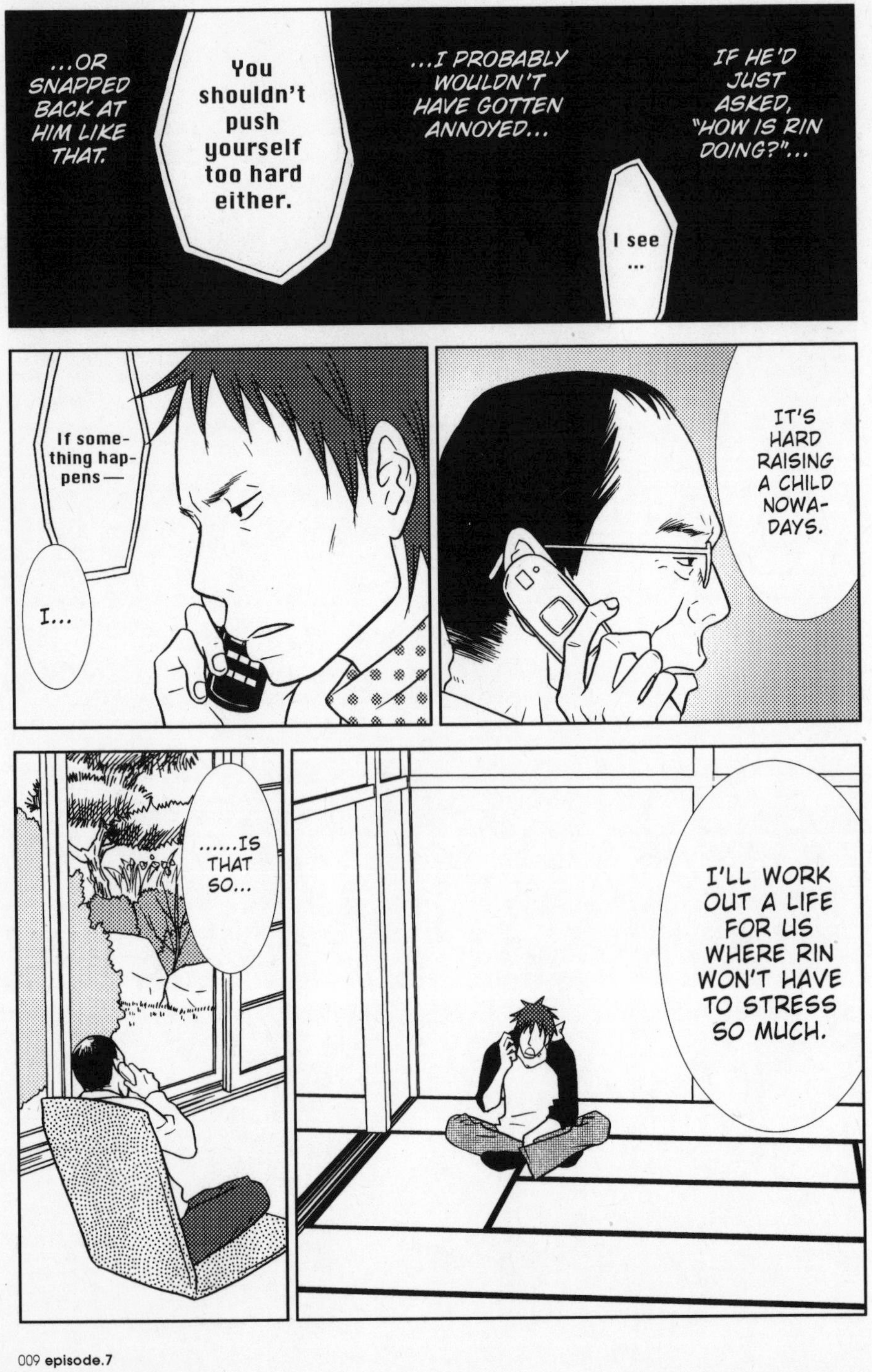
IF HE'D JUST ASKED, "HOW IS RIN DOING?"...
I see ...
...I PROBABLY WOULDN'T HAVE GOTTEN ANNOYED...
You shouldn't push yourself too hard either.
...OR SNAPPED BACK AT HIM LIKE THAT.
IT'S HARD RAISING A CHILD NOWA-DAYS.
If some-thing hap-pens—
I...
I'LL WORK OUT A LIFE FOR US WHERE RIN WON'T HAVE TO STRESS SO MUCH.
......IS THAT SO...

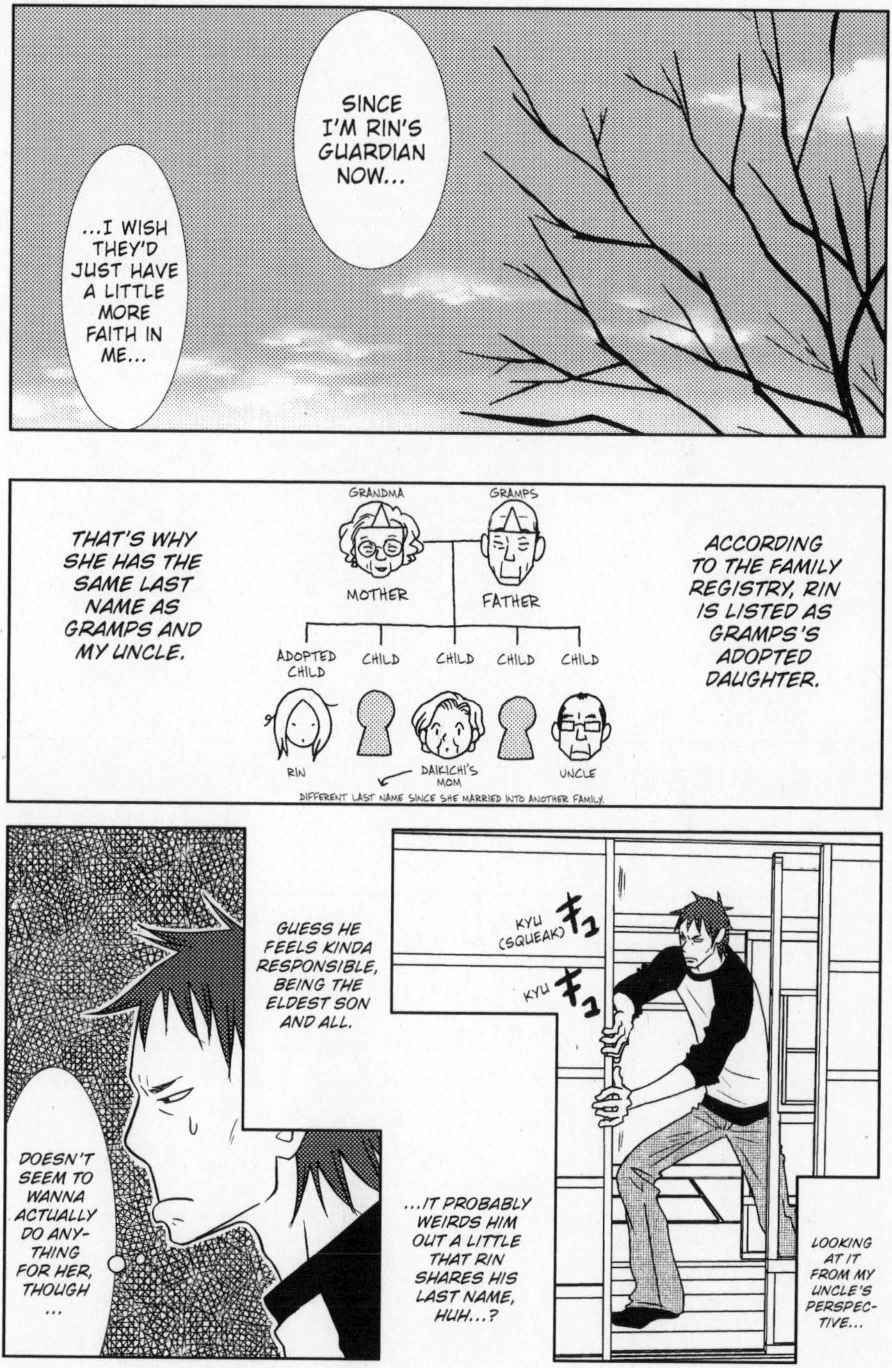
SINCE I'M RIN'S GUARDIAN NOW...
...I WISH THEY'D JUST HAVE A LITTLE MORE FAITH IN ME...
ACCORDING TO THE FAMILY REGISTRY, RIN IS LISTED AS GRAMPS'S ADOPTED DAUGHTER.
GRANDMA
GRAMPS
MOTHER
FATHER
ADOPTED CHILD
CHILD
CHILD
CHILD
CHILD
RIN
DAIKICHI'S MOM
UNCLE
DIFFERENT LAST NAME SINCE SHE MARRIED INTO ANOTHER FAMILY.
THAT'S WHY SHE HAS THE SAME LAST NAME AS GRAMPS AND MY UNCLE.
LOOKING AT IT FROM MY UNCLE'S PERSPECTIVE...
KYU (SQUEAK)
KYU
...IT PROBABLY WEIRDS HIM OUT A LITTLE THAT RIN SHARES HIS LAST NAME, HUH...?
GUESS HE FEELS KINDA RESPONSIBLE, BEING THE ELDEST SON AND ALL.
DOESN'T SEEM TO WANNA ACTUALLY DO ANYTHING FOR HER, THOUGH...

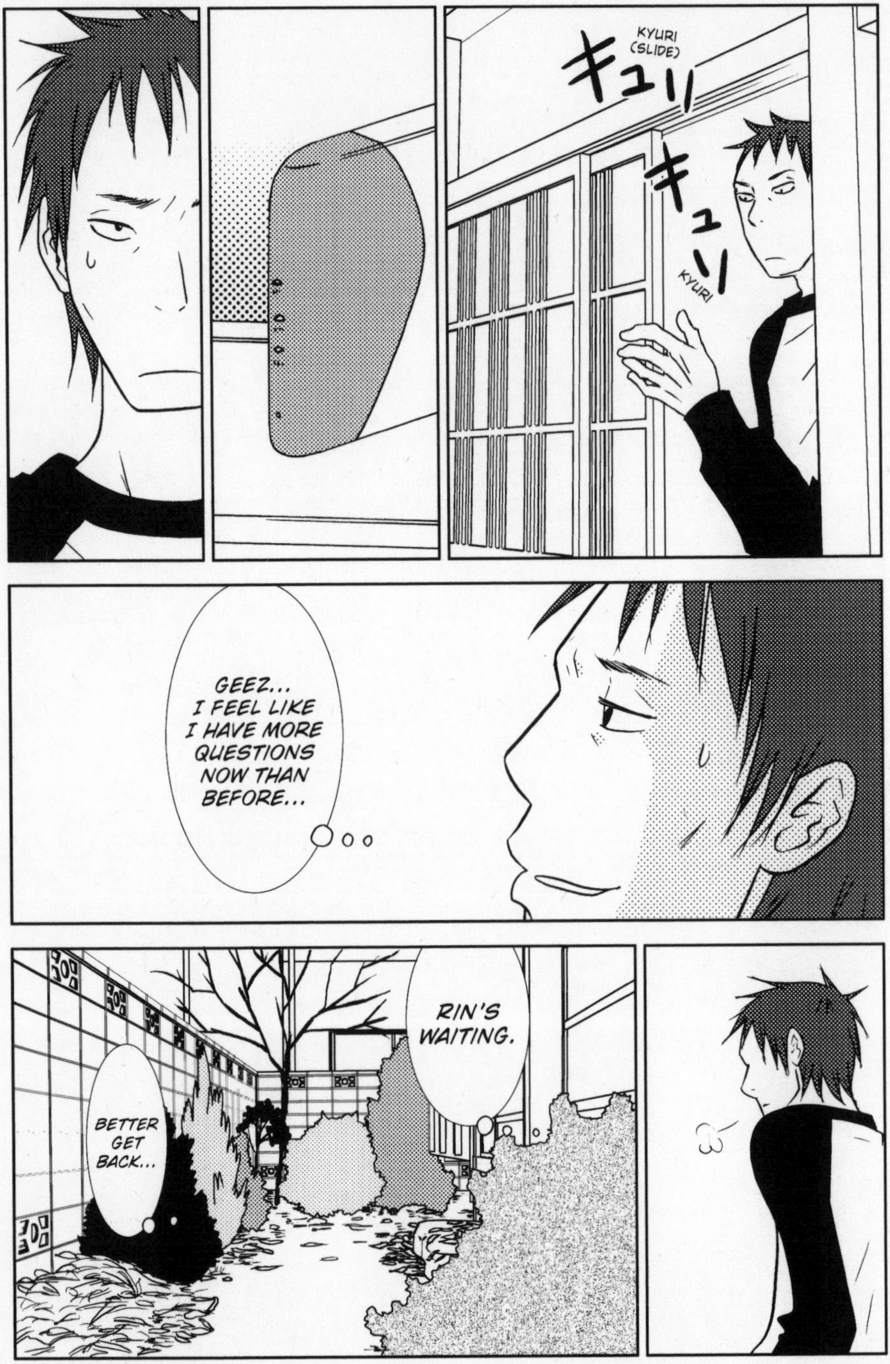
KYURI (SLIDE)
キュリ
キュリ
KYURI
GEEZ... I FEEL LIKE I HAVE MORE QUESTIONS NOW THAN BEFORE...
RIN'S WAITING.
BETTER GET BACK...

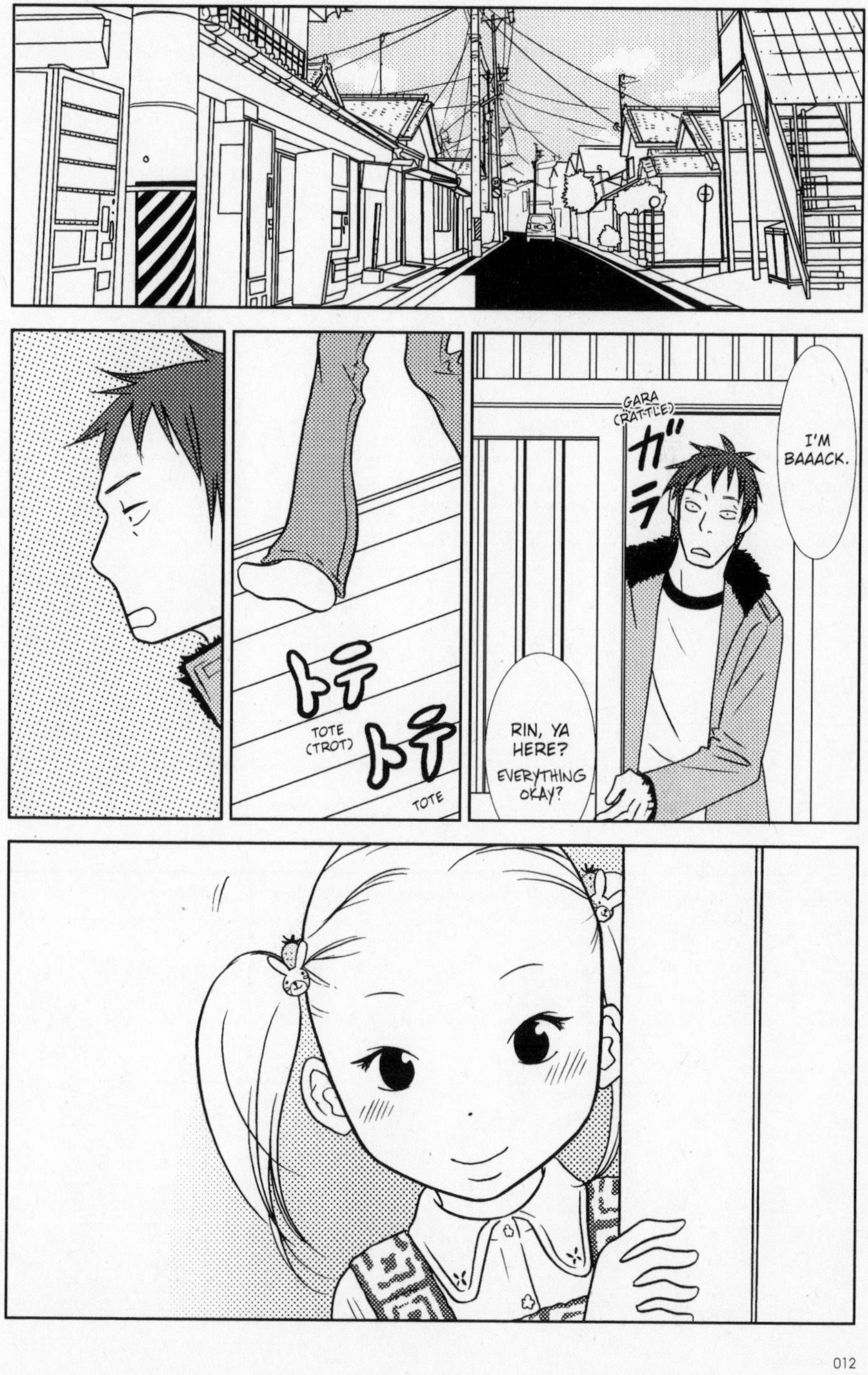
I'M BAAACK.
GARA (RATTLE)
ガラ
RIN, YA HERE?
EVERYTHING OKAY?
トテ
TOTE (TROT)
トテ
TOTE

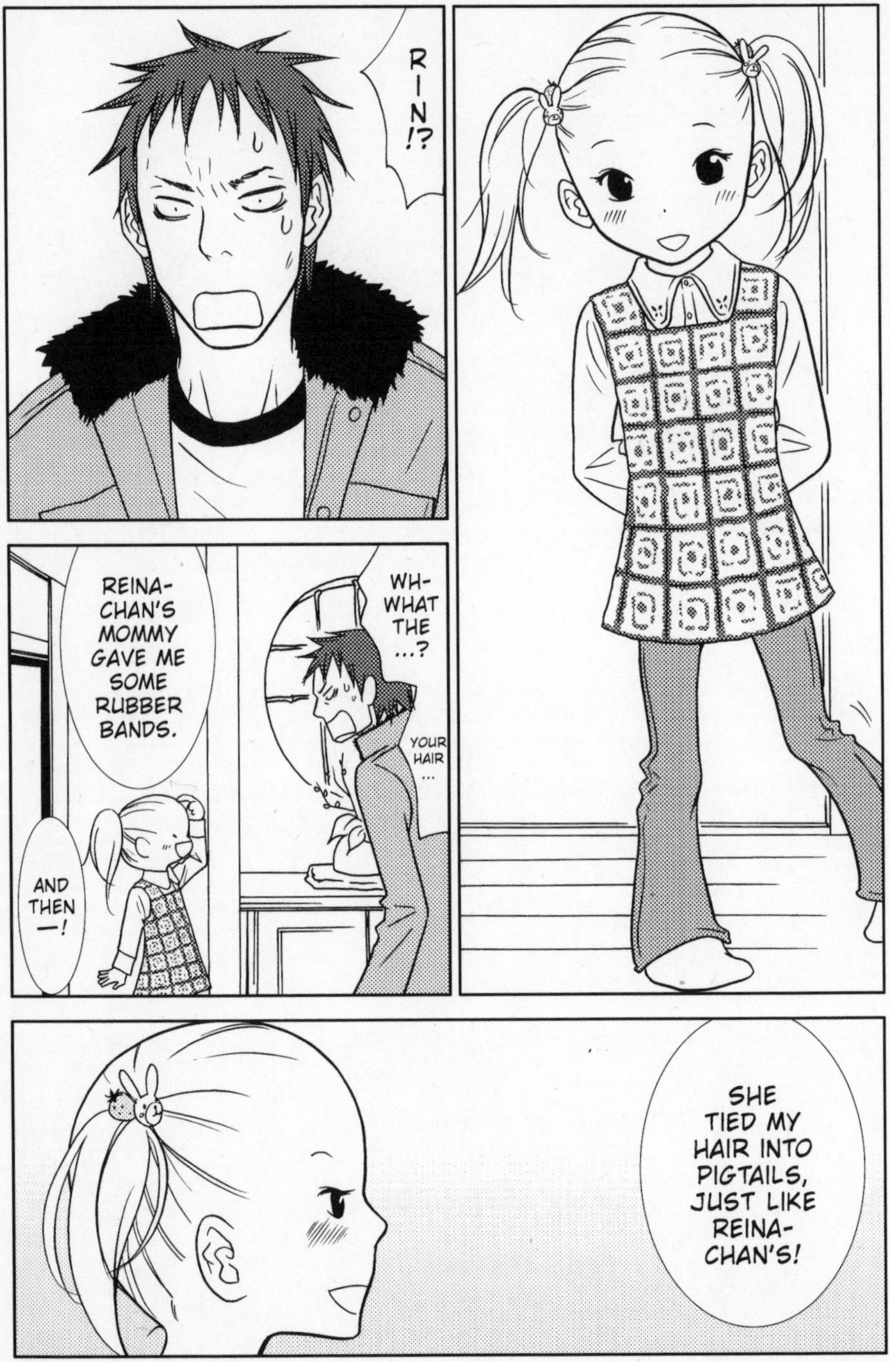
RIN!?
WH-WHAT THE ...?
YOUR HAIR ...
REINA-CHAN'S MOMMY GAVE ME SOME RUBBER BANDS.
AND THEN—!
SHE TIED MY HAIR INTO PIGTAILS, JUST LIKE REINA-CHAN'S!

WAIT A SEC, IS THAT EVEN WHAT YOU HAD ON BEFORE ...?
THESE ARE BIG SIS KAZUMI'S...
HUH?
KAZUMI GAVE—
HANG ON, MOM!!
KIDS THESE DAYS CAN'T WEAR THIS ANCIENT STUFF!!
WOULD YOU GIVE IT UP ALREADY!!?
BUT WHYYY? THEY'RE SO CUTE! AND THEY'RE ALL HAND-KNITTED!
AH, WELL, I USED A KNITTER FOR THIS ONE!
BRINGS BACK MEMO-RIES, RIIIGHT ...?
YOU WORE THIS WHEN YOU WERE FOUR, KAZU-MI...
THESE REEK OF THE SHOWA ERA AND CAMPHOR!!
CALLING IT "CAMPHOR" MAKES YOU REEK OF THE SHOWA ERA TOO, YA KNOW...
THIS ONE'S IN AN AFGHAN KNIT PAT-TERN ...
キィー
KII (SCREECH)
キィー
KII
I DON'T GIVE A DAMN WHAT KIND OF KNIT PATTERN IT IS!!

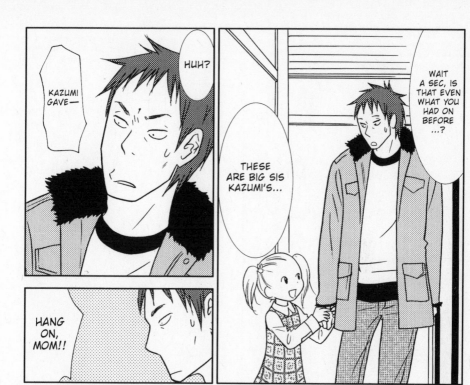

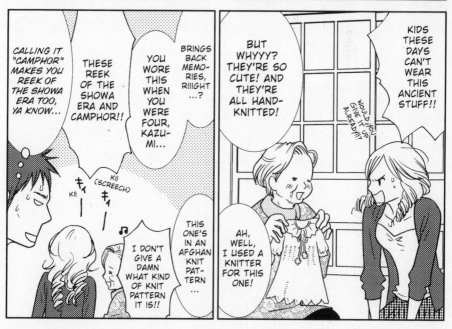

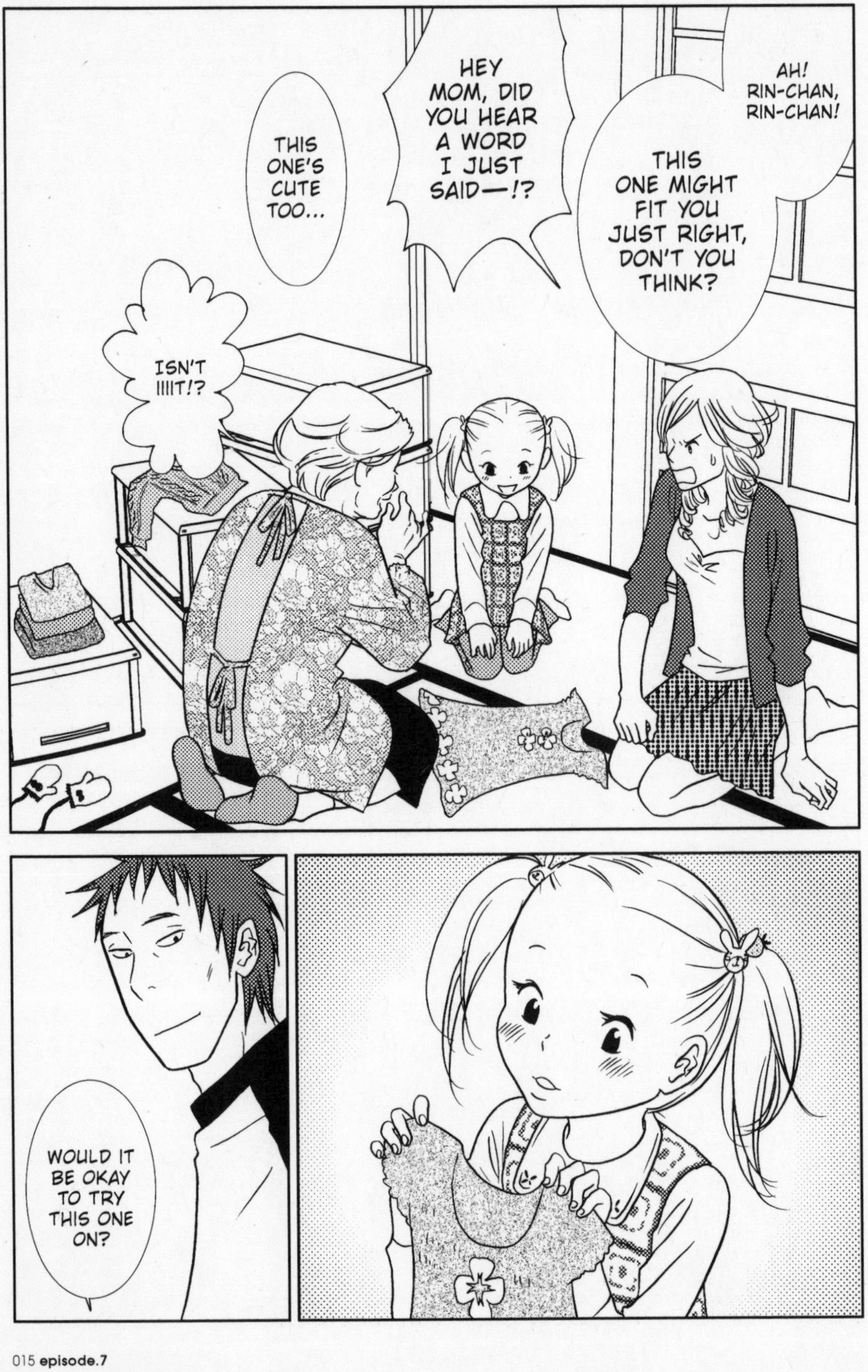
AH! RIN-CHAN, RIN-CHAN!
THIS ONE MIGHT FIT YOU JUST RIGHT, DON'T YOU THINK?
HEY MOM, DID YOU HEAR A WORD I JUST SAID—!?
THIS ONE'S CUTE TOO...
ISN'T IIIIT!?
WOULD IT BE OKAY TO TRY THIS ONE ON?

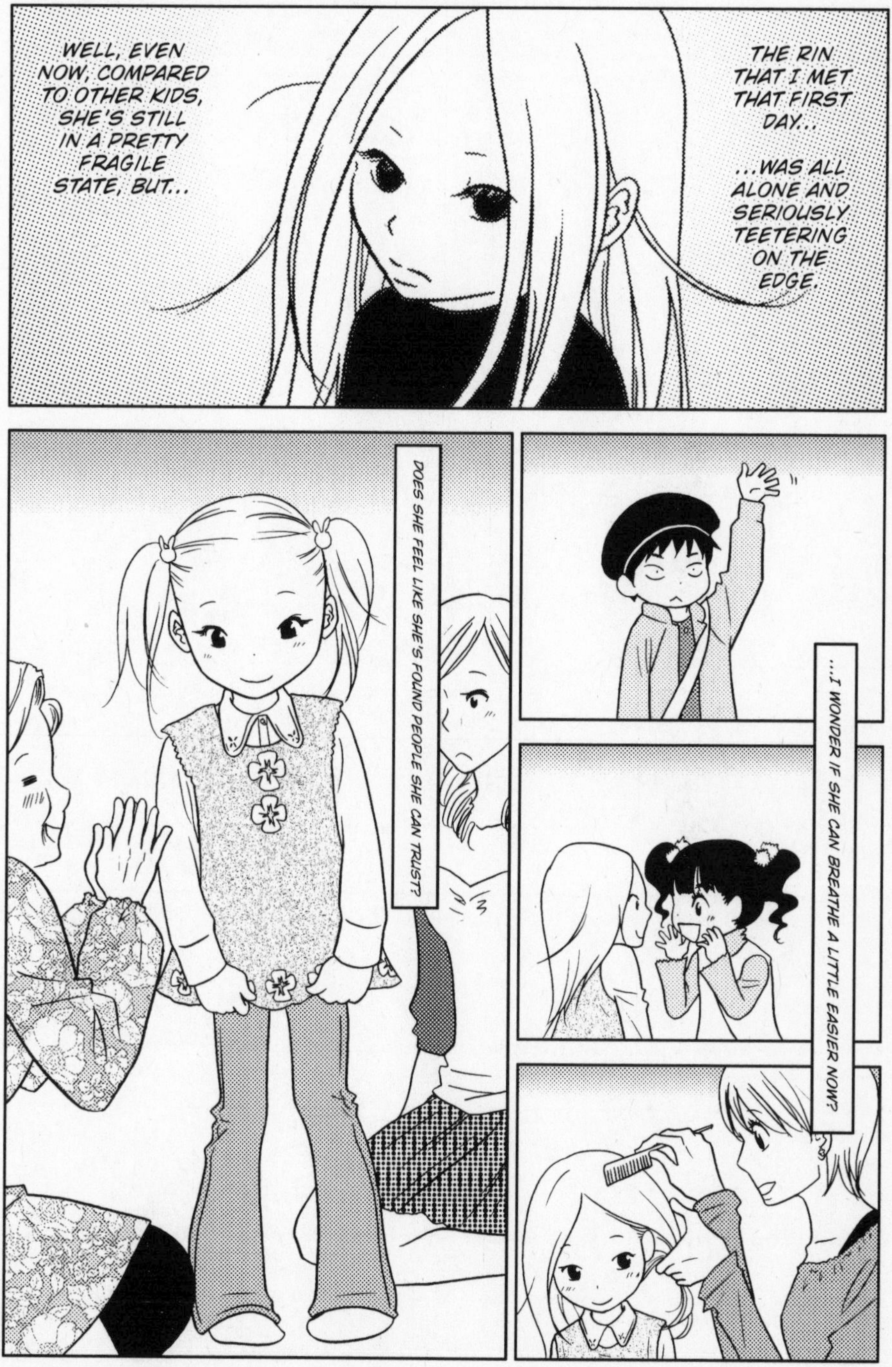
THE RIN THAT I MET THAT FIRST DAY...
...WAS ALL ALONE AND SERIOUSLY TEETERING ON THE EDGE.
WELL, EVEN NOW, COMPARED TO OTHER KIDS, SHE'S STILL IN A PRETTY FRAGILE STATE, BUT...
...I WONDER IF SHE CAN BREATHE A LITTLE EASIER NOW?
DOES SHE FEEL LIKE SHE'S FOUND PEOPLE SHE CAN TRUST?

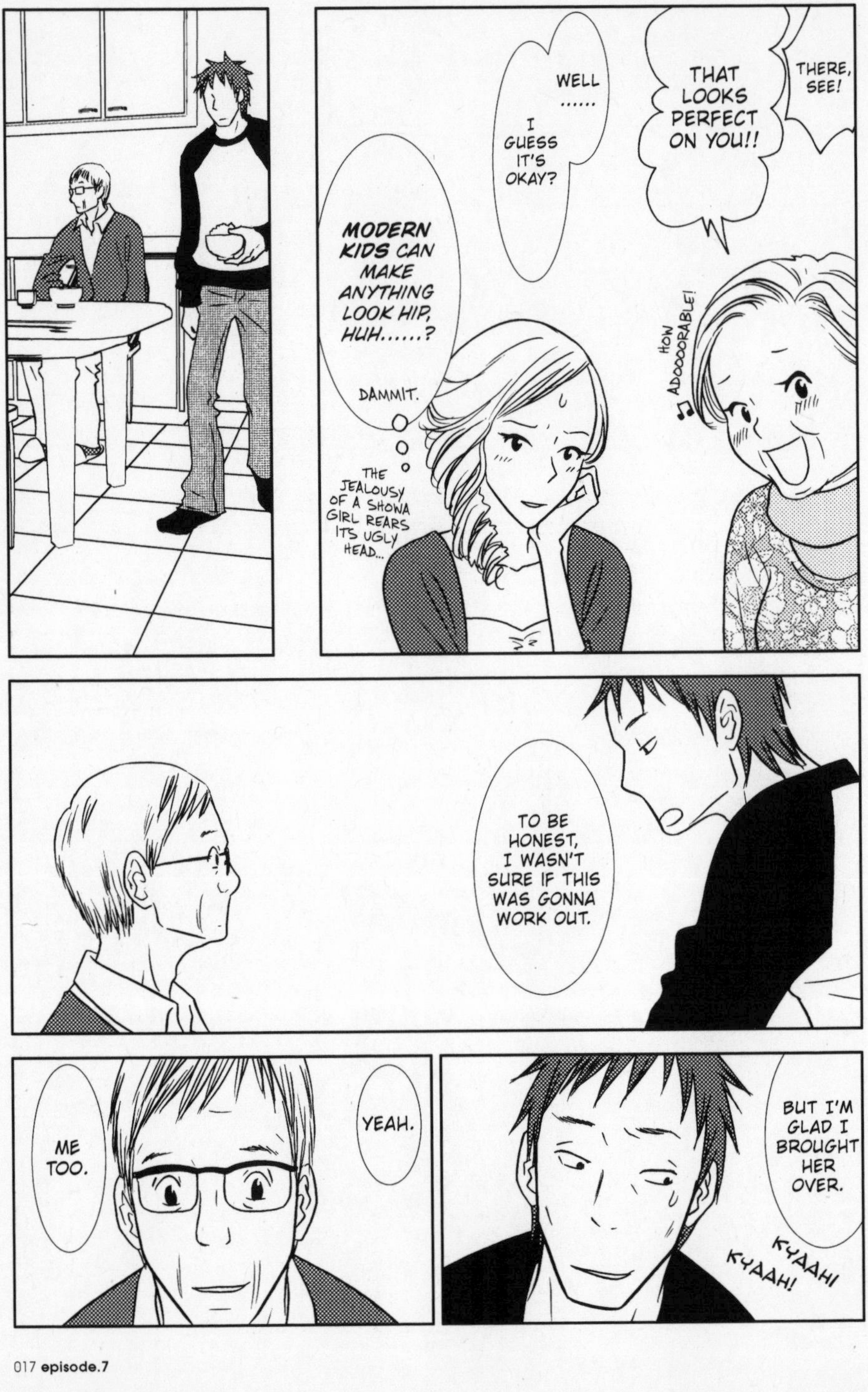
THERE, SEE!
THAT LOOKS PERFECT ON YOU!!
HOW ADOOOORABLE!
WELL...... I GUESS IT'S OKAY?
MODERN KIDS CAN MAKE ANYTHING LOOK HIP, HUH......?
DAMMIT.
THE JEALOUSY OF A SHOWA GIRL REARS ITS UGLY HEAD...
TO BE HONEST, I WASN'T SURE IF THIS WAS GONNA WORK OUT.
BUT I'M GLAD I BROUGHT HER OVER.
KYAAH! KYAAH!
YEAH.
ME TOO.

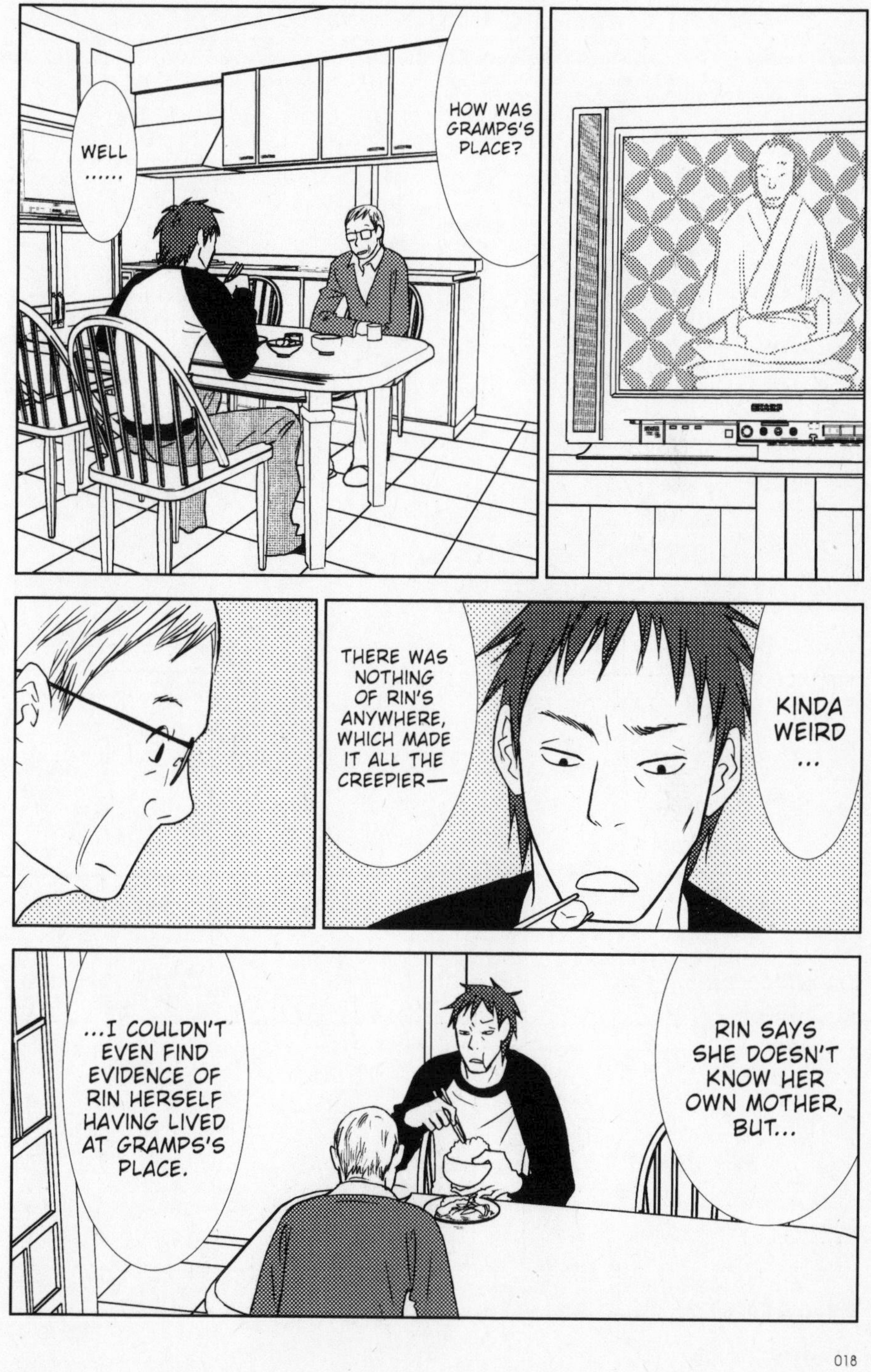
HOW WAS GRAMPS'S PLACE?
WELL ......
KINDA WEIRD ...
THERE WAS NOTHING OF RIN'S ANYWHERE, WHICH MADE IT ALL THE CREEPIER—
RIN SAYS SHE DOESN'T KNOW HER OWN MOTHER, BUT...
...I COULDN'T EVEN FIND EVIDENCE OF RIN HERSELF HAVING LIVED AT GRAMPS'S PLACE.

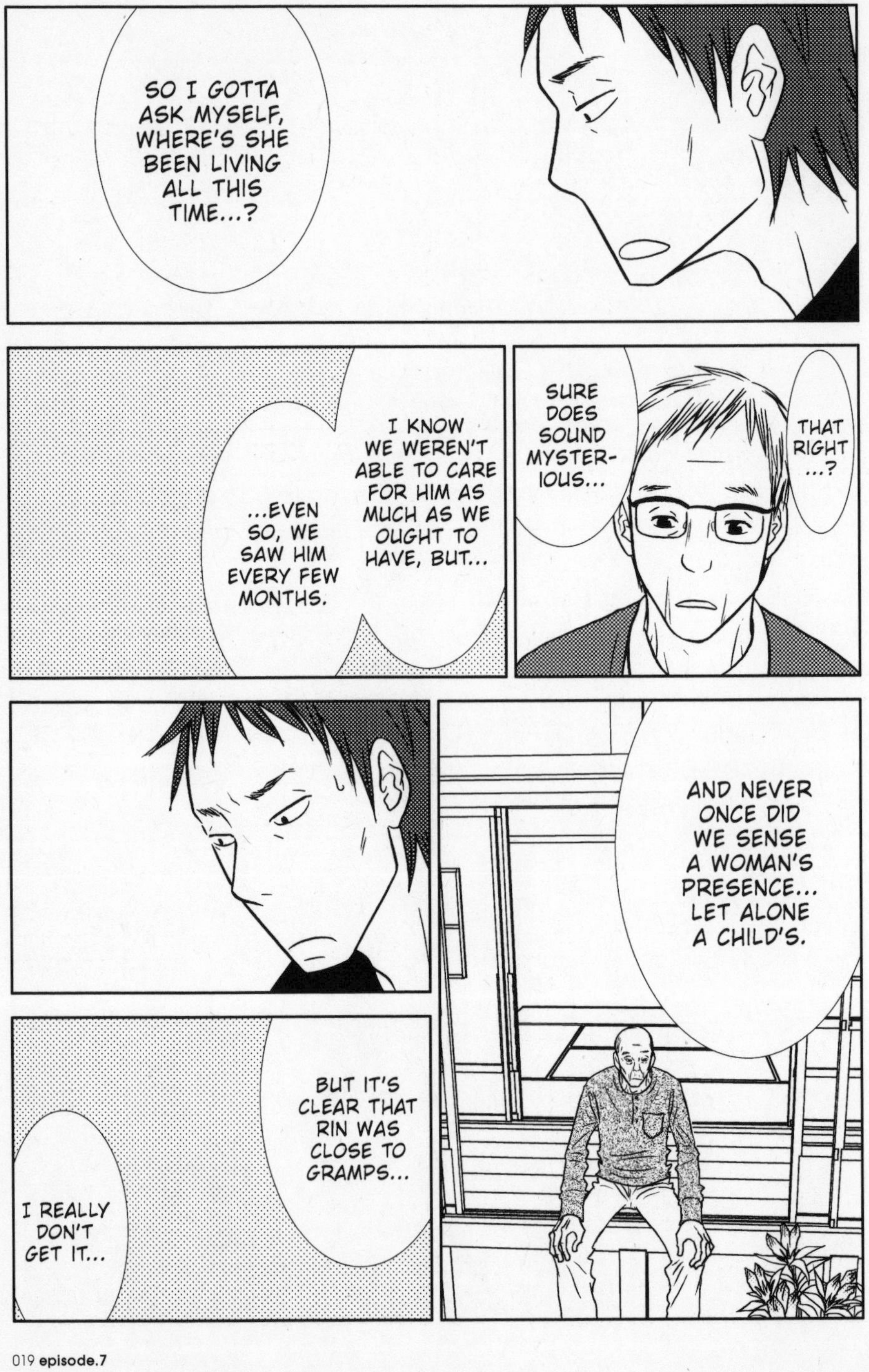
SO I GOTTA ASK MYSELF, WHERE'S SHE BEEN LIVING ALL THIS TIME...?
THAT RIGHT...?
SURE DOES SOUND MYSTERIOUS...
I KNOW WE WEREN'T ABLE TO CARE FOR HIM AS MUCH AS WE OUGHT TO HAVE, BUT...
...EVEN SO, WE SAW HIM EVERY FEW MONTHS.
AND NEVER ONCE DID WE SENSE A WOMAN'S PRESENCE... LET ALONE A CHILD'S.
BUT IT'S CLEAR THAT RIN WAS CLOSE TO GRAMPS...
I REALLY DON'T GET IT...

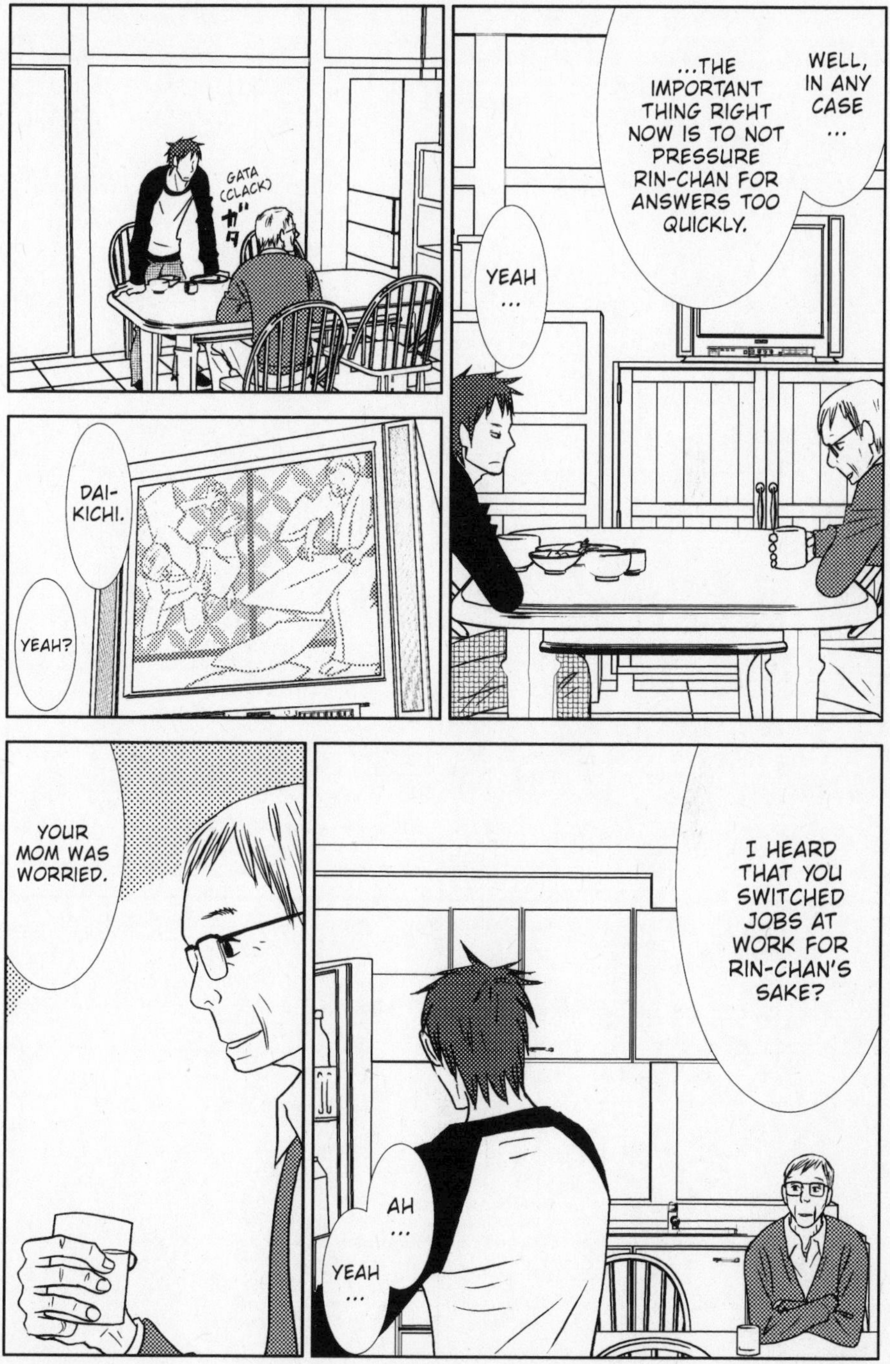
WELL, IN ANY CASE ...
...THE IMPORTANT THING RIGHT NOW IS TO NOT PRESSURE RIN-CHAN FOR ANSWERS TOO QUICKLY.
YEAH ...
GATA (CLACK)
ガタ
DAI-KICHI.
YEAH?
I HEARD THAT YOU SWITCHED JOBS AT WORK FOR RIN-CHAN'S SAKE?
AH ...
YEAH ...
YOUR MOM WAS WORRIED.

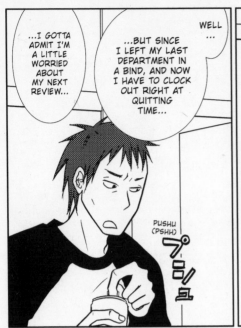

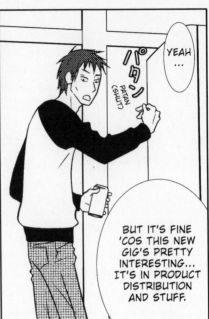

YEAH ...
PATAN (SHUT)
BUT IT'S FINE 'COS THIS NEW GIG'S PRETTY INTERESTING... IT'S IN PRODUCT DISTRIBUTION AND STUFF.
WELL ...
...BUT SINCE I LEFT MY LAST DEPARTMENT IN A BIND, AND NOW I HAVE TO CLOCK OUT RIGHT AT QUITTING TIME...
...I GOTTA ADMIT I'M A LITTLE WORRIED ABOUT MY NEXT REVIEW...
PUSHU (PSHH)
BUT STILL, THIS SEEMS BETTER THAN GETTING BEAT UP AT SALES CONFERENCES AND GOING BALD.
AAH.
THOSE ARE A PAIN, AREN'T THEY?
CAN'T SAY FOR SURE, SINCE I WAS IN HR AND ALL, BUT I BET THEY CAN LEAD TO HAIR LOSS.
AND LOTS OF IT TOO.
SAY, DAD, WHAT BRAND HAIR GROWTH PRODUCT DO YOU USE?
U-FU-FU! FOR ME, IT'S GOTTA BE...
WANT SOME GRILLED SQUID?
SURE ...

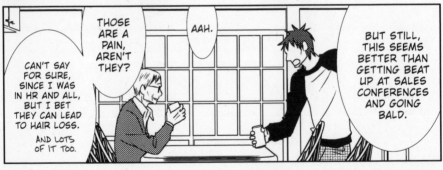

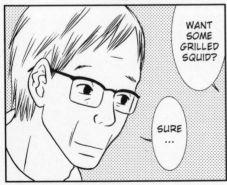

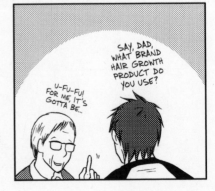

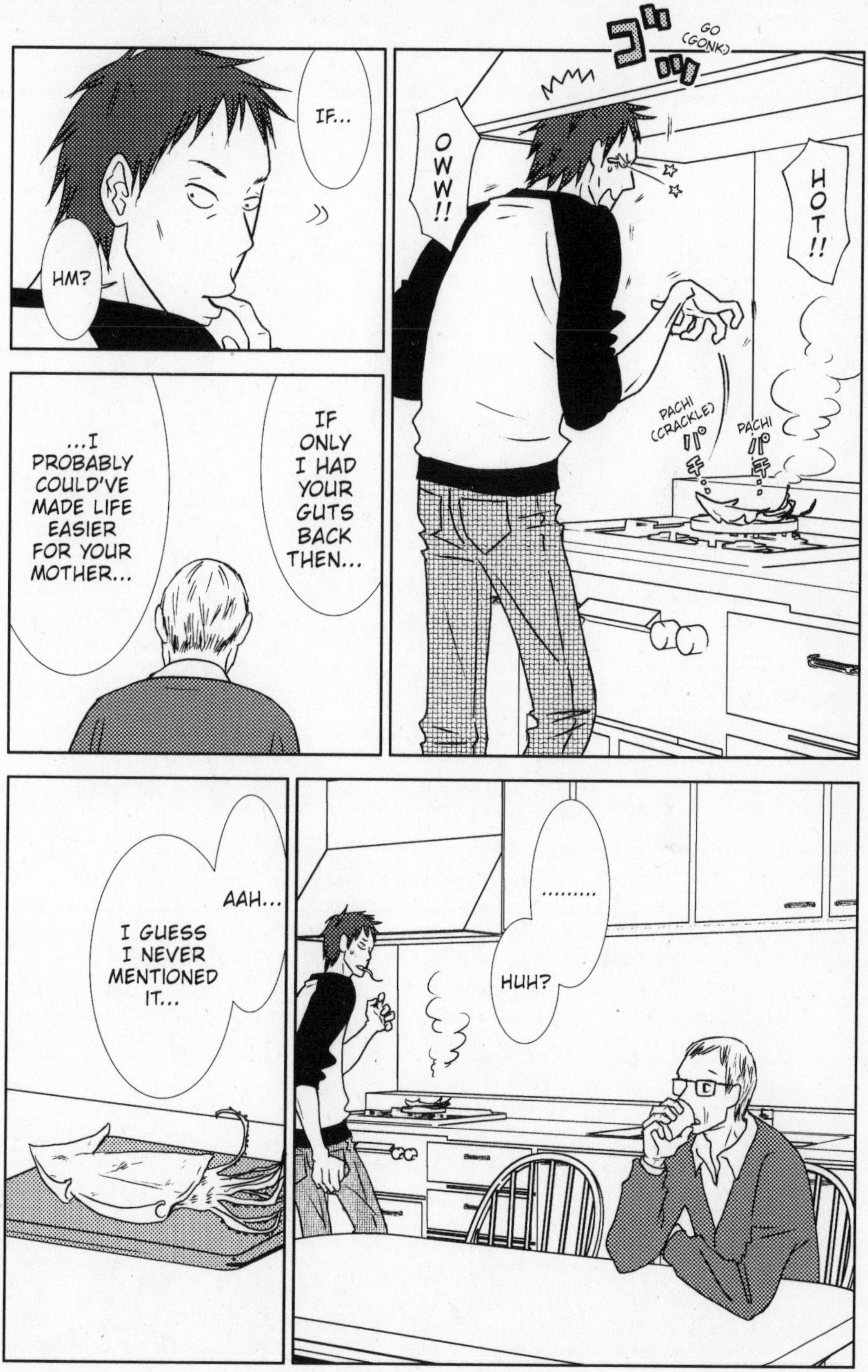

GO (GONK)
HOT!!
OWW!!
PACHI
PACHI (CRACKLE)
IF...
HM?
IF ONLY I HAD YOUR GUTS BACK THEN...
...I PROBABLY COULD'VE MADE LIFE EASIER FOR YOUR MOTHER...
....
HUH?
AAH...
I GUESS I NEVER MENTIONED IT...

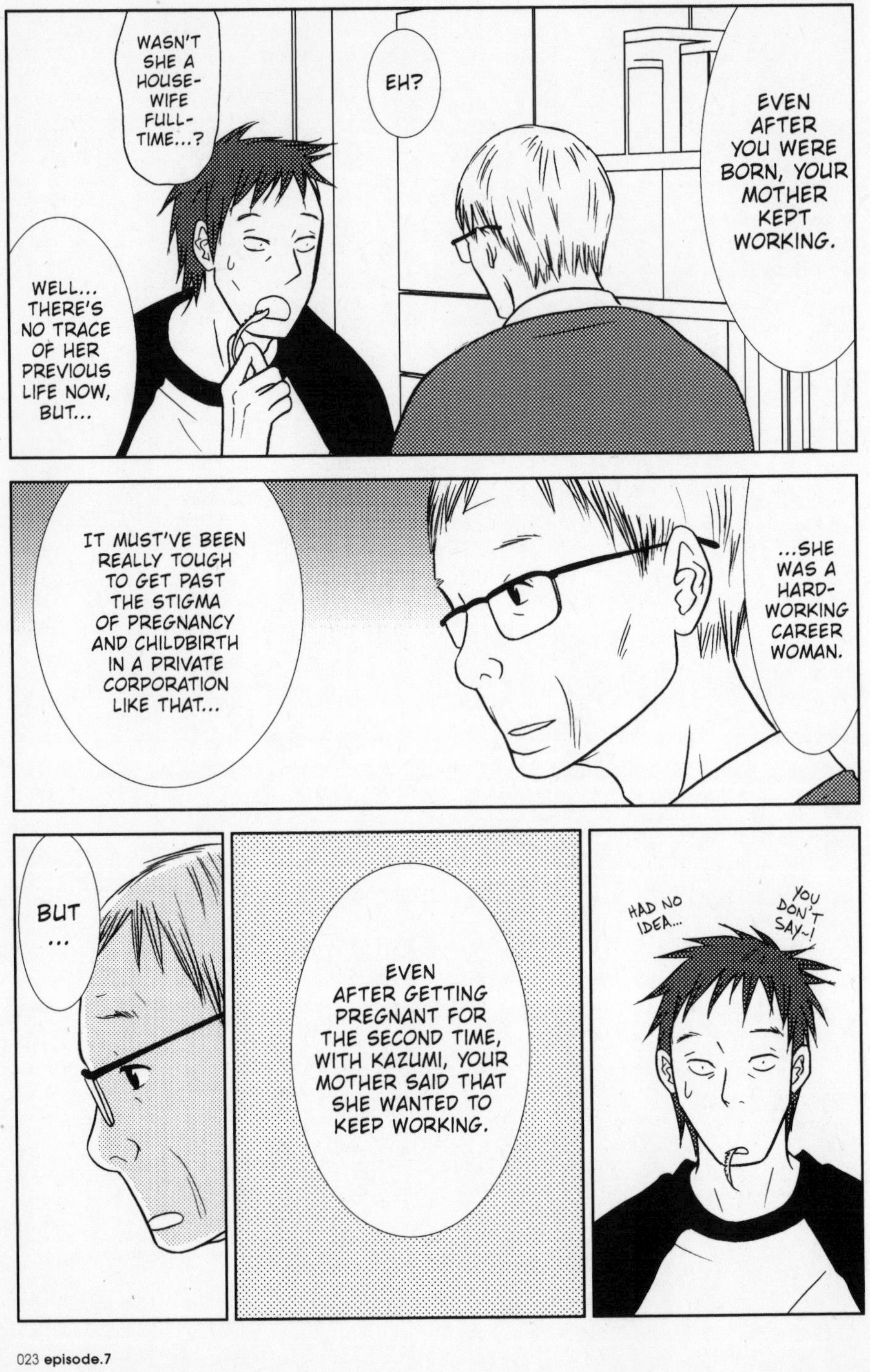
EVEN AFTER YOU WERE BORN, YOUR MOTHER KEPT WORKING.
EH?
WASN'T SHE A HOUSE-WIFE FULL-TIME...?
WELL... THERE'S NO TRACE OF HER PREVIOUS LIFE NOW, BUT...
...SHE WAS A HARD-WORKING CAREER WOMAN.
IT MUST'VE BEEN REALLY TOUGH TO GET PAST THE STIGMA OF PREGNANCY AND CHILDBIRTH IN A PRIVATE CORPORATION LIKE THAT...
YOU DON'T SAY~!
HAD NO IDEA...
EVEN AFTER GETTING PREGNANT FOR THE SECOND TIME, WITH KAZUMI, YOUR MOTHER SAID THAT SHE WANTED TO KEEP WORKING.
BUT ...

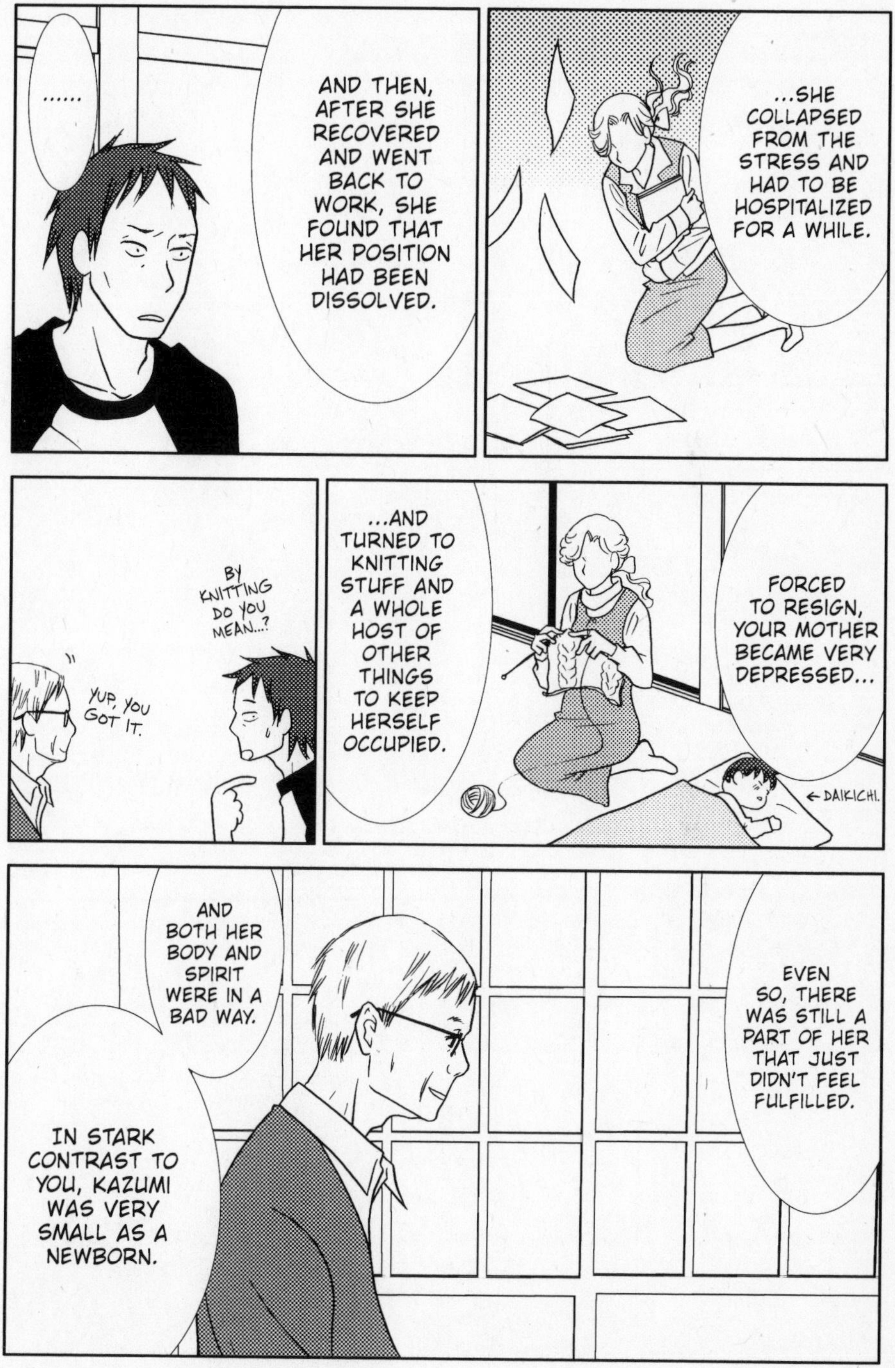
...SHE COLLAPSED FROM THE STRESS AND HAD TO BE HOSPITALIZED FOR A WHILE.
AND THEN, AFTER SHE RECOVERED AND WENT BACK TO WORK, SHE FOUND THAT HER POSITION HAD BEEN DISSOLVED.
......
FORCED TO RESIGN, YOUR MOTHER BECAME VERY DEPRESSED...
...AND TURNED TO KNITTING STUFF AND A WHOLE HOST OF OTHER THINGS TO KEEP HERSELF OCCUPIED.
← DAIKICHI.
BY KNITTING DO YOU MEAN...?
YUP, YOU GOT IT.
EVEN SO, THERE WAS STILL A PART OF HER THAT JUST DIDN'T FEEL FULFILLED.
AND BOTH HER BODY AND SPIRIT WERE IN A BAD WAY.
IN STARK CONTRAST TO YOU, KAZUMI WAS VERY SMALL AS A NEWBORN.

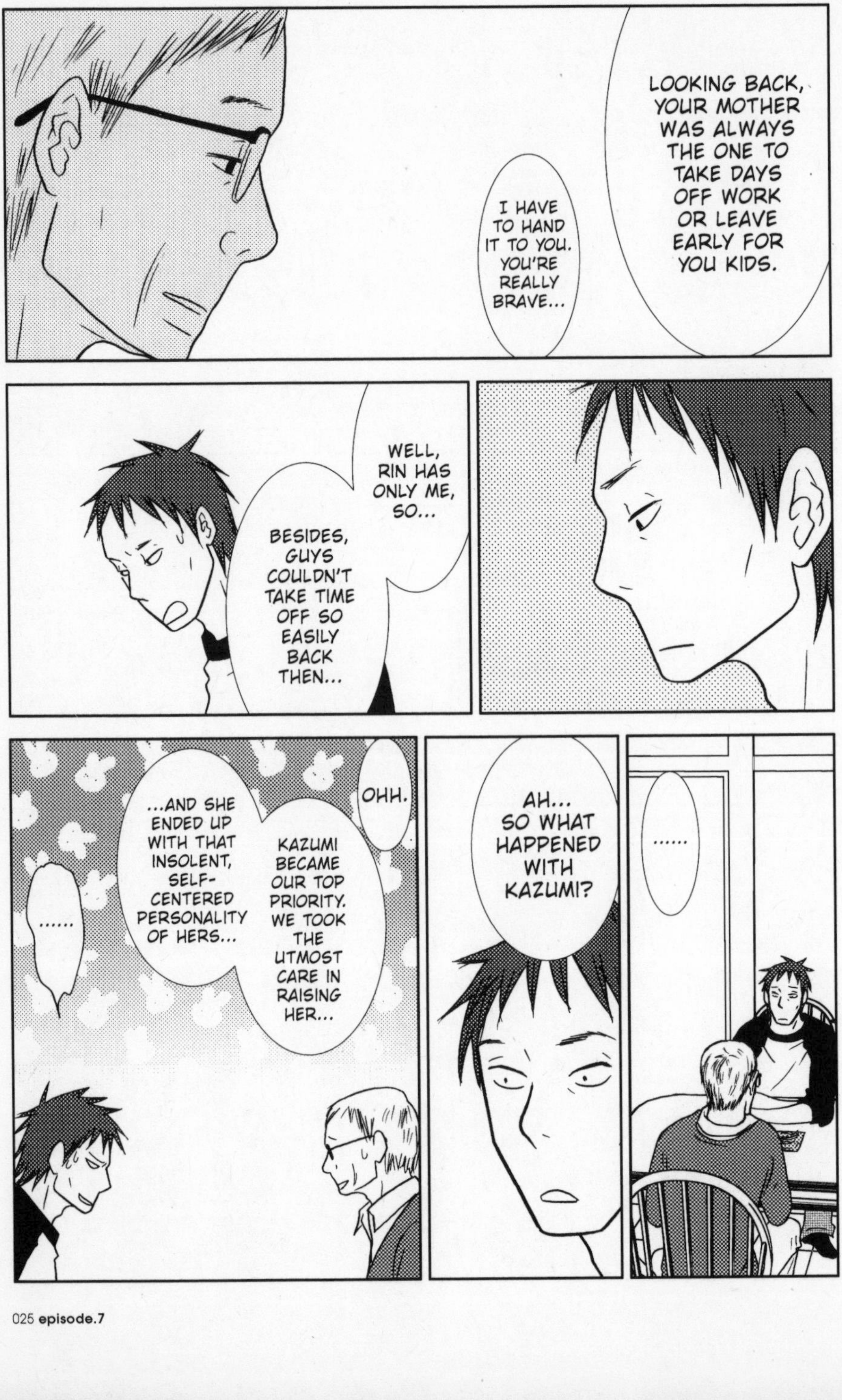
LOOKING BACK, YOUR MOTHER WAS ALWAYS THE ONE TO TAKE DAYS OFF WORK OR LEAVE EARLY FOR YOU KIDS.
I HAVE TO HAND IT TO YOU. YOU'RE REALLY BRAVE...
WELL, RIN HAS ONLY ME, SO...
BESIDES, GUYS COULDN'T TAKE TIME OFF SO EASILY BACK THEN...
......
AH... SO WHAT HAPPENED WITH KAZUMI?
OHH.
KAZUMI BECAME OUR TOP PRIORITY. WE TOOK THE UTMOST CARE IN RAISING HER...
...AND SHE ENDED UP WITH THAT INSOLENT, SELF-CENTERED PERSONALITY OF HERS...
......

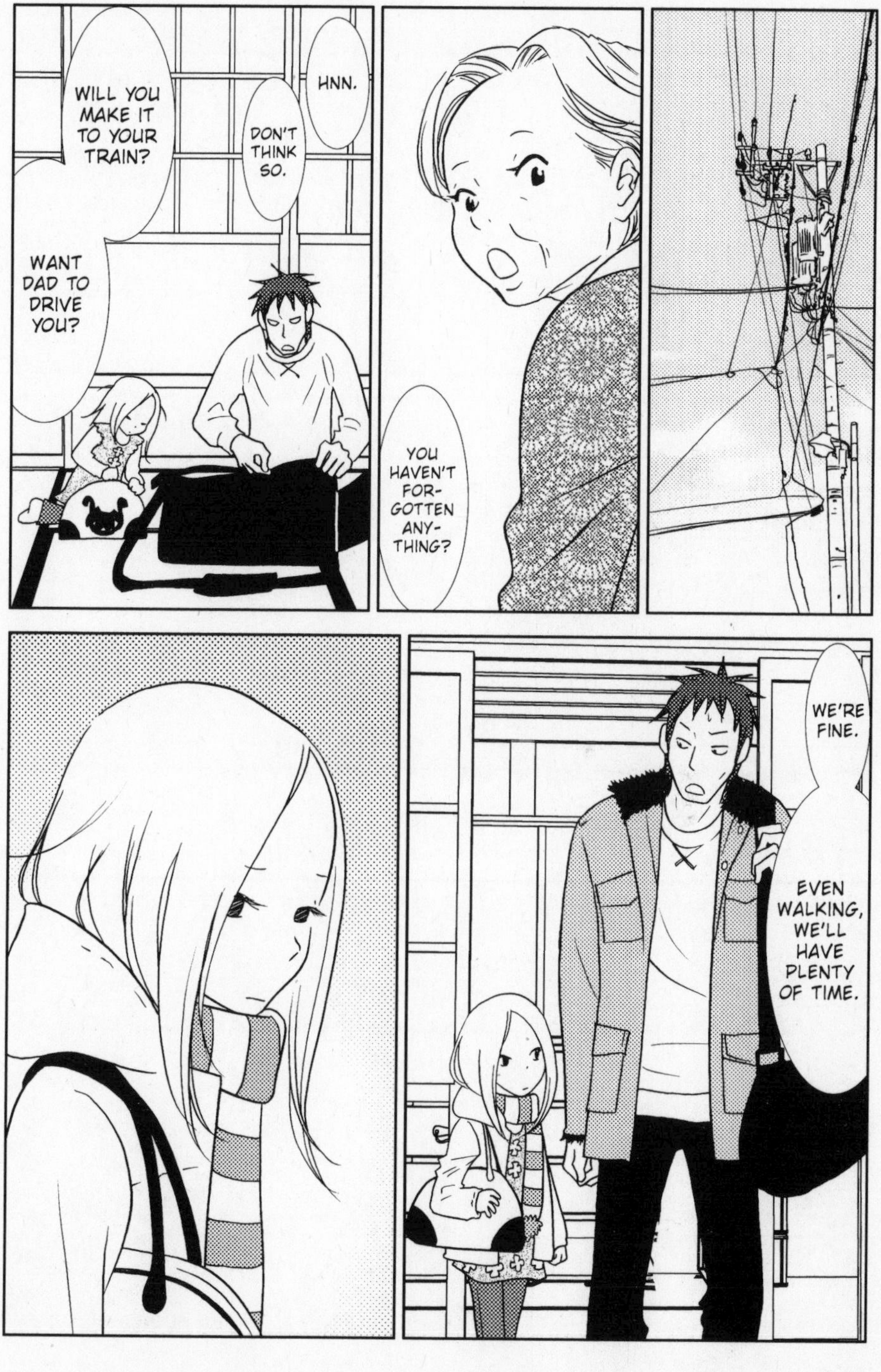
YOU HAVEN'T FOR-GOTTEN ANY-THING?
HNN.
DON'T THINK SO.
WILL YOU MAKE IT TO YOUR TRAIN?
WANT DAD TO DRIVE YOU?
WE'RE FINE.
EVEN WALKING, WE'LL HAVE PLENTY OF TIME.

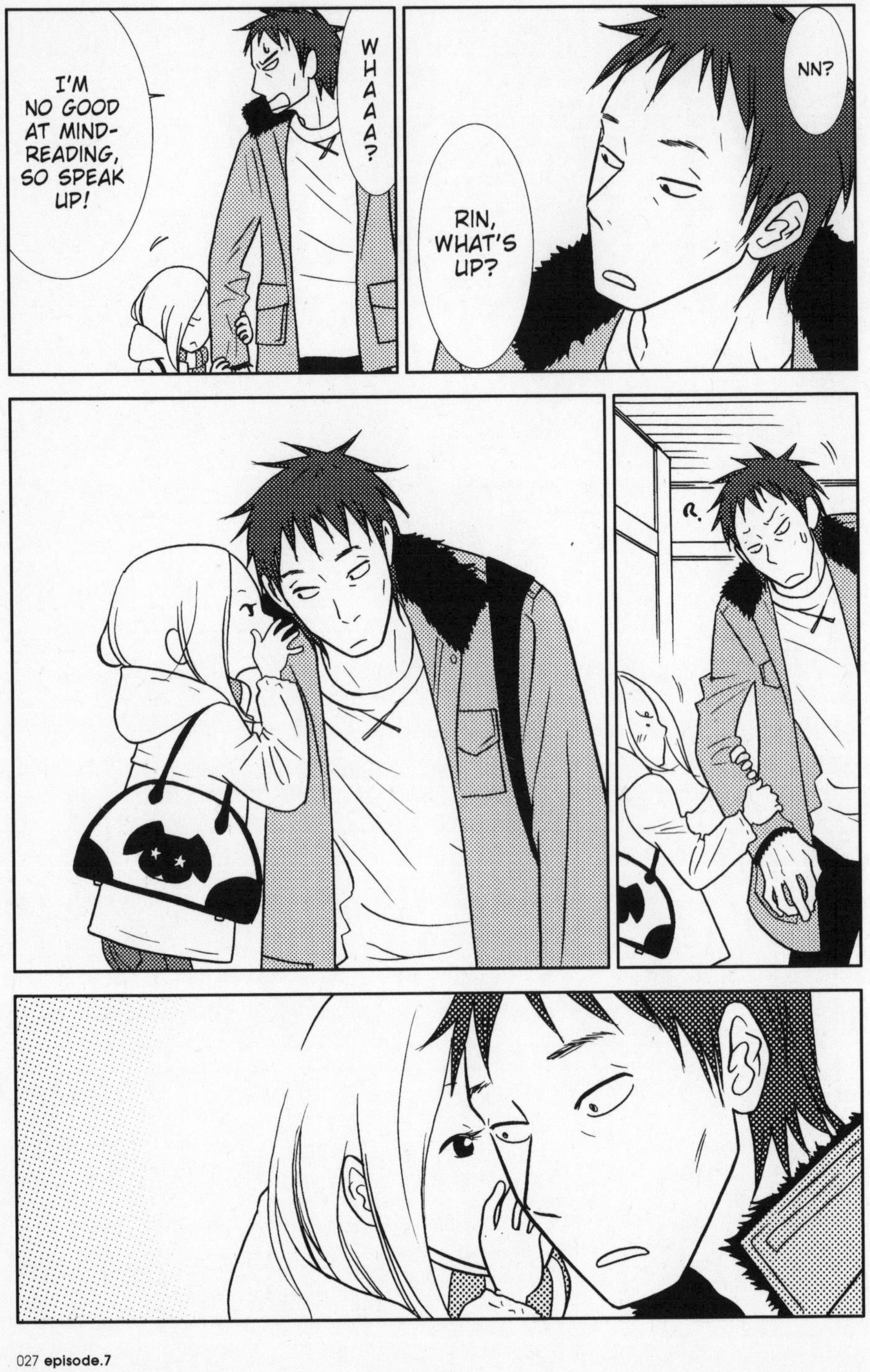
NN?
RIN, WHAT'S UP?
WHAAAA?
I'M NO GOOD AT MIND-READING, SO SPEAK UP!

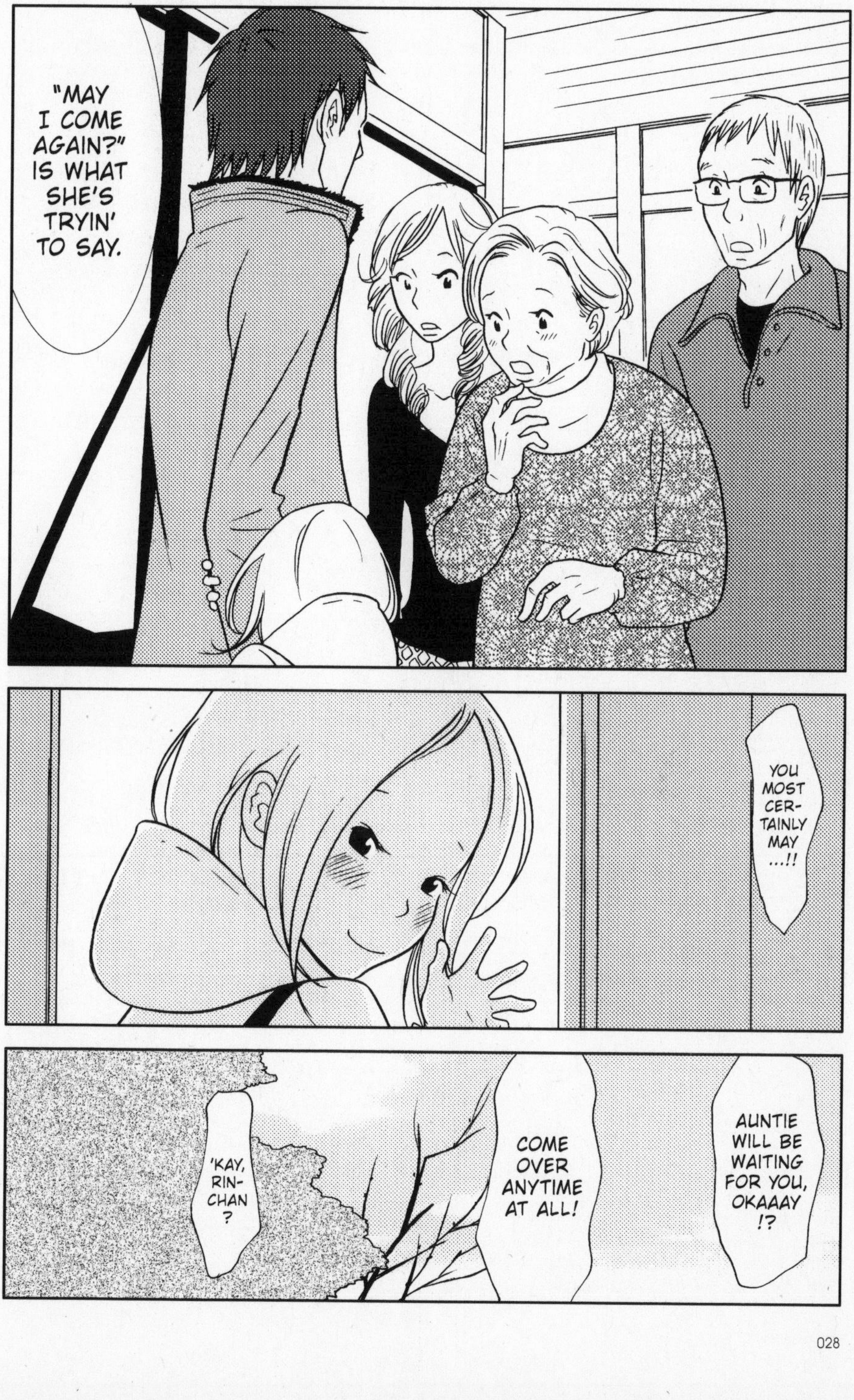
"MAY I COME AGAIN?" IS WHAT SHE'S TRYIN' TO SAY.
YOU MOST CERTAINLY MAY ...!!
AUNTIE WILL BE WAITING FOR YOU, OKAAAY!?
COME OVER ANYTIME AT ALL!
'KAY, RIN-CHAN?

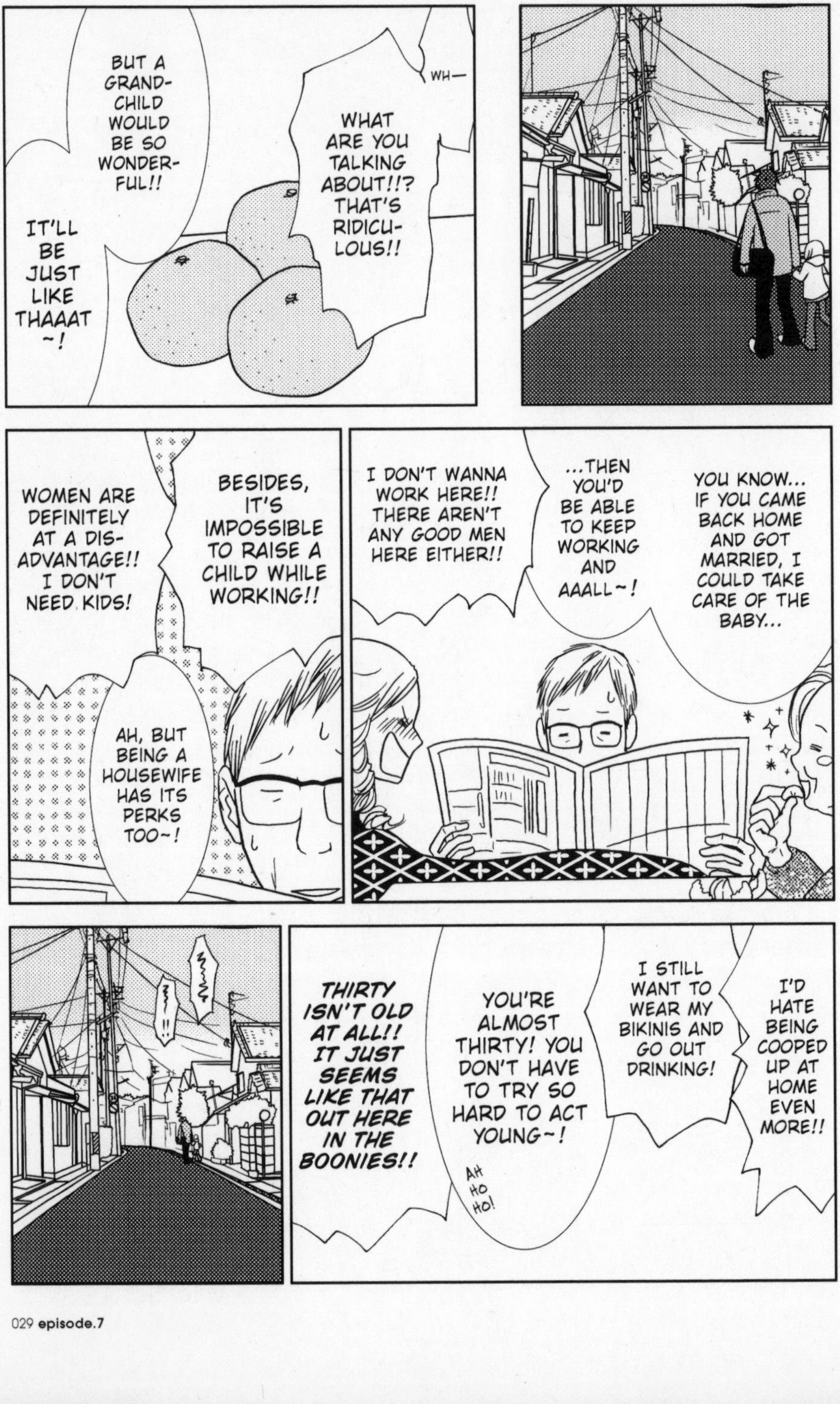
WH—
WHAT ARE YOU TALKING ABOUT!!? THAT'S RIDICULOUS!!
BUT A GRANDCHILD WOULD BE SO WONDERFUL!!
IT'LL BE JUST LIKE THAAAT~!
YOU KNOW... IF YOU CAME BACK HOME AND GOT MARRIED, I COULD TAKE CARE OF THE BABY...
...THEN YOU'D BE ABLE TO KEEP WORKING AND AAALL~!
I DON'T WANNA WORK HERE!! THERE AREN'T ANY GOOD MEN HERE EITHER!!
BESIDES, IT'S IMPOSSIBLE TO RAISE A CHILD WHILE WORKING!!
WOMEN ARE DEFINITELY AT A DISADVANTAGE!! I DON'T NEED KIDS!
AH, BUT BEING A HOUSEWIFE HAS ITS PERKS TOO~!
I'D HATE BEING COOPED UP AT HOME EVEN MORE!!
I STILL WANT TO WEAR MY BIKINIS AND GO OUT DRINKING!
YOU'RE ALMOST THIRTY! YOU DON'T HAVE TO TRY SO HARD TO ACT YOUNG~!
AH HO HO!
THIRTY ISN'T OLD AT ALL!! IT JUST SEEMS LIKE THAT OUT HERE IN THE BOONIES!!

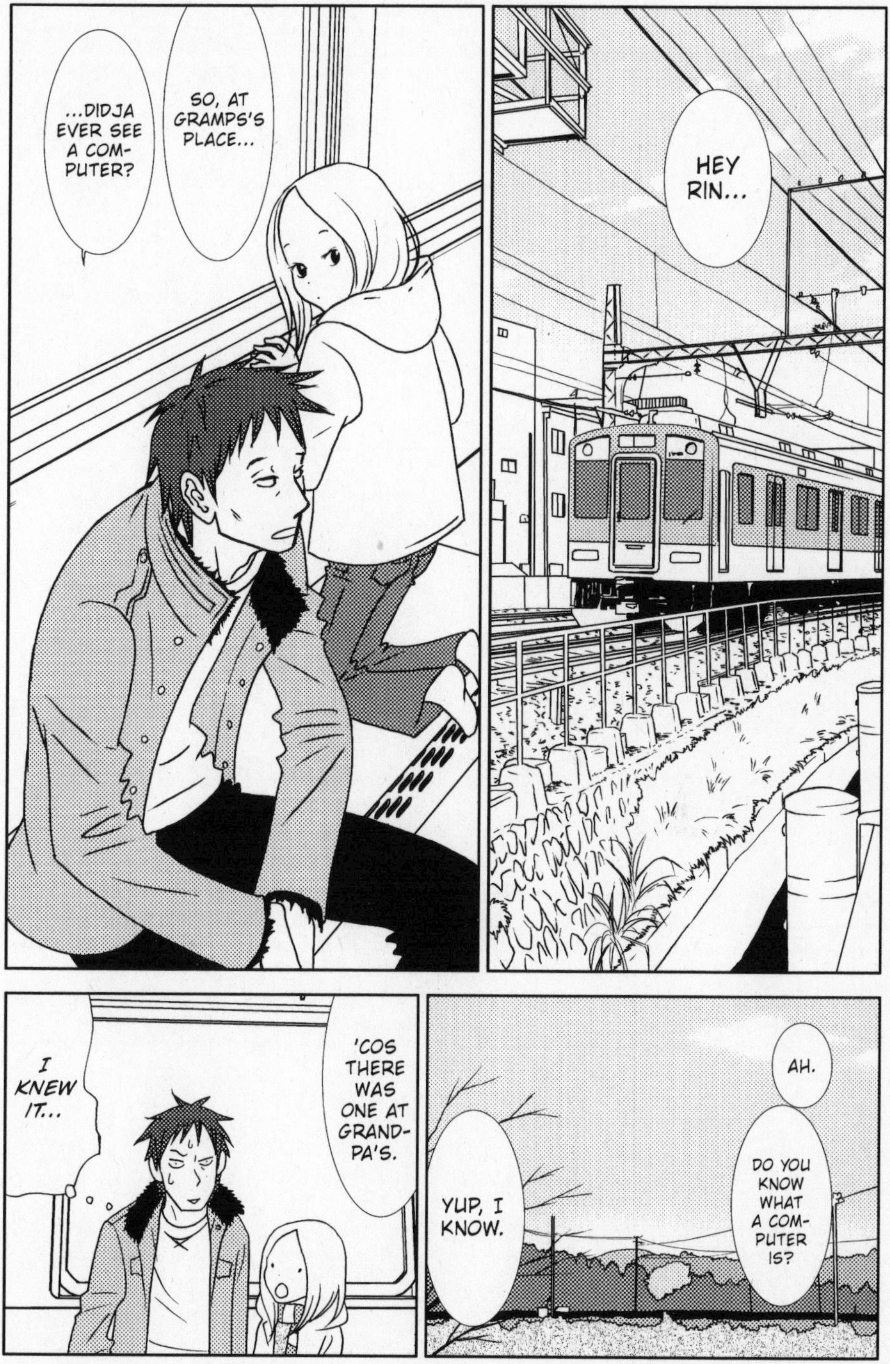
HEY RIN...
SO, AT GRAMPS'S PLACE...
...DIDJA EVER SEE A COMPUTER?
AH.
DO YOU KNOW WHAT A COMPUTER IS?
YUP, I KNOW.
'COS THERE WAS ONE AT GRANDPA'S.
I KNEW IT...

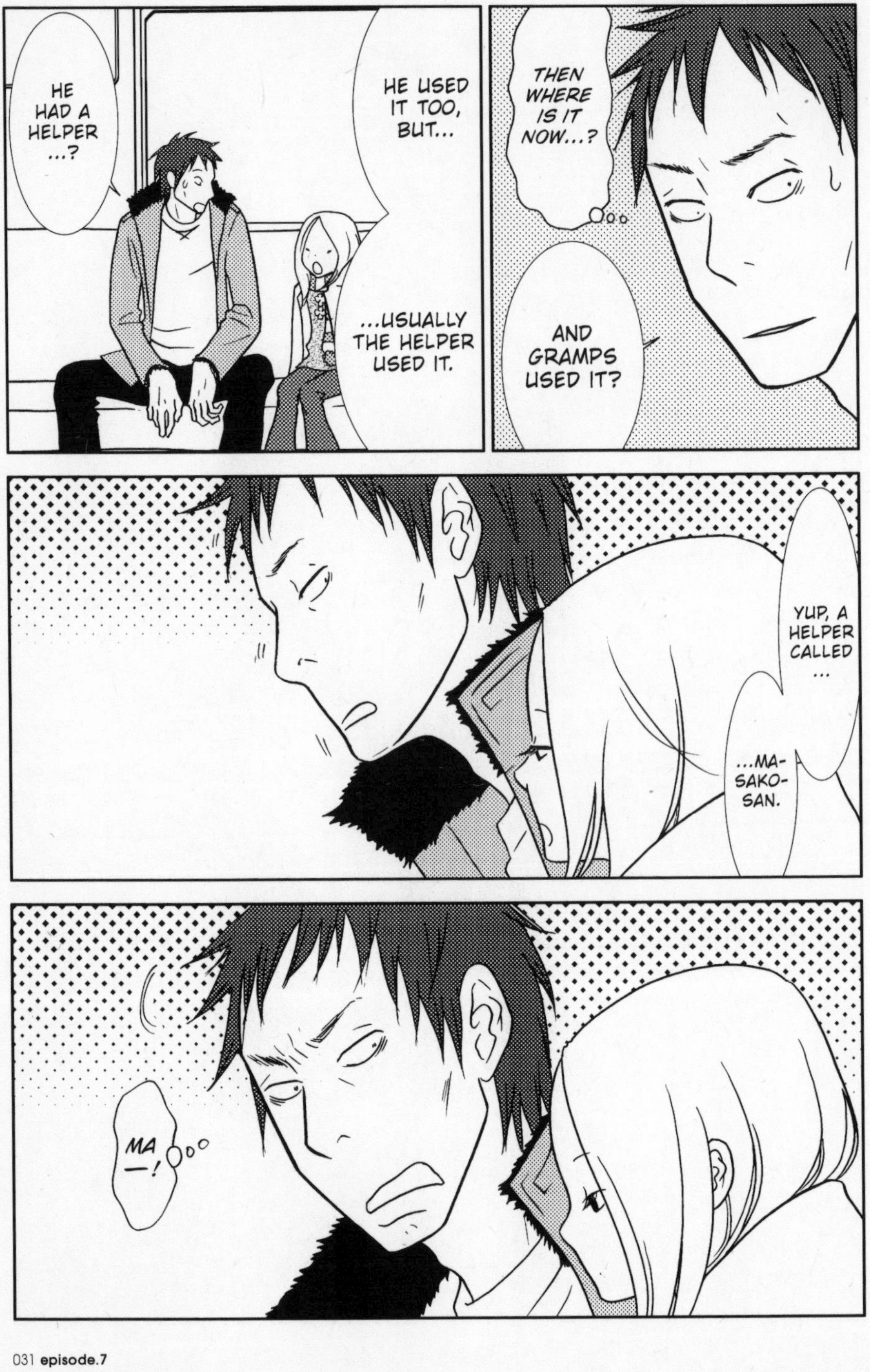
THEN WHERE IS IT NOW...?
AND GRAMPS USED IT?
HE USED IT TOO, BUT...
...USUALLY THE HELPER USED IT.
HE HAD A HELPER ...?
YUP, A HELPER CALLED ...
...MA-SAKO-SAN.
MA—!

BOOK: MOTHER-CHILD HEALTH RECORD BOOK

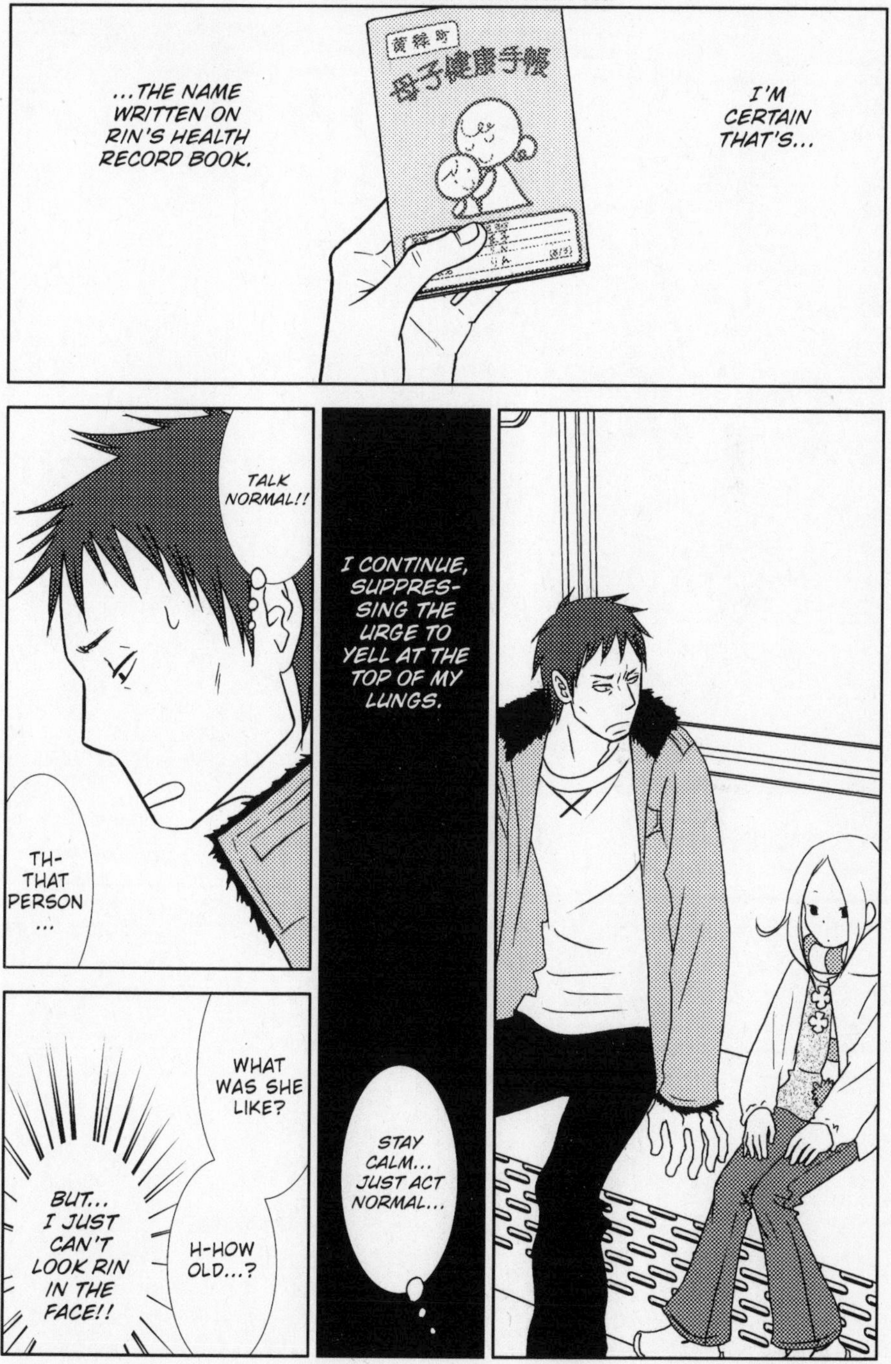

母子健康手帳
I'M CERTAIN THAT'S...
...THE NAME WRITTEN ON RIN'S HEALTH RECORD BOOK.
I CONTINUE, SUPPRES-SING THE URGE TO YELL AT THE TOP OF MY LUNGS.
STAY CALM... JUST ACT NORMAL...
TALK NORMAL!!
TH-THAT PERSON...
WHAT WAS SHE LIKE?
H-HOW OLD...?
BUT... I JUST CAN'T LOOK RIN IN THE FACE!!

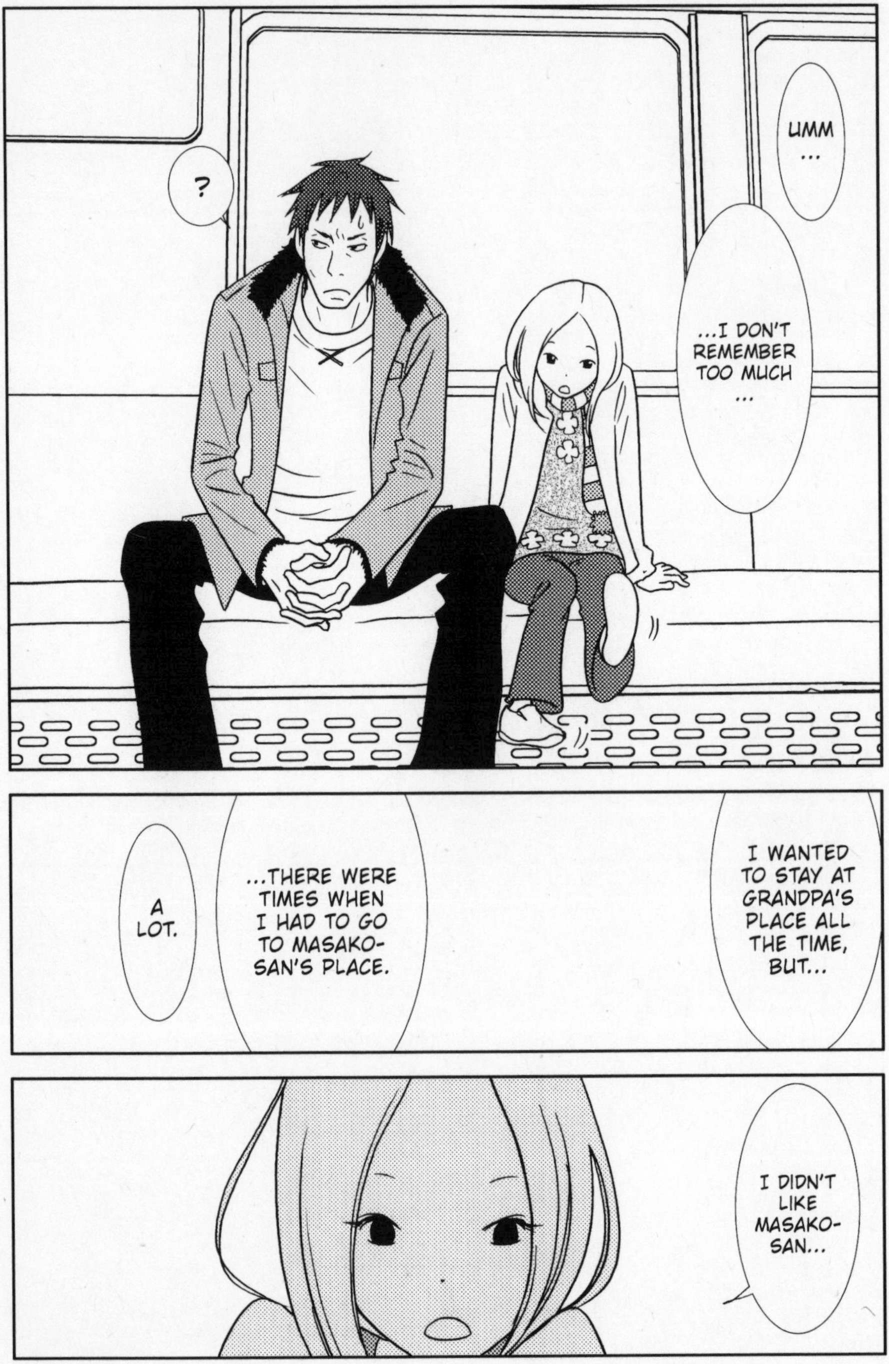
UMM ...
...I DON'T REMEMBER TOO MUCH ...
?
I WANTED TO STAY AT GRANDPA'S PLACE ALL THE TIME, BUT...
...THERE WERE TIMES WHEN I HAD TO GO TO MASAKO-SAN'S PLACE.
A LOT.
I DIDN'T LIKE MASAKO-SAN...

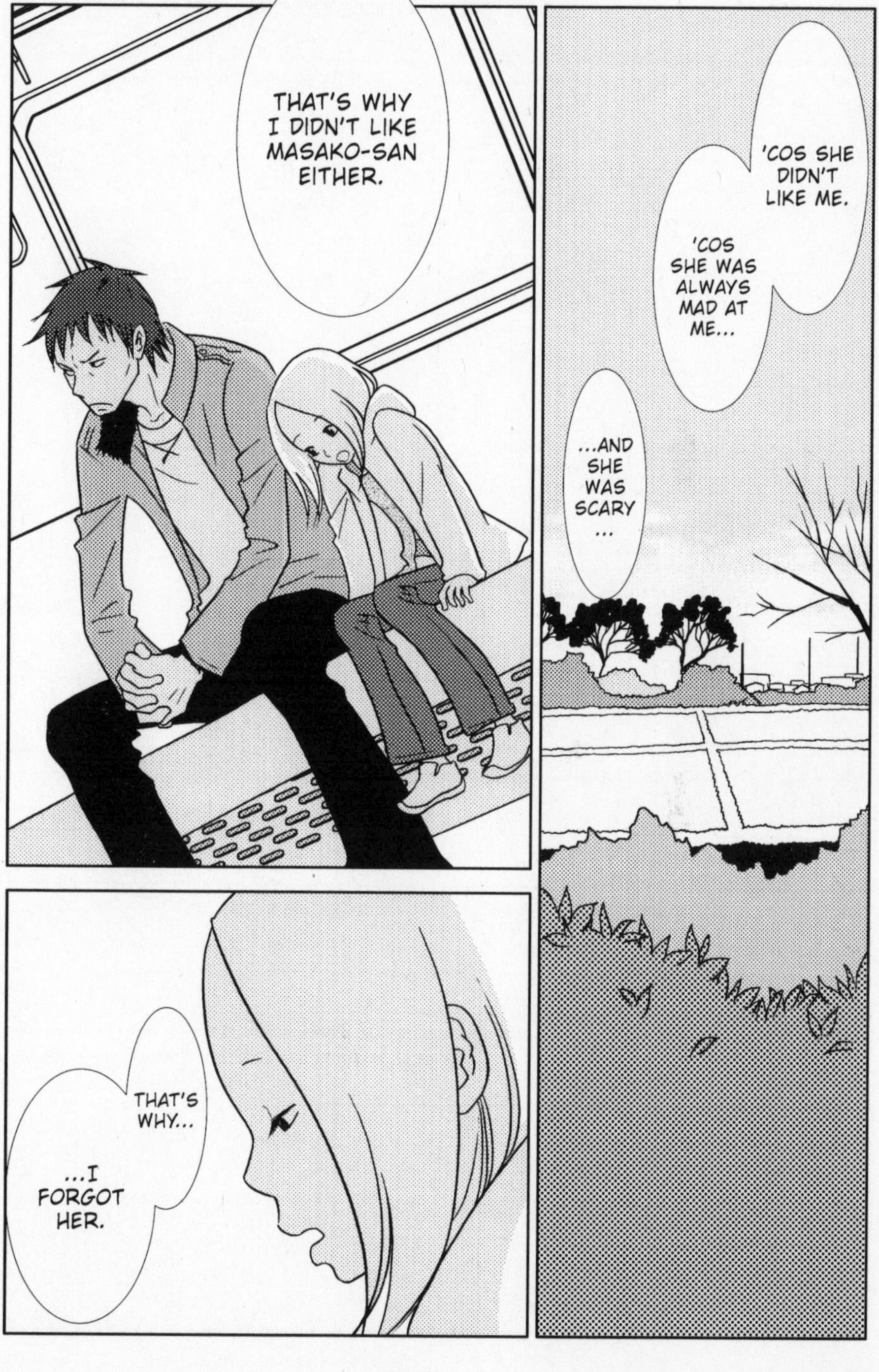

'COS SHE DIDN'T LIKE ME.
'COS SHE WAS ALWAYS MAD AT ME...
...AND SHE WAS SCARY...
THAT'S WHY I DIDN'T LIKE MASAKO-SAN EITHER.
THAT'S WHY...
...I FORGOT HER.

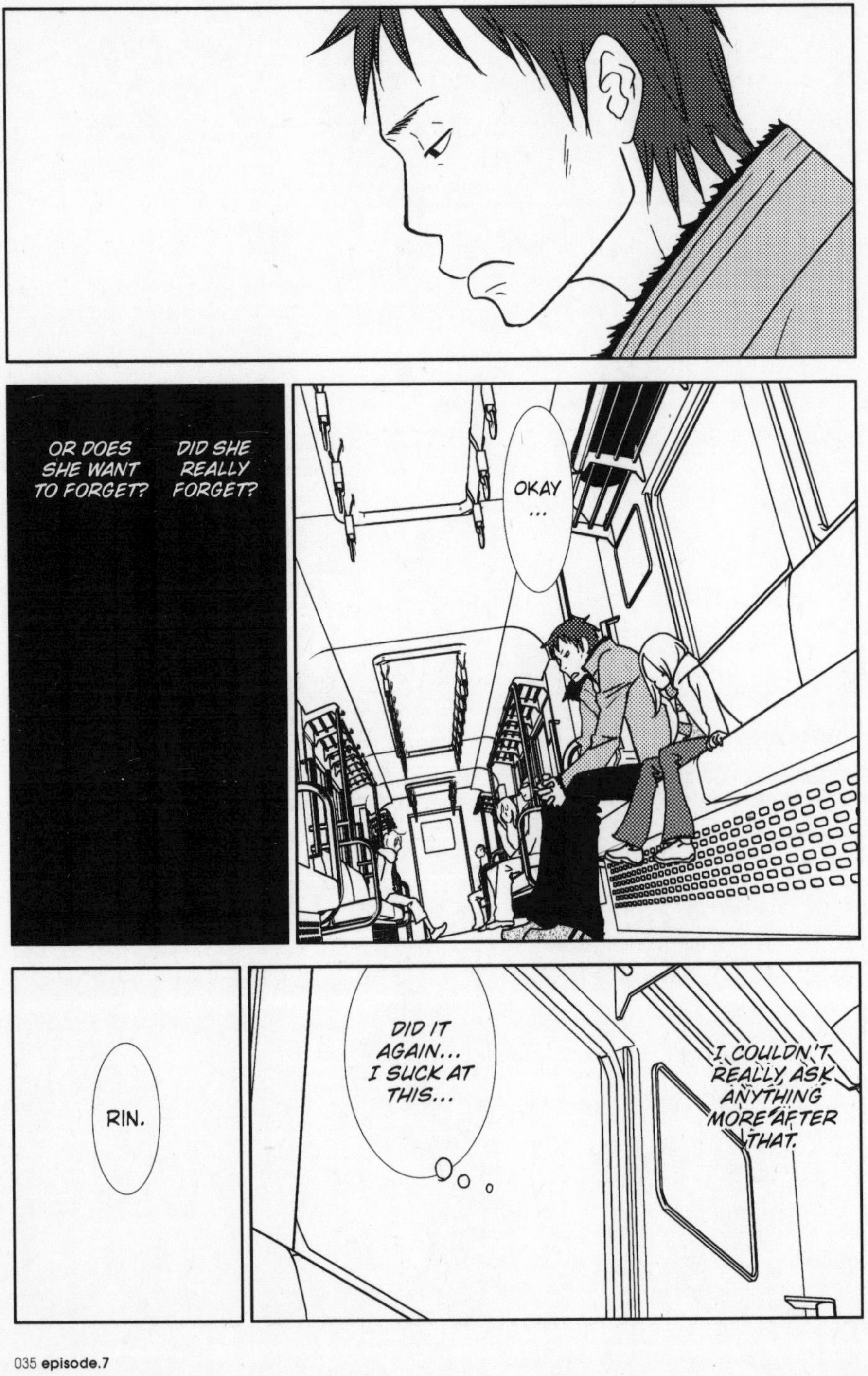
OKAY ...
DID SHE REALLY FORGET?
OR DOES SHE WANT TO FORGET?
I COULDN'T REALLY ASK ANYTHING MORE AFTER THAT.
DID IT AGAIN... I SUCK AT THIS...
RIN.

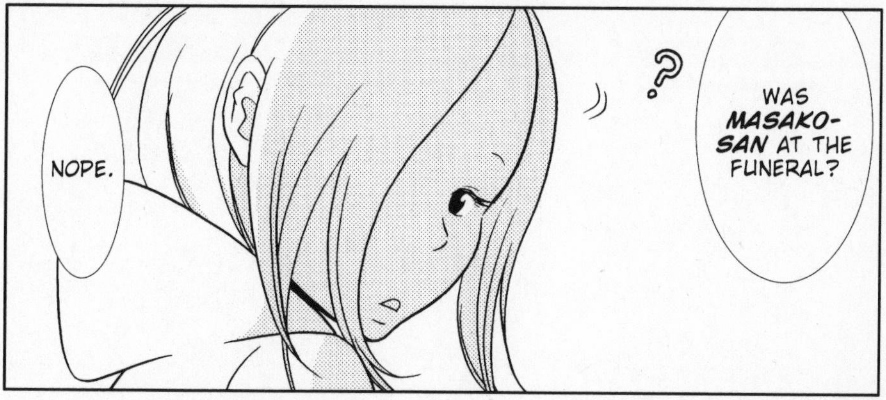
WAS MASAKO-SAN AT THE FUNERAL?
?
NOPE.

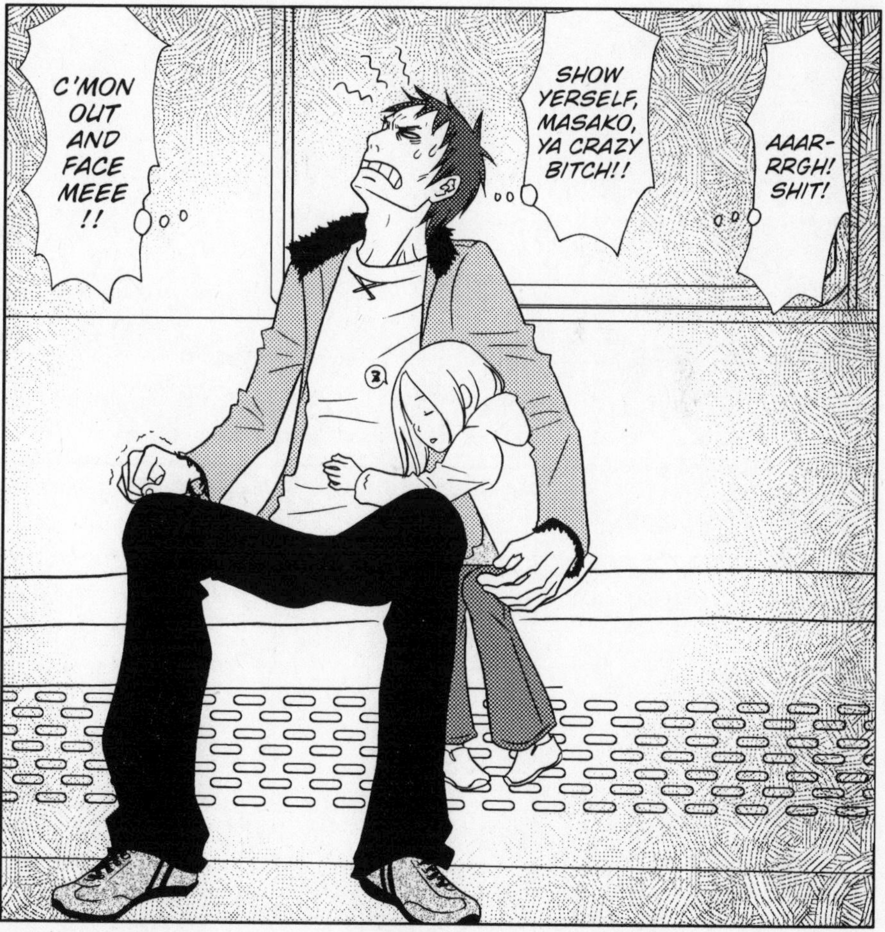
AAAR-RRGH! SHIT!
SHOW YERSELF, MASAKO, YA CRAZY BITCH!!
C'MON OUT AND FACE MEEE!!

BUNNY**DROP**

episode.8

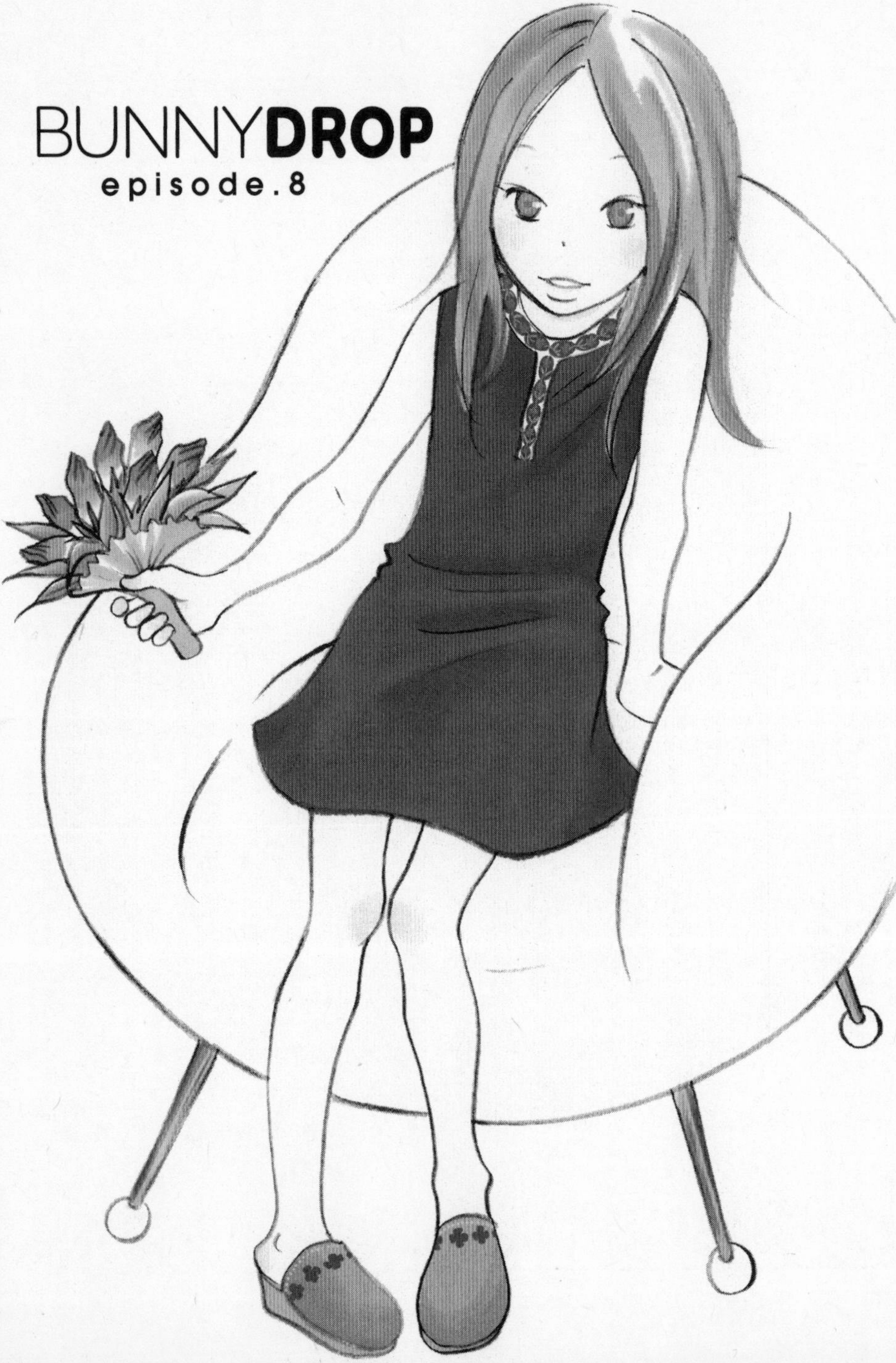

BUNNY**DROP**

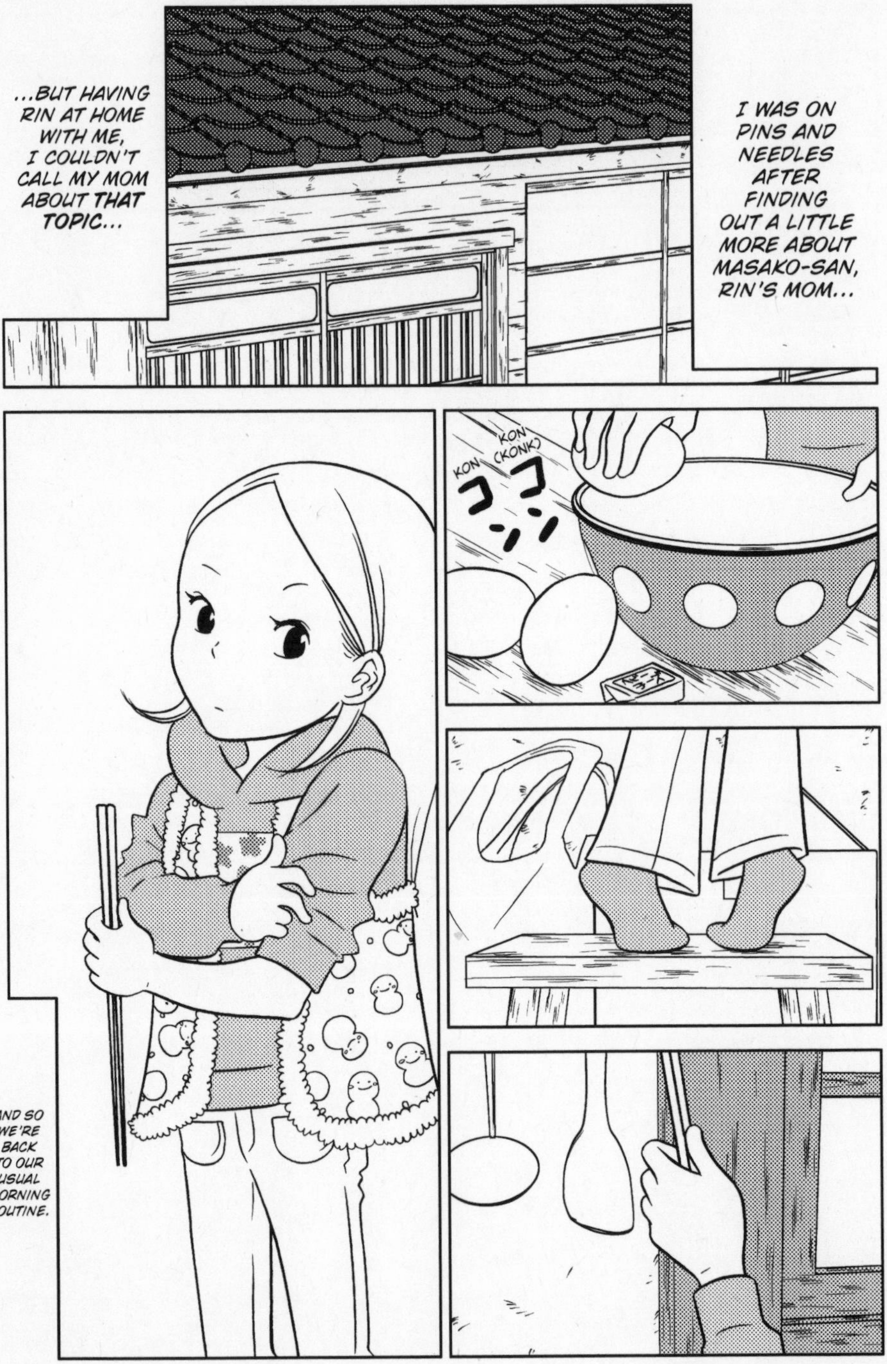
I WAS ON PINS AND NEEDLES AFTER FINDING OUT A LITTLE MORE ABOUT MASAKO-SAN, RIN'S MOM...
...BUT HAVING RIN AT HOME WITH ME, I COULDN'T CALL MY MOM ABOUT THAT TOPIC...
KON (KONK)
KON
AND SO WE'RE BACK TO OUR USUAL MORNING ROUTINE.

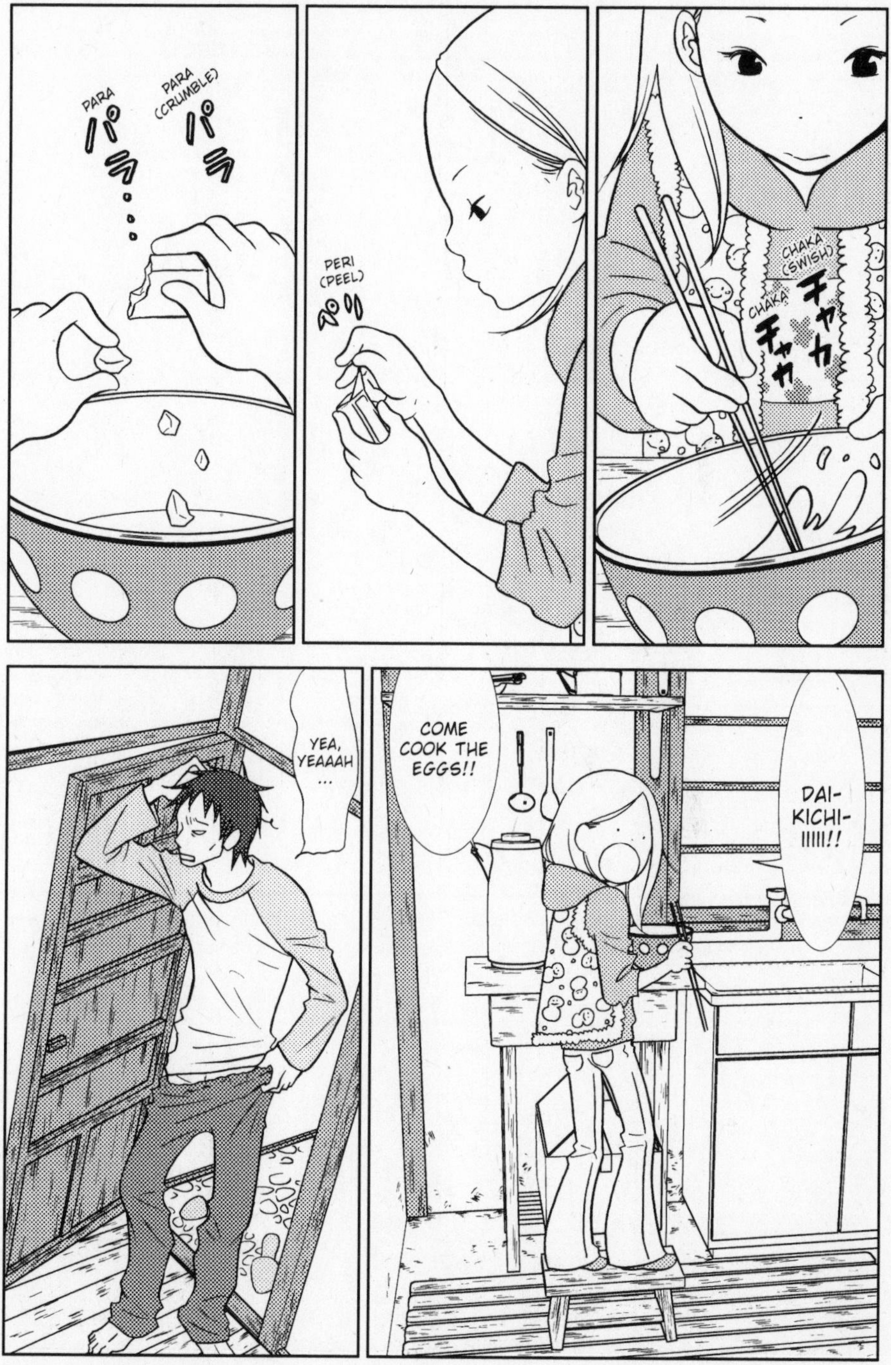
CHAKA (SWISH)
チャカ
CHAKA
チャカ
PERI (PEEL)
ペリ
PARA (CRUMBLE)
パラ
PARA
パラ…
DAI-KICHI-IIIIII!!
COME COOK THE EGGS!!
YEA, YEAAAH …

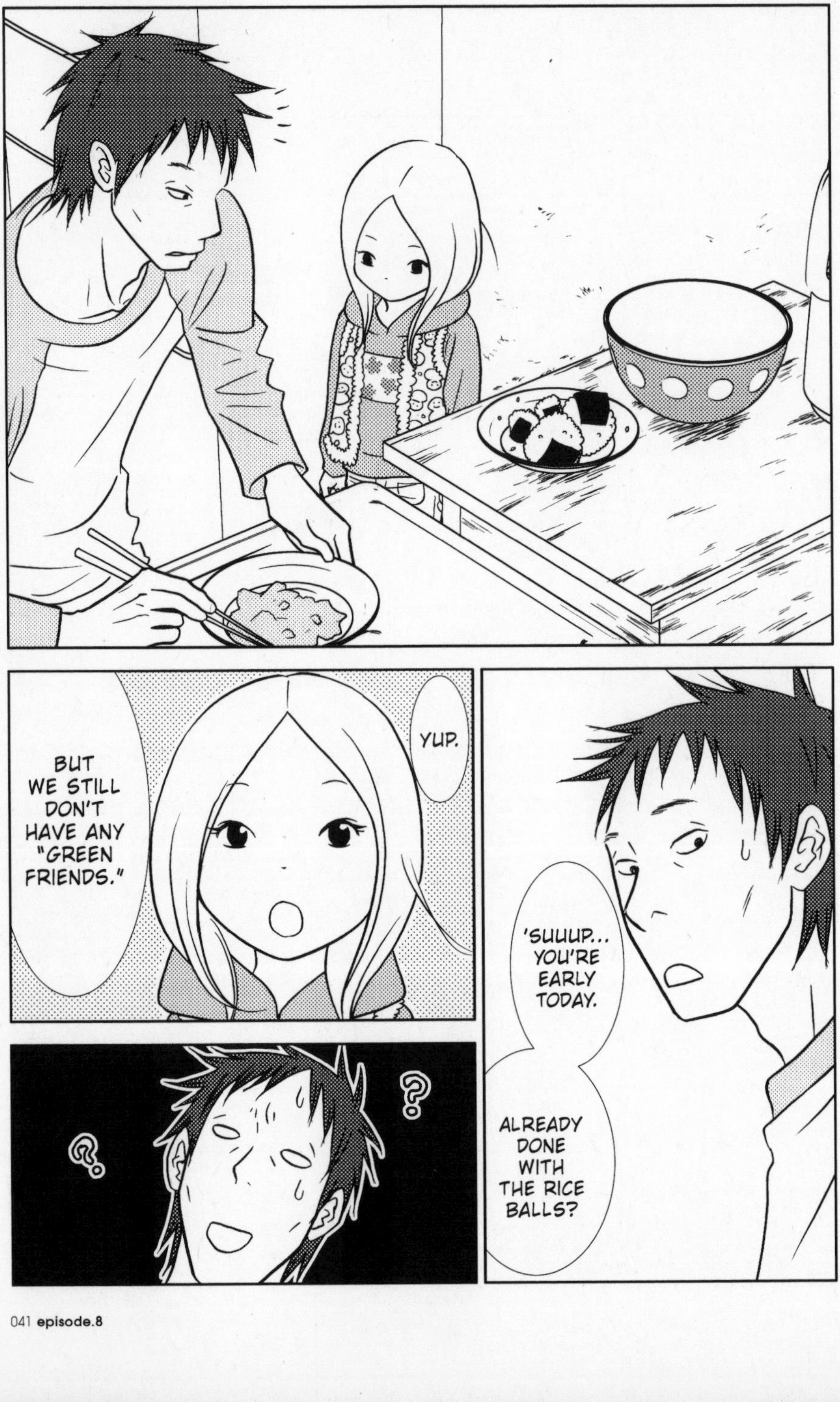
'SUUUP... YOU'RE EARLY TODAY.
ALREADY DONE WITH THE RICE BALLS?
YUP.
BUT WE STILL DON'T HAVE ANY "GREEN FRIENDS."

WH-WHAT WAS THAT AGAIN ...?
RICE BALLS ARE "YELLOW FRIENDS."
EGGS AND CHEESE ARE "RED FRIENDS."
AH ...!
AH, YEAH ...
DID YOU FORGET ALREADY?
THOSE!!
UMMM... HNNN... GREEN WOULD BE...
WHAT'S LEFT? FRUITS AND VEGGIES ...?
INCIDENTALLY, IT TURNS OUT THAT KINDER-GARTNERS THESE DAYS ARE TAUGHT NUTRITION... (SIMPLE STUFF)...
H-HOW ABOUT AN ORANGE!!?
(STAB IN THE DARK).
OKAY!!
HOW DO I PUT IT... SHE'S REALLY RESPON-SIBLE... AND ALSO HARD TO TRICK...

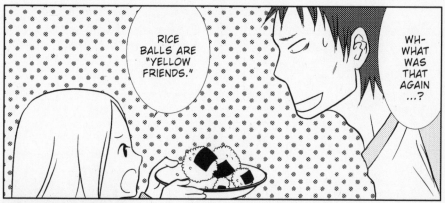

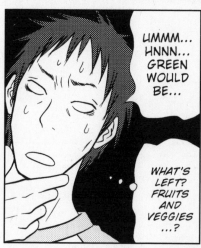

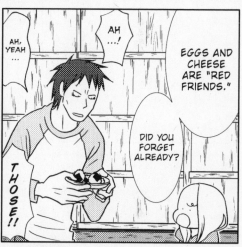

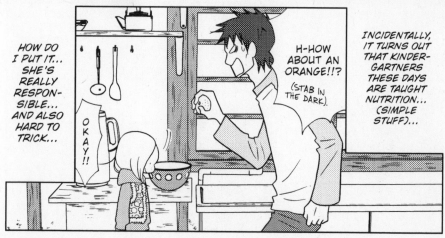

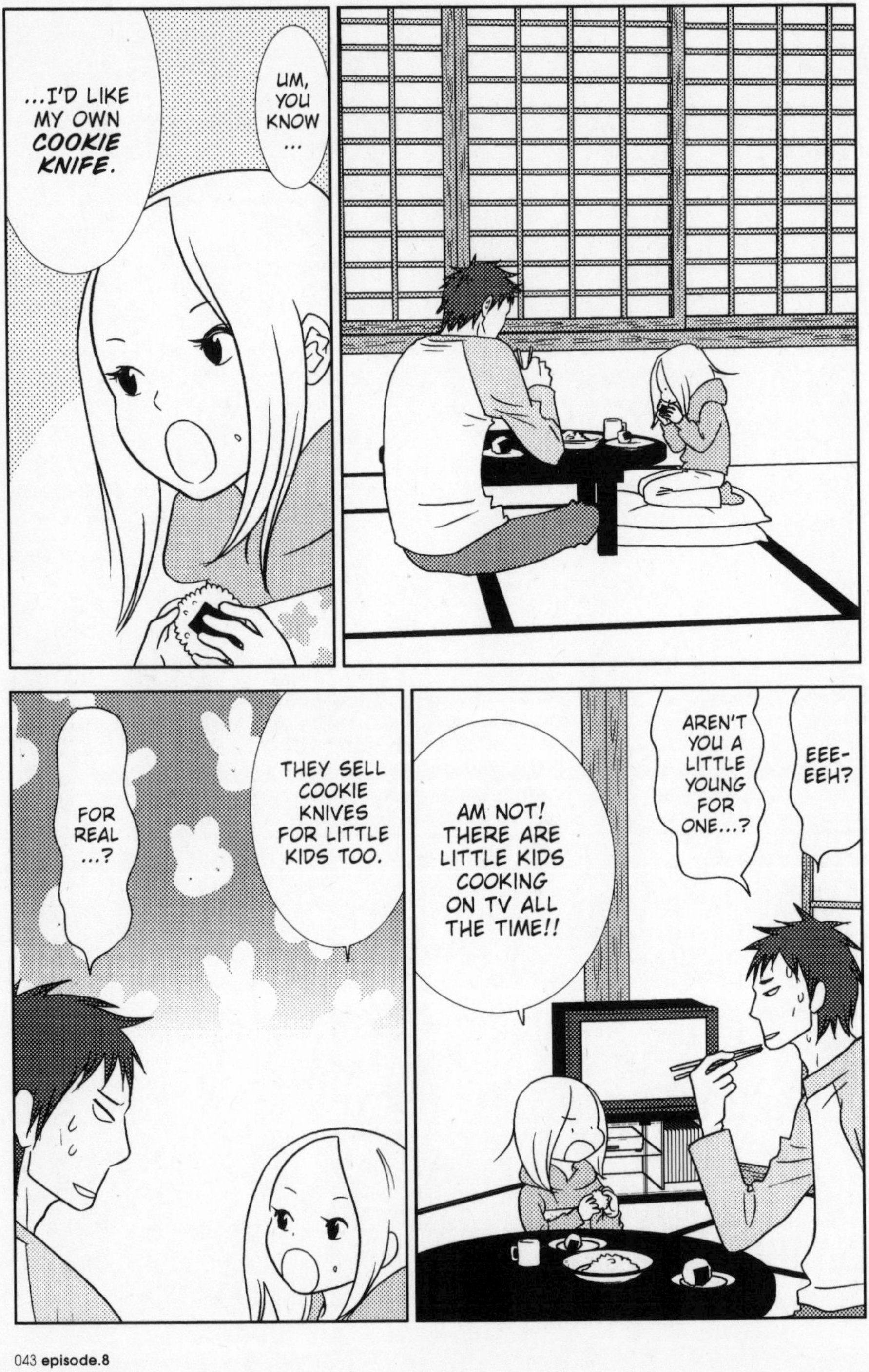
UM, YOU KNOW ...
...I'D LIKE MY OWN **COOKIE KNIFE**.
EEE-EEH?
AREN'T YOU A LITTLE YOUNG FOR ONE...?
AM NOT! THERE ARE LITTLE KIDS COOKING ON TV ALL THE TIME!!
THEY SELL COOKIE KNIVES FOR LITTLE KIDS TOO.
FOR REAL ...?

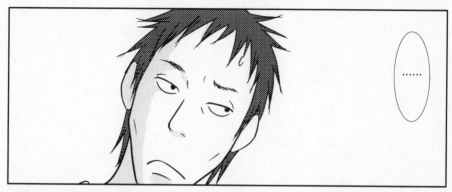

......

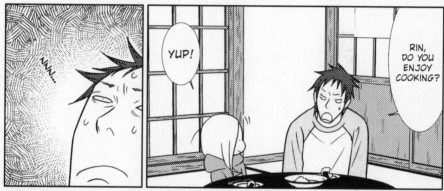

NN!..

YUP!

RIN, DO YOU ENJOY COOKING?

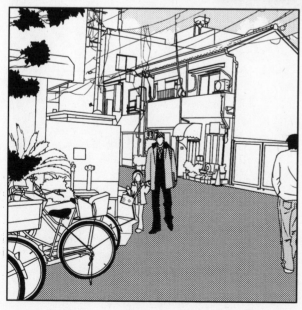

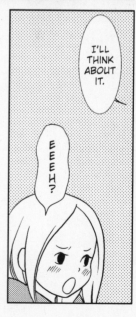

I'LL THINK ABOUT IT.

EEEH?

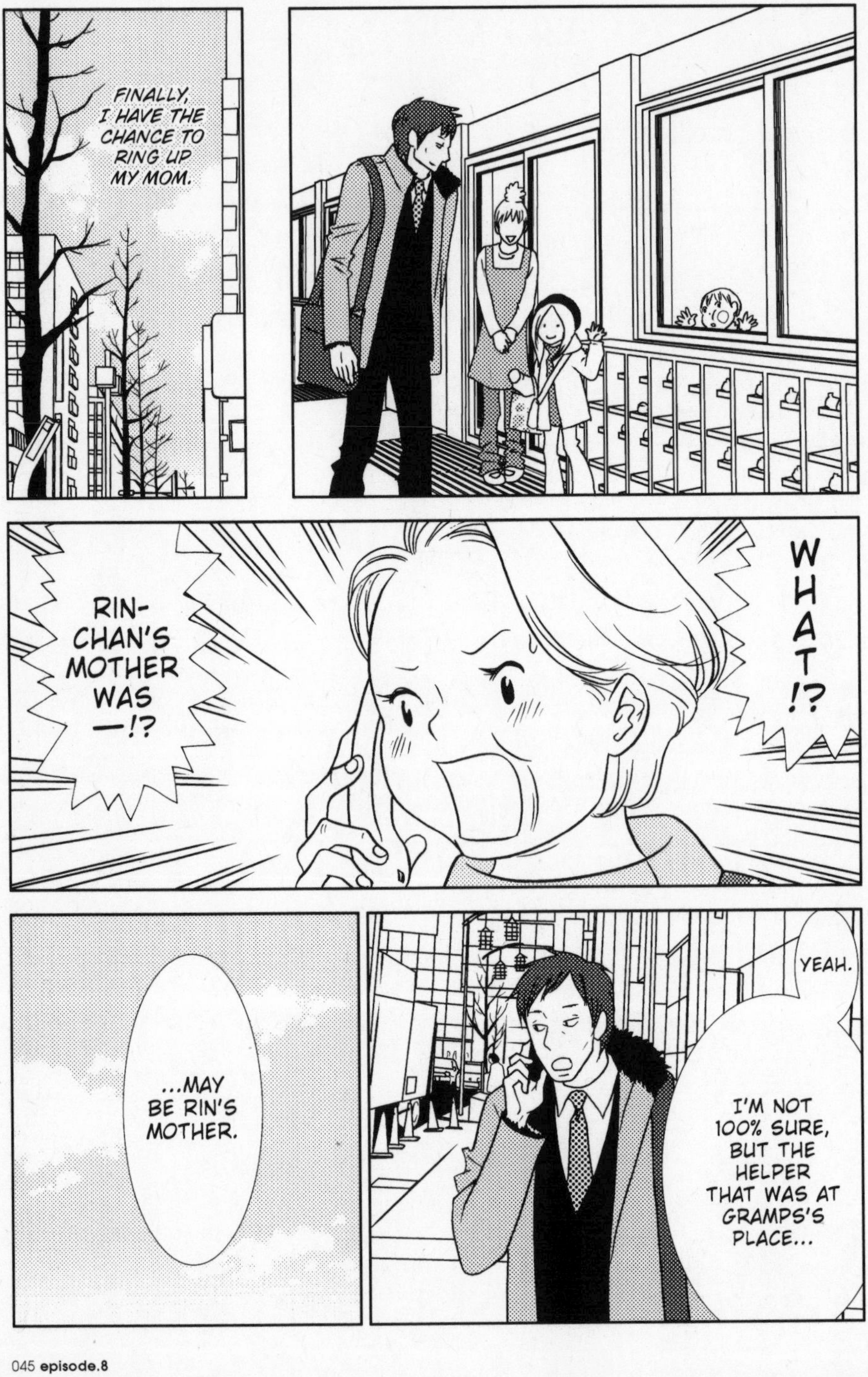
FINALLY, I HAVE THE CHANCE TO RING UP MY MOM.
WHAT!?
RIN-CHAN'S MOTHER WAS—!?
YEAH.
I'M NOT 100% SURE, BUT THE HELPER THAT WAS AT GRAMPS'S PLACE...
...MAY BE RIN'S MOTHER.

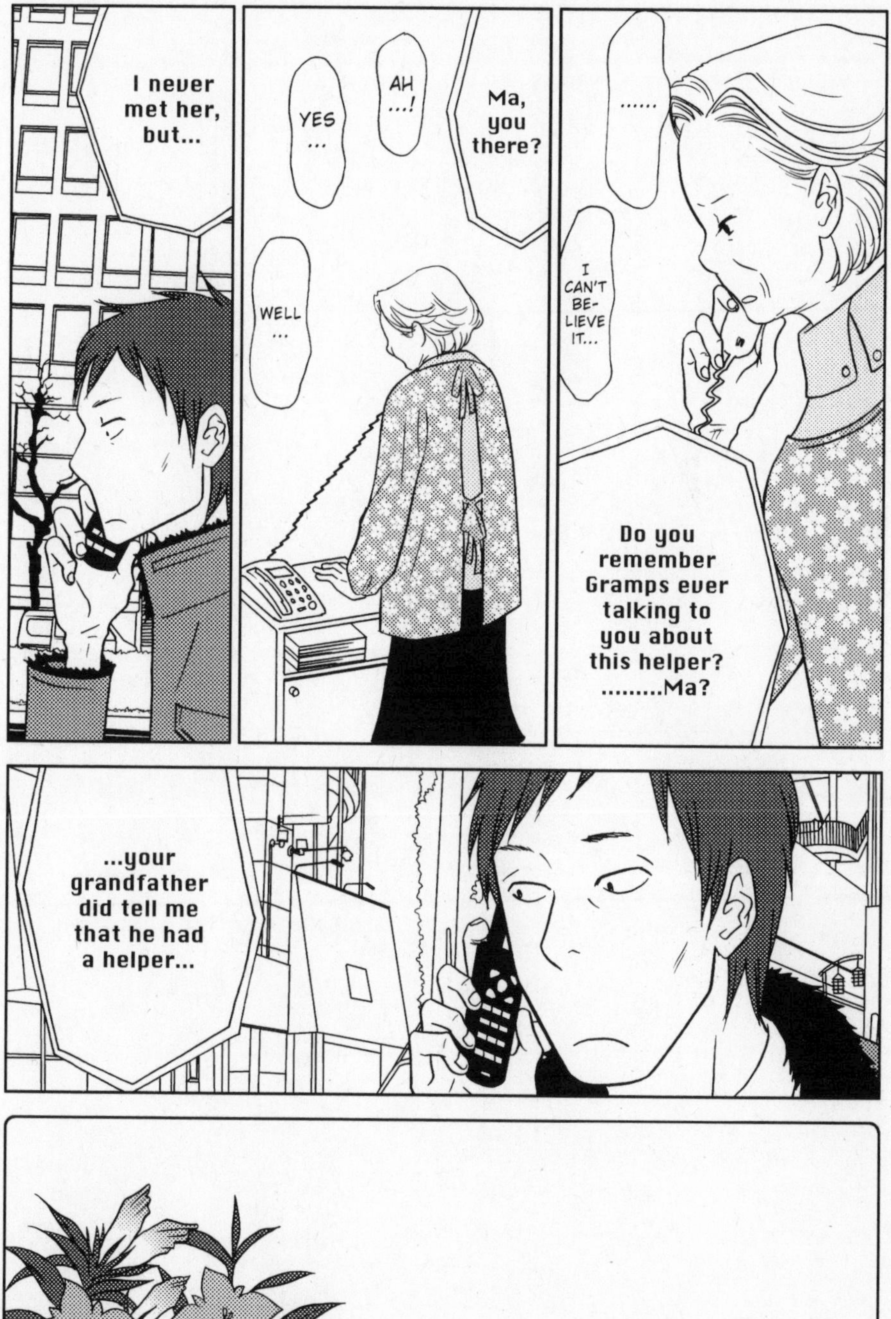

......
I CAN'T BE-LIEVE IT...
Do you remember Gramps ever talking to you about this helper? ....Ma?
Ma, you there?
AH ...!
YES ...
WELL ...
I never met her, but...
...your grandfather did tell me that he had a helper...

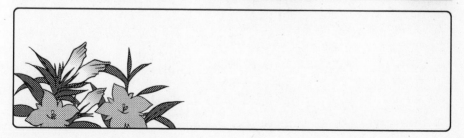

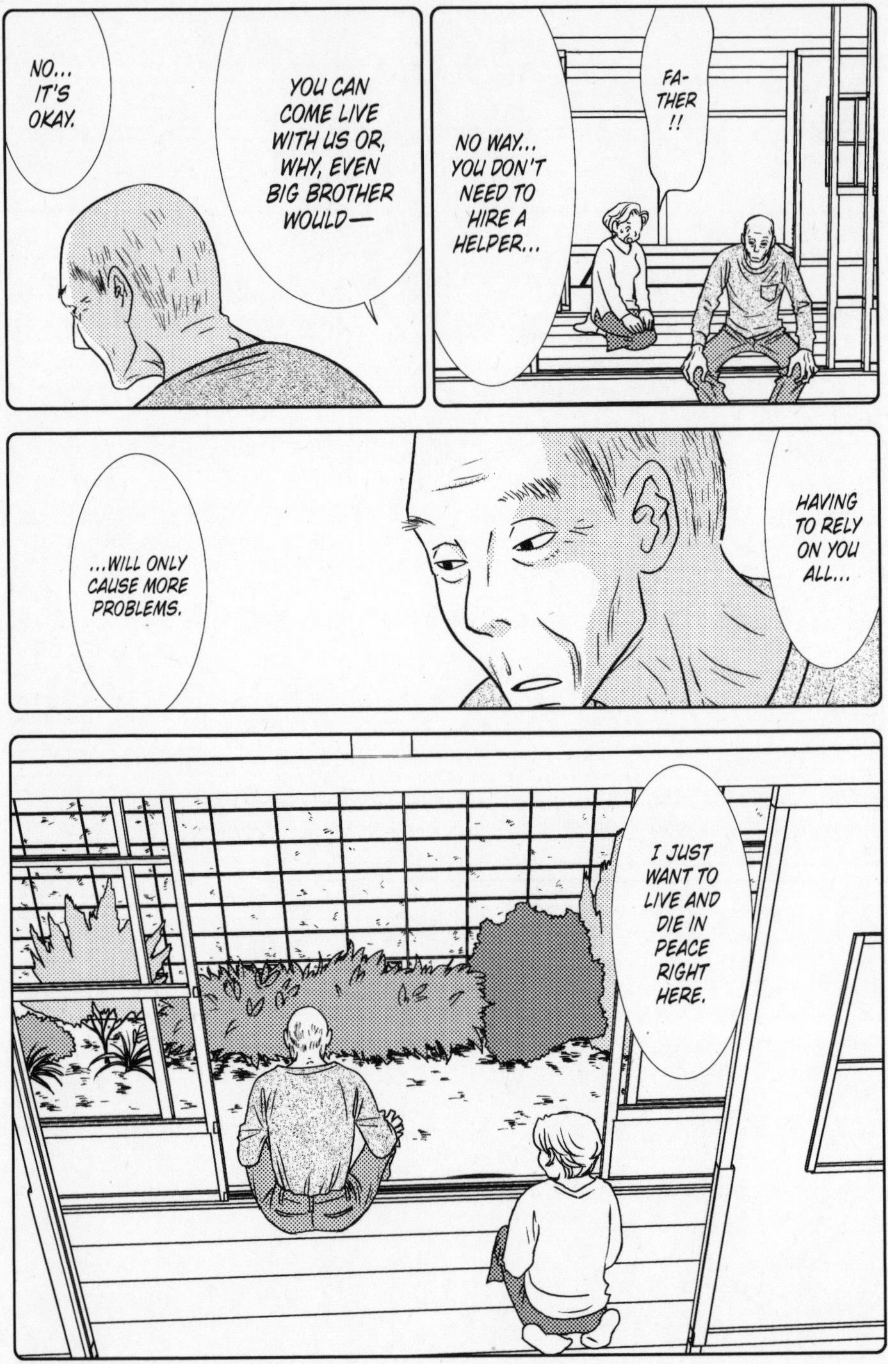
FA-THER!!
NO WAY... YOU DON'T NEED TO HIRE A HELPER...
YOU CAN COME LIVE WITH US OR, WHY, EVEN BIG BROTHER WOULD—
NO... IT'S OKAY.
HAVING TO RELY ON YOU ALL...
...WILL ONLY CAUSE MORE PROBLEMS.
I JUST WANT TO LIVE AND DIE IN PEACE RIGHT HERE.

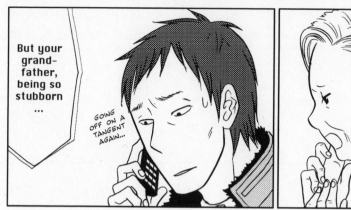

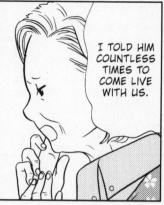

I TOLD HIM COUNTLESS TIMES TO COME LIVE WITH US.
But your grand-father, being so stubborn ...
GOING OFF ON A TANGENT AGAIN...
MA, I JUST GOT TO WORK NOW, SO...
...IF YOU FIND OUT ANYTHING ABOUT THIS HELPER, COULD YOU LET ME KNOW?
BYE ...

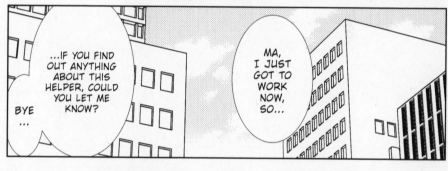

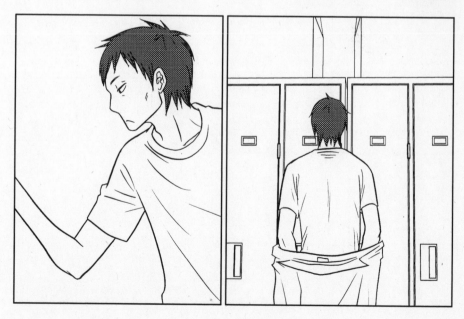

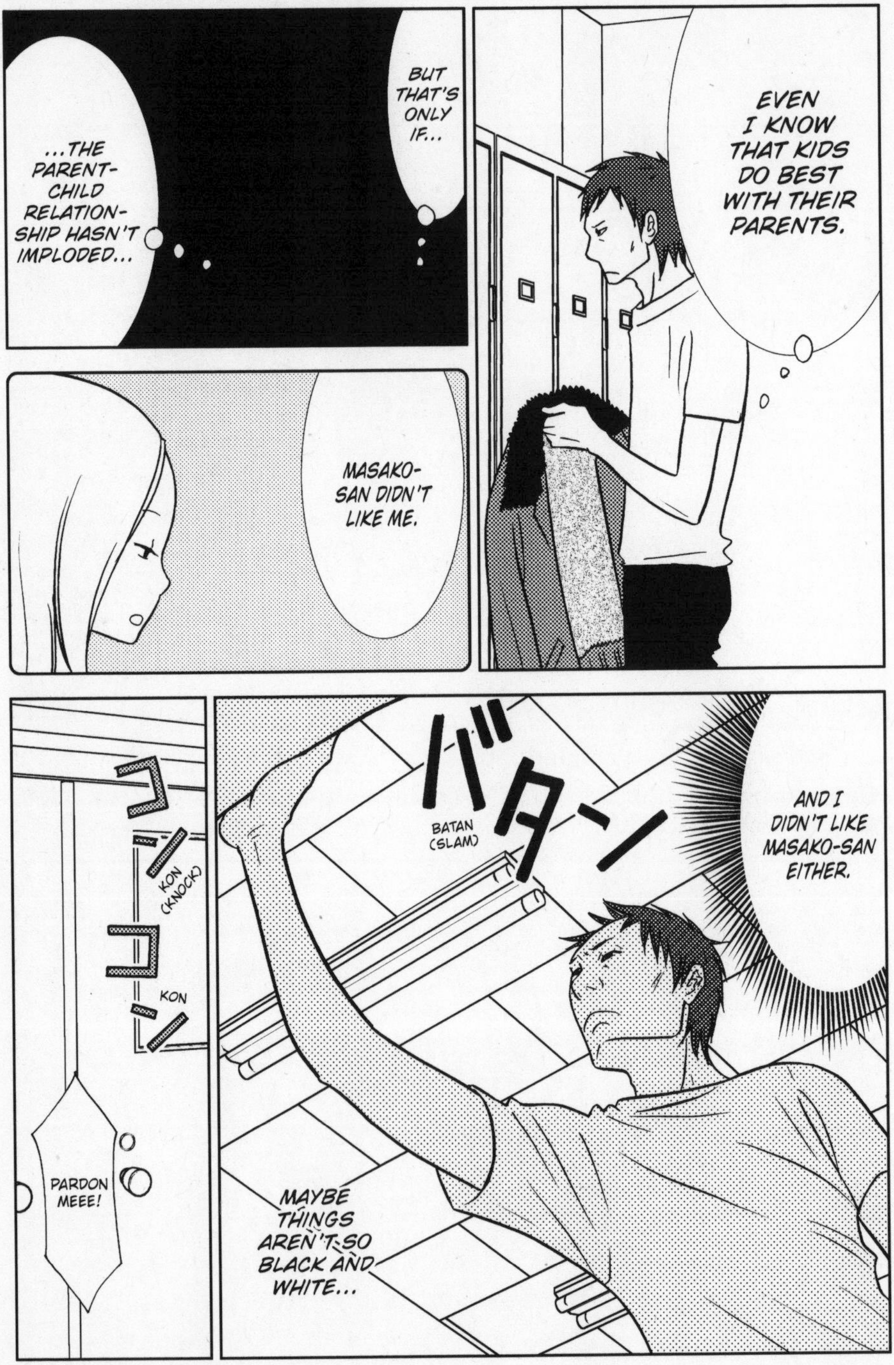
EVEN I KNOW THAT KIDS DO BEST WITH THEIR PARENTS.
BUT THAT'S ONLY IF...
...THE PARENT-CHILD RELATIONSHIP HASN'T IMPLODED...
MASAKO-SAN DIDN'T LIKE ME.
AND I DIDN'T LIKE MASAKO-SAN EITHER.
バタン
BATAN (SLAM)
MAYBE THINGS AREN'T SO BLACK AND WHITE...
コン
KON (KNOCK)
コン
KON
PARDON MEEE!

JACKET: DAIKICHI

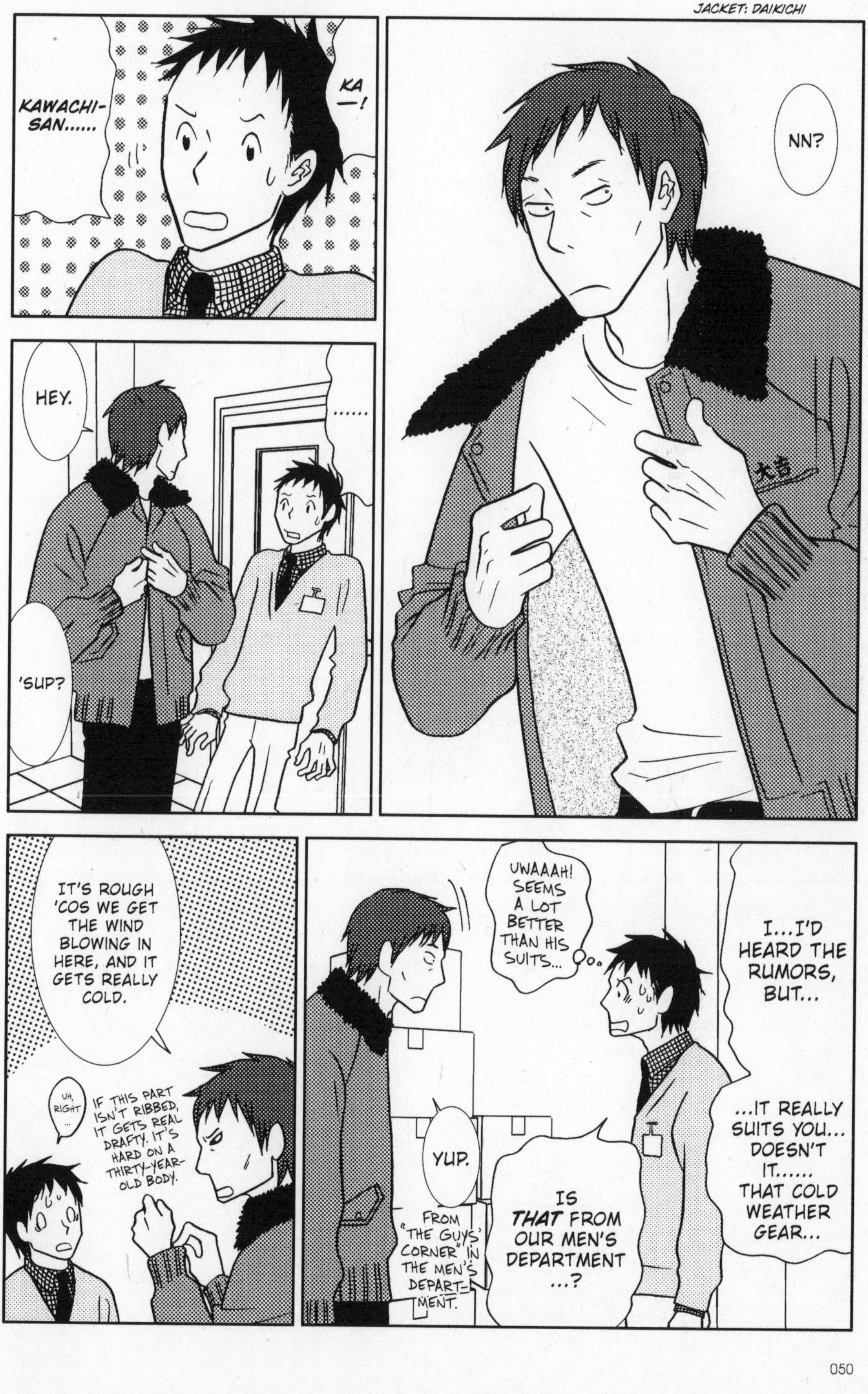
NN?
KA—!
KAWACHI-SAN......
......
HEY.
'SUP?
I...I'D HEARD THE RUMORS, BUT...
UWAAAH! SEEMS A LOT BETTER THAN HIS SUITS...
...IT REALLY SUITS YOU... DOESN'T IT...... THAT COLD WEATHER GEAR...
IS THAT FROM OUR MEN'S DEPARTMENT ...?
YUP.
FROM "THE GUYS' CORNER" IN THE MEN'S DEPART-MENT.
IT'S ROUGH 'COS WE GET THE WIND BLOWING IN HERE, AND IT GETS REALLY COLD.
IF THIS PART ISN'T RIBBED, IT GETS REAL DRAFTY. IT'S HARD ON A THIRTY-YEAR-OLD BODY.
UH, RIGHT ...

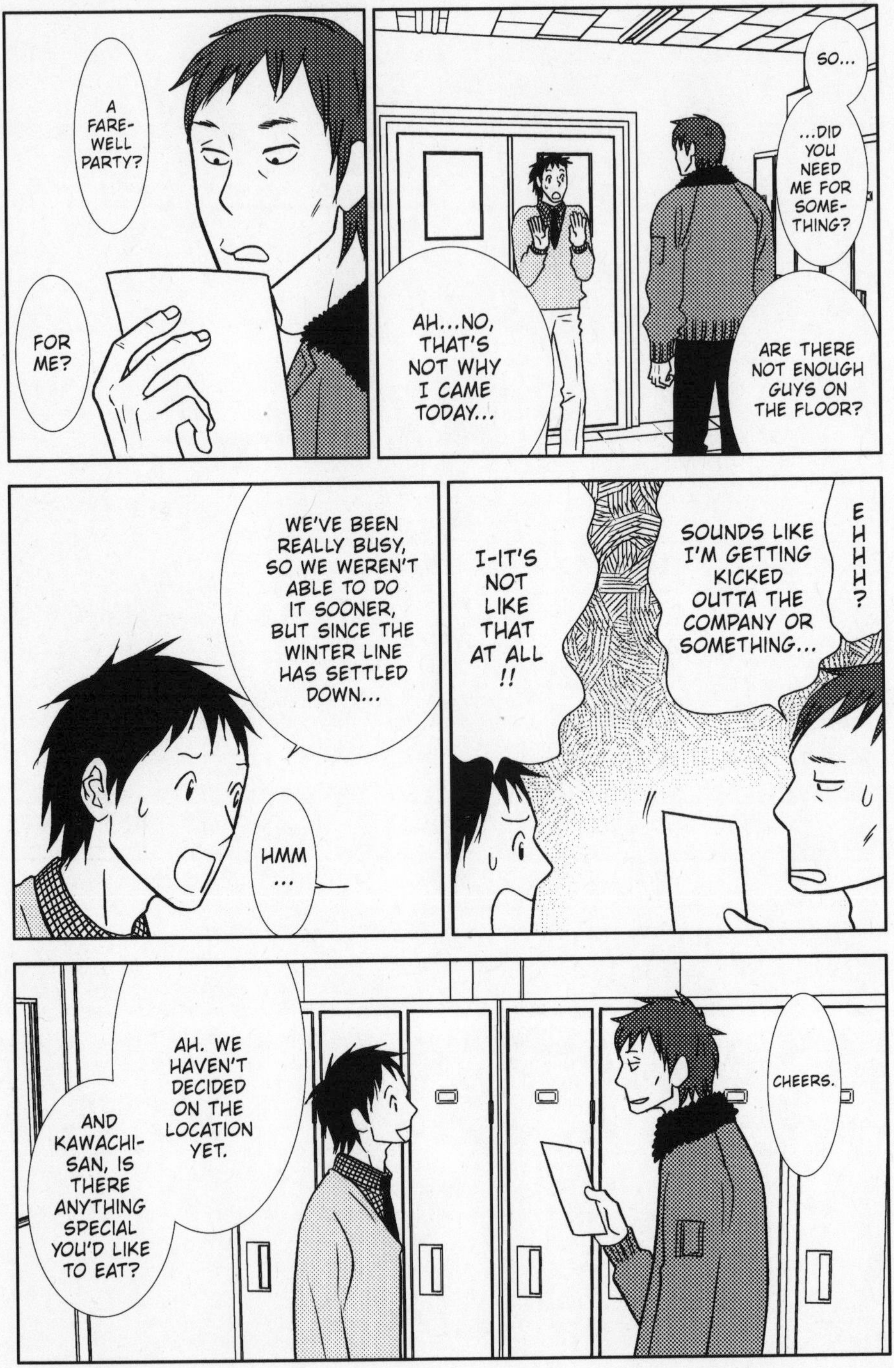
SO...
...DID YOU NEED ME FOR SOMETHING?
ARE THERE NOT ENOUGH GUYS ON THE FLOOR?
AH...NO, THAT'S NOT WHY I CAME TODAY...
A FAREWELL PARTY?
FOR ME?
EHHH?
SOUNDS LIKE I'M GETTING KICKED OUTTA THE COMPANY OR SOMETHING...
I-IT'S NOT LIKE THAT AT ALL!!
WE'VE BEEN REALLY BUSY, SO WE WEREN'T ABLE TO DO IT SOONER, BUT SINCE THE WINTER LINE HAS SETTLED DOWN...
HMM...
CHEERS.
AH. WE HAVEN'T DECIDED ON THE LOCATION YET.
AND KAWACHI-SAN, IS THERE ANYTHING SPECIAL YOU'D LIKE TO EAT?

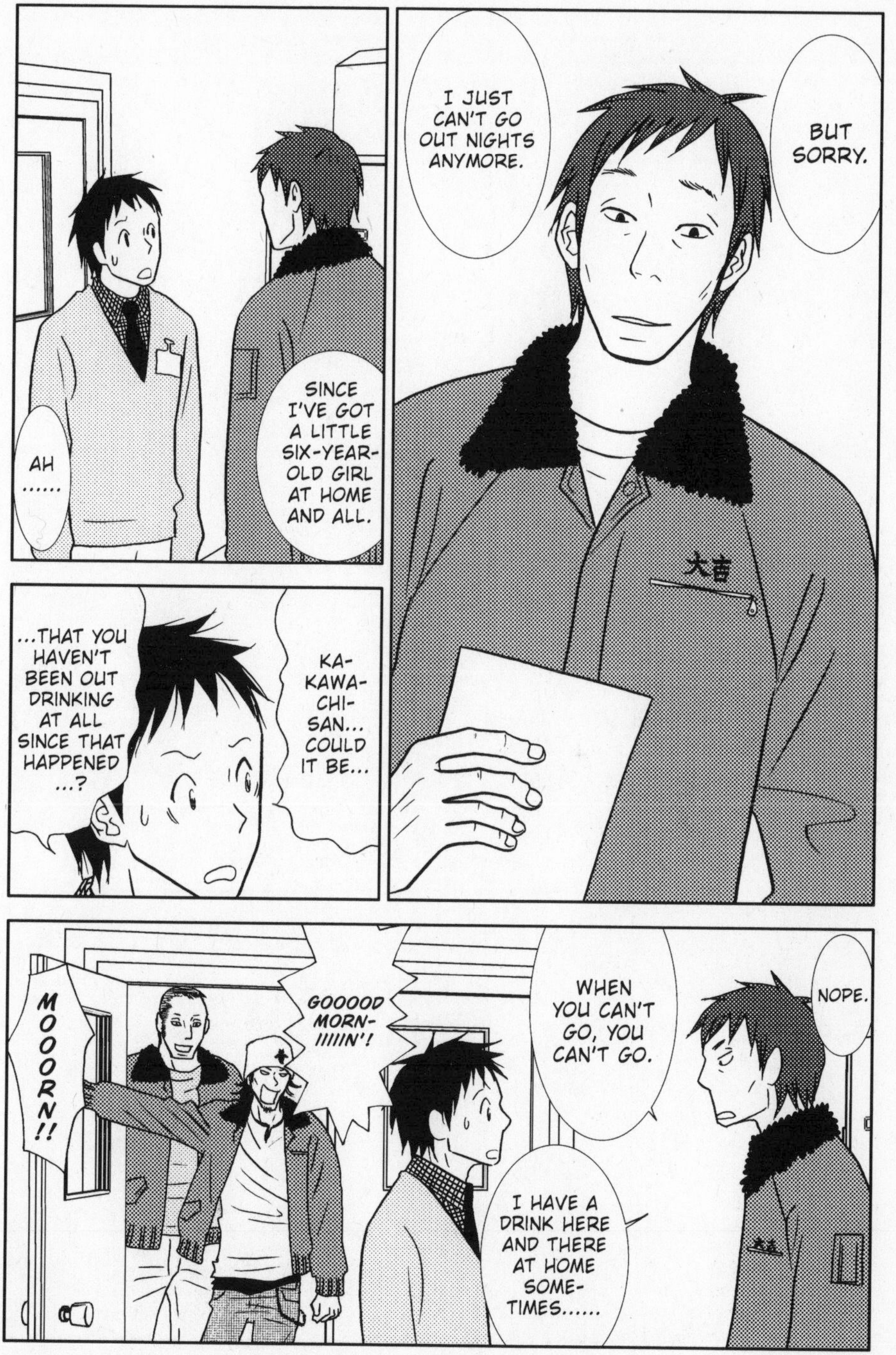
BUT SORRY.
I JUST CAN'T GO OUT NIGHTS ANYMORE.
大吉
SINCE I'VE GOT A LITTLE SIX-YEAR-OLD GIRL AT HOME AND ALL.
AH ......
KA-KAWACHI-SAN... COULD IT BE...
...THAT YOU HAVEN'T BEEN OUT DRINKING AT ALL SINCE THAT HAPPENED ...?
NOPE.
WHEN YOU CAN'T GO, YOU CAN'T GO.
I HAVE A DRINK HERE AND THERE AT HOME SOME-TIMES......
GOOOOD MORN-IIIIIN'!
MOOORN!!

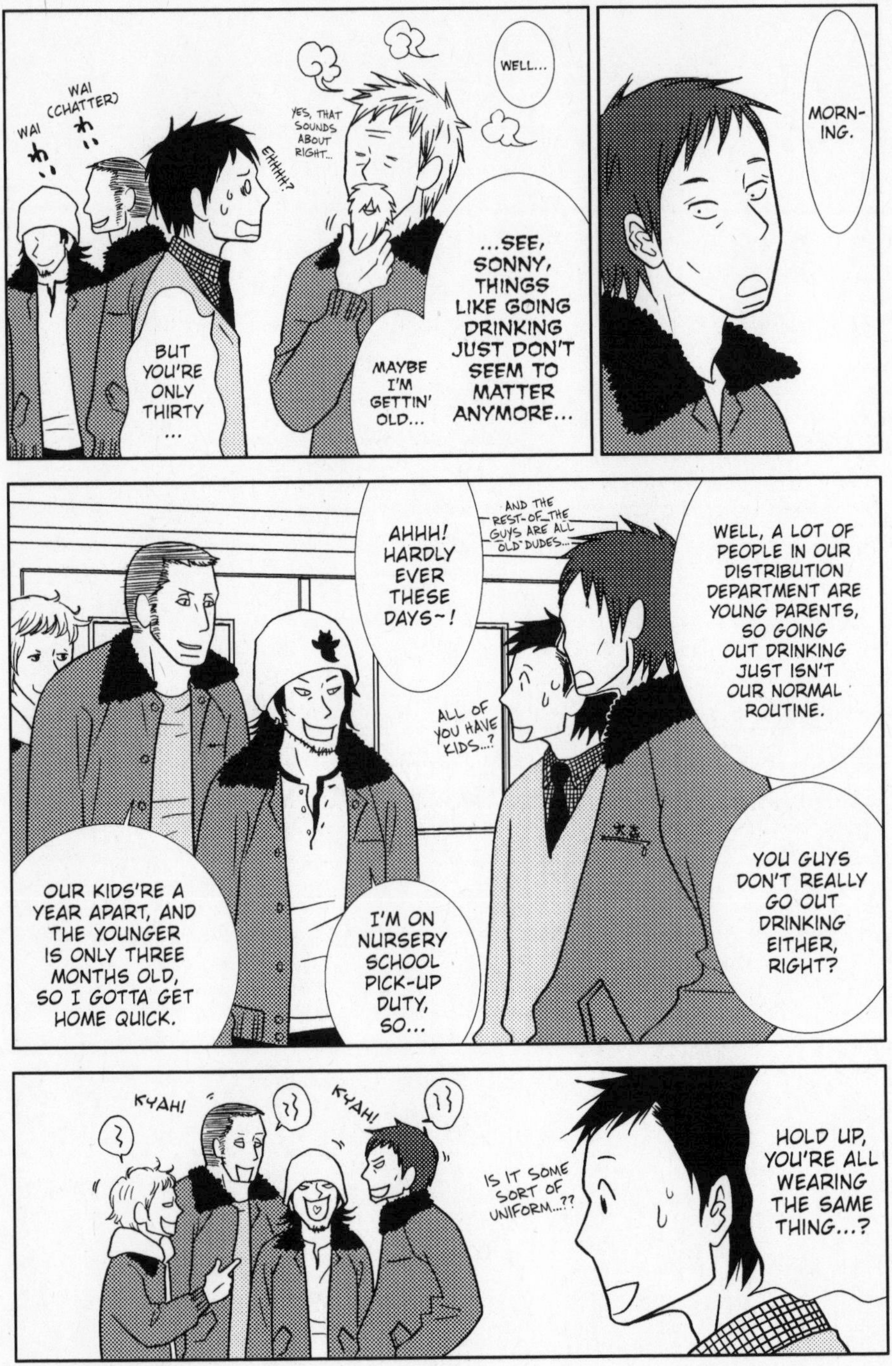
MORN-ING.
WELL...
...SEE, SONNY, THINGS LIKE GOING DRINKING JUST DON'T SEEM TO MATTER ANYMORE...
YES, THAT SOUNDS ABOUT RIGHT...
MAYBE I'M GETTIN' OLD...
EHHHH?
BUT YOU'RE ONLY THIRTY...
WAI (CHATTER) わい
WAI わい
WELL, A LOT OF PEOPLE IN OUR DISTRIBUTION DEPARTMENT ARE YOUNG PARENTS, SO GOING OUT DRINKING JUST ISN'T OUR NORMAL ROUTINE.
AND THE REST OF THE GUYS ARE ALL OLD DUDES...
AHHH! HARDLY EVER THESE DAYS~!
YOU GUYS DON'T REALLY GO OUT DRINKING EITHER, RIGHT?
ALL OF YOU HAVE KIDS...?
I'M ON NURSERY SCHOOL PICK-UP DUTY, SO...
OUR KIDS'RE A YEAR APART, AND THE YOUNGER IS ONLY THREE MONTHS OLD, SO I GOTTA GET HOME QUICK.
HOLD UP, YOU'RE ALL WEARING THE SAME THING...?
IS IT SOME SORT OF UNIFORM...??
KYAH!
KYAH!

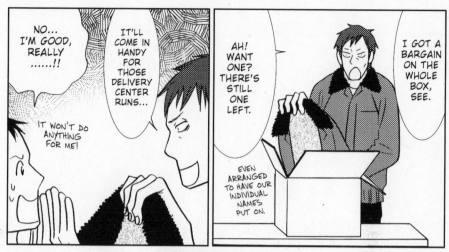

I GOT A BARGAIN ON THE WHOLE BOX, SEE.
EVEN ARRANGED TO HAVE OUR INDIVIDUAL NAMES PUT ON.
AH! WANT ONE? THERE'S STILL ONE LEFT.
IT'LL COME IN HANDY FOR THOSE DELIVERY CENTER RUNS...
NO... I'M GOOD, REALLY ......!!
IT WON'T DO ANYTHING FOR ME!
BUT SERIOUSLY, THINK ABOUT IT, OKAY, KAWACHI-SAN!?
PYUU (DASH)
FASHION SNOB.
I TOLD YOU I CAN'T...
GASHAN (CRASH)
BACHIN (SNAP)

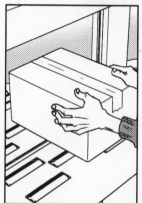

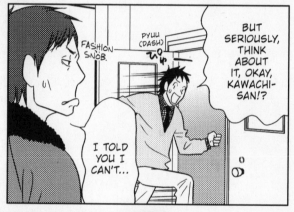

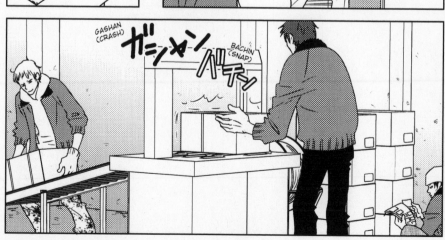

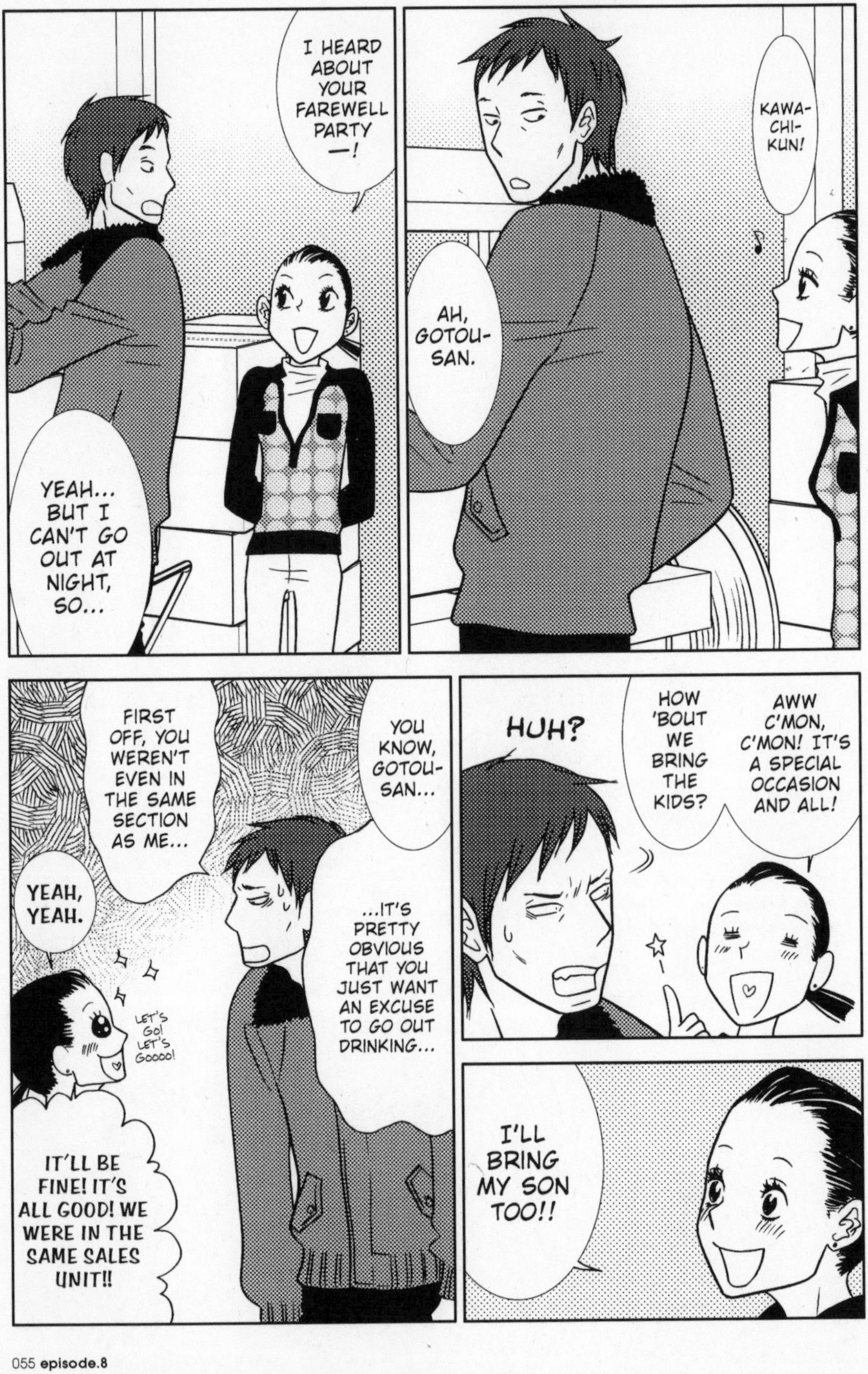
KAWA-CHI-KUN!
AH, GOTOU-SAN.
I HEARD ABOUT YOUR FAREWELL PARTY—!
YEAH... BUT I CAN'T GO OUT AT NIGHT, SO...
AWW C'MON, C'MON! IT'S A SPECIAL OCCASION AND ALL!
HOW 'BOUT WE BRING THE KIDS?
HUH?
I'LL BRING MY SON TOO!!
YOU KNOW, GOTOU-SAN...
FIRST OFF, YOU WEREN'T EVEN IN THE SAME SECTION AS ME...
...IT'S PRETTY OBVIOUS THAT YOU JUST WANT AN EXCUSE TO GO OUT DRINKING...
YEAH, YEAH.
LET'S GO! LET'S GOOOO!
IT'LL BE FINE! IT'S ALL GOOD! WE WERE IN THE SAME SALES UNIT!!

WHADDAYA SAY, HUH? I'LL TELL THEM TO PLAN FOR THAT, 'KAAY!!?
AND I'LL GET THEM TO PUT IN A REQUEST FOR A TATAMI ROOM, OF COURSE!
ARE YOU FOR REAL!?
MY NEW WORKPLACE IS A DIVISION THAT'S ALWAYS DEPENDED HEAVILY ON CONTRACTORS AND PART-TIMERS, SO...
...MY FIRST PROJECT WAS TO REVIEW THE MANUFACTURING PROCESS.
CHANGE ISN'T SO BAD ONCE IN A WHILE...

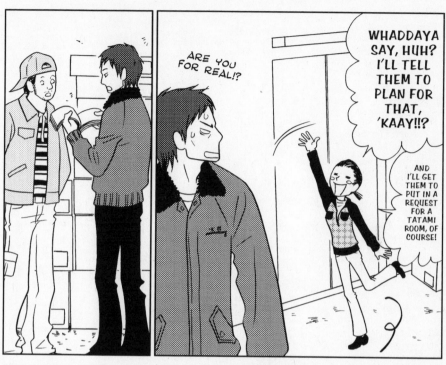

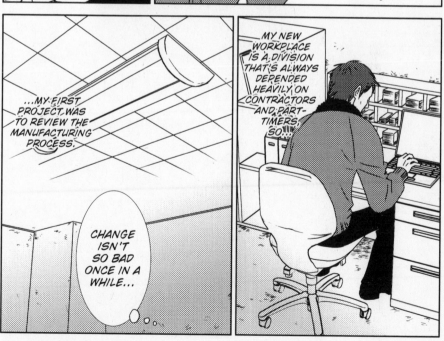

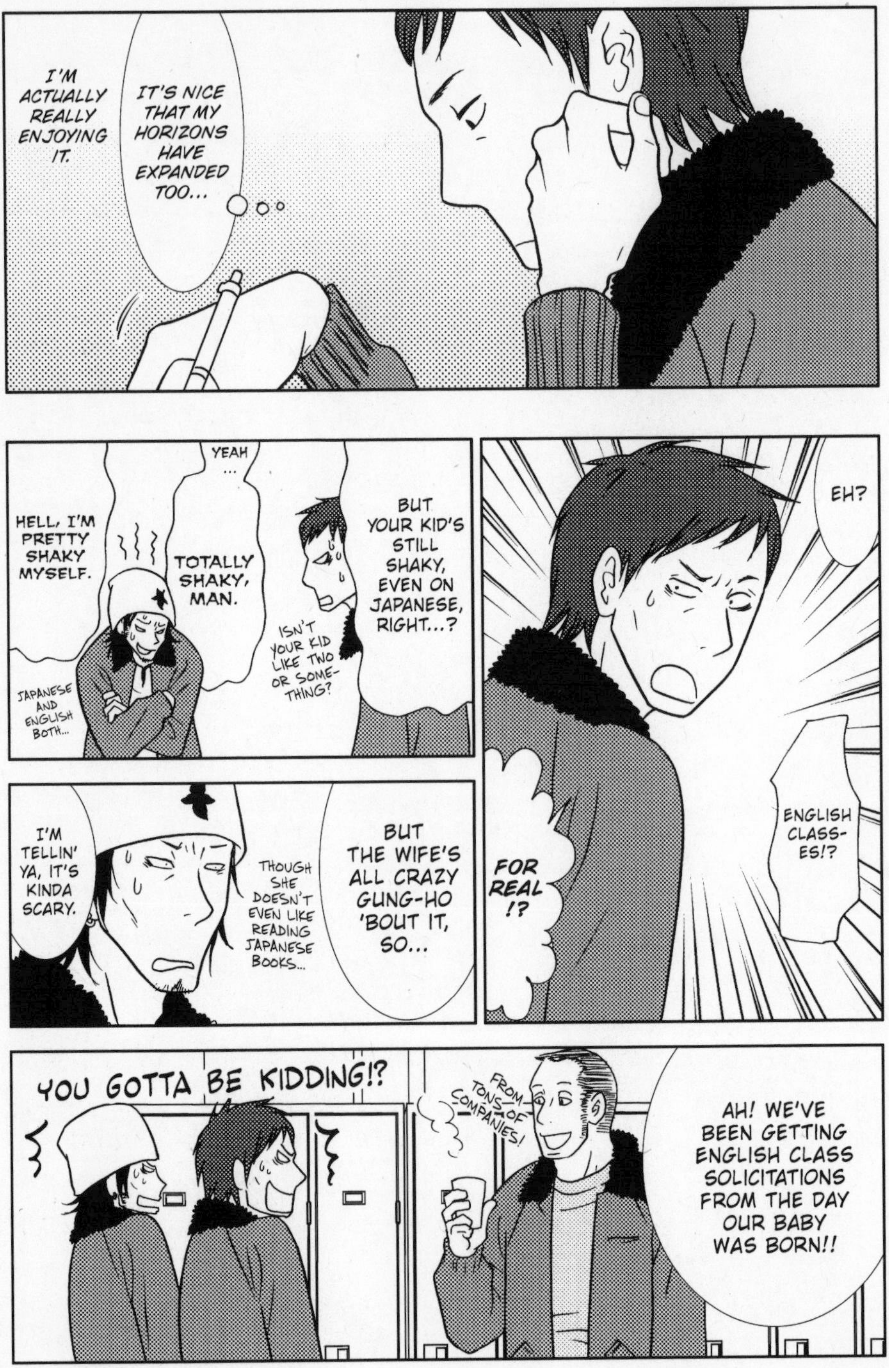
IT'S NICE THAT MY HORIZONS HAVE EXPANDED TOO...
I'M ACTUALLY REALLY ENJOYING IT.
EH?
ENGLISH CLASSES!?
FOR REAL!?
BUT YOUR KID'S STILL SHAKY, EVEN ON JAPANESE, RIGHT...?
ISN'T YOUR KID LIKE TWO OR SOME-THING?
YEAH ...
TOTALLY SHAKY, MAN.
HELL, I'M PRETTY SHAKY MYSELF.
JAPANESE AND ENGLISH BOTH...
BUT THE WIFE'S ALL CRAZY GUNG-HO 'BOUT IT, SO...
THOUGH SHE DOESN'T EVEN LIKE READING JAPANESE BOOKS...
I'M TELLIN' YA, IT'S KINDA SCARY.
AH! WE'VE BEEN GETTING ENGLISH CLASS SOLICITATIONS FROM THE DAY OUR BABY WAS BORN!!
FROM TONS OF COMPANIES!
YOU GOTTA BE KIDDING!?

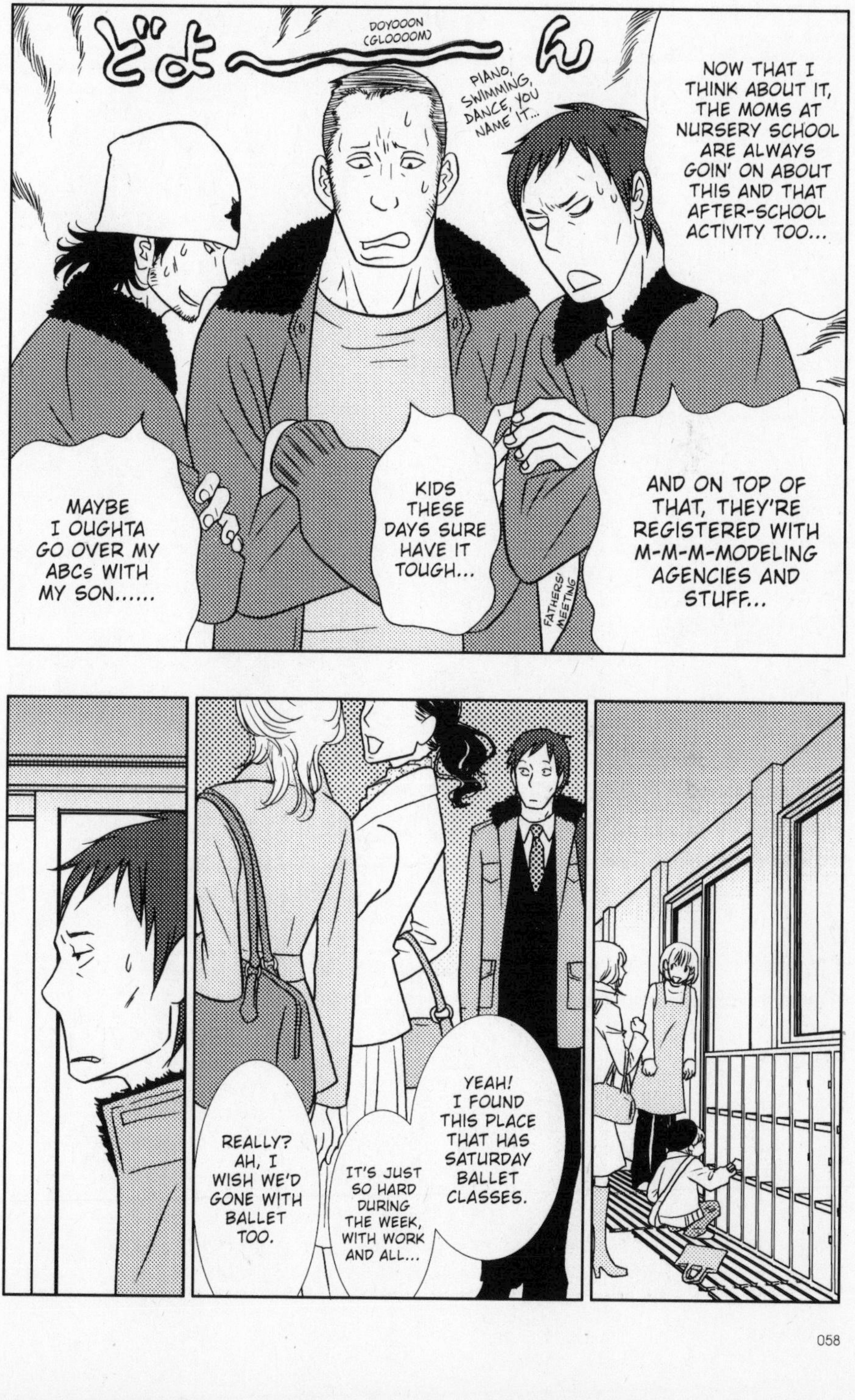
NOW THAT I THINK ABOUT IT, THE MOMS AT NURSERY SCHOOL ARE ALWAYS GOIN' ON ABOUT THIS AND THAT AFTER-SCHOOL ACTIVITY TOO...
PIANO, SWIMMING, DANCE, YOU NAME IT...
どよ〜〜ん
DOYOOON (GLOOOOM)
AND ON TOP OF THAT, THEY'RE REGISTERED WITH M-M-M-MODELING AGENCIES AND STUFF...
FATHERS' MEETING
KIDS THESE DAYS SURE HAVE IT TOUGH...
MAYBE I OUGHTA GO OVER MY ABCs WITH MY SON......
YEAH! I FOUND THIS PLACE THAT HAS SATURDAY BALLET CLASSES.
IT'S JUST SO HARD DURING THE WEEK, WITH WORK AND ALL...
REALLY? AH, I WISH WE'D GONE WITH BALLET TOO.

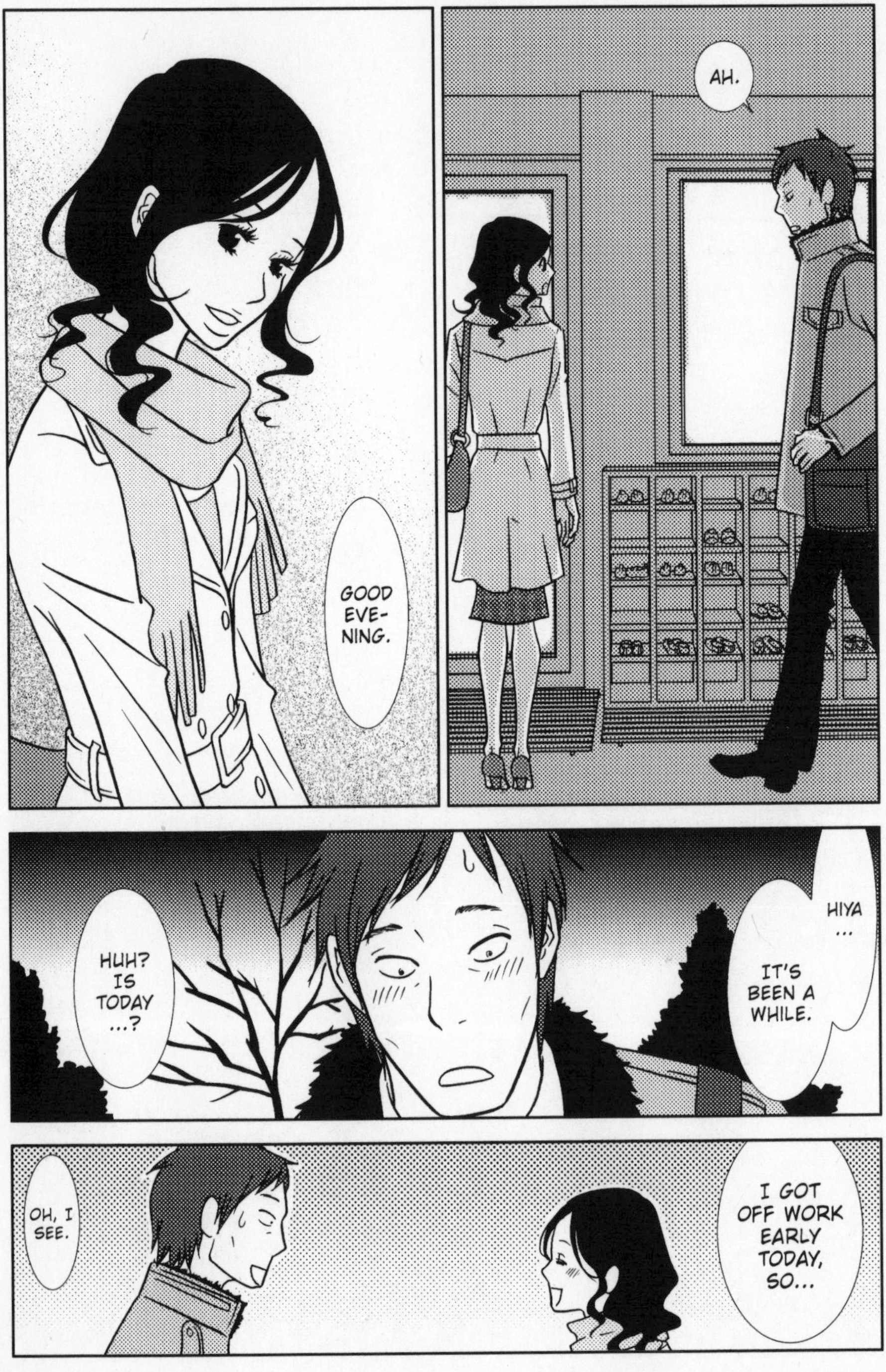
AH.
GOOD EVE-NING.
HIYA ...
IT'S BEEN A WHILE.
HUH? IS TODAY ...?
I GOT OFF WORK EARLY TODAY, SO...
OH, I SEE.

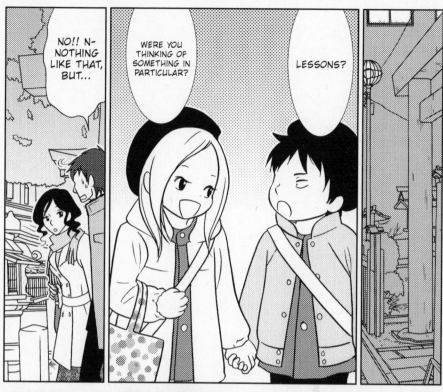

LESSONS?
WERE YOU THINKING OF SOMETHING IN PARTICULAR?
NO!! N-NOTHING LIKE THAT, BUT...
IT JUST SEEMS LIKE EVERYONE ELSE IS DOING STUFF LIKE THAT, SO...
OHH...
...I WAS WONDERING WHAT KIND OF THINGS I SHOULD BE LOOKING INTO...
RIN IS A LITTLE GIRL, AFTER ALL.
AND SHE'S STUCK GETTING RAISED BY A GEEZER LIKE ME, SO...
...I WORRY ABOUT HER FUTURE SOMETIMES.

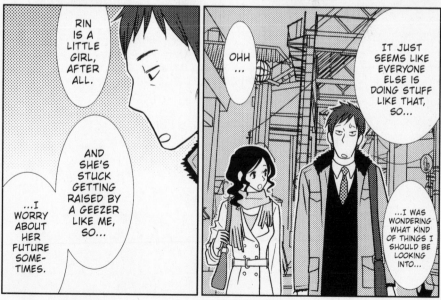

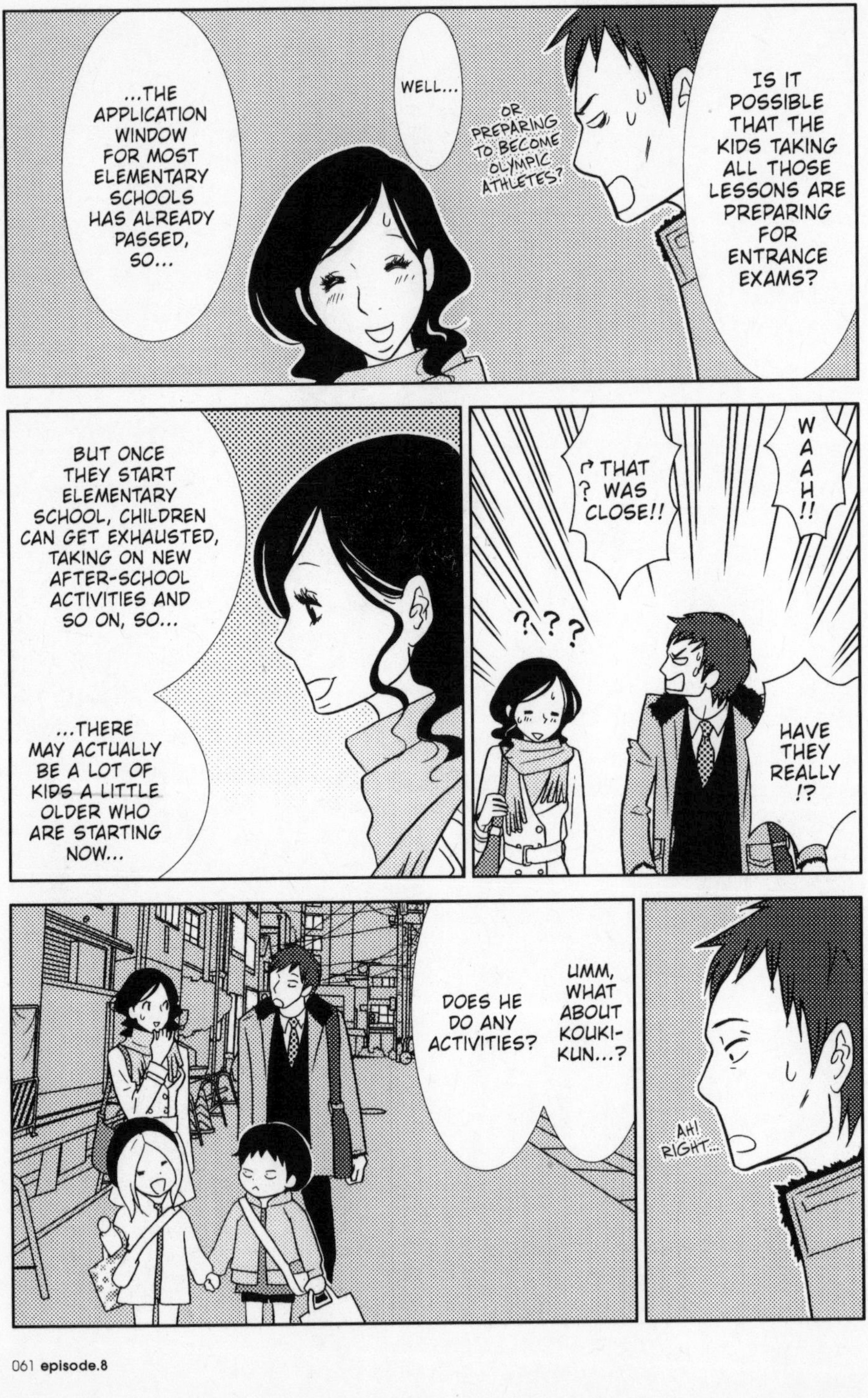
IS IT POSSIBLE THAT THE KIDS TAKING ALL THOSE LESSONS ARE PREPARING FOR ENTRANCE EXAMS?
OR PREPARING TO BECOME OLYMPIC ATHLETES?
WELL...
...THE APPLICATION WINDOW FOR MOST ELEMENTARY SCHOOLS HAS ALREADY PASSED, SO...
WAAH!!
THAT WAS CLOSE!!
???
HAVE THEY REALLY!?
BUT ONCE THEY START ELEMENTARY SCHOOL, CHILDREN CAN GET EXHAUSTED, TAKING ON NEW AFTER-SCHOOL ACTIVITIES AND SO ON, SO...
...THERE MAY ACTUALLY BE A LOT OF KIDS A LITTLE OLDER WHO ARE STARTING NOW...
AH! RIGHT...
UMM, WHAT ABOUT KOUKI-KUN...?
DOES HE DO ANY ACTIVITIES?

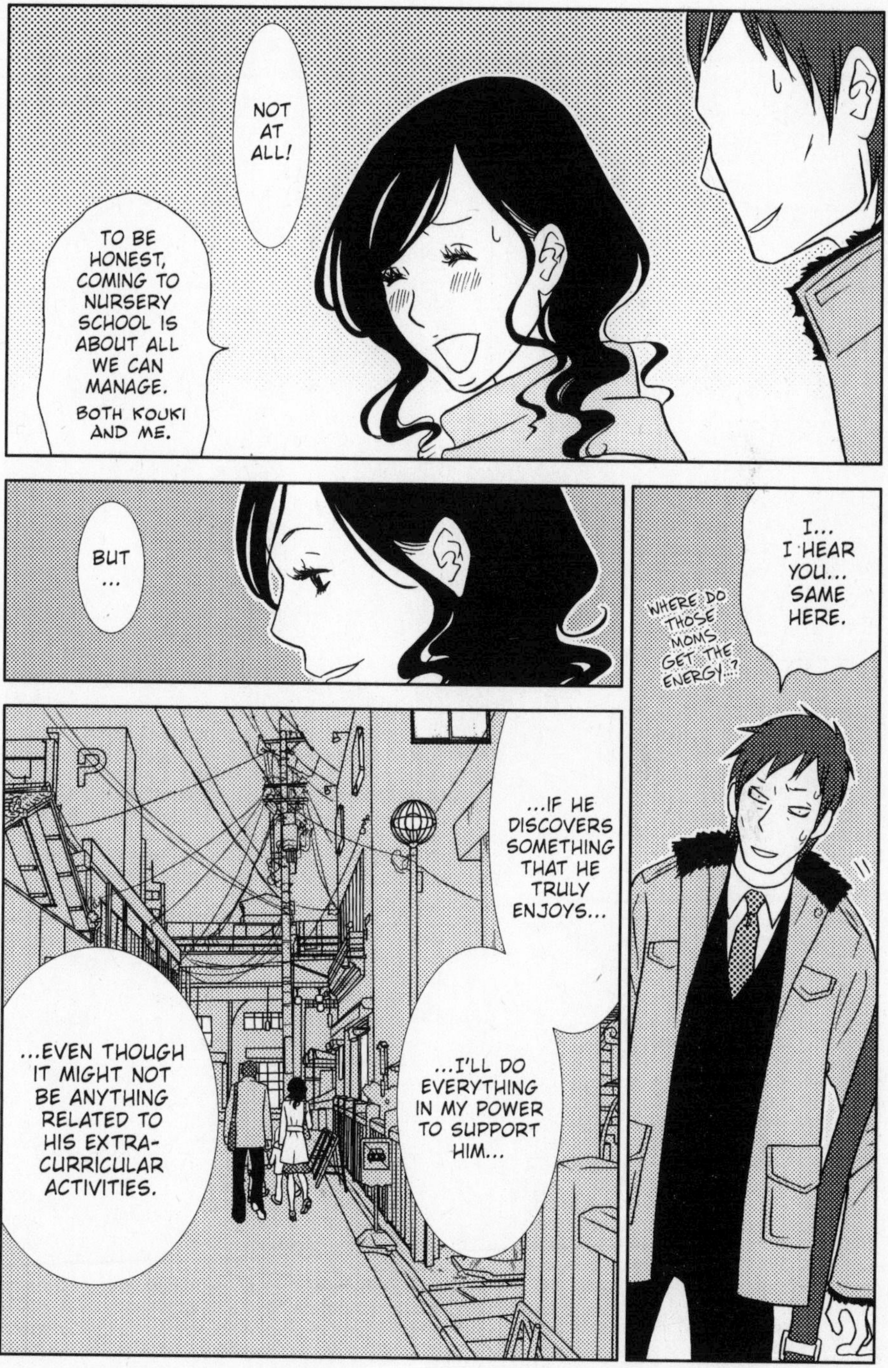
NOT AT ALL!
TO BE HONEST, COMING TO NURSERY SCHOOL IS ABOUT ALL WE CAN MANAGE. BOTH KOUKI AND ME.
I... I HEAR YOU... SAME HERE.
WHERE DO THOSE MOMS GET THE ENERGY...?
BUT...
...IF HE DISCOVERS SOMETHING THAT HE TRULY ENJOYS...
...I'LL DO EVERYTHING IN MY POWER TO SUPPORT HIM...
...EVEN THOUGH IT MIGHT NOT BE ANYTHING RELATED TO HIS EXTRA-CURRICULAR ACTIVITIES.

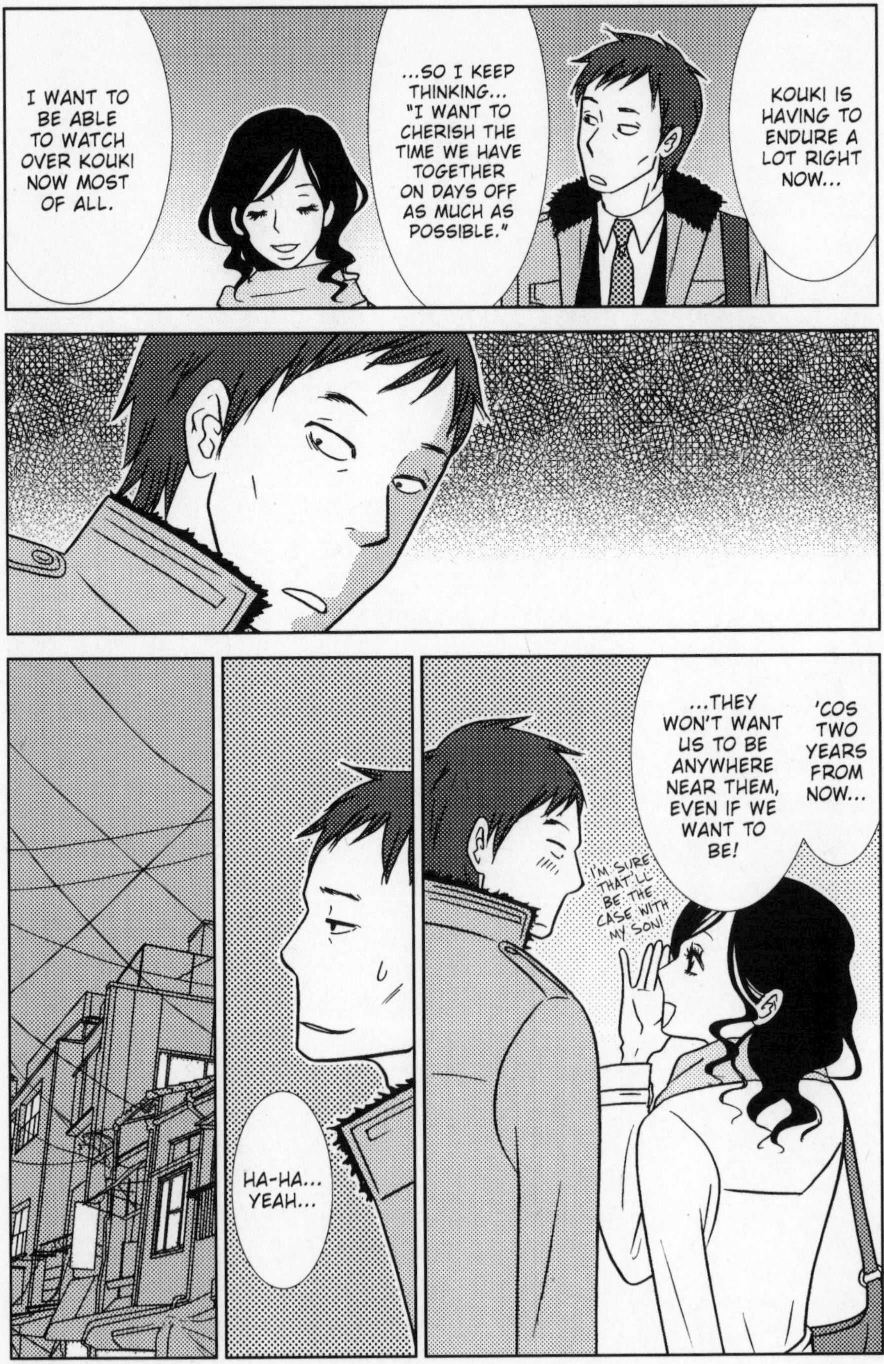
KOUKI IS HAVING TO ENDURE A LOT RIGHT NOW...
...SO I KEEP THINKING... "I WANT TO CHERISH THE TIME WE HAVE TOGETHER ON DAYS OFF AS MUCH AS POSSIBLE."
I WANT TO BE ABLE TO WATCH OVER KOUKI NOW MOST OF ALL.
'COS TWO YEARS FROM NOW...
...THEY WON'T WANT US TO BE ANYWHERE NEAR THEM, EVEN IF WE WANT TO BE!
I'M SURE THAT'LL BE THE CASE WITH MY SON!
HA-HA... YEAH...

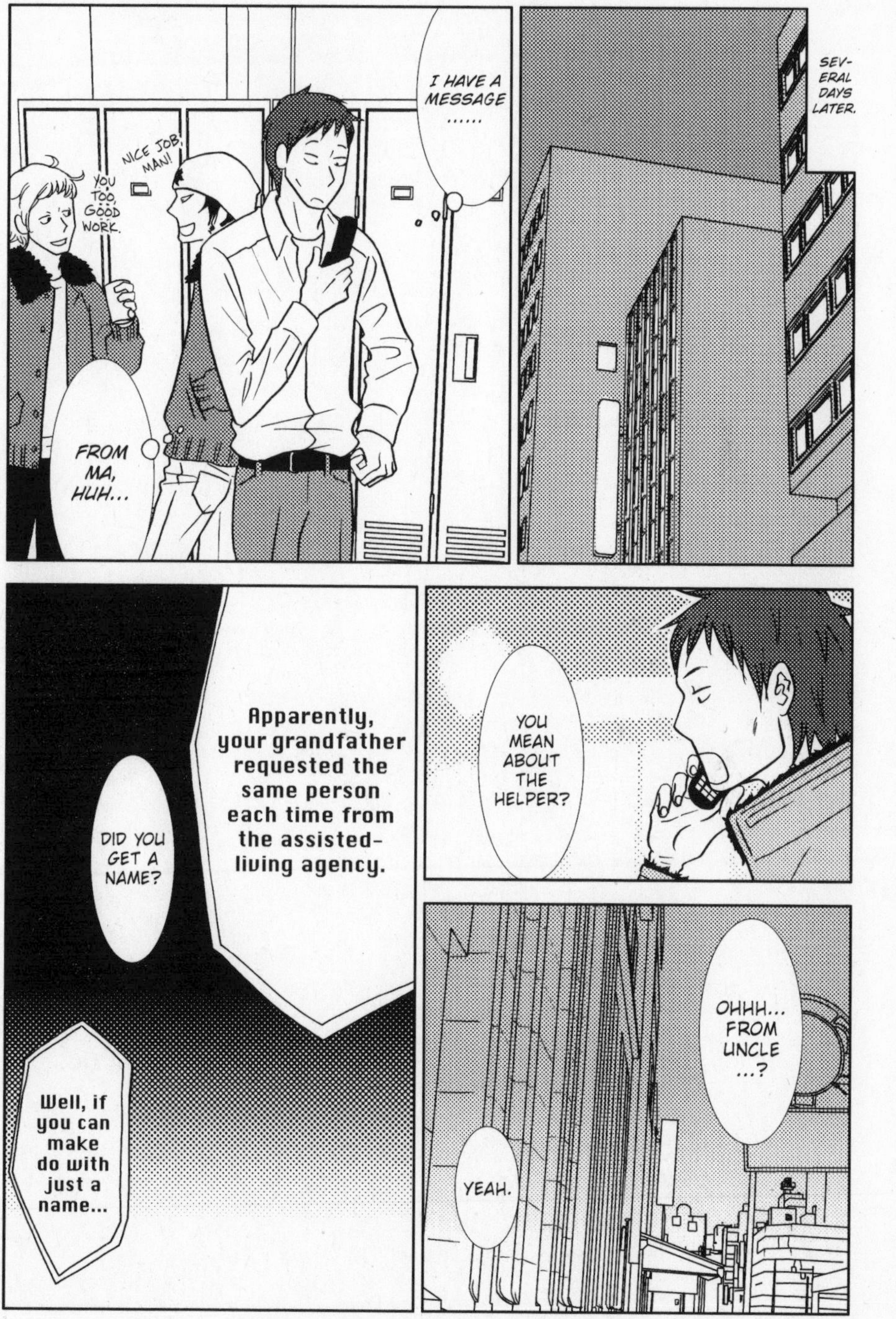
SEVERAL DAYS LATER.
I HAVE A MESSAGE ......
NICE JOB, MAN!
YOU TOO, GOOD WORK.
FROM MA, HUH...
YOU MEAN ABOUT THE HELPER?
OHHH... FROM UNCLE ...?
YEAH.
Apparently, your grandfather requested the same person each time from the assisted-living agency.
DID YOU GET A NAME?
Well, if you can make do with just a name...

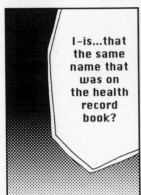

Masako Yoshii-san......
Written with the characters for "correct" and "child" ...
I KNEW IT...
I-is...that the same name that was on the health record book?
YUP...... SAME NAME.
HEY... CALM DOWN ...
...THERE'S A LOT WE STILL DON'T KNOW.
YEAH... THANKS, MA.
I'LL CALL YOU AGAIN LATER.
AH, AND KEEP THIS ALL A SECRET FROM RIN.
'KAY.
TIME FOR ME TO KEEP DIGGING NICE-'N'-STEADY TOO...
MY RAGE IS BEGINNING TO BOIL OVER WITH THIS WHOLE CONFUSING SITUATION.
STILL ...

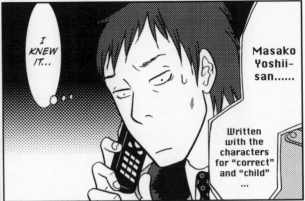

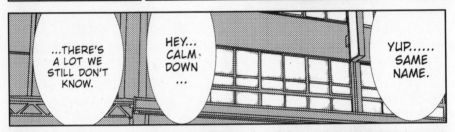

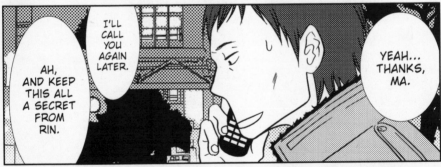

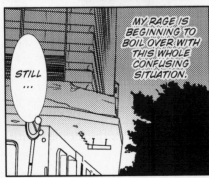

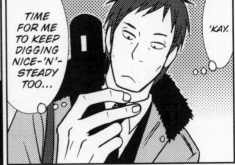

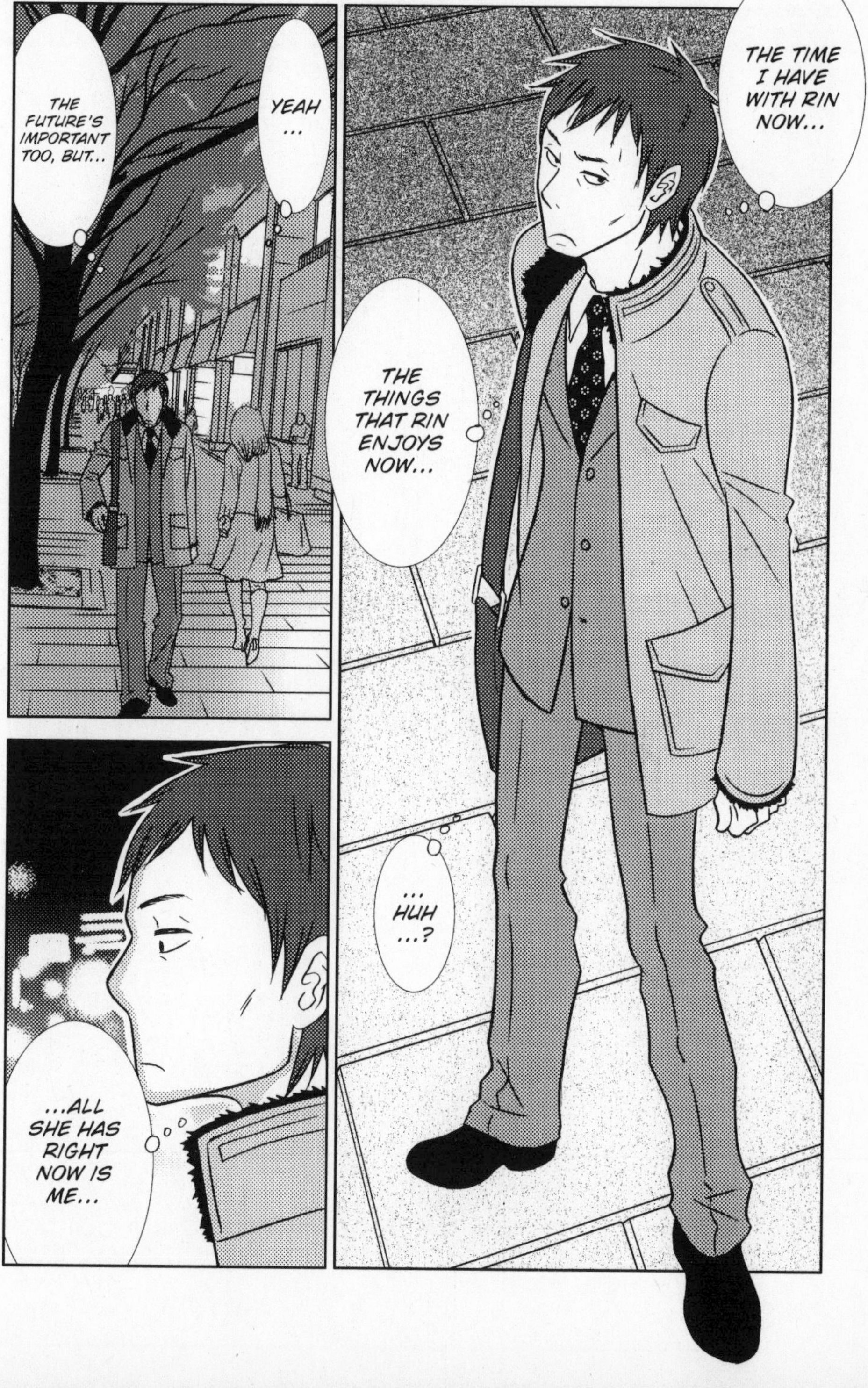
THE TIME I HAVE WITH RIN NOW...
THE THINGS THAT RIN ENJOYS NOW...
...HUH...?
YEAH...
THE FUTURE'S IMPORTANT TOO, BUT...
...ALL SHE HAS RIGHT NOW IS ME...

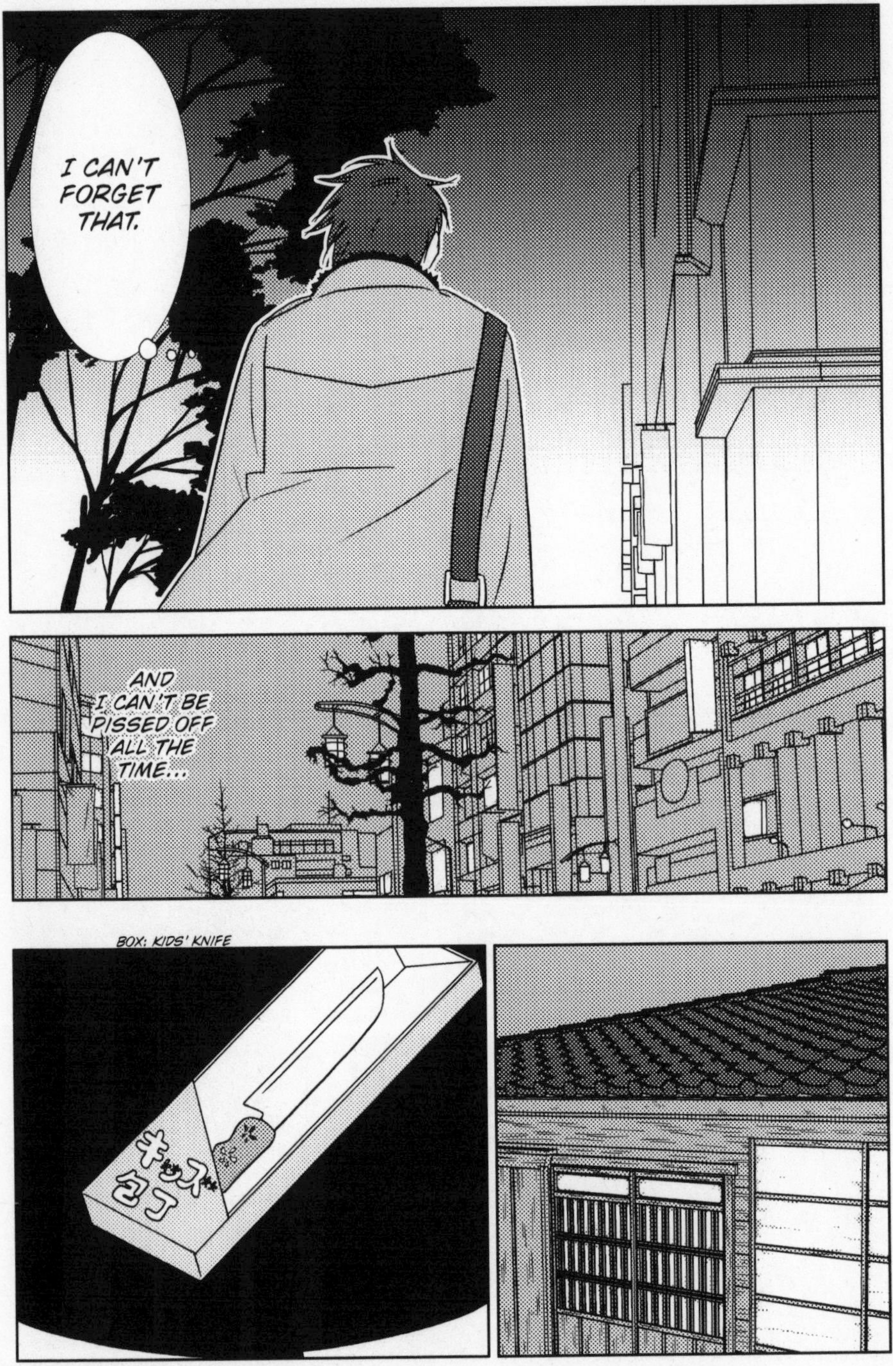
I CAN'T FORGET THAT.
AND I CAN'T BE PISSED OFF ALL THE TIME...
BOX: KIDS' KNIFE
キッズ包丁

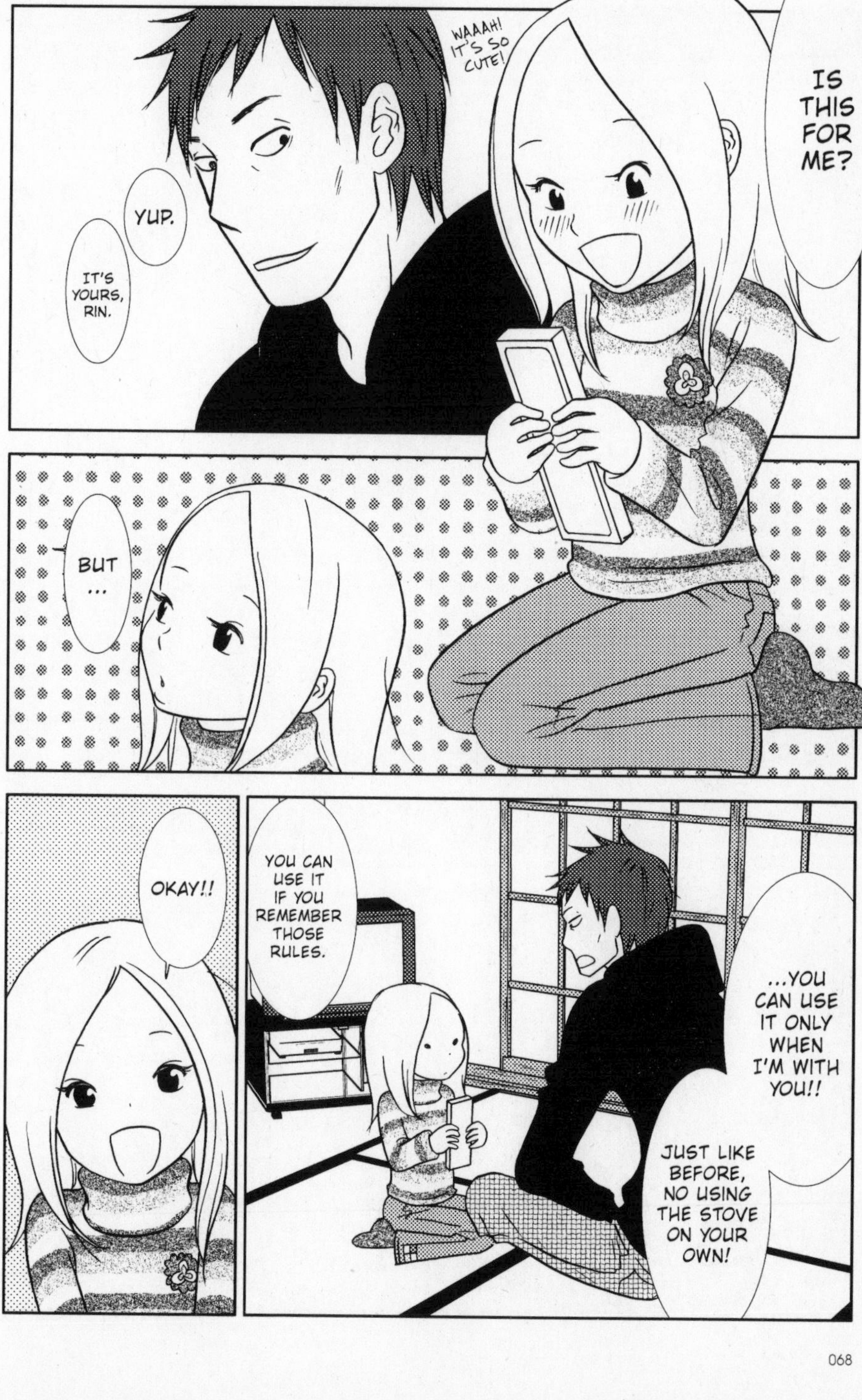
IS THIS FOR ME?
WAAAH! IT'S SO CUTE!
YUP.
IT'S YOURS, RIN.
BUT ...
...YOU CAN USE IT ONLY WHEN I'M WITH YOU!!
JUST LIKE BEFORE, NO USING THE STOVE ON YOUR OWN!
YOU CAN USE IT IF YOU REMEMBER THOSE RULES.
OKAY!!

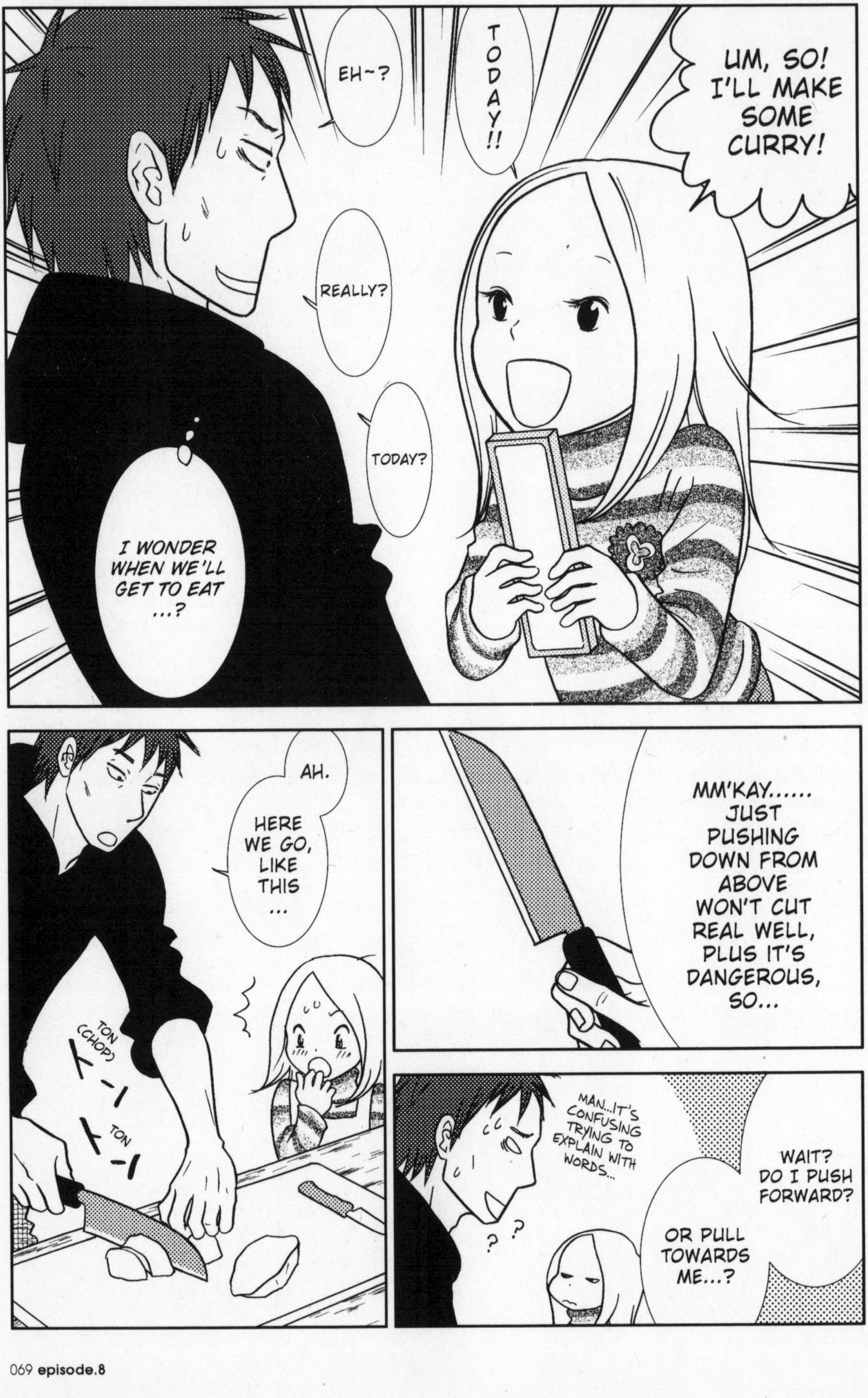
UM, SO! I'LL MAKE SOME CURRY!
TODAY!!
EH~?
REALLY?
TODAY?
I WONDER WHEN WE'LL GET TO EAT ...?
MM'KAY...... JUST PUSHING DOWN FROM ABOVE WON'T CUT REAL WELL, PLUS IT'S DANGEROUS, SO...
WAIT? DO I PUSH FORWARD?
MAN...IT'S CONFUSING TRYING TO EXPLAIN WITH WORDS...
OR PULL TOWARDS ME...?
? ?
AH.
HERE WE GO, LIKE THIS ...
TON (CHOP)
TON

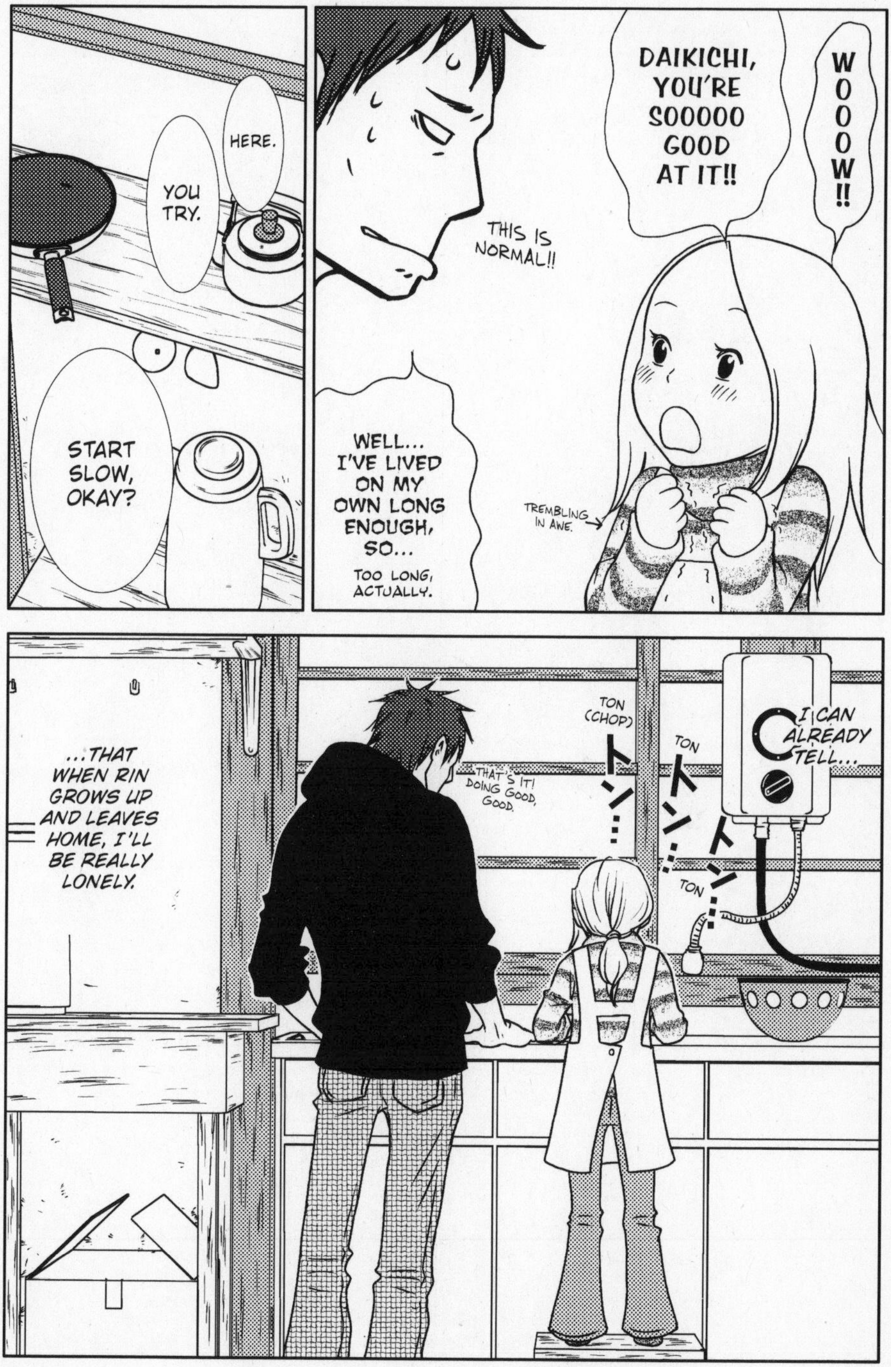
WOOOOW!!
DAIKICHI, YOU'RE SOOOOO GOOD AT IT!!
TREMBLING IN AWE.
THIS IS NORMAL!!
WELL... I'VE LIVED ON MY OWN LONG ENOUGH, SO...
TOO LONG, ACTUALLY.
HERE.
YOU TRY.
START SLOW, OKAY?
I CAN ALREADY TELL...
TON
TON
TON (CHOP)
THAT'S IT! DOING GOOD, GOOD.
...THAT WHEN RIN GROWS UP AND LEAVES HOME, I'LL BE REALLY LONELY.

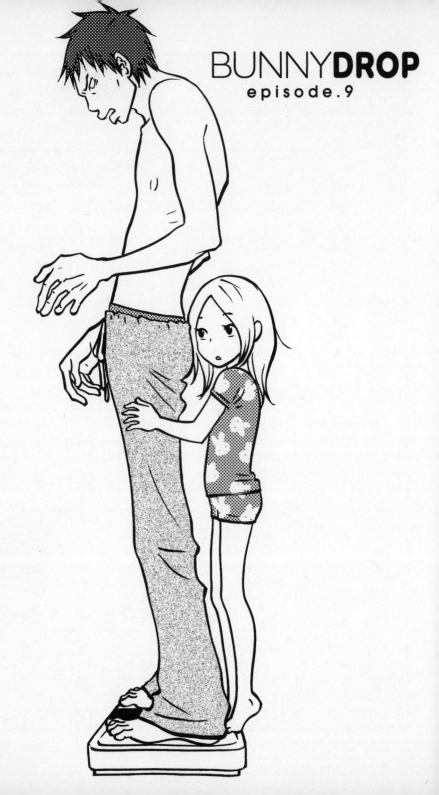

BUNNY**DROP**
episode.9

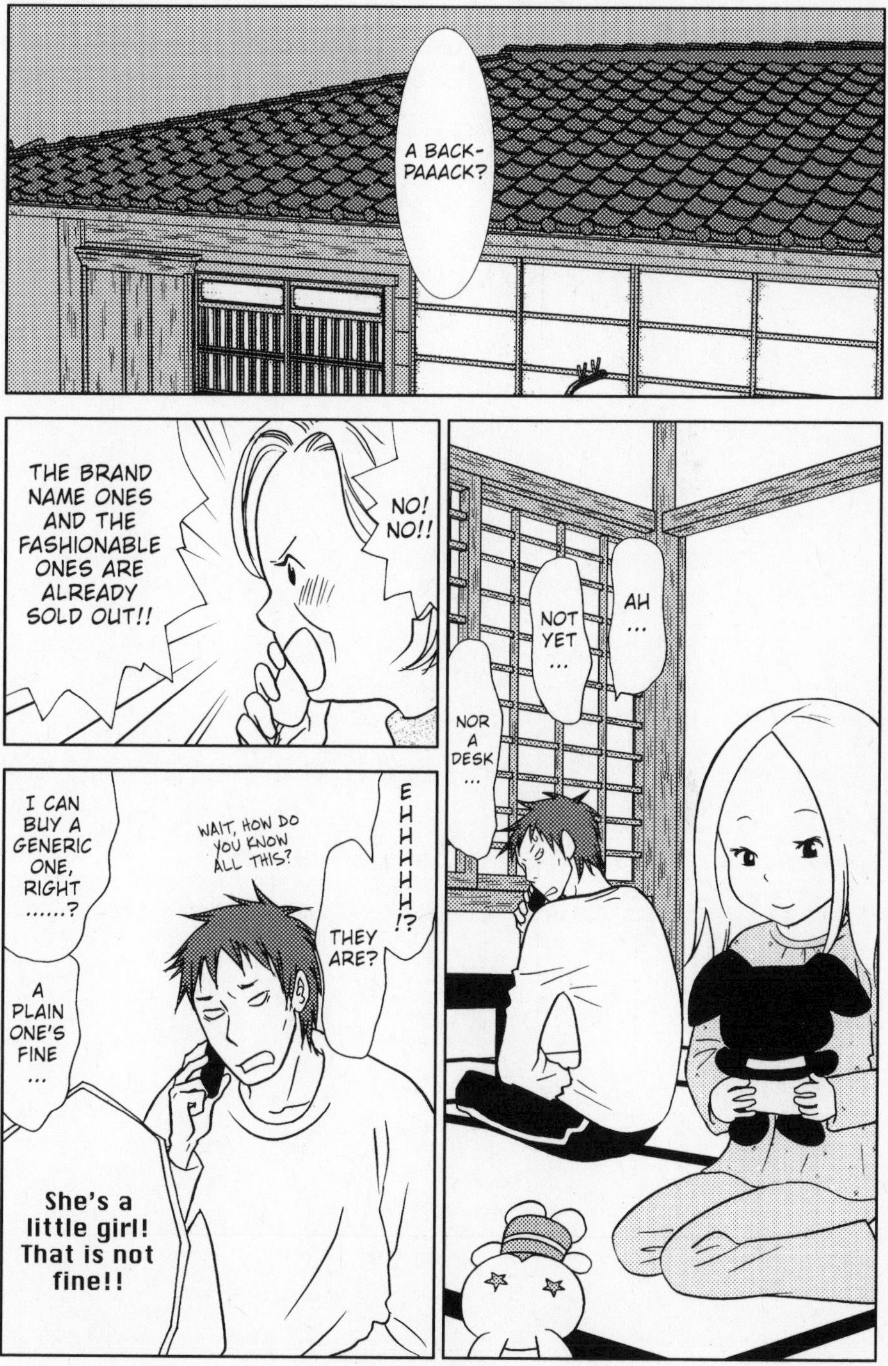
A BACK-PAAACK?
AH ...
NOT YET ...
NOR A DESK ...
NO! NO!!
THE BRAND NAME ONES AND THE FASHIONABLE ONES ARE ALREADY SOLD OUT!!
EHHHHH!?
THEY ARE?
WAIT, HOW DO YOU KNOW ALL THIS?
I CAN BUY A GENERIC ONE, RIGHT ......?
A PLAIN ONE'S FINE ...
She's a little girl! That is not fine!!

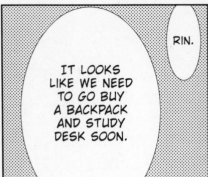

ふう
FUU (SIGH)
RIN.
IT LOOKS LIKE WE NEED TO GO BUY A BACKPACK AND STUDY DESK SOON.
WHAT KIND DO YOU WANT?
WHAT'S A STUDY DESK?
ERM ...
A DESK FOR YOU TO USE WHEN YOU STUDY AT HOME. YOU KNOW, SINCE YOU'LL GET HOMEWORK WHEN YOU GO TO ELEMENTARY SCHOOL.
HMM...
I DON'T KNOW WHAT KINDS THERE ARE.
.... YEAH, TELL ME ABOUT IT...
WELL, WHY DON'T WE GO LOOK AT SOME ON MY DAY OFF?
'KAY.

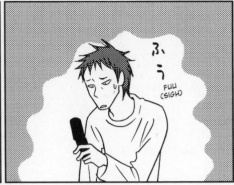

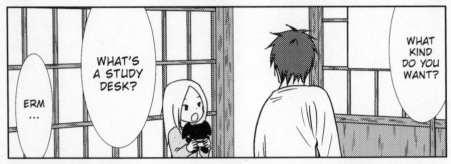

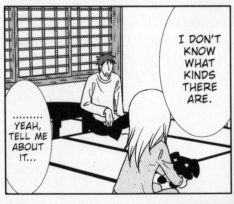

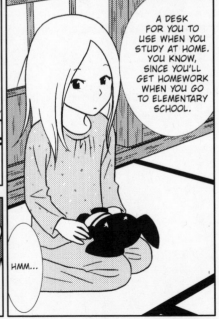

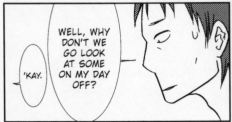

JUST WHEN I THOUGHT RIN AND I HAD OUR ROUTINE DOWN WITH THE NURSERY SCHOOL...
...NOW WE HAVE TO GO THROUGH ELEMENTARY SCHOOL ENTRANCE PREP.
PROBABLY MORE FUMBLING AROUND, PREPPING LIKE BEFORE...
MORE IMPORTANTLY, HOW DO I GET HER INTO ELEMENTARY SCHOOL...?
DO I NEED TO GO TO SOME GOVERNMENT OFFICE ...?
AND WHERE DO I PUT A STUDY DESK...?
ARE ELEMENTARY SCHOOLGIRLS AT AN AGE WHERE THEY NEED THEIR OWN ROOMS ...?
TILL WHEN CAN WE TAKE BATHS TOGETHER?
SLEEP IN THE SAME ROOM?
BUT SINCE SHE CAN'T WASH HER OWN HAIR YET...!

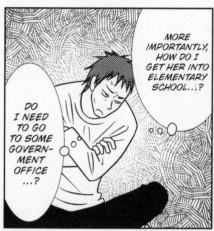

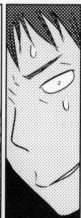

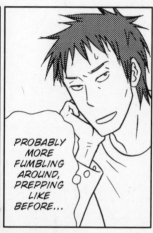

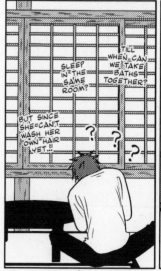

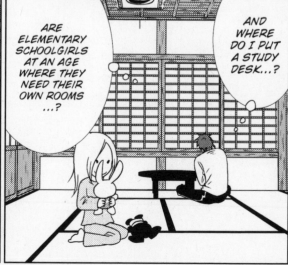

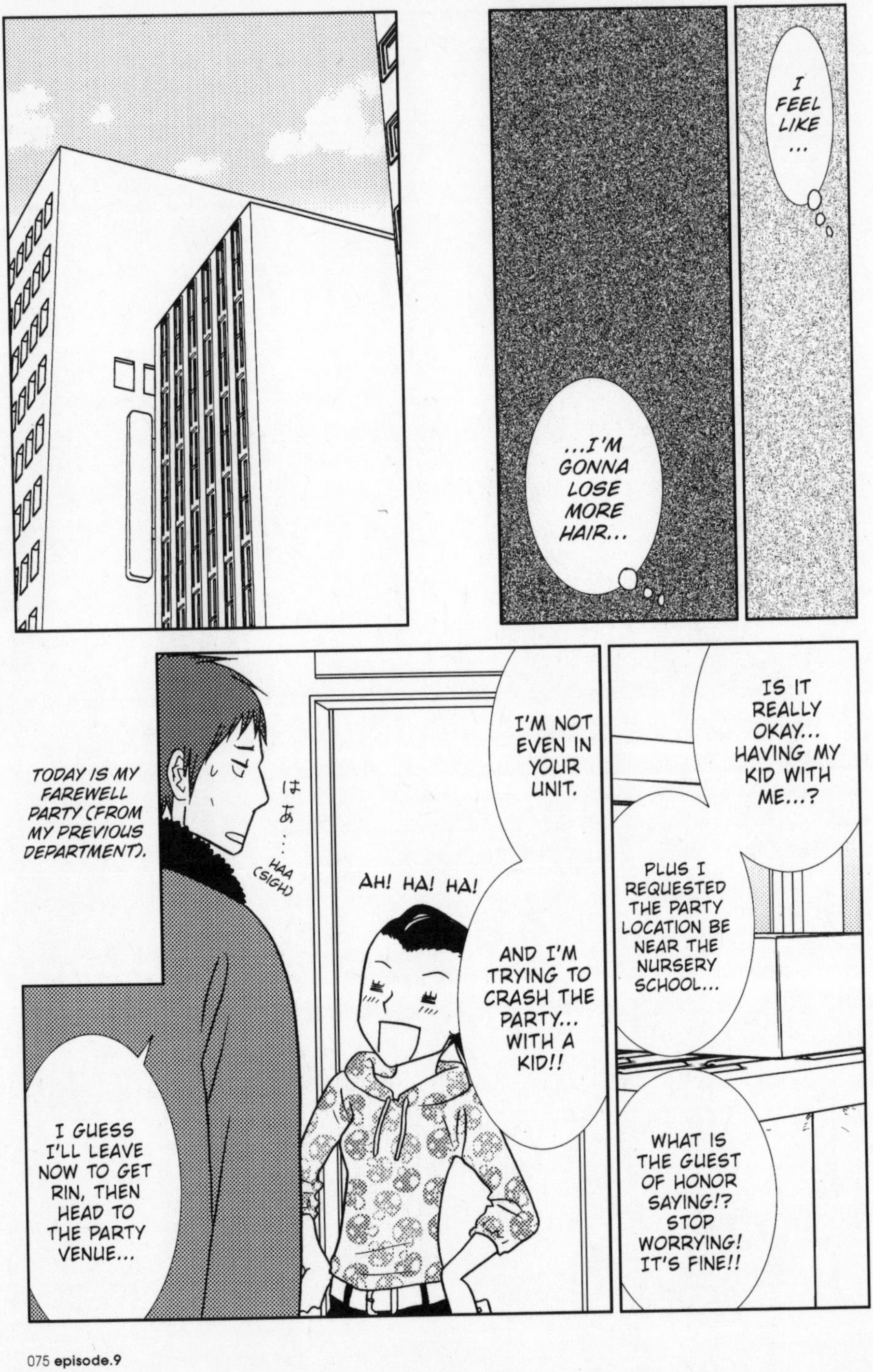
I FEEL LIKE ...
...I'M GONNA LOSE MORE HAIR...
IS IT REALLY OKAY... HAVING MY KID WITH ME...?
PLUS I REQUESTED THE PARTY LOCATION BE NEAR THE NURSERY SCHOOL...
WHAT IS THE GUEST OF HONOR SAYING!? STOP WORRYING! IT'S FINE!!
I'M NOT EVEN IN YOUR UNIT.
AND I'M TRYING TO CRASH THE PARTY... WITH A KID!!
AH! HA! HA!
はあ…
HAA (SIGH)
TODAY IS MY FAREWELL PARTY (FROM MY PREVIOUS DEPARTMENT).
I GUESS I'LL LEAVE NOW TO GET RIN, THEN HEAD TO THE PARTY VENUE...

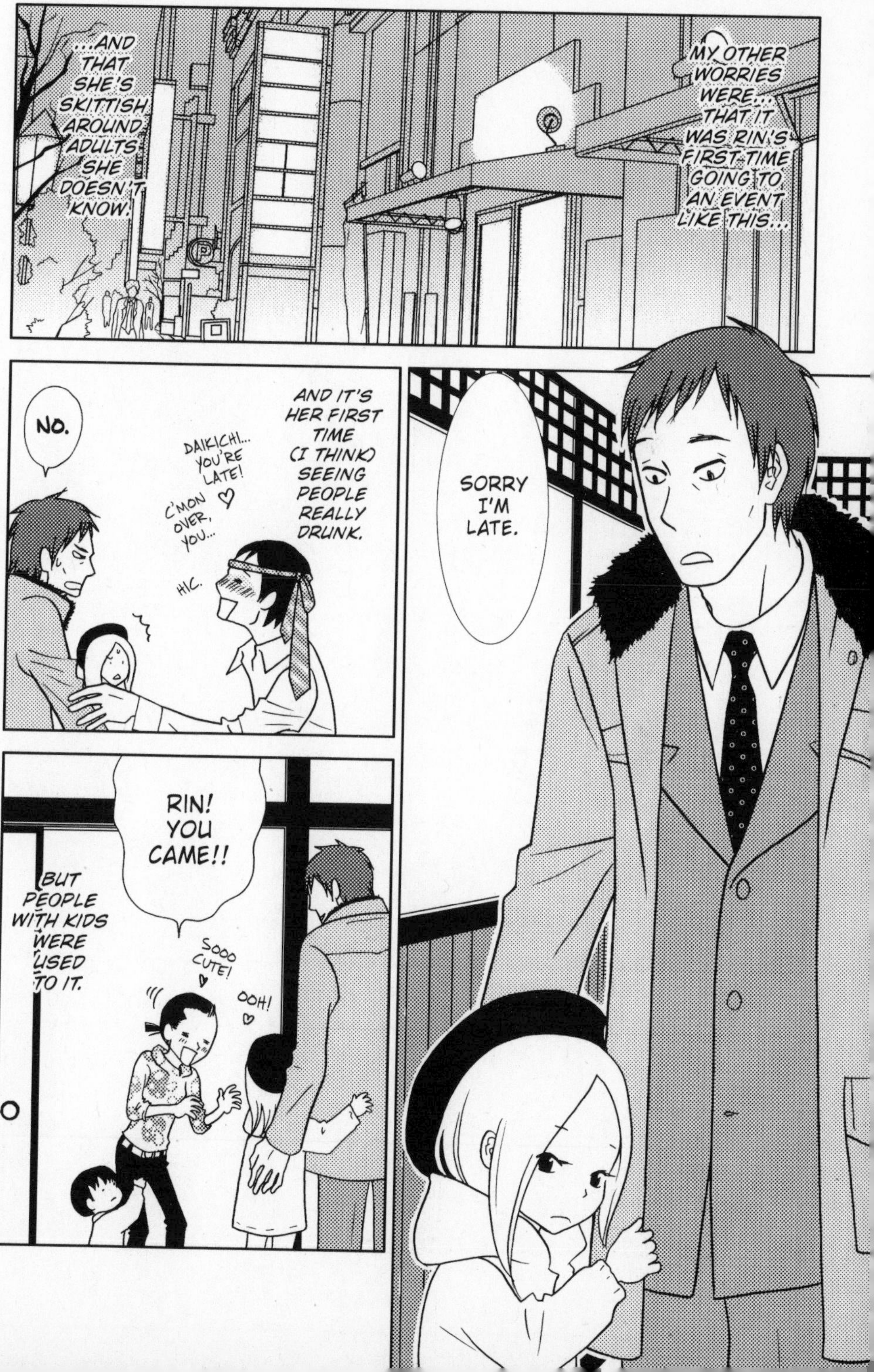
MY OTHER WORRIES WERE... THAT IT WAS RIN'S FIRST TIME GOING TO AN EVENT LIKE THIS...
...AND THAT SHE'S SKITTISH AROUND ADULTS SHE DOESN'T KNOW.
SORRY I'M LATE.
AND IT'S HER FIRST TIME (I THINK) SEEING PEOPLE REALLY DRUNK.
DAIKICHI... YOU'RE LATE!
C'MON OVER, YOU... ♡
HIC.
NO.
RIN! YOU CAME!!
BUT PEOPLE WITH KIDS WERE USED TO IT.
SOOO CUTE! ♡
OOH! ♡

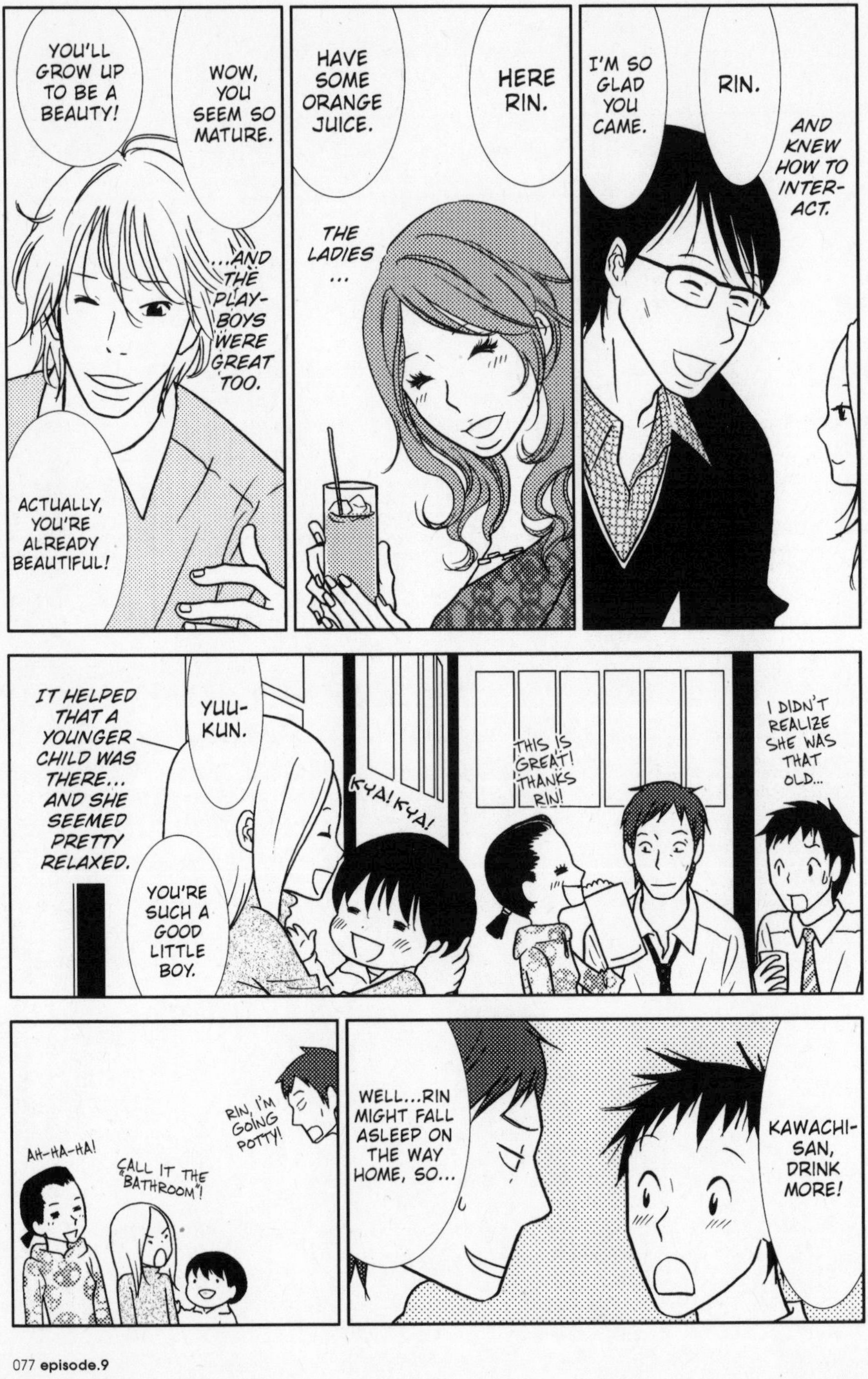
RIN.
I'M SO GLAD YOU CAME.
AND KNEW HOW TO INTER-ACT.
HERE RIN.
HAVE SOME ORANGE JUICE.
THE LADIES ...
WOW, YOU SEEM SO MATURE.
YOU'LL GROW UP TO BE A BEAUTY!
...AND THE PLAY-BOYS WERE GREAT TOO.
ACTUALLY, YOU'RE ALREADY BEAUTIFUL!
I DIDN'T REALIZE SHE WAS THAT OLD...
THIS IS GREAT! THANKS RIN!
KYA! KYA!
YUU-KUN.
IT HELPED THAT A YOUNGER CHILD WAS THERE... AND SHE SEEMED PRETTY RELAXED.
YOU'RE SUCH A GOOD LITTLE BOY.
KAWACHI-SAN, DRINK MORE!
WELL...RIN MIGHT FALL ASLEEP ON THE WAY HOME, SO...
RIN, I'M GOING POTTY!
CALL IT THE "BATHROOM"!
AH-HA-HA!

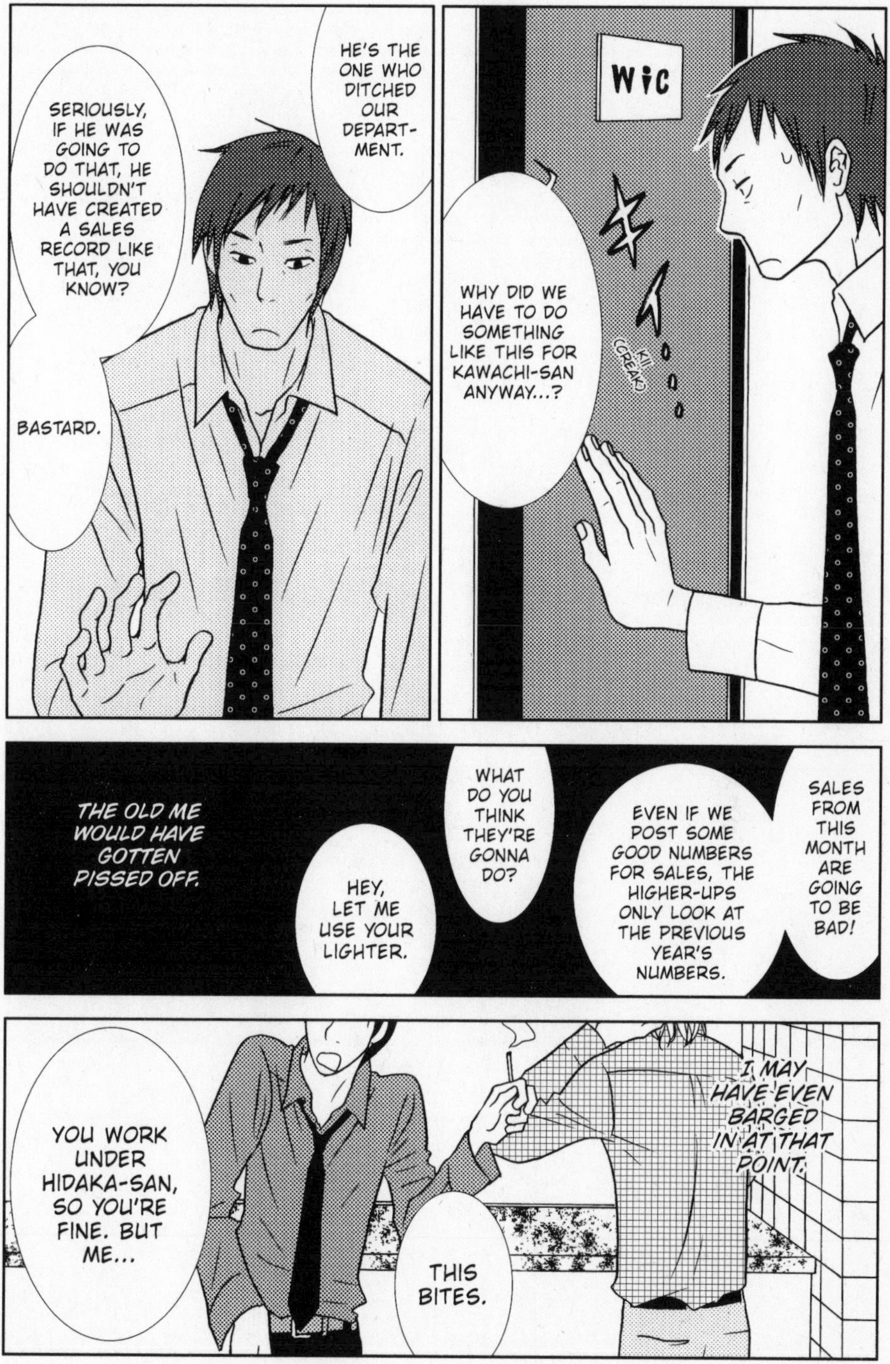
WIC
KI (CREAK)
WHY DID WE HAVE TO DO SOMETHING LIKE THIS FOR KAWACHI-SAN ANYWAY...?
HE'S THE ONE WHO DITCHED OUR DEPARTMENT.
SERIOUSLY, IF HE WAS GOING TO DO THAT, HE SHOULDN'T HAVE CREATED A SALES RECORD LIKE THAT, YOU KNOW?
BASTARD.
SALES FROM THIS MONTH ARE GOING TO BE BAD!
EVEN IF WE POST SOME GOOD NUMBERS FOR SALES, THE HIGHER-UPS ONLY LOOK AT THE PREVIOUS YEAR'S NUMBERS.
WHAT DO YOU THINK THEY'RE GONNA DO?
HEY, LET ME USE YOUR LIGHTER.
THE OLD ME WOULD HAVE GOTTEN PISSED OFF.
I MAY HAVE EVEN BARGED IN AT THAT POINT.
THIS BITES.
YOU WORK UNDER HIDAKA-SAN, SO YOU'RE FINE. BUT ME...

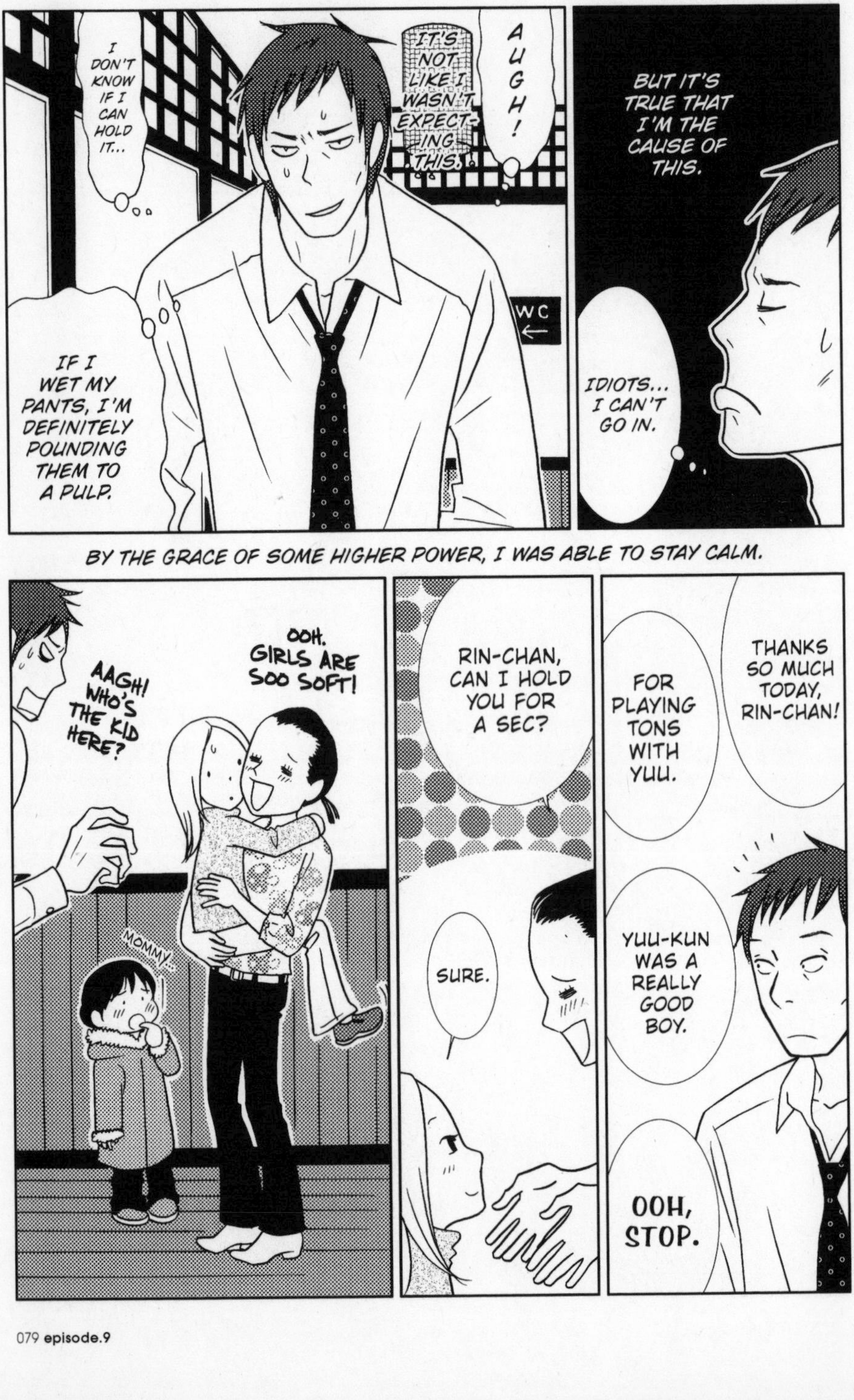
BUT IT'S TRUE THAT I'M THE CAUSE OF THIS.
IDIOTS... I CAN'T GO IN.
AUGH!
IT'S NOT LIKE I WASN'T EXPECTING THIS.
I DON'T KNOW IF I CAN HOLD IT...
WC
IF I WET MY PANTS, I'M DEFINITELY POUNDING THEM TO A PULP.
BY THE GRACE OF SOME HIGHER POWER, I WAS ABLE TO STAY CALM.
THANKS SO MUCH TODAY, RIN-CHAN!
FOR PLAYING TONS WITH YUU.
YUU-KUN WAS A REALLY GOOD BOY.
OOH, STOP.
RIN-CHAN, CAN I HOLD YOU FOR A SEC?
SURE.
OOH. GIRLS ARE SOO SOFT!
AAGH! WHO'S THE KID HERE?
MOMMY...

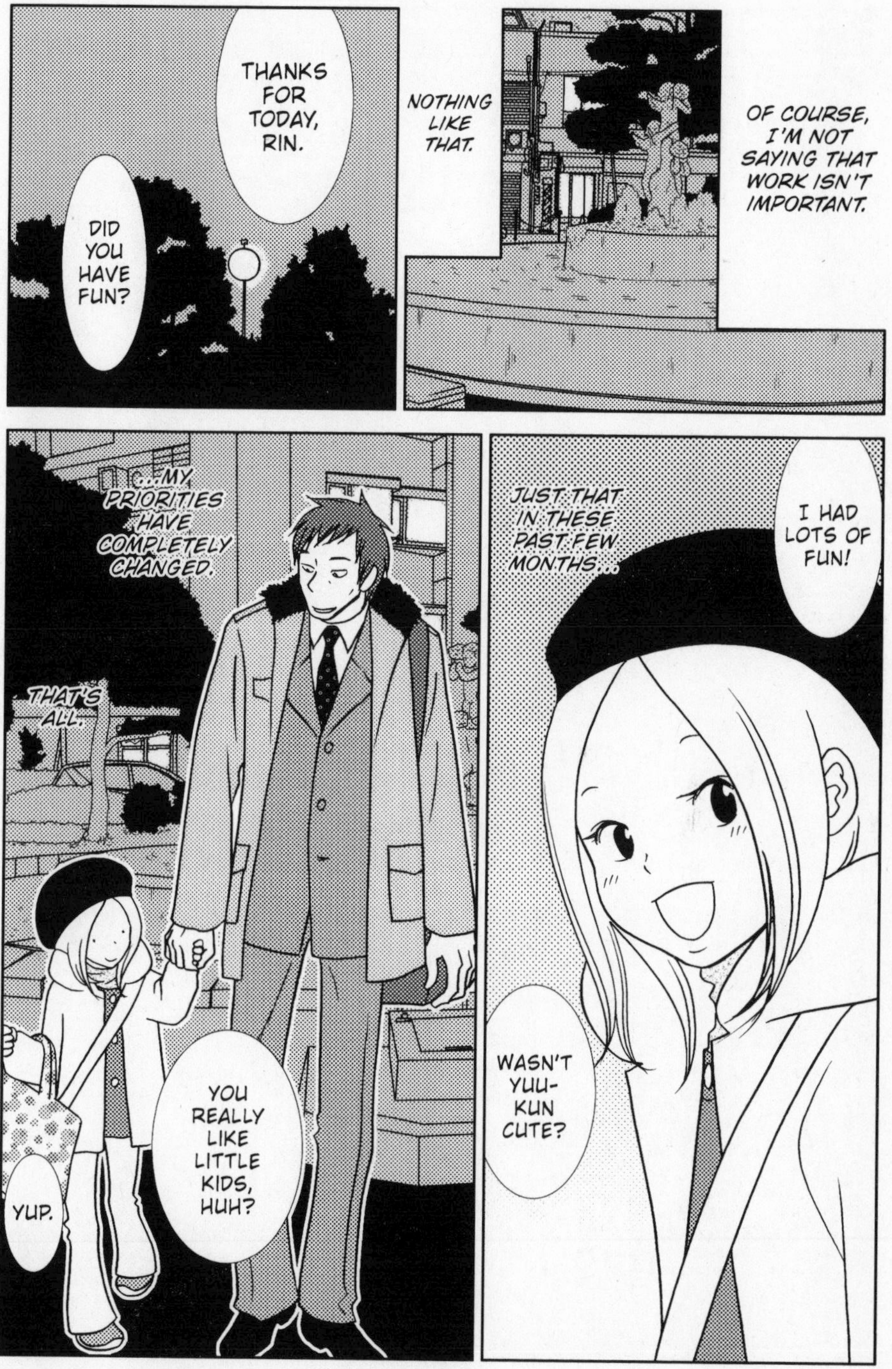
NOTHING LIKE THAT.
OF COURSE, I'M NOT SAYING THAT WORK ISN'T IMPORTANT.
THANKS FOR TODAY, RIN.
DID YOU HAVE FUN?
I HAD LOTS OF FUN!
JUST THAT IN THESE PAST FEW MONTHS...
WASN'T YUU-KUN CUTE?
...MY PRIORITIES HAVE COMPLETELY CHANGED.
THAT'S ALL.
YOU REALLY LIKE LITTLE KIDS, HUH?
YUP.

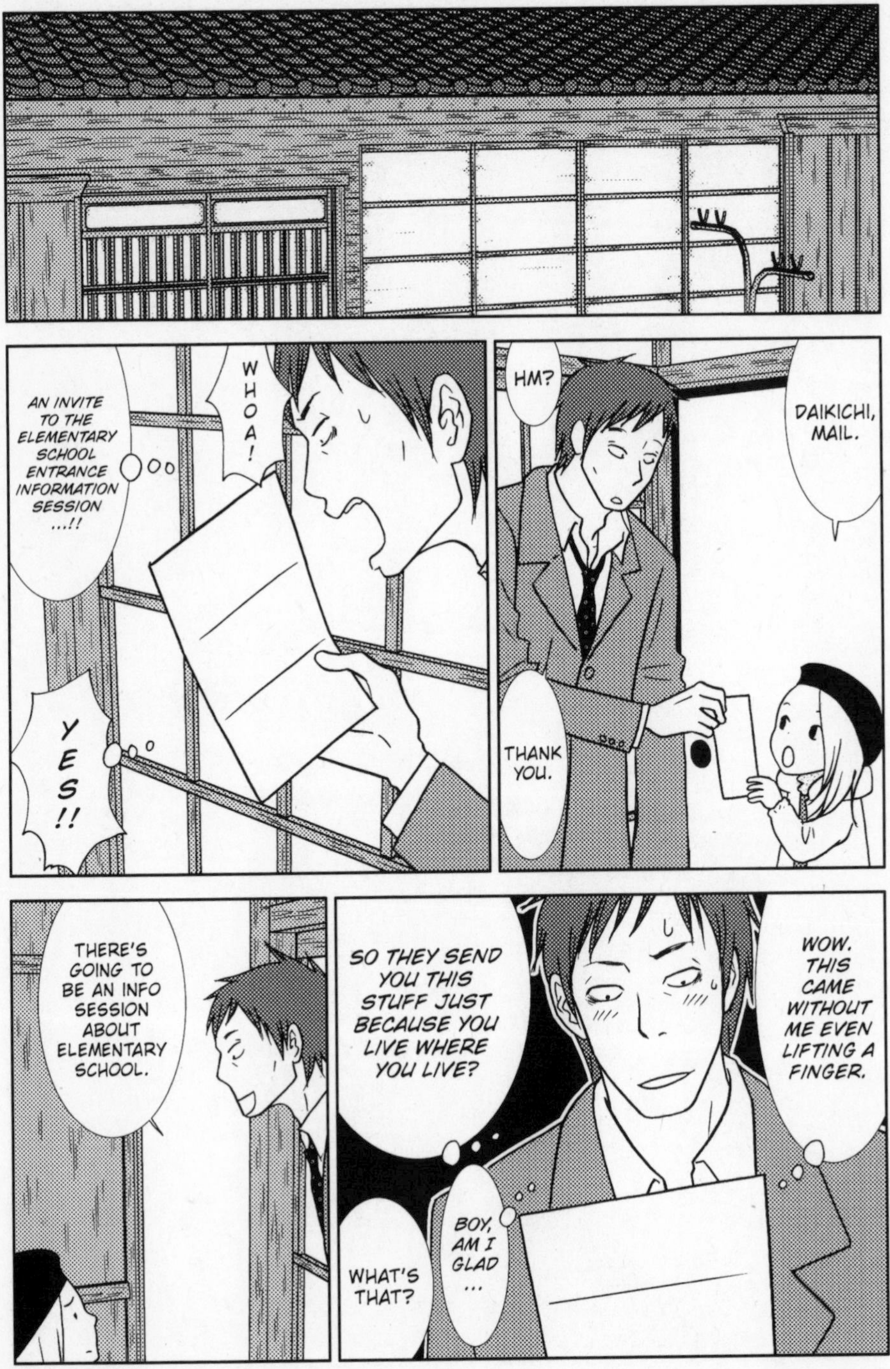
DAIKICHI, MAIL.
HM?
THANK YOU.
WHOA!
AN INVITE TO THE ELEMENTARY SCHOOL ENTRANCE INFORMATION SESSION ...!!
YES!!
WOW. THIS CAME WITHOUT ME EVEN LIFTING A FINGER.
SO THEY SEND YOU THIS STUFF JUST BECAUSE YOU LIVE WHERE YOU LIVE?
BOY, AM I GLAD ...
WHAT'S THAT?
THERE'S GOING TO BE AN INFO SESSION ABOUT ELEMENTARY SCHOOL.

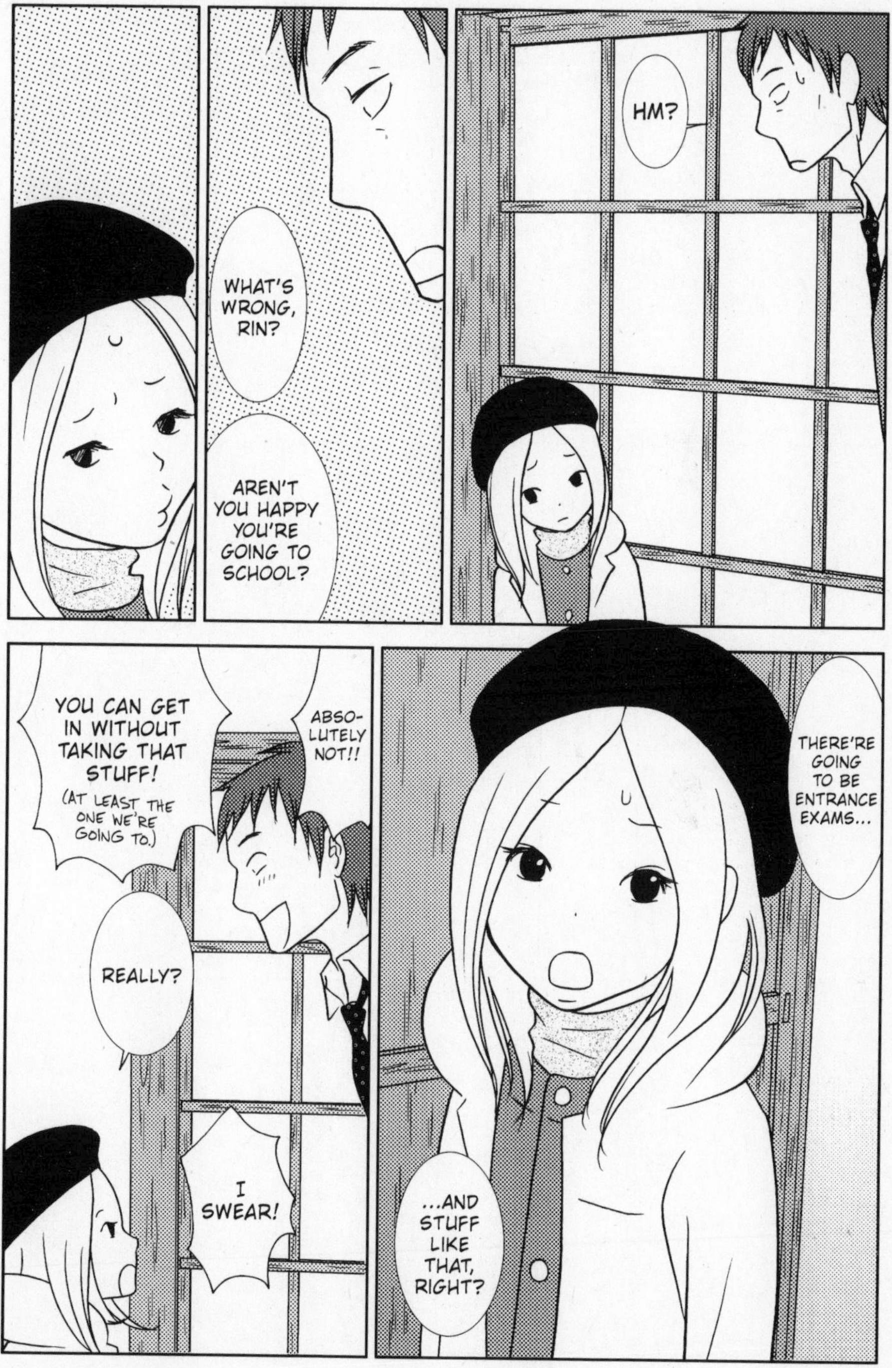
HM?
WHAT'S WRONG, RIN?
AREN'T YOU HAPPY YOU'RE GOING TO SCHOOL?
THERE'RE GOING TO BE ENTRANCE EXAMS...
...AND STUFF LIKE THAT, RIGHT?
ABSO-LUTELY NOT!!
YOU CAN GET IN WITHOUT TAKING THAT STUFF!
(AT LEAST THE ONE WE'RE GOING TO.)
REALLY?
I SWEAR!

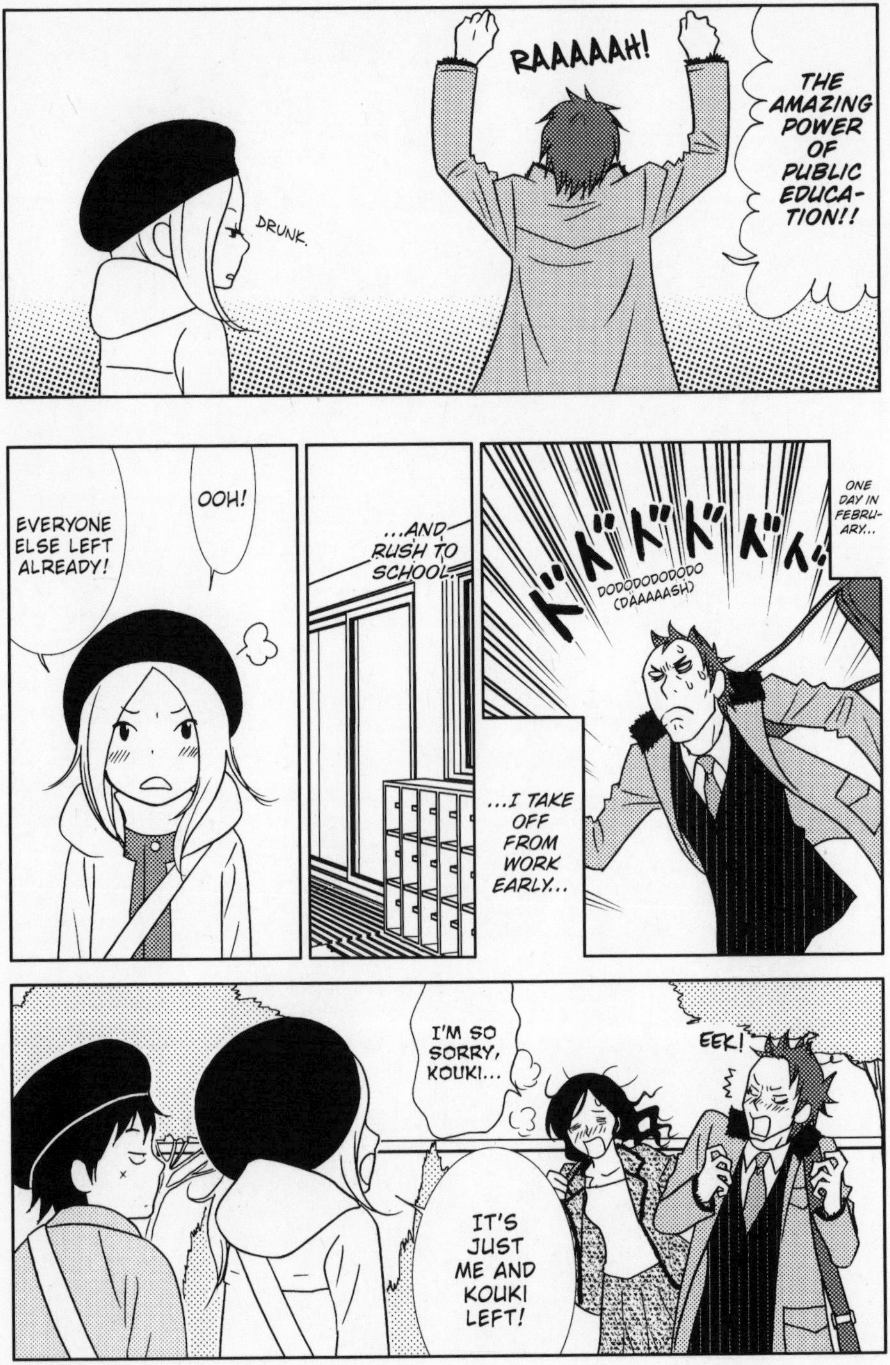
THE AMAZING POWER OF PUBLIC EDUCATION!!
RAAAAAH!
DRUNK.
ONE DAY IN FEBRUARY...
ドドドドド
DODODODODO (DAAAAASH)
...I TAKE OFF FROM WORK EARLY...
...AND RUSH TO SCHOOL.
OOH!
EVERYONE ELSE LEFT ALREADY!
EEK!
I'M SO SORRY, KOUKI...
IT'S JUST ME AND KOUKI LEFT!

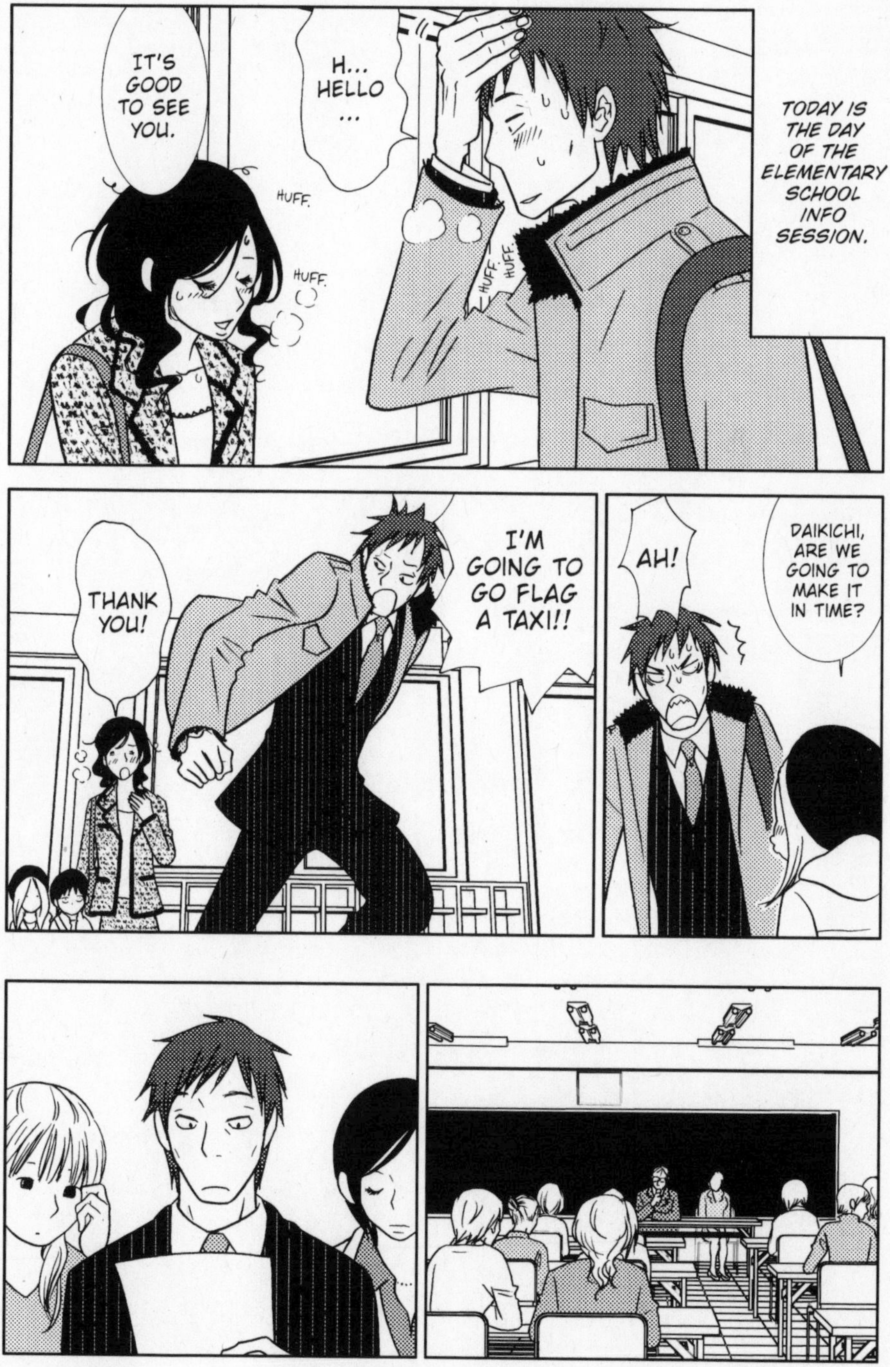
TODAY IS THE DAY OF THE ELEMENTARY SCHOOL INFO SESSION.
H... HELLO ...
HUFF. HUFF.
IT'S GOOD TO SEE YOU.
HUFF.
HUFF.
DAIKICHI, ARE WE GOING TO MAKE IT IN TIME?
AH!
I'M GOING TO GO FLAG A TAXI!!
THANK YOU!

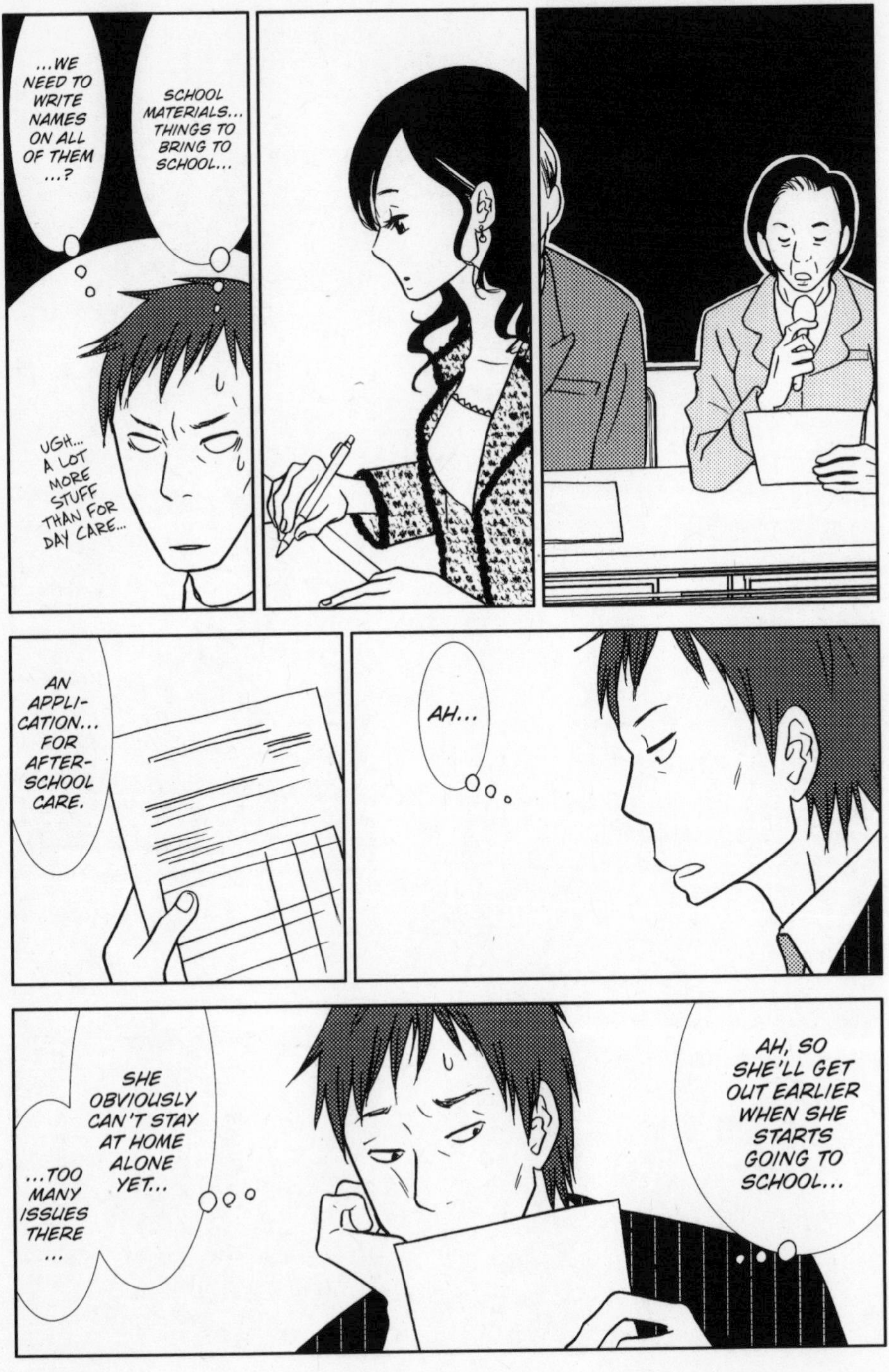
SCHOOL MATERIALS... THINGS TO BRING TO SCHOOL...
...WE NEED TO WRITE NAMES ON ALL OF THEM ...?
UGH... A LOT MORE STUFF THAN FOR DAY CARE...
AH...
AN APPLICATION... FOR AFTER-SCHOOL CARE.
AH, SO SHE'LL GET OUT EARLIER WHEN SHE STARTS GOING TO SCHOOL...
SHE OBVIOUSLY CAN'T STAY AT HOME ALONE YET...
...TOO MANY ISSUES THERE ...

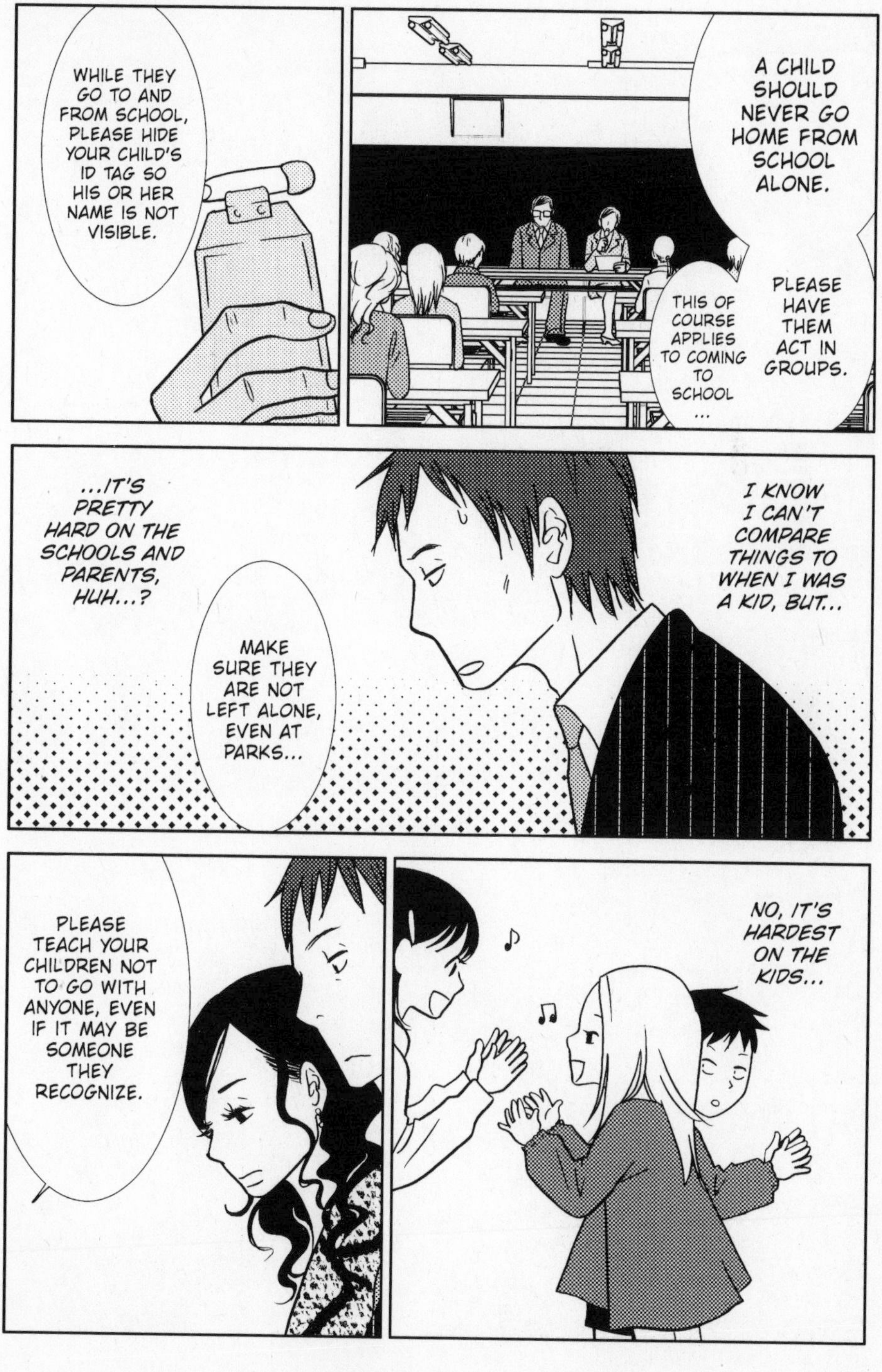
A CHILD SHOULD NEVER GO HOME FROM SCHOOL ALONE.
PLEASE HAVE THEM ACT IN GROUPS.
THIS OF COURSE APPLIES TO COMING TO SCHOOL ...
WHILE THEY GO TO AND FROM SCHOOL, PLEASE HIDE YOUR CHILD'S ID TAG SO HIS OR HER NAME IS NOT VISIBLE.
I KNOW I CAN'T COMPARE THINGS TO WHEN I WAS A KID, BUT...
...IT'S PRETTY HARD ON THE SCHOOLS AND PARENTS, HUH...?
MAKE SURE THEY ARE NOT LEFT ALONE, EVEN AT PARKS...
NO, IT'S HARDEST ON THE KIDS...
PLEASE TEACH YOUR CHILDREN NOT TO GO WITH ANYONE, EVEN IF IT MAY BE SOMEONE THEY RECOGNIZE.

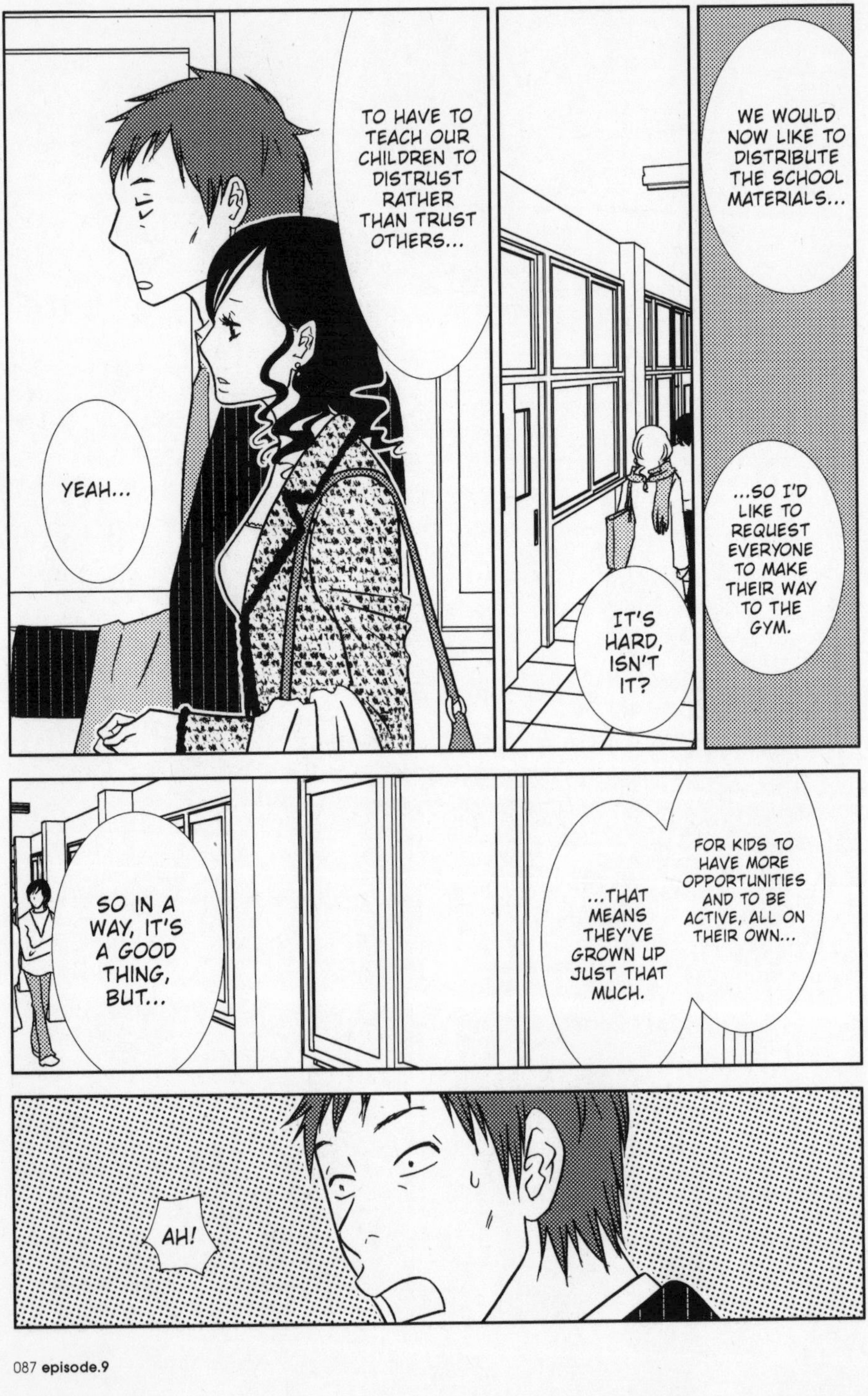
WE WOULD NOW LIKE TO DISTRIBUTE THE SCHOOL MATERIALS...
...SO I'D LIKE TO REQUEST EVERYONE TO MAKE THEIR WAY TO THE GYM.
IT'S HARD, ISN'T IT?
TO HAVE TO TEACH OUR CHILDREN TO DISTRUST RATHER THAN TRUST OTHERS...
YEAH...
FOR KIDS TO HAVE MORE OPPORTUNITIES AND TO BE ACTIVE, ALL ON THEIR OWN...
...THAT MEANS THEY'VE GROWN UP JUST THAT MUCH.
SO IN A WAY, IT'S A GOOD THING, BUT...
AH!

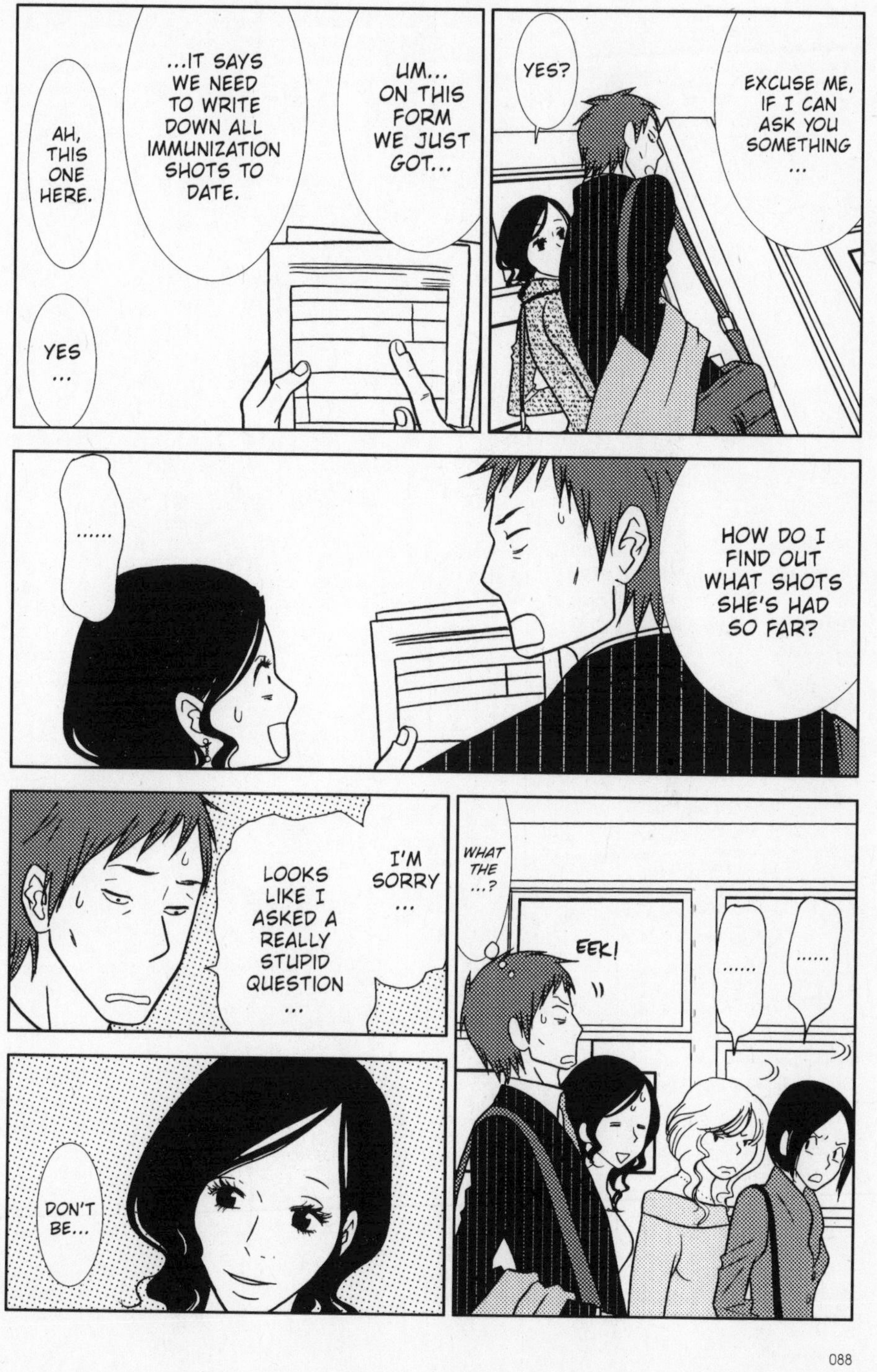
EXCUSE ME, IF I CAN ASK YOU SOMETHING ...
YES?
UM... ON THIS FORM WE JUST GOT...
...IT SAYS WE NEED TO WRITE DOWN ALL IMMUNIZATION SHOTS TO DATE.
AH, THIS ONE HERE.
YES ...
HOW DO I FIND OUT WHAT SHOTS SHE'S HAD SO FAR?
......
WHAT THE ...?
EEK!
......
......
I'M SORRY ...
LOOKS LIKE I ASKED A REALLY STUPID QUESTION ...
DON'T BE...

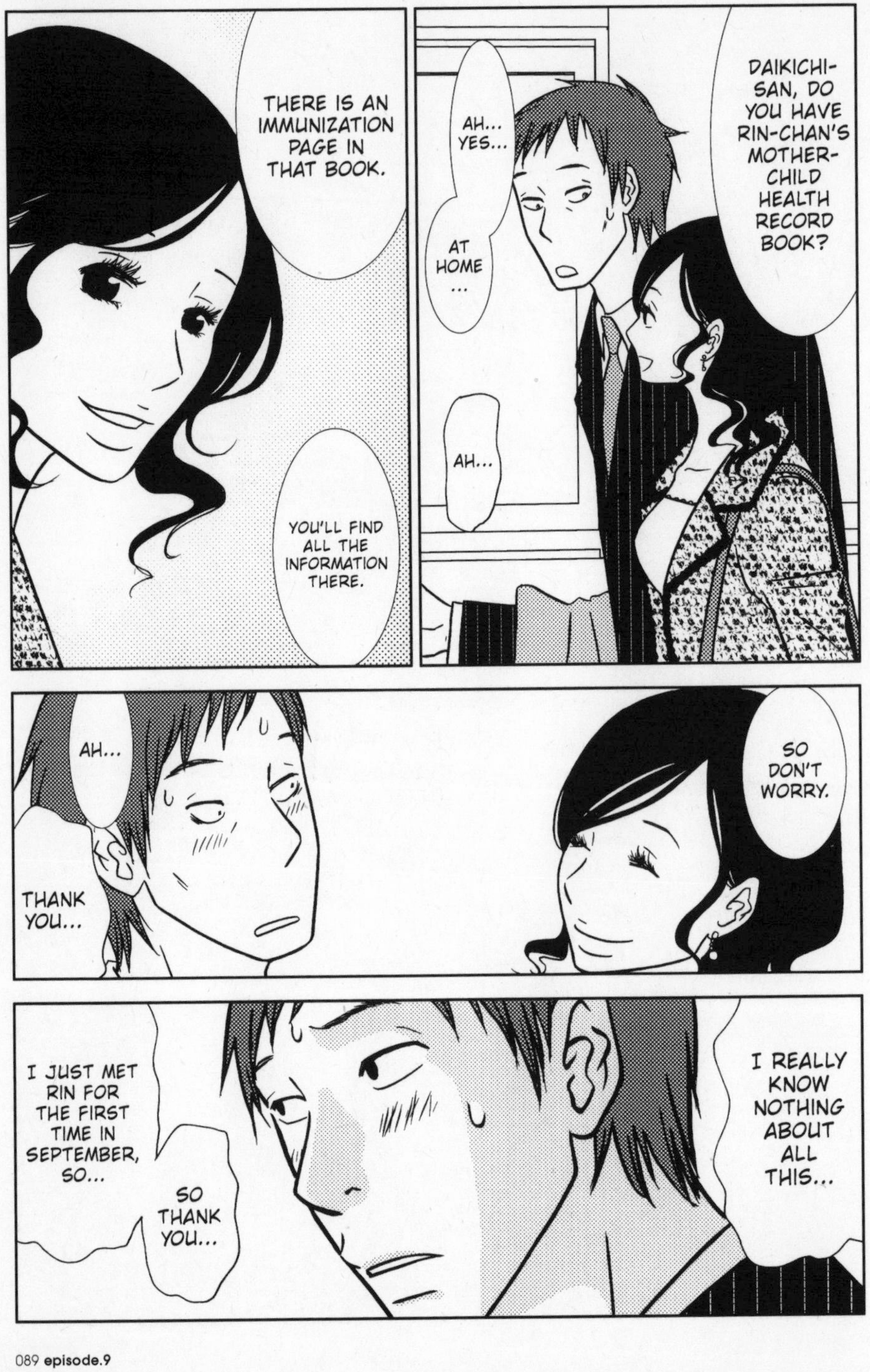
DAIKICHI-SAN, DO YOU HAVE RIN-CHAN'S MOTHER-CHILD HEALTH RECORD BOOK?
AH... YES...
AT HOME ...
AH...
THERE IS AN IMMUNIZATION PAGE IN THAT BOOK.
YOU'LL FIND ALL THE INFORMATION THERE.
SO DON'T WORRY.
AH...
THANK YOU...
I REALLY KNOW NOTHING ABOUT ALL THIS...
I JUST MET RIN FOR THE FIRST TIME IN SEPTEMBER, SO...
SO THANK YOU...

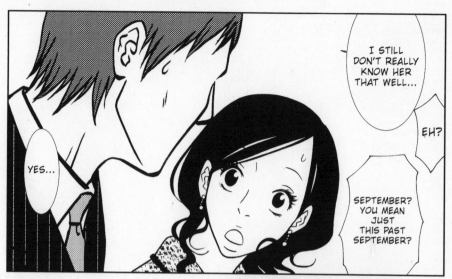

I STILL DON'T REALLY KNOW HER THAT WELL...

EH?

SEPTEMBER? YOU MEAN JUST THIS PAST SEPTEMBER?

YES...

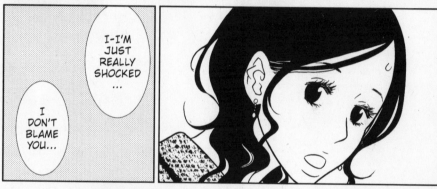

I-I'M JUST REALLY SHOCKED...

I DON'T BLAME YOU...

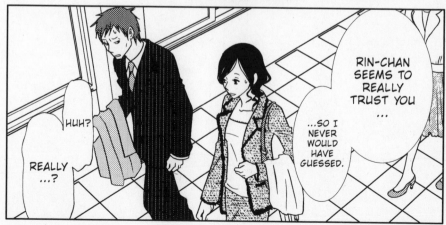

RIN-CHAN SEEMS TO REALLY TRUST YOU...

...SO I NEVER WOULD HAVE GUESSED.

HUH?

REALLY...?

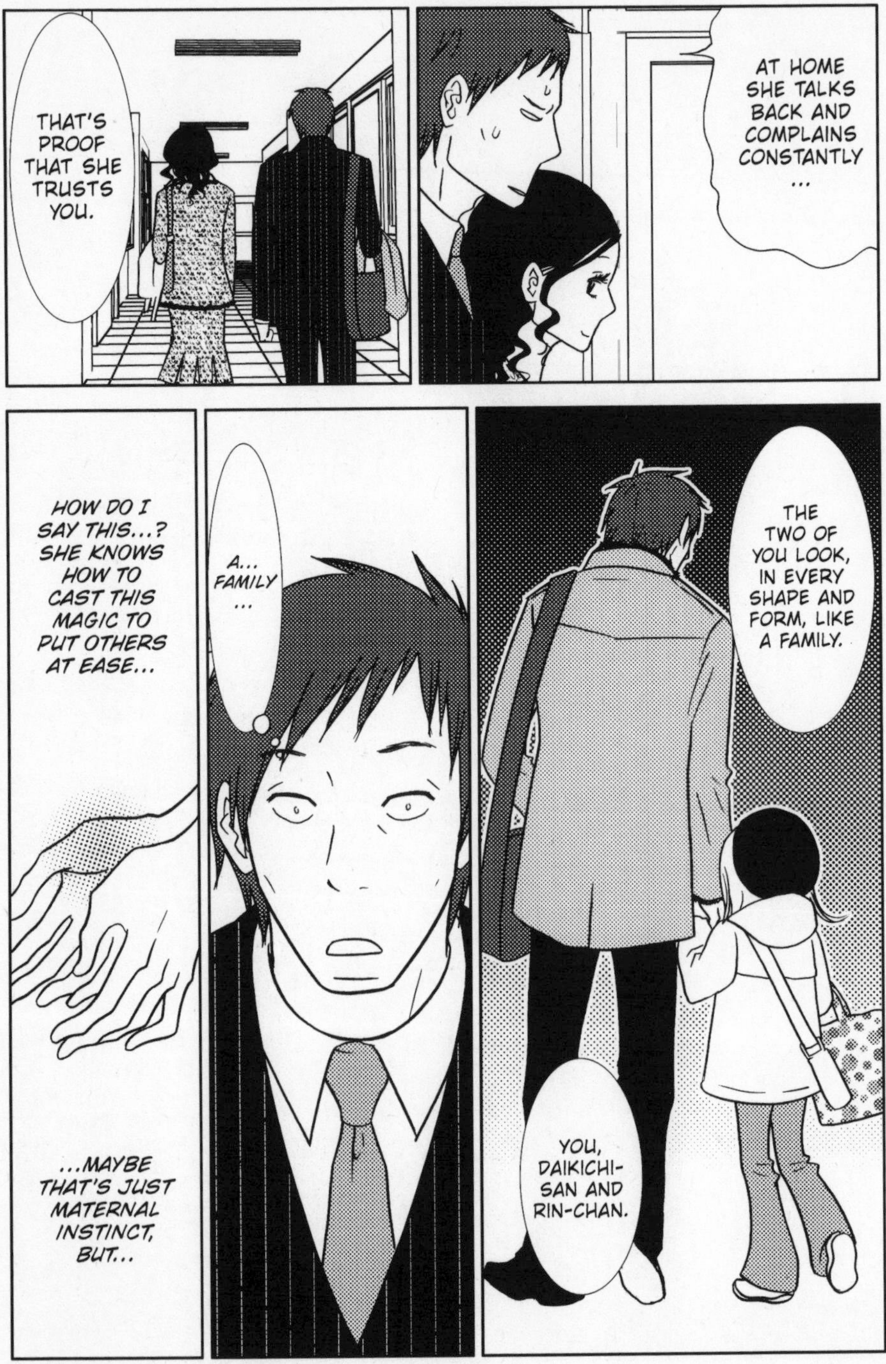
AT HOME SHE TALKS BACK AND COMPLAINS CONSTANTLY ...
THAT'S PROOF THAT SHE TRUSTS YOU.
THE TWO OF YOU LOOK, IN EVERY SHAPE AND FORM, LIKE A FAMILY.
YOU, DAIKICHI-SAN AND RIN-CHAN.
A... FAMILY ...
HOW DO I SAY THIS...? SHE KNOWS HOW TO CAST THIS MAGIC TO PUT OTHERS AT EASE...
...MAYBE THAT'S JUST MATERNAL INSTINCT, BUT...

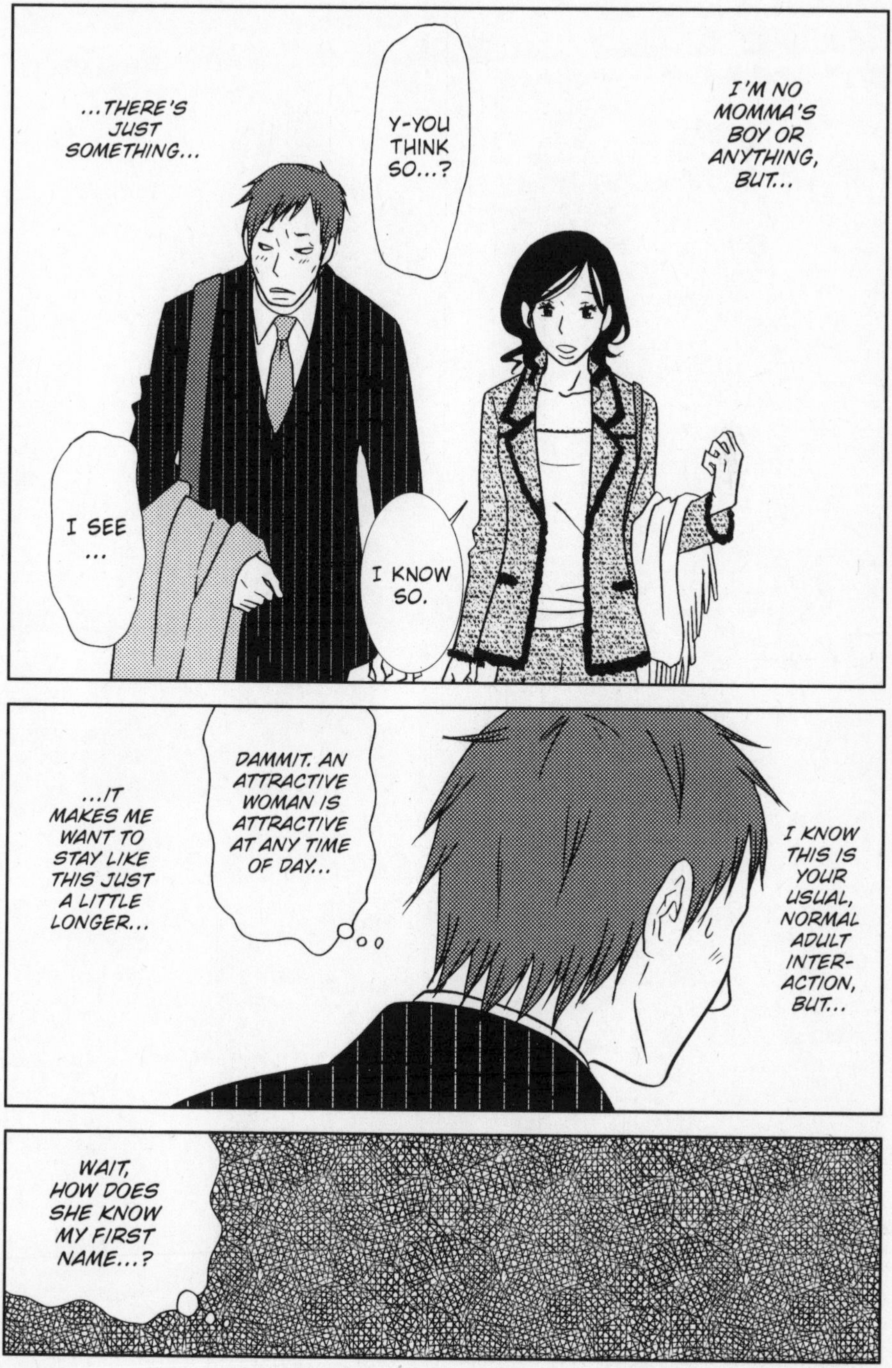
I'M NO MOMMA'S BOY OR ANYTHING, BUT...
Y-YOU THINK SO...?
...THERE'S JUST SOMETHING...
I KNOW SO.
I SEE ...
I KNOW THIS IS YOUR USUAL, NORMAL ADULT INTER-ACTION, BUT...
DAMMIT. AN ATTRACTIVE WOMAN IS ATTRACTIVE AT ANY TIME OF DAY...
...IT MAKES ME WANT TO STAY LIKE THIS JUST A LITTLE LONGER...
WAIT, HOW DOES SHE KNOW MY FIRST NAME...?

BOX: MATH ACTIVITY SET

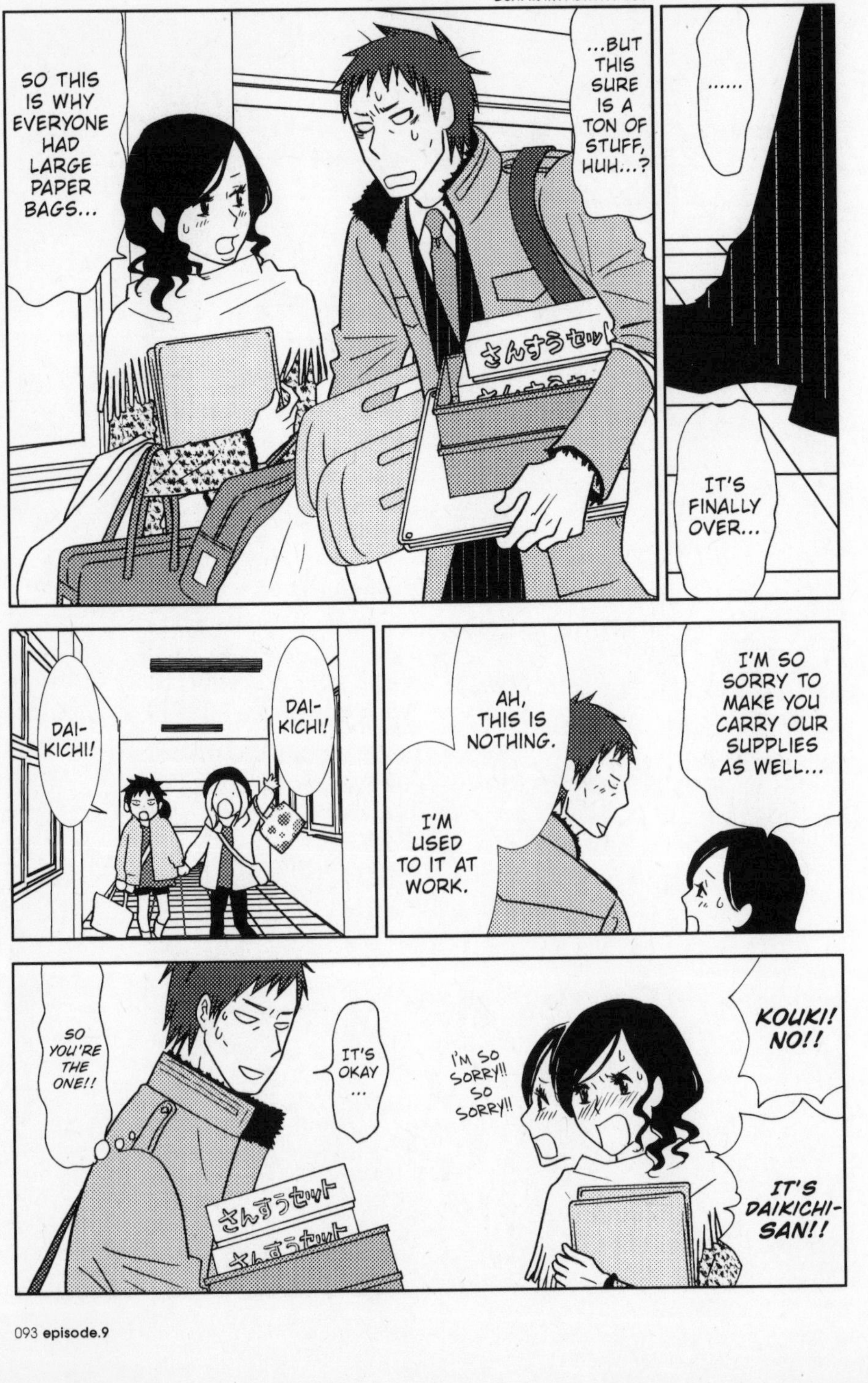
......
IT'S FINALLY OVER...
...BUT THIS SURE IS A TON OF STUFF, HUH...?
SO THIS IS WHY EVERYONE HAD LARGE PAPER BAGS...
さんすうセット
I'M SO SORRY TO MAKE YOU CARRY OUR SUPPLIES AS WELL...
AH, THIS IS NOTHING.
I'M USED TO IT AT WORK.
DAI-KICHI!
DAI-KICHI!
KOUKI! NO!!
IT'S DAIKICHI-SAN!!
I'M SO SORRY!! SO SORRY!!
IT'S OKAY ...
SO YOU'RE THE ONE!!
さんすうセット
さんすうセット

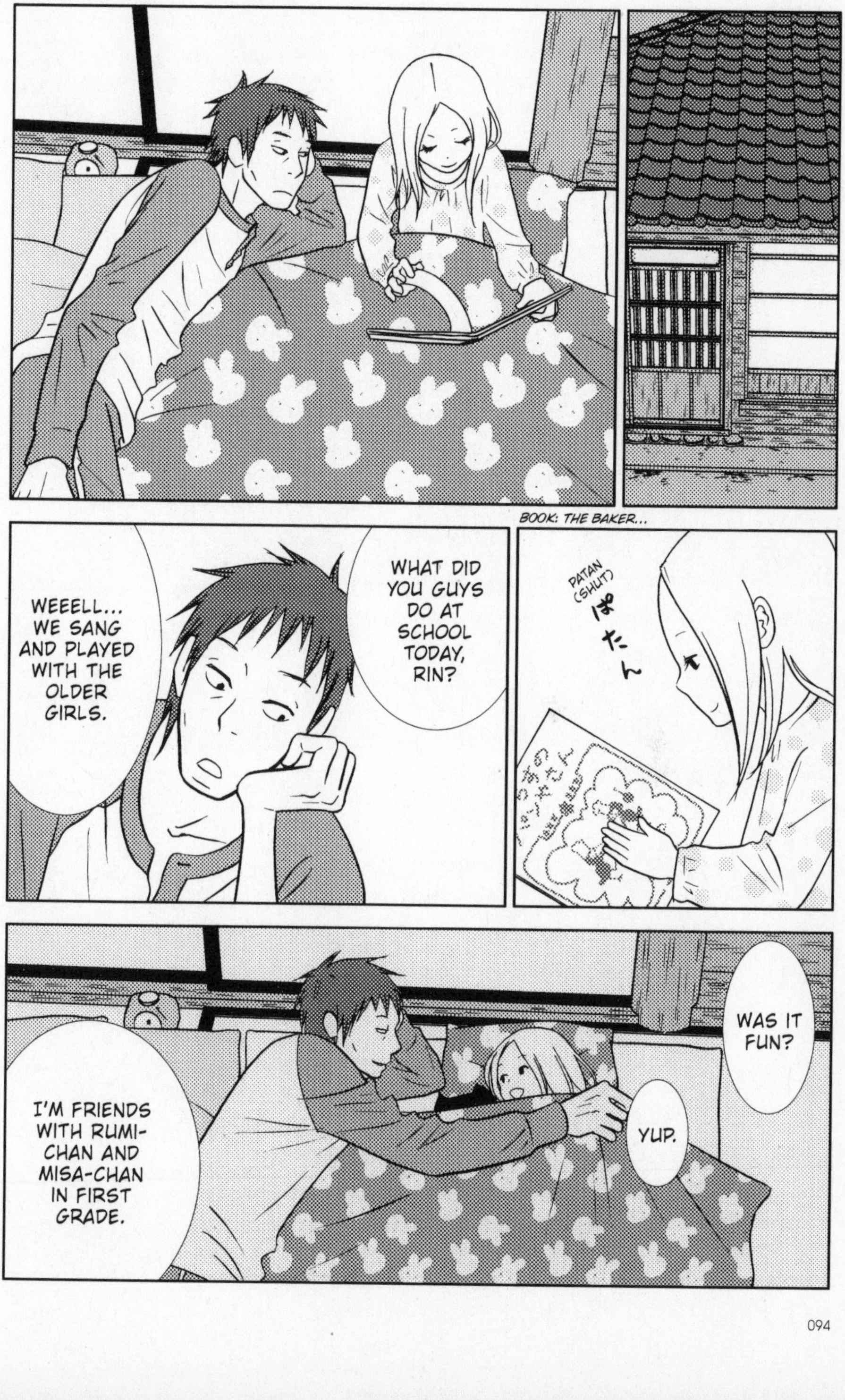
BOOK: THE BAKER...
PATAN (SHUT)
ぱたん
WHAT DID YOU GUYS DO AT SCHOOL TODAY, RIN?
WEEELL... WE SANG AND PLAYED WITH THE OLDER GIRLS.
WAS IT FUN?
YUP.
I'M FRIENDS WITH RUMI-CHAN AND MISA-CHAN IN FIRST GRADE.

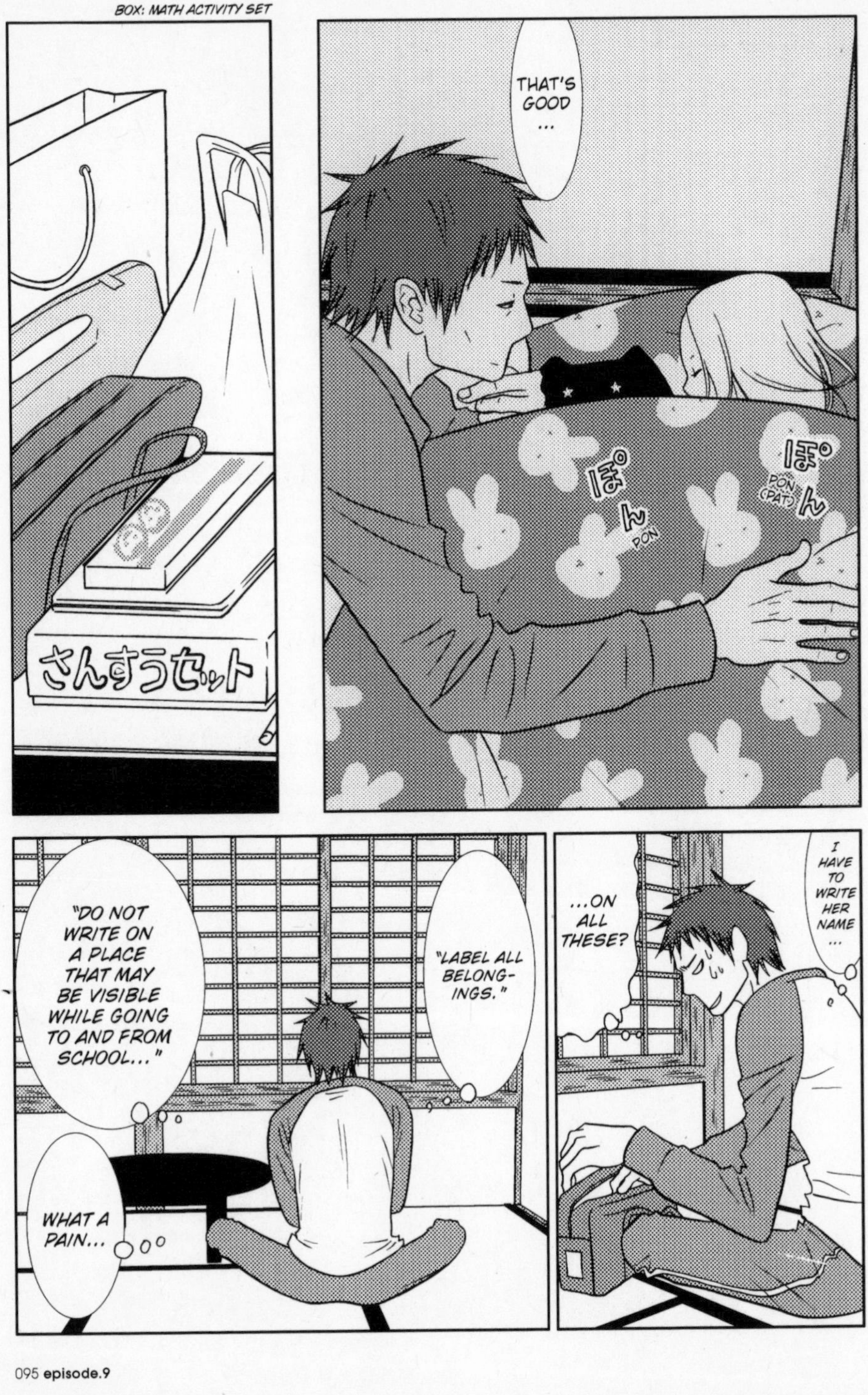
THAT'S GOOD ...
ぽん
PON (PAT)
ぽん
PON
BOX: MATH ACTIVITY SET
さんすうセット
I HAVE TO WRITE HER NAME ...
...ON ALL THESE?
"LABEL ALL BELONGINGS."
"DO NOT WRITE ON A PLACE THAT MAY BE VISIBLE WHILE GOING TO AND FROM SCHOOL..."
WHAT A PAIN...

BOOK: MOTHER-CHILD HEALTH RECORD BOOK

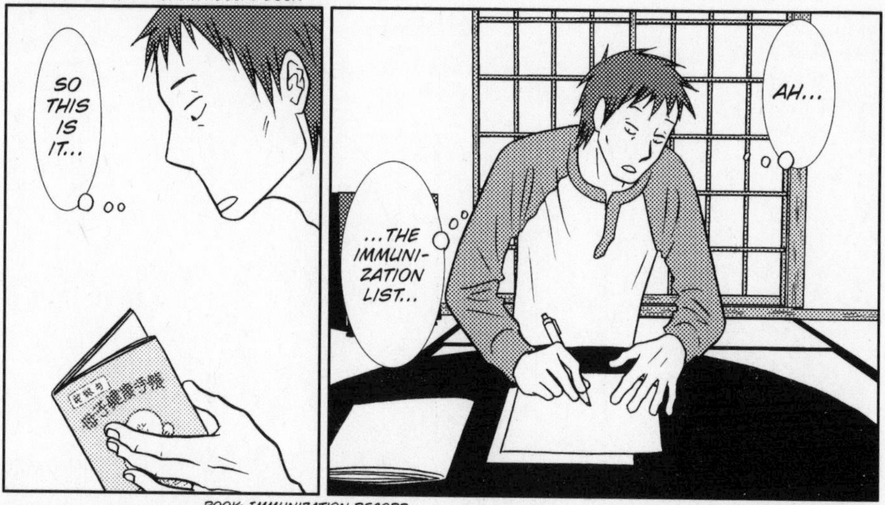
AH...
...THE IMMUNIZATION LIST...
SO THIS IS IT...

BOOK: IMMUNIZATION RECORD

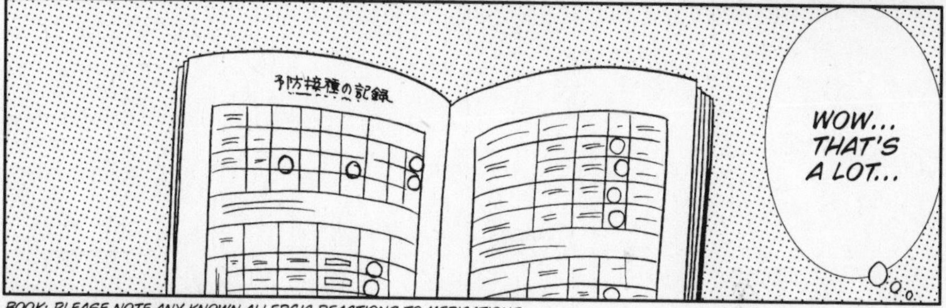
WOW... THAT'S A LOT...
予防接種の記録

BOOK: PLEASE NOTE ANY KNOWN ALLERGIC REACTIONS TO MEDICATIONS...

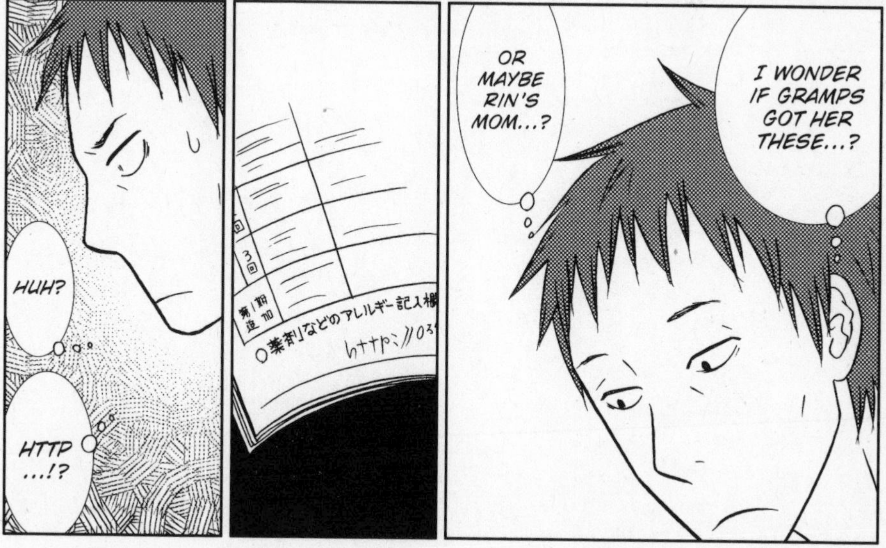
I WONDER IF GRAMPS GOT HER THESE...?
OR MAYBE RIN'S MOM...?
HUH?
HTTP ...!?

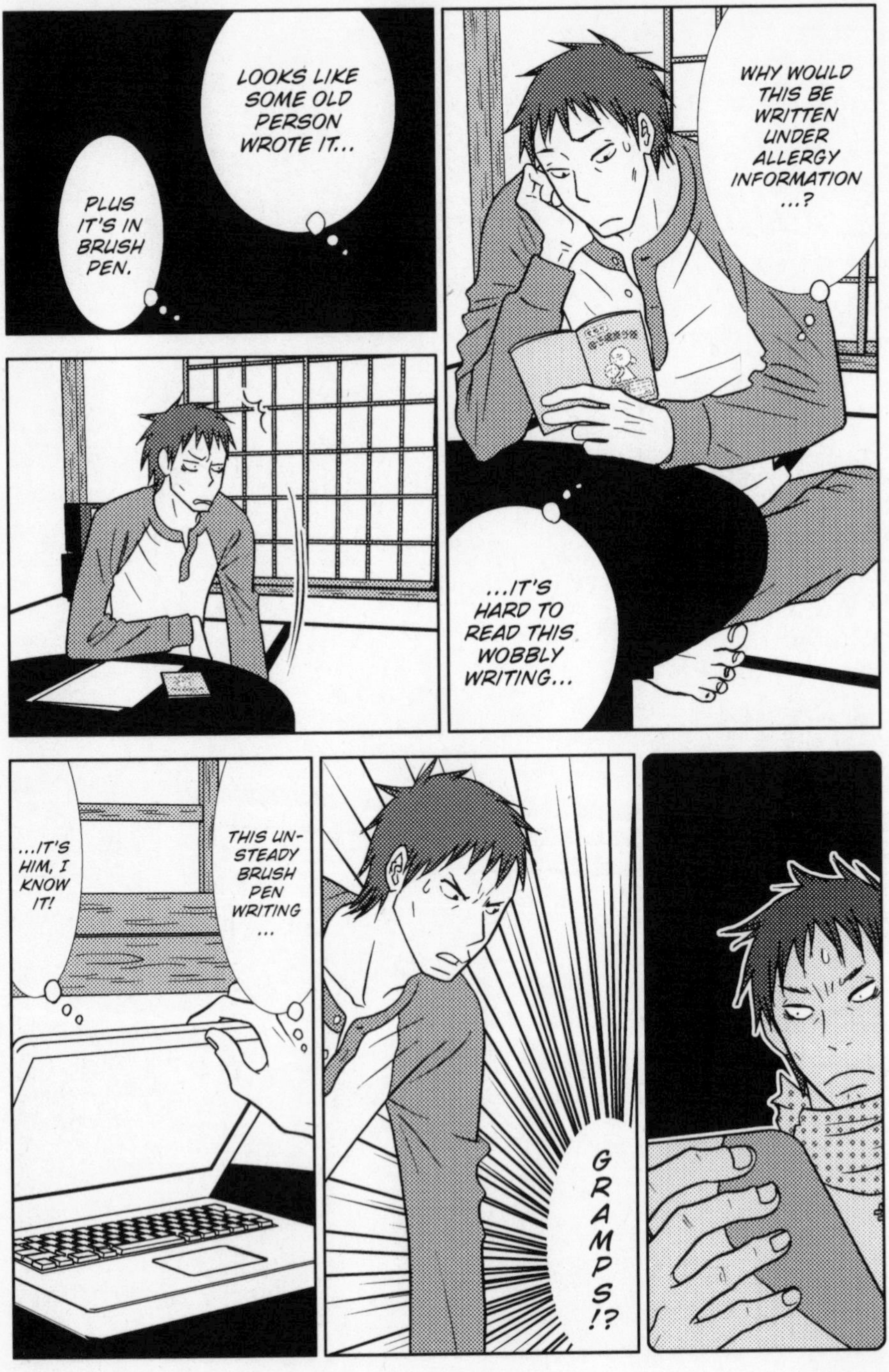
WHY WOULD THIS BE WRITTEN UNDER ALLERGY INFORMATION ...?
...IT'S HARD TO READ THIS WOBBLY WRITING...
LOOKS LIKE SOME OLD PERSON WROTE IT...
PLUS IT'S IN BRUSH PEN.
GRAMPS!?
THIS UN-STEADY BRUSH PEN WRITING ...
...IT'S HIM, I KNOW IT!

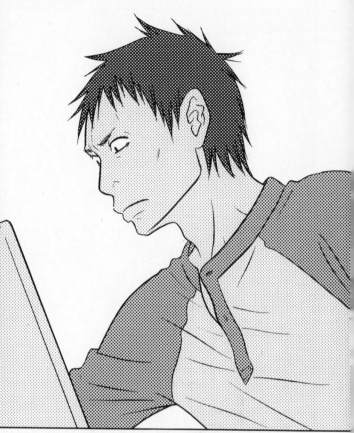

HIS LAST WILL AND TESTAMENT ...!?
WEBSITE: SOUICHI'S WILL. "TA-DAA!"
PUTTING HIS LAST TESTAMENT UP ON A BLOG...
...ARE YOU FOR REAL ...?
GRAMPS...
AT LEAST HE CAN TYPE ...!!

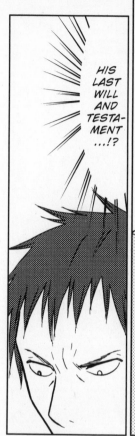

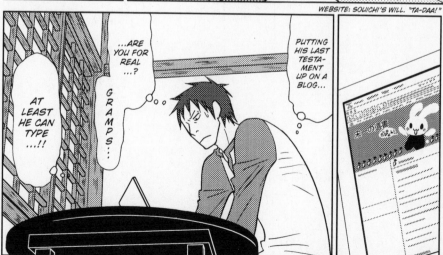

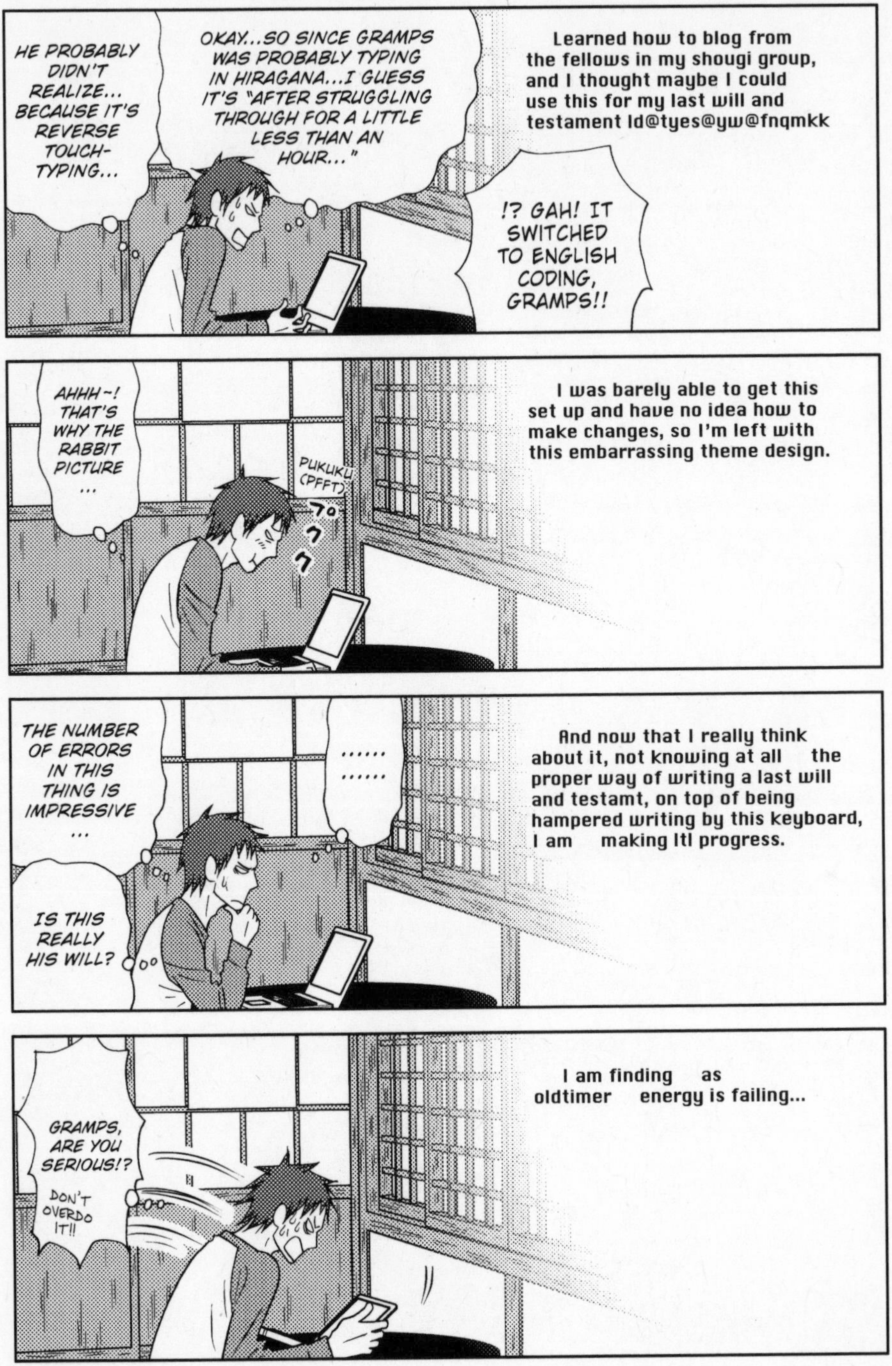
Learned how to blog from the fellows in my shougi group, and I thought maybe I could use this for my last will and testament ld@tyes@yw@fnqmkk
!? GAH! IT SWITCHED TO ENGLISH CODING, GRAMPS!!
OKAY...SO SINCE GRAMPS WAS PROBABLY TYPING IN HIRAGANA...I GUESS IT'S "AFTER STRUGGLING THROUGH FOR A LITTLE LESS THAN AN HOUR..."
HE PROBABLY DIDN'T REALIZE... BECAUSE IT'S REVERSE TOUCH-TYPING...
I was barely able to get this set up and have no idea how to make changes, so I'm left with this embarrassing theme design.
PUKUKU (PFFFT)
AHHH~! THAT'S WHY THE RABBIT PICTURE ...
And now that I really think about it, not knowing at all the proper way of writing a last will and testamt, on top of being hampered writing by this keyboard, I am making ltl progress.
....
THE NUMBER OF ERRORS IN THIS THING IS IMPRESSIVE ...
IS THIS REALLY HIS WILL?
I am finding as oldtimer energy is failing...
GRAMPS, ARE YOU SERIOUS!?
DON'T OVERDO IT!!

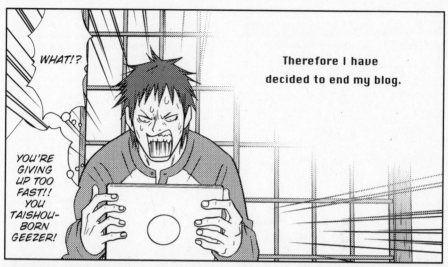

Therefore I have decided to end my blog.
WHAT!?
YOU'RE GIVING UP TOO FAST!! YOU TAISHOU-BORN GEEZER!
To be continued in Rin's Mother-Child
July 2005
Souichi Kaga
......EH?
TO BE CONTINUED...?
THE MOTHER-CHILD HEALTH RECORD BOOK...?
WAIT A SEC. WAS THERE ANYTHING LIKE THAT IN THERE?
BUT WOULDN'T ANYONE NOTICE SOMETHING LIKE THAT!?
GRAMPS, ARE YOU SERIOUS?

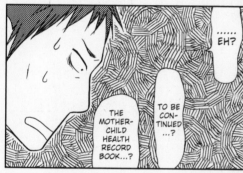

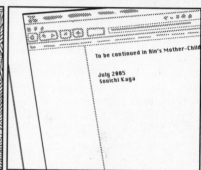

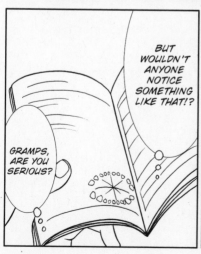

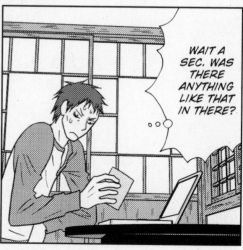

BOOK: MOTHER-CHILD HEALTH RECORD BOOK.

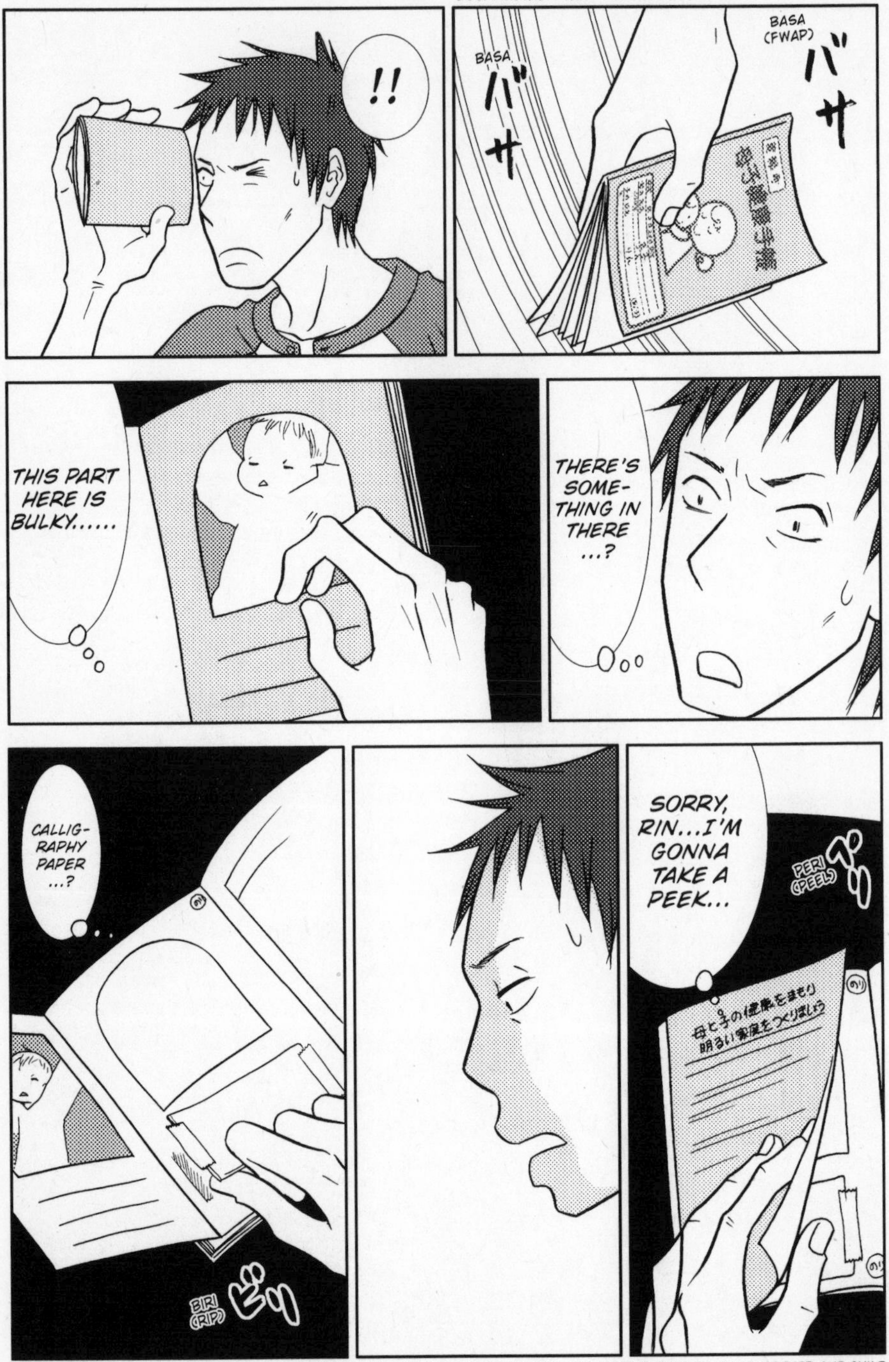
BASA (FWAP)
バサ
BASA
バサ
母子健康手帳
!!
THERE'S SOME-THING IN THERE ...?
THIS PART HERE IS BULKY......
SORRY, RIN...I'M GONNA TAKE A PEEK...
PERI (PEEL)
ペリ
母と子の健康をまもり
明るい家庭をつくりましょう
CALLIG-RAPHY PAPER ...?
BIRI (RIP)
ビリ

BOOK: TOWARDS A BRIGHTER FUTURE - PROTECING THE HEALTH OF MOTHER AND CHILD.

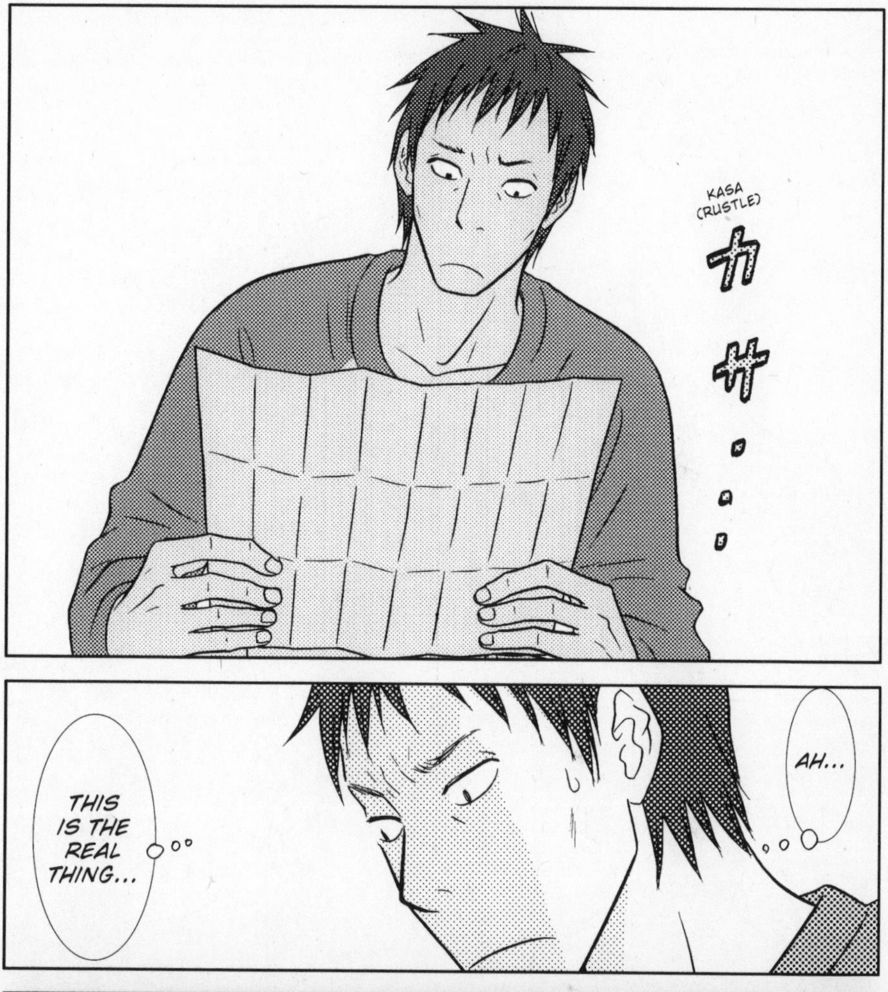
KASA (RUSTLE)
カサ...
AH...
THIS IS THE REAL THING...
I'VE FINALLY DISCOVERED...
...GRAMPS'S FEELINGS TOWARDS RIN AND MASAKO-SAN.

BUNNY**DROP**
episode.10

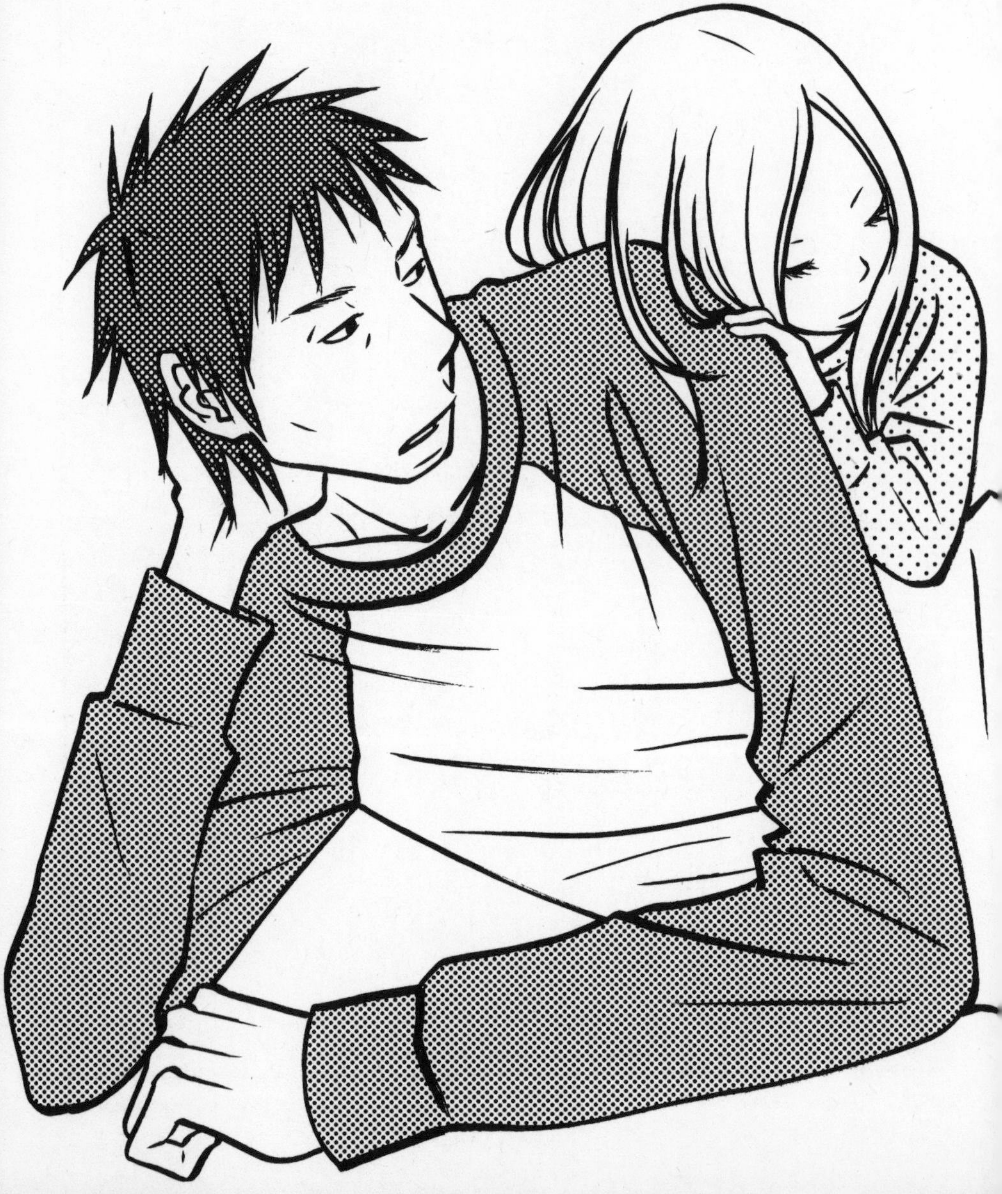

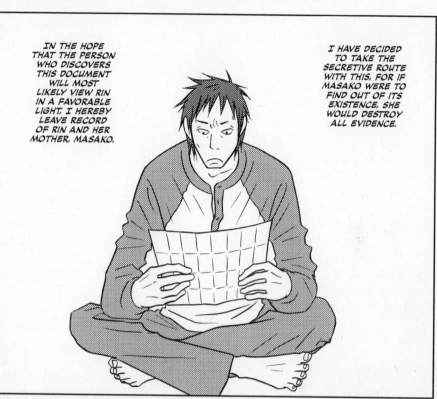

I HAVE DECIDED TO TAKE THE SECRETIVE ROUTE WITH THIS, FOR IF MASAKO WERE TO FIND OUT OF ITS EXISTENCE, SHE WOULD DESTROY ALL EVIDENCE.
IN THE HOPE THAT THE PERSON WHO DISCOVERS THIS DOCUMENT WILL MOST LIKELY VIEW RIN IN A FAVORABLE LIGHT, I HEREBY LEAVE RECORD OF RIN AND HER MOTHER, MASAKO.
GOKURI (GULP)
ALTHOUGH MASAKO IS APT TO BE MISUNDER-STOOD, I WOULD LIKE TO STATE FOR THE RECORD THAT SHE IS NOT A BAD GIRL.

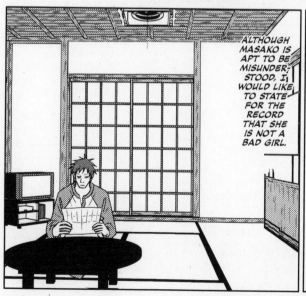

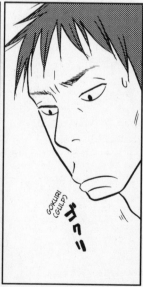

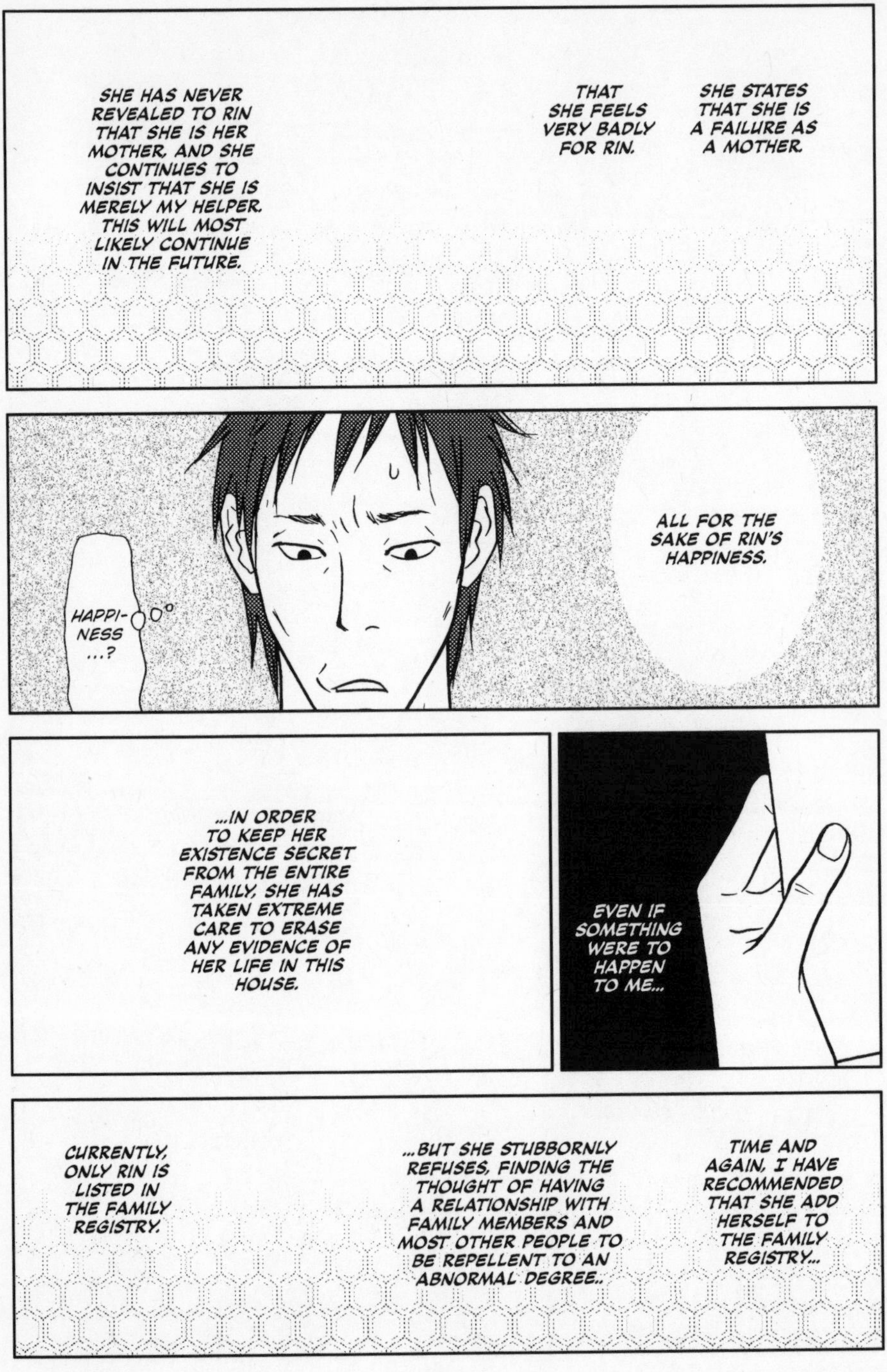
SHE STATES THAT SHE IS A FAILURE AS A MOTHER.
THAT SHE FEELS VERY BADLY FOR RIN.
SHE HAS NEVER REVEALED TO RIN THAT SHE IS HER MOTHER, AND SHE CONTINUES TO INSIST THAT SHE IS MERELY MY HELPER. THIS WILL MOST LIKELY CONTINUE IN THE FUTURE.
ALL FOR THE SAKE OF RIN'S HAPPINESS.
HAPPINESS...?
EVEN IF SOMETHING WERE TO HAPPEN TO ME...
...IN ORDER TO KEEP HER EXISTENCE SECRET FROM THE ENTIRE FAMILY, SHE HAS TAKEN EXTREME CARE TO ERASE ANY EVIDENCE OF HER LIFE IN THIS HOUSE.
TIME AND AGAIN, I HAVE RECOMMENDED THAT SHE ADD HERSELF TO THE FAMILY REGISTRY...
...BUT SHE STUBBORNLY REFUSES, FINDING THE THOUGHT OF HAVING A RELATIONSHIP WITH FAMILY MEMBERS AND MOST OTHER PEOPLE TO BE REPELLENT TO AN ABNORMAL DEGREE..
CURRENTLY, ONLY RIN IS LISTED IN THE FAMILY REGISTRY.

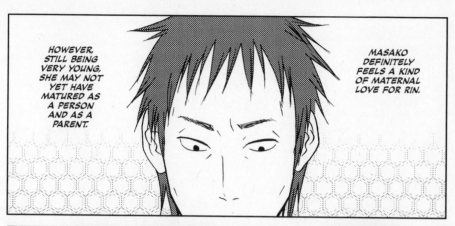

MASAKO DEFINITELY FEELS A KIND OF MATERNAL LOVE FOR RIN.
HOWEVER, STILL BEING VERY YOUNG, SHE MAY NOT YET HAVE MATURED AS A PERSON AND AS A PARENT.
I DON'T UNDER-STAND THIS.
IS IT BECAUSE GRAMPS CAN'T WRITE?
OR AM I JUST STUPID ...?
......
SOMEHOW, I SLOGGED THROUGH THAT BARELY LEGIBLE, WOBBLY WRITING, AND A LOT OF IT JUST DIDN'T SIT RIGHT INSIDE.
BUT...
...THE ONE THING THAT CAME ACROSS LOUD AND CLEAR...

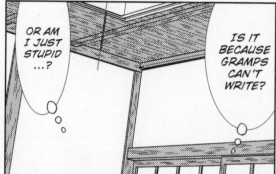

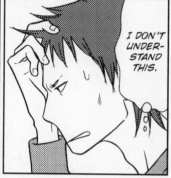

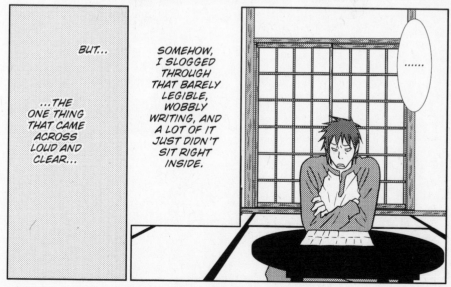

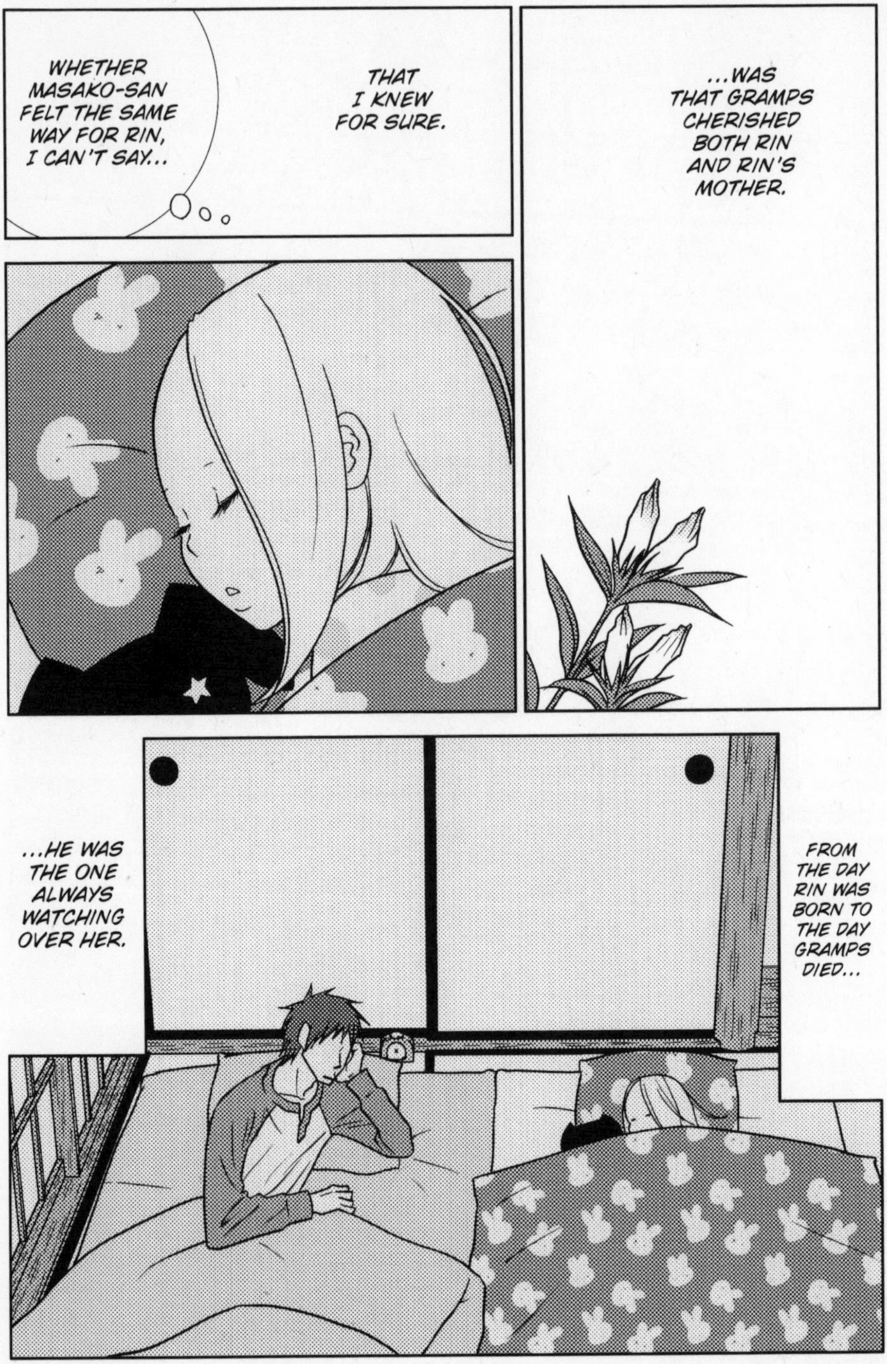
WHETHER MASAKO-SAN FELT THE SAME WAY FOR RIN, I CAN'T SAY...
THAT I KNEW FOR SURE.
...WAS THAT GRAMPS CHERISHED BOTH RIN AND RIN'S MOTHER.
FROM THE DAY RIN WAS BORN TO THE DAY GRAMPS DIED...
...HE WAS THE ONE ALWAYS WATCHING OVER HER.

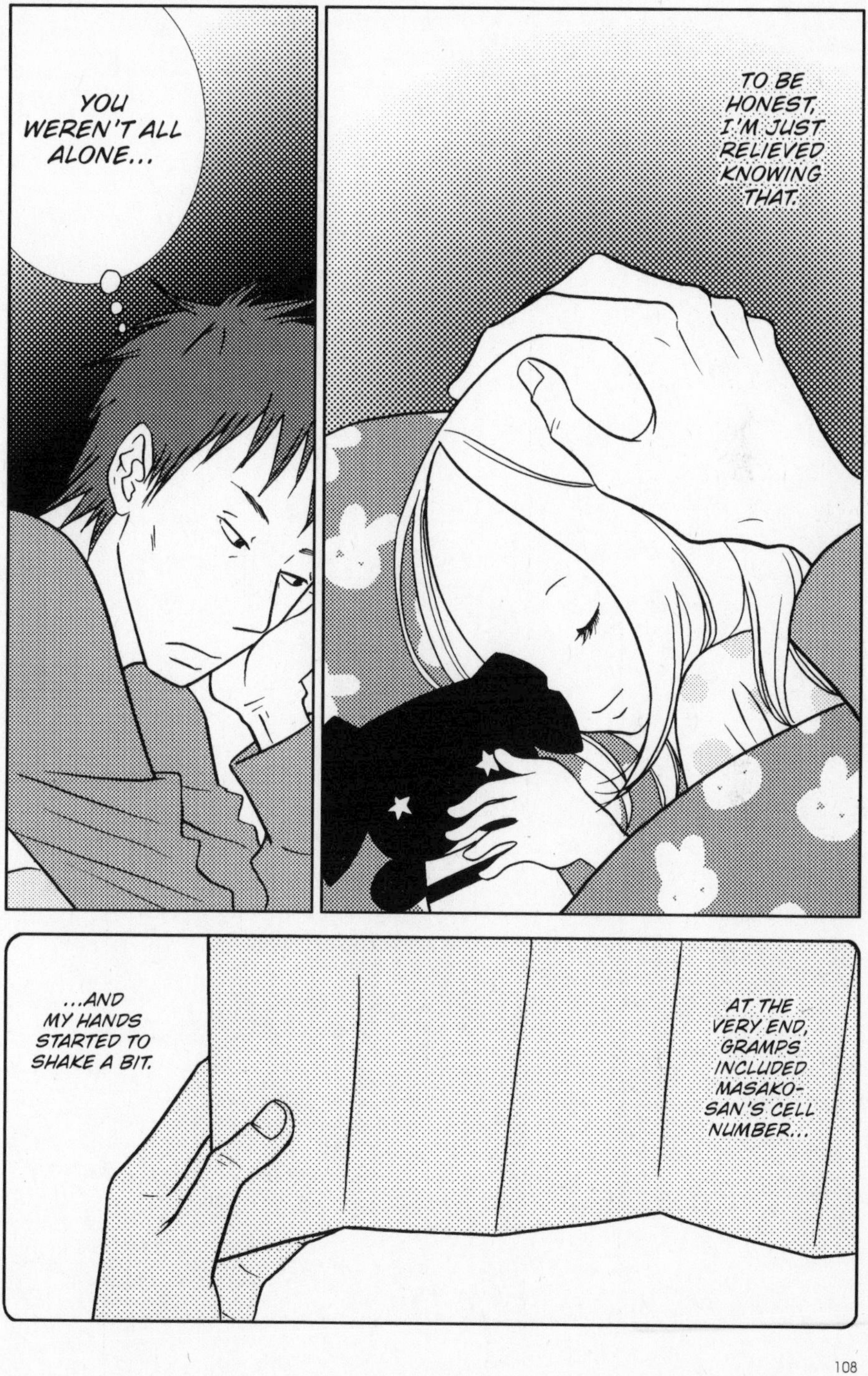
TO BE HONEST, I'M JUST RELIEVED KNOWING THAT.
YOU WEREN'T ALL ALONE...
AT THE VERY END, GRAMPS INCLUDED MASAKO-SAN'S CELL NUMBER...
...AND MY HANDS STARTED TO SHAKE A BIT.

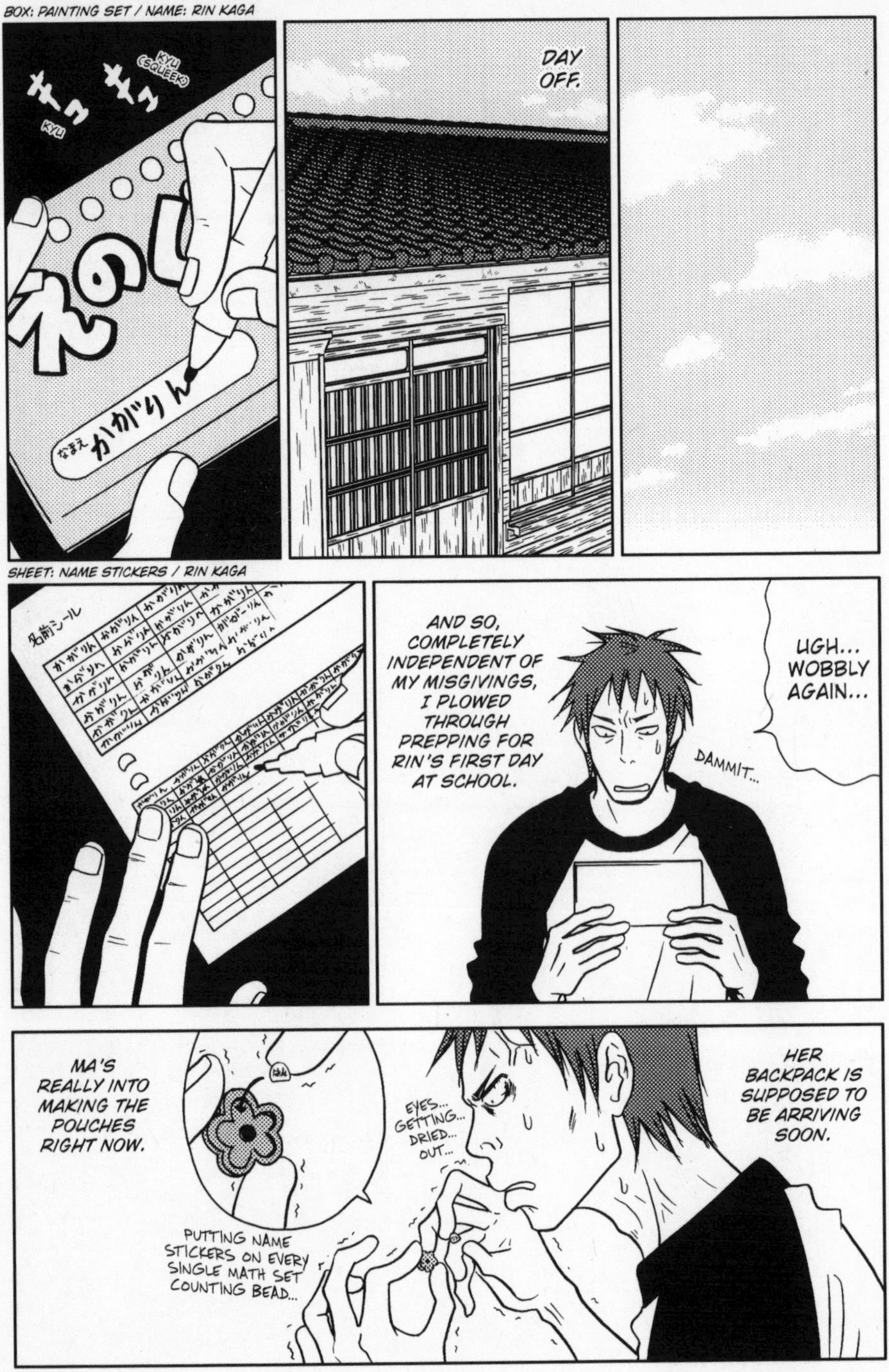
DAY OFF.
BOX: PAINTING SET / NAME: RIN KAGA
KYU (SQUEEK) KYU
AND SO, COMPLETELY INDEPENDENT OF MY MISGIVINGS, I PLOWED THROUGH PREPPING FOR RIN'S FIRST DAY AT SCHOOL.
UGH... WOBBLY AGAIN...
DAMMIT...
SHEET: NAME STICKERS / RIN KAGA
HER BACKPACK IS SUPPOSED TO BE ARRIVING SOON.
EYES... GETTING... DRIED... OUT...
MA'S REALLY INTO MAKING THE POUCHES RIGHT NOW.
PUTTING NAME STICKERS ON EVERY SINGLE MATH SET COUNTING BEAD...

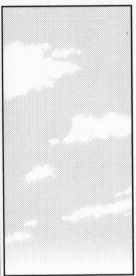

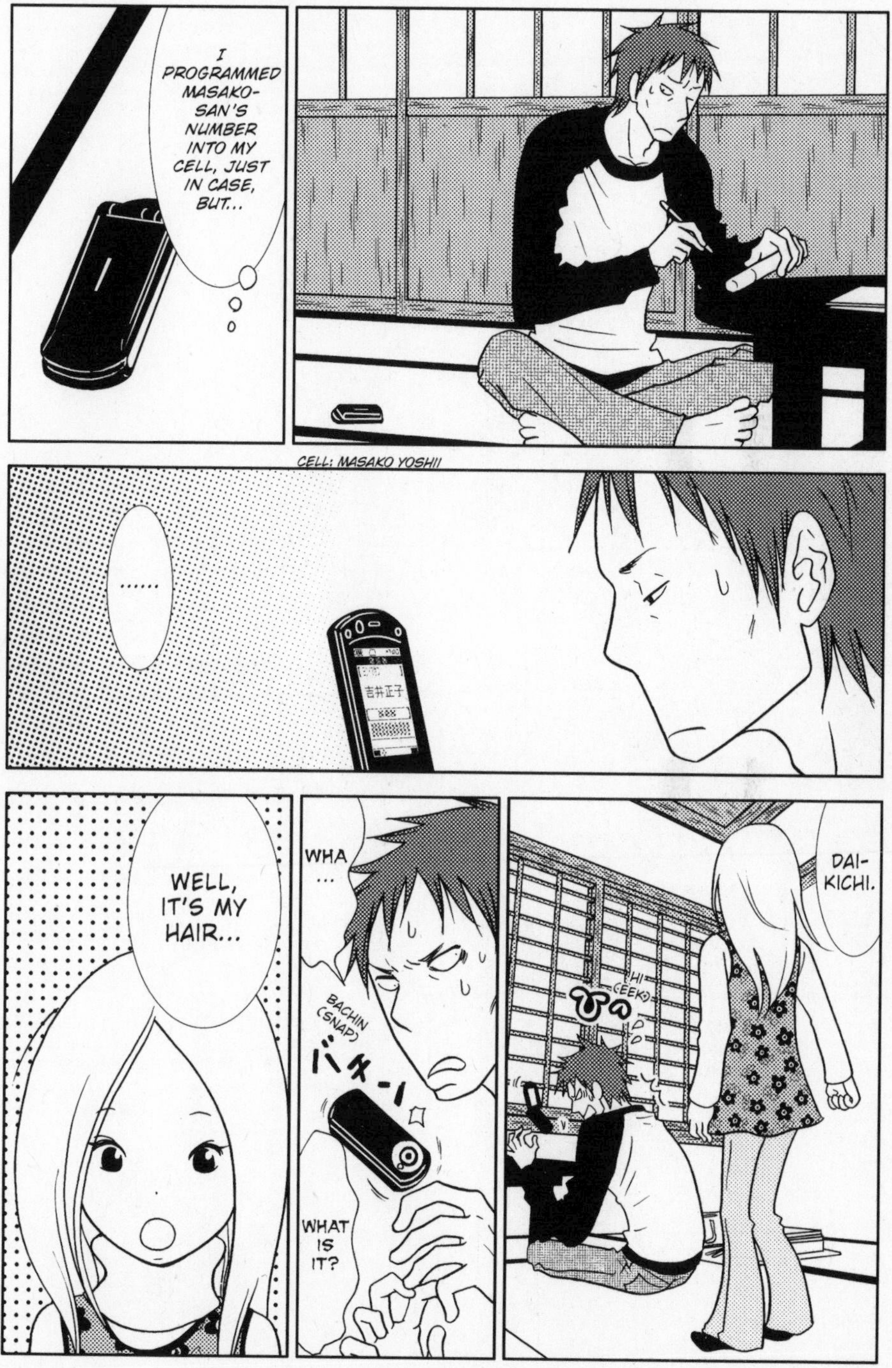
I PROGRAMMED MASAKO-SAN'S NUMBER INTO MY CELL, JUST IN CASE, BUT...
CELL: MASAKO YOSHII
......
吉井正子
DAI-KICHI.
HI (EEK)
WHA ...
BACHIN (SNAP)
WHAT IS IT?
WELL, IT'S MY HAIR...

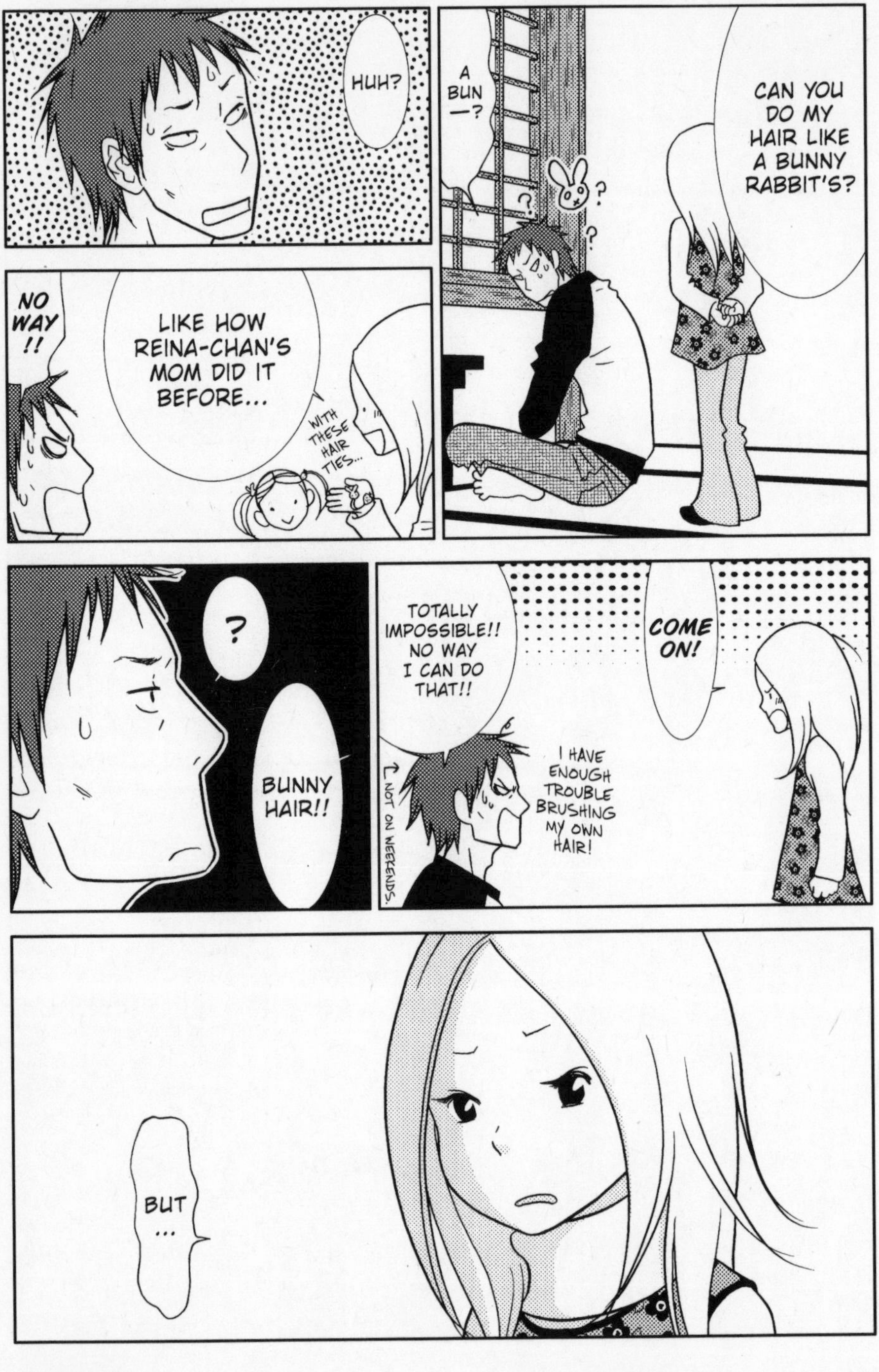
CAN YOU DO MY HAIR LIKE A BUNNY RABBIT'S?
A BUN—?
HUH?
LIKE HOW REINA-CHAN'S MOM DID IT BEFORE...
WITH THESE HAIR TIES...
NO WAY!!
COME ON!
TOTALLY IMPOSSIBLE!! NO WAY I CAN DO THAT!!
I HAVE ENOUGH TROUBLE BRUSHING MY OWN HAIR!
NOT ON WEEKENDS.
?
BUNNY HAIR!!
BUT ...

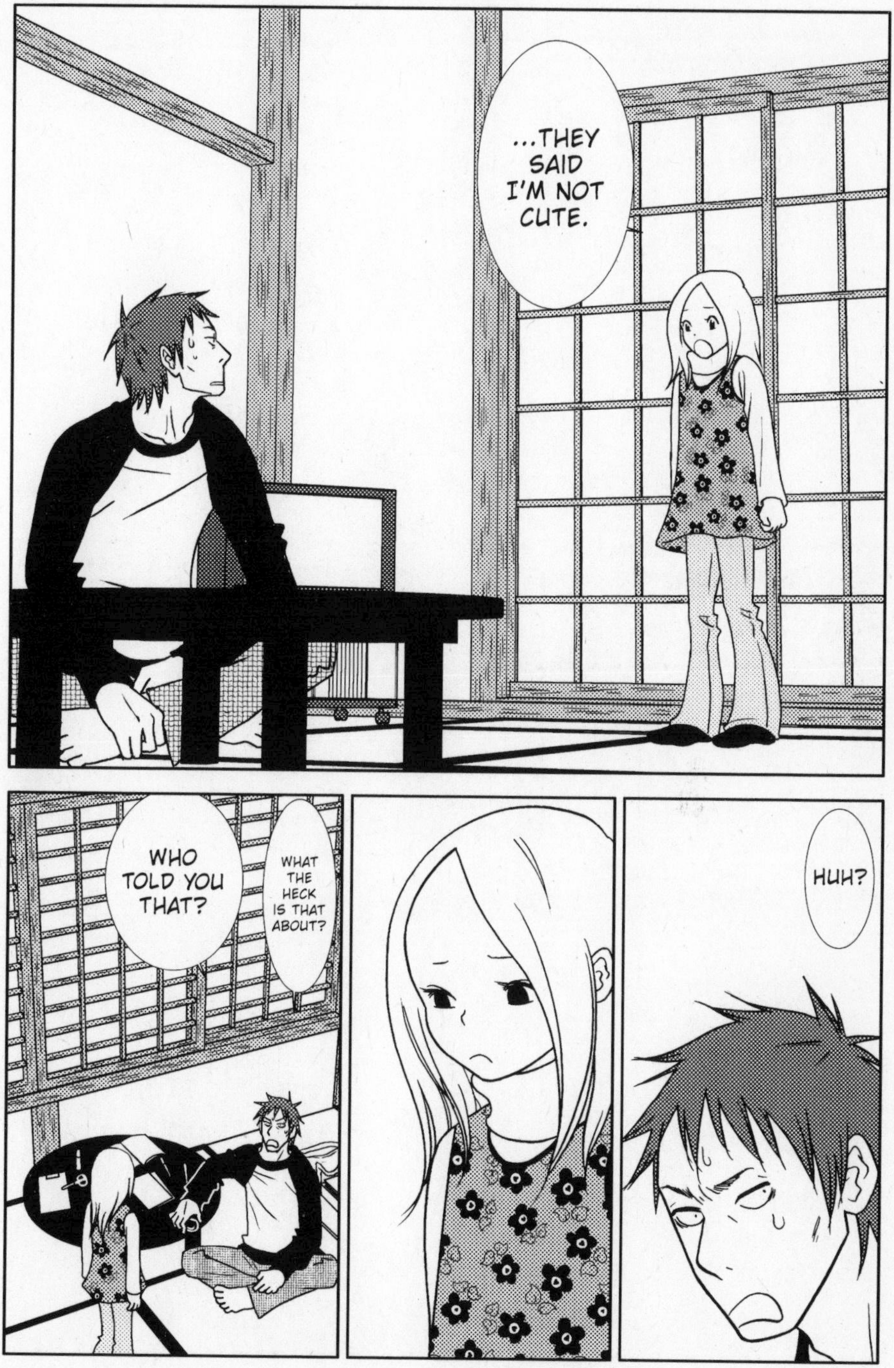
...THEY SAID I'M NOT CUTE.
HUH?
WHAT THE HECK IS THAT ABOUT?
WHO TOLD YOU THAT?

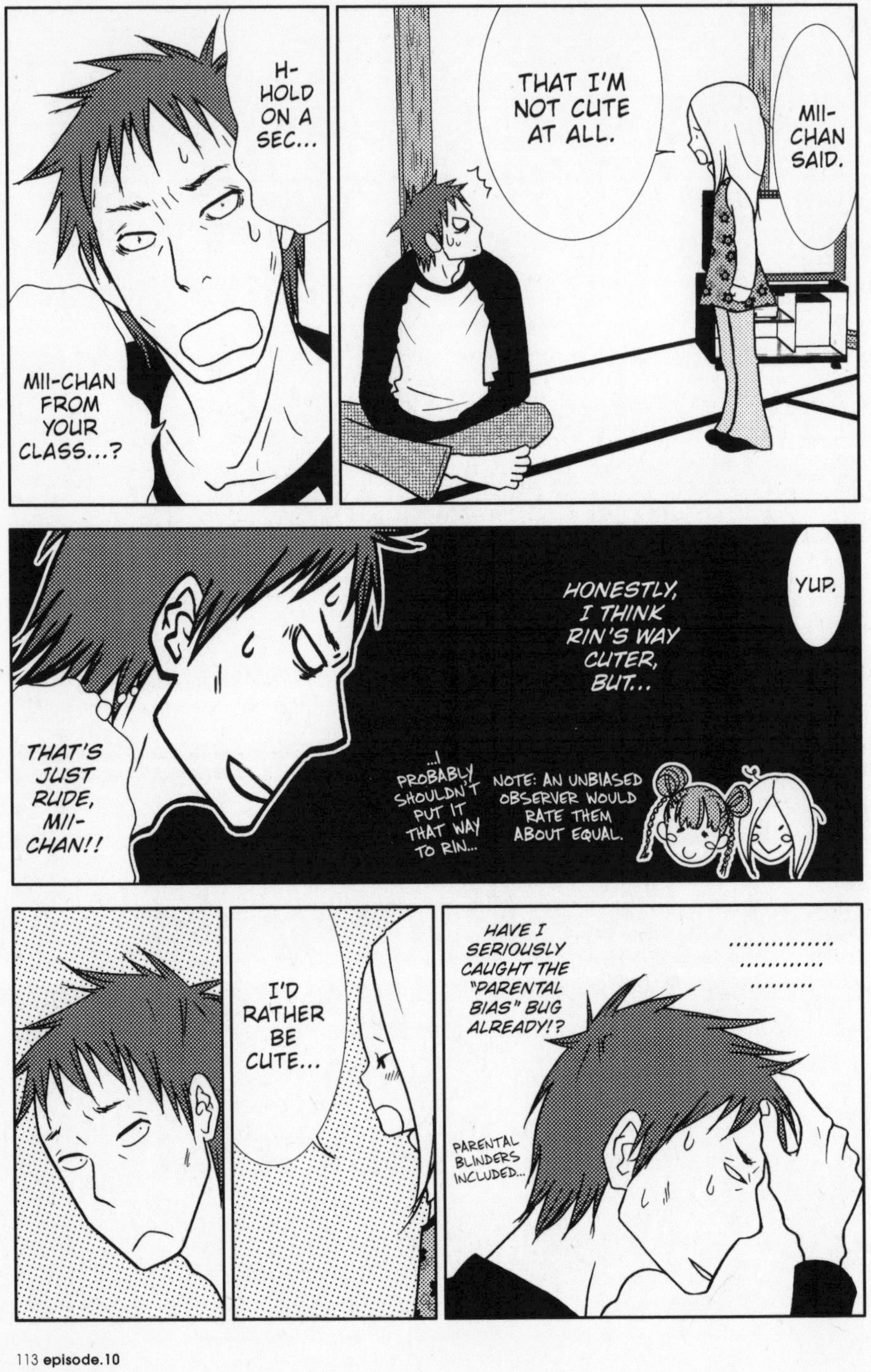
MII-CHAN SAID.
THAT I'M NOT CUTE AT ALL.
H-HOLD ON A SEC...
MII-CHAN FROM YOUR CLASS...?
YUP.
HONESTLY, I THINK RIN'S WAY CUTER, BUT...
NOTE: AN UNBIASED OBSERVER WOULD RATE THEM ABOUT EQUAL.
...I PROBABLY SHOULDN'T PUT IT THAT WAY TO RIN...
THAT'S JUST RUDE, MII-CHAN!!
....
....
....
HAVE I SERIOUSLY CAUGHT THE "PARENTAL BIAS" BUG ALREADY!?
PARENTAL BLINDERS INCLUDED...
I'D RATHER BE CUTE...

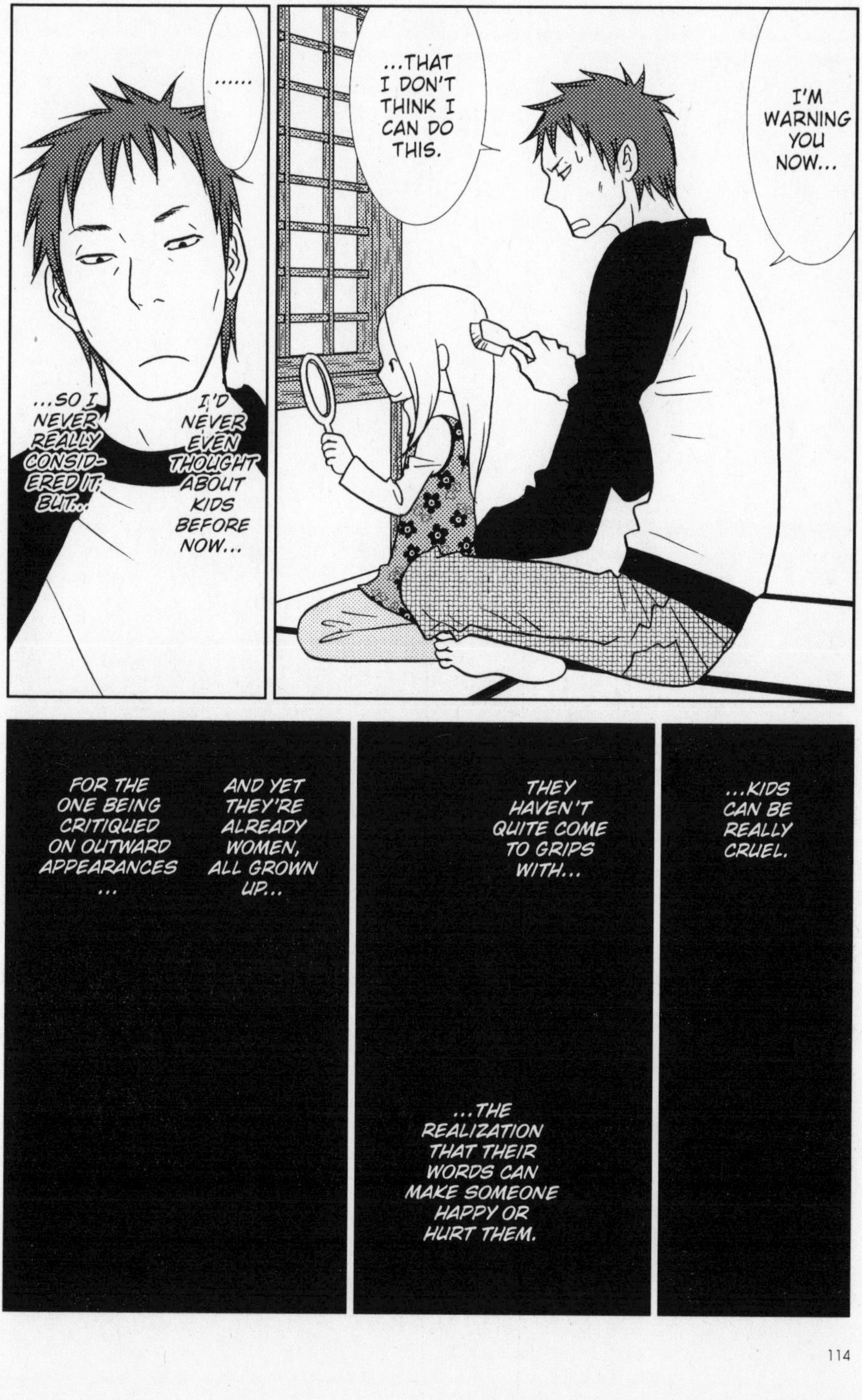
I'M WARNING YOU NOW...
...THAT I DON'T THINK I CAN DO THIS.
......
I'D NEVER EVEN THOUGHT ABOUT KIDS BEFORE NOW...
...SO I NEVER REALLY CONSIDERED IT, BUT...
...KIDS CAN BE REALLY CRUEL.
THEY HAVEN'T QUITE COME TO GRIPS WITH...
...THE REALIZATION THAT THEIR WORDS CAN MAKE SOMEONE HAPPY OR HURT THEM.
AND YET THEY'RE ALREADY WOMEN, ALL GROWN UP...
FOR THE ONE BEING CRITIQUED ON OUTWARD APPEARANCES...

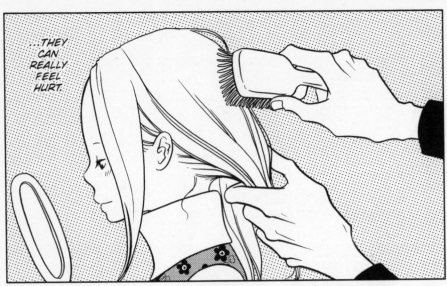

...THEY CAN REALLY FEEL HURT.

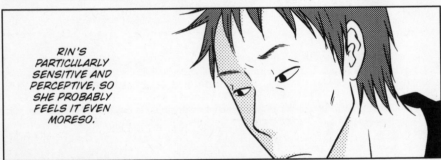

RIN'S PARTICULARLY SENSITIVE AND PERCEPTIVE, SO SHE PROBABLY FEELS IT EVEN MORESO.

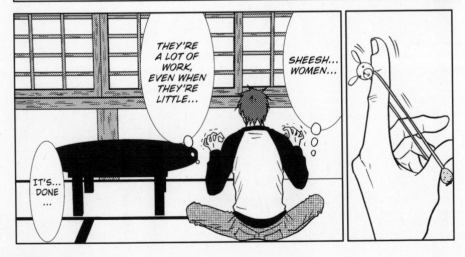

THEY'RE A LOT OF WORK, EVEN WHEN THEY'RE LITTLE...

SHEESH... WOMEN...

IT'S... DONE ...

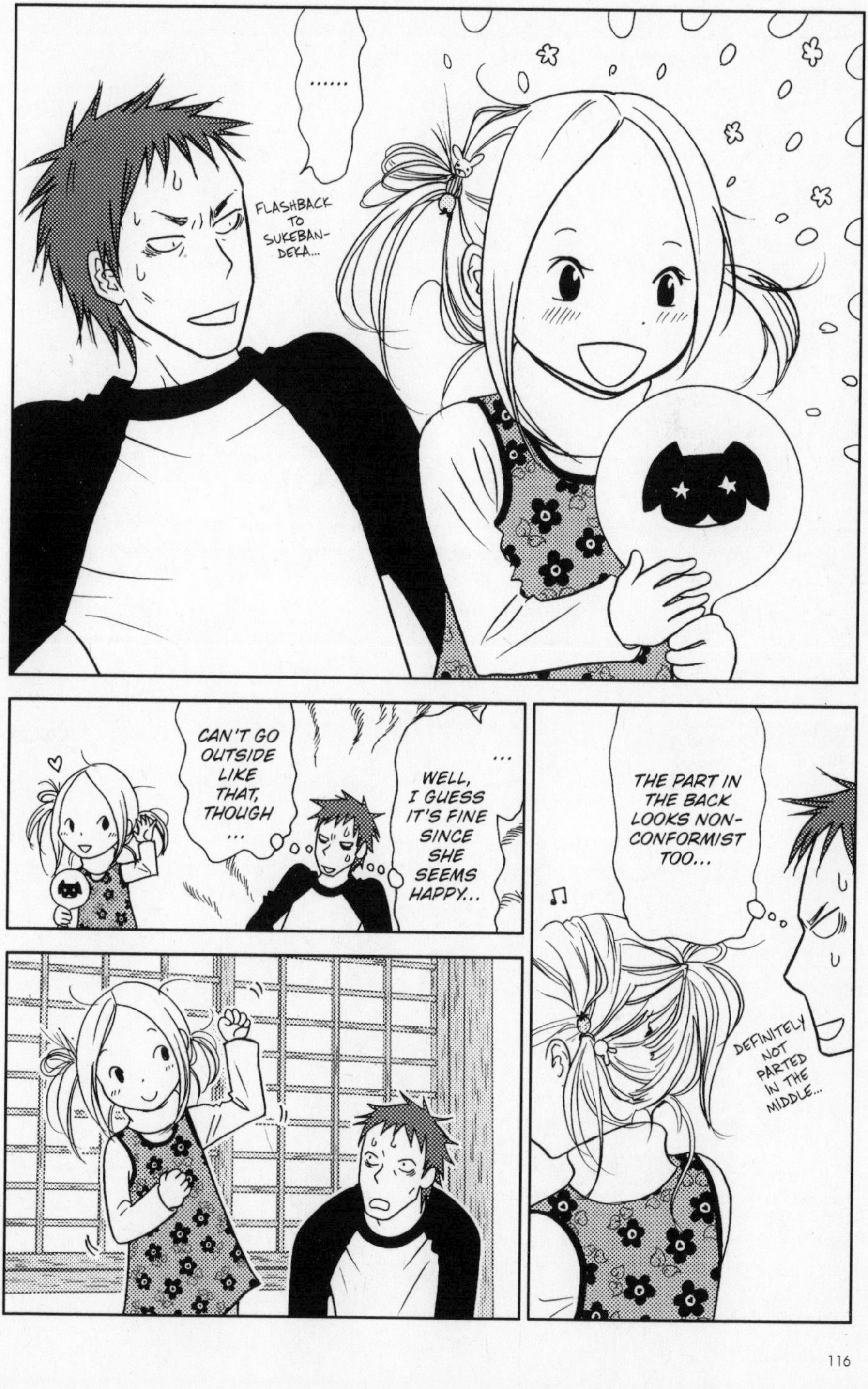
......
FLASHBACK TO SUKEBAN-DEKA...
THE PART IN THE BACK LOOKS NON-CONFORMIST TOO...
DEFINITELY NOT PARTED IN THE MIDDLE...
...
WELL, I GUESS IT'S FINE SINCE SHE SEEMS HAPPY...
CAN'T GO OUTSIDE LIKE THAT, THOUGH ...

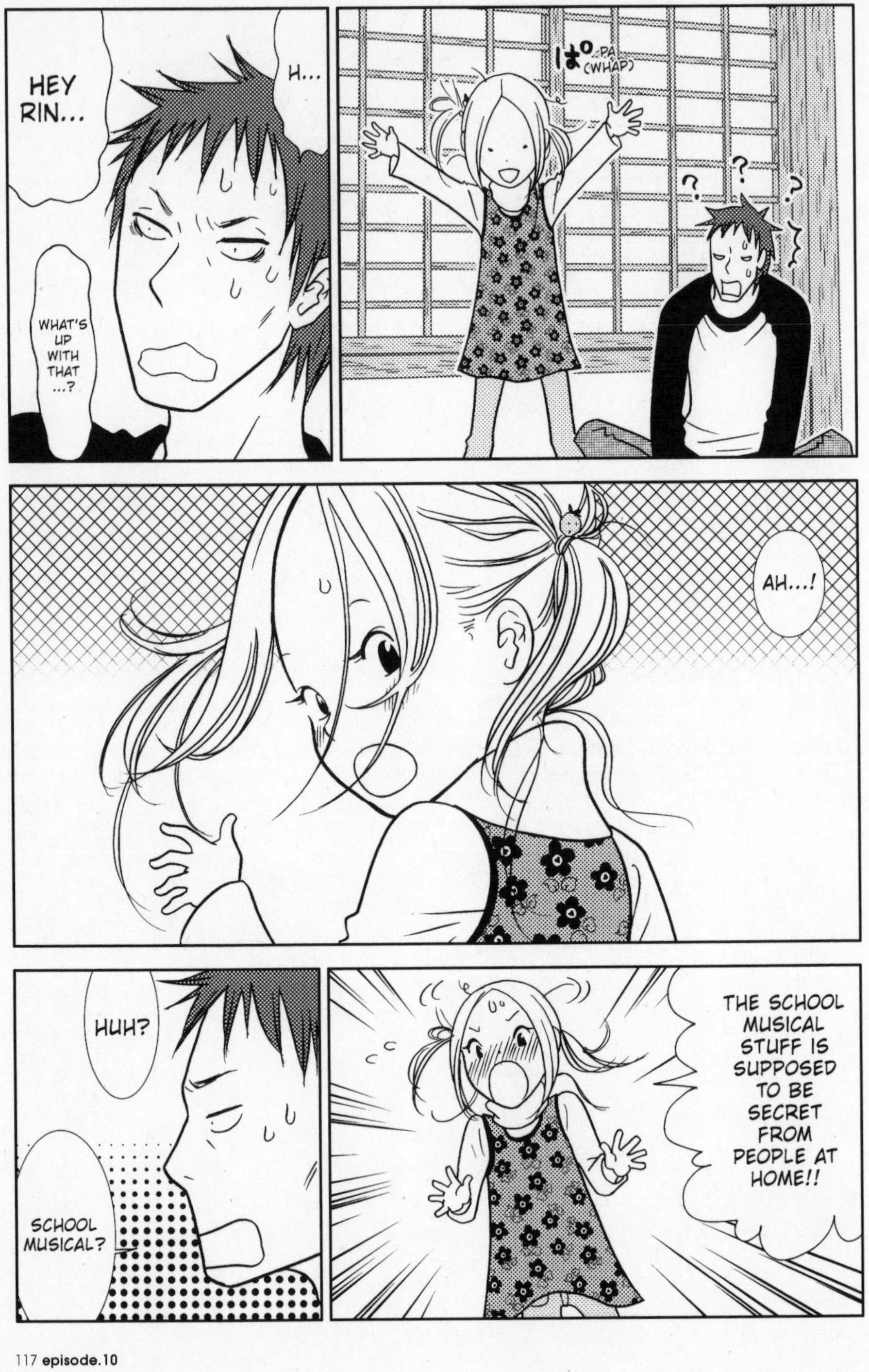
ぱ PA (WHAP)
? ? ?
H...
HEY RIN...
WHAT'S UP WITH THAT ...?
AH...!
THE SCHOOL MUSICAL STUFF IS SUPPOSED TO BE SECRET FROM PEOPLE AT HOME!!
HUH?
SCHOOL MUSICAL?

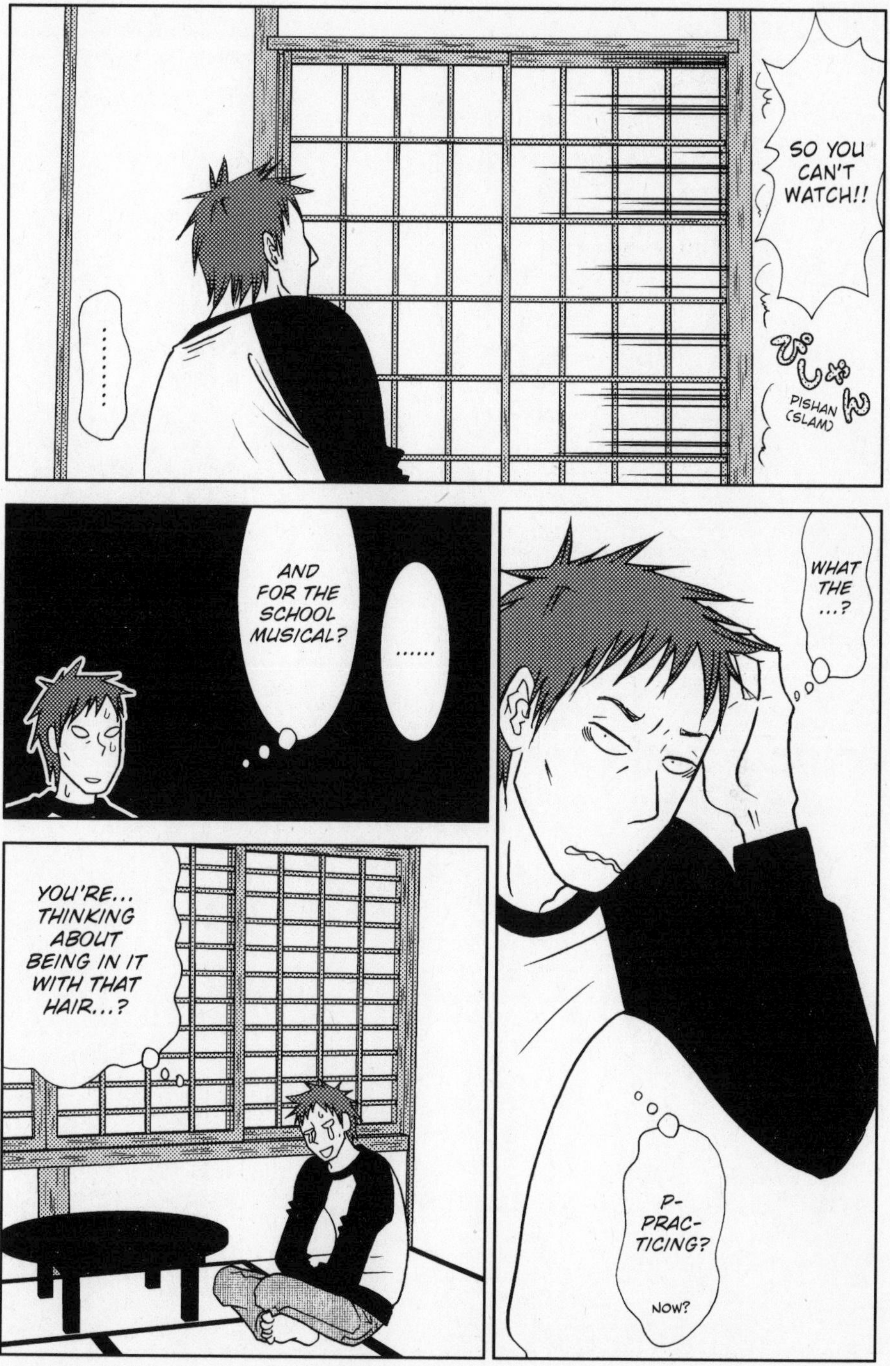
SO YOU CAN'T WATCH!!
ぴしゃん
PISHAN (SLAM)
……
WHAT THE ...?
P-PRAC-TICING?
NOW?
......
AND FOR THE SCHOOL MUSICAL?
YOU'RE... THINKING ABOUT BEING IN IT WITH THAT HAIR...?

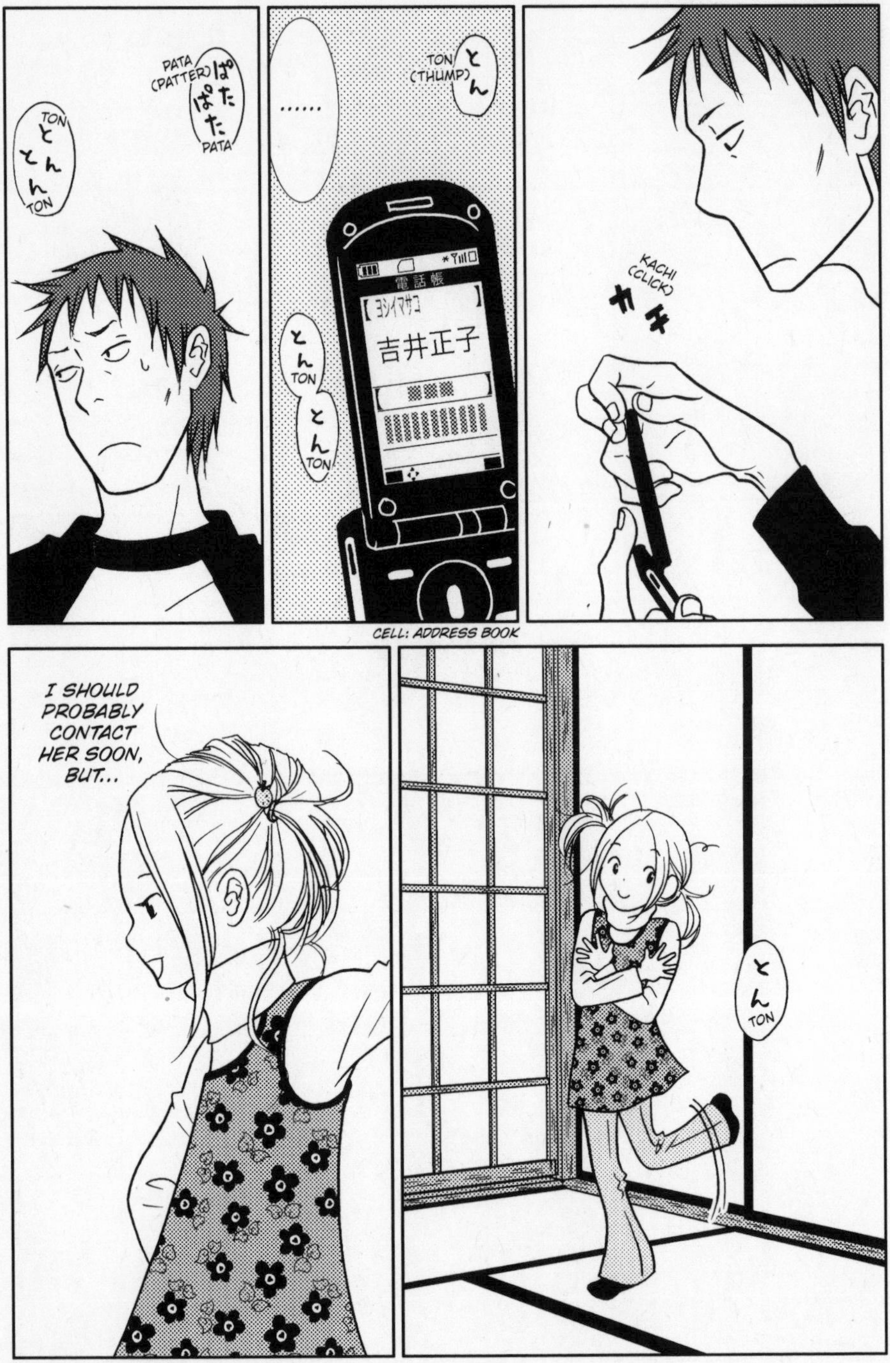
KACHI (CLICK)
カチ
とん
TON (THUMP)
......
電話帳
ヨシイマサコ
吉井正子
とん TON
とん TON
CELL: ADDRESS BOOK
ぱたぱた
PATA (PATTER) PATA
とんとん
TON TON
とん TON
I SHOULD PROBABLY CONTACT HER SOON, BUT...

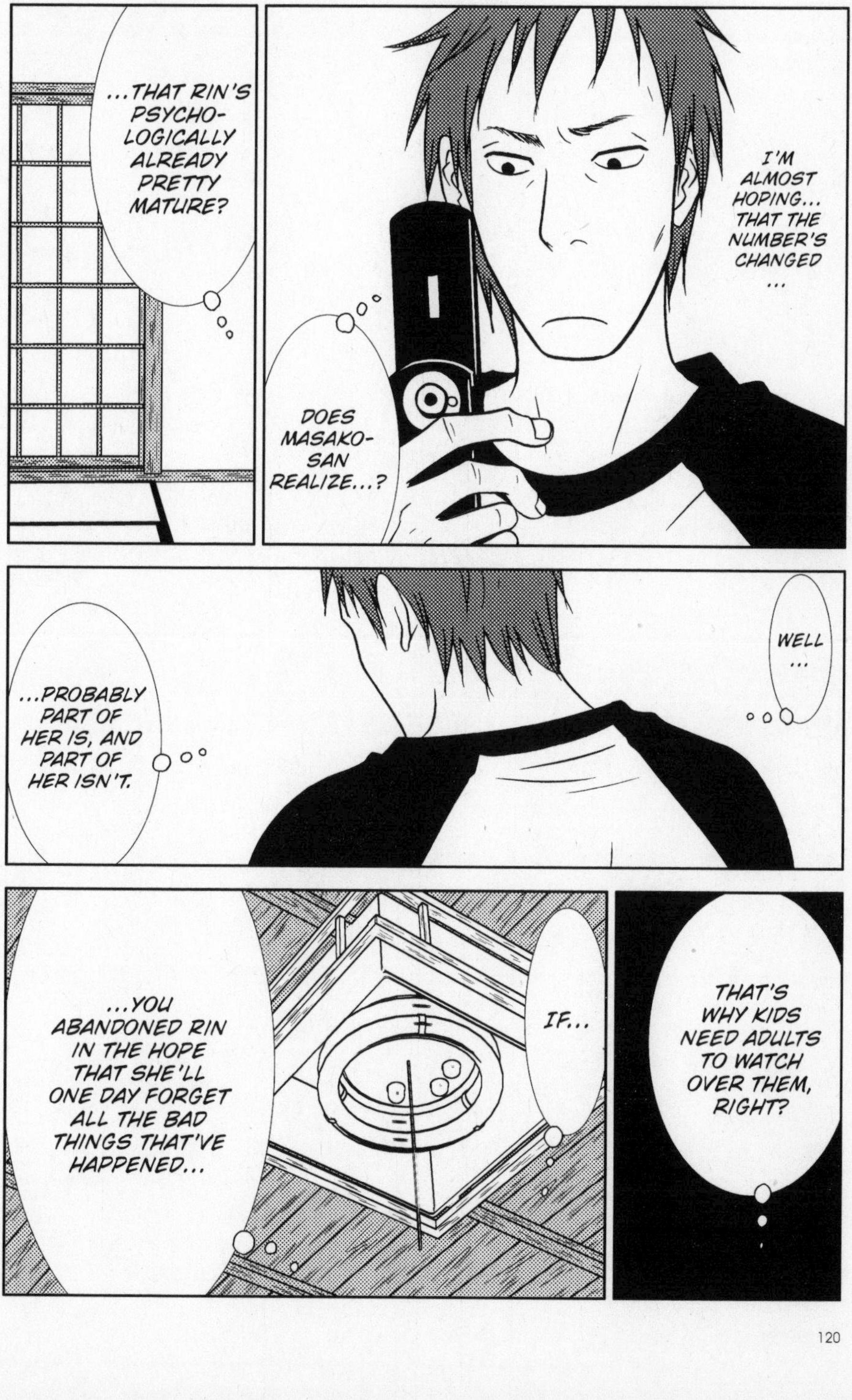
I'M ALMOST HOPING... THAT THE NUMBER'S CHANGED...
DOES MASAKO-SAN REALIZE...?
...THAT RIN'S PSYCHOLOGICALLY ALREADY PRETTY MATURE?
WELL...
...PROBABLY PART OF HER IS, AND PART OF HER ISN'T.
THAT'S WHY KIDS NEED ADULTS TO WATCH OVER THEM, RIGHT?
IF...
...YOU ABANDONED RIN IN THE HOPE THAT SHE'LL ONE DAY FORGET ALL THE BAD THINGS THAT'VE HAPPENED...

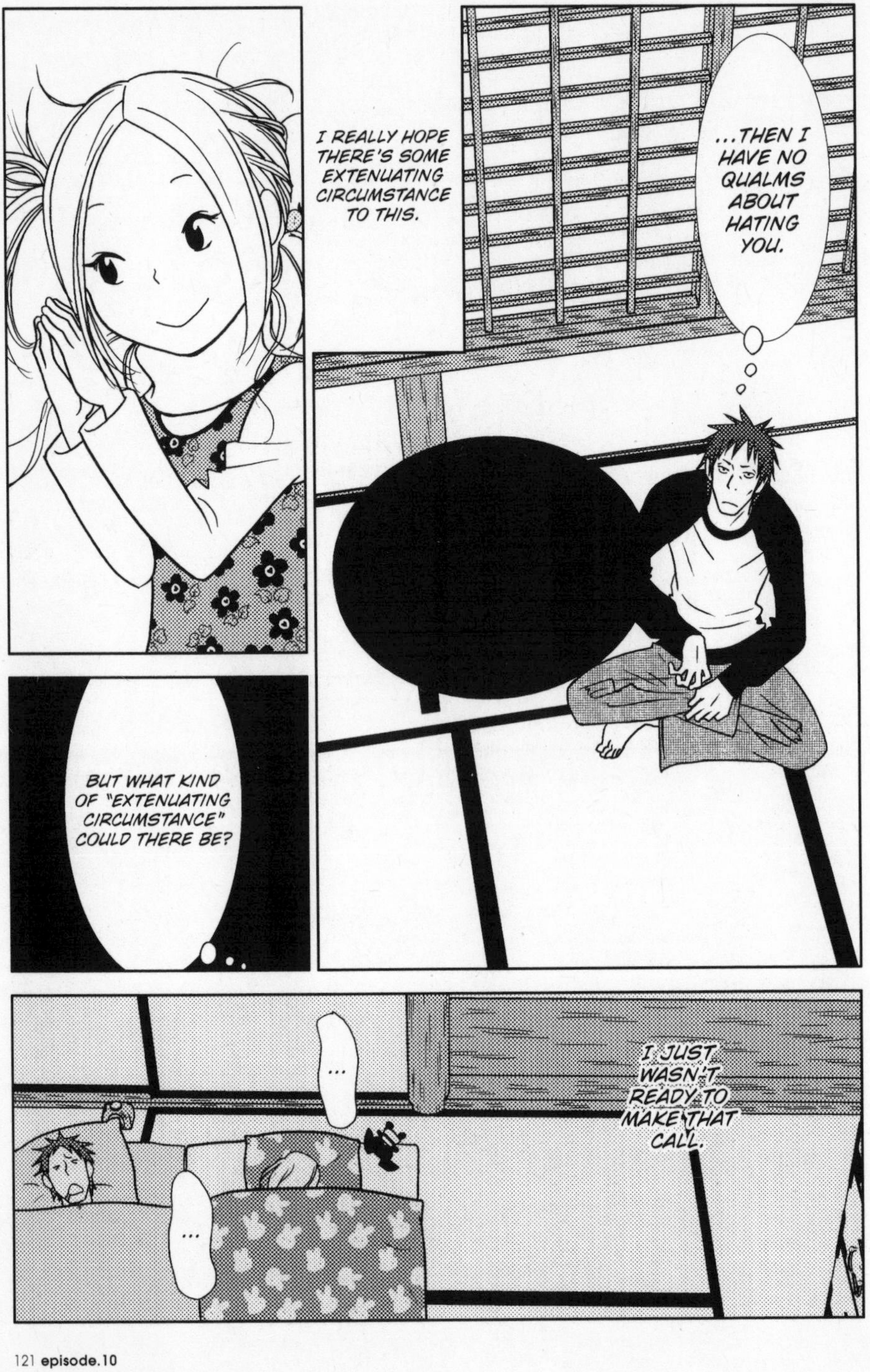
...THEN I HAVE NO QUALMS ABOUT HATING YOU.
I REALLY HOPE THERE'S SOME EXTENUATING CIRCUMSTANCE TO THIS.
BUT WHAT KIND OF "EXTENUATING CIRCUMSTANCE" COULD THERE BE?
I JUST WASN'T READY TO MAKE THAT CALL.
...
...

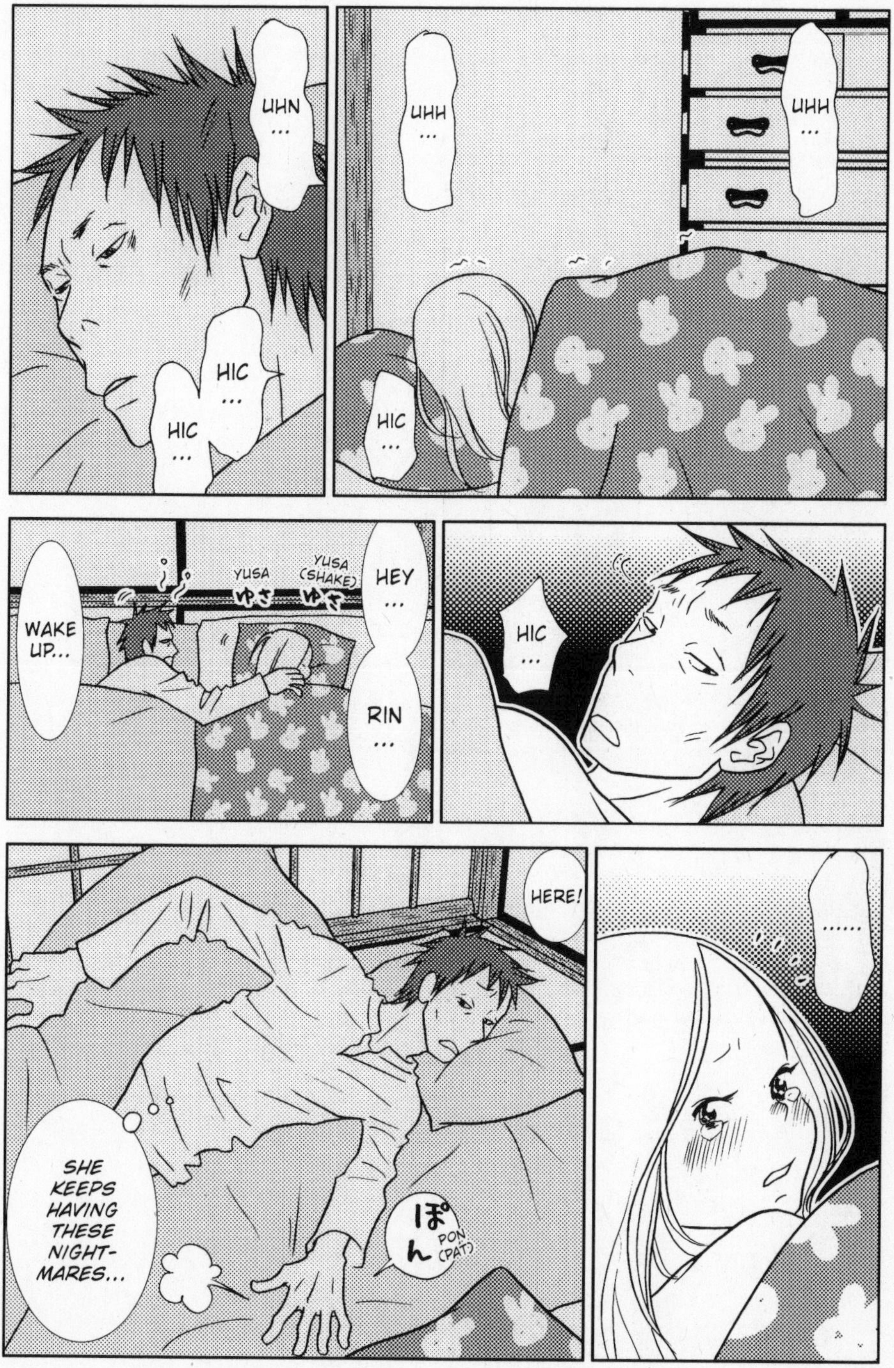
UHH ...
UHH ...
HIC ...
UHN ...
HIC ...
HIC ...
HIC ...
HEY ...
RIN ...
YUSA (SHAKE) ゆさ
YUSA ゆさ
WAKE UP...
......
HERE!
ぽん PON (PAT)
SHE KEEPS HAVING THESE NIGHT-MARES...

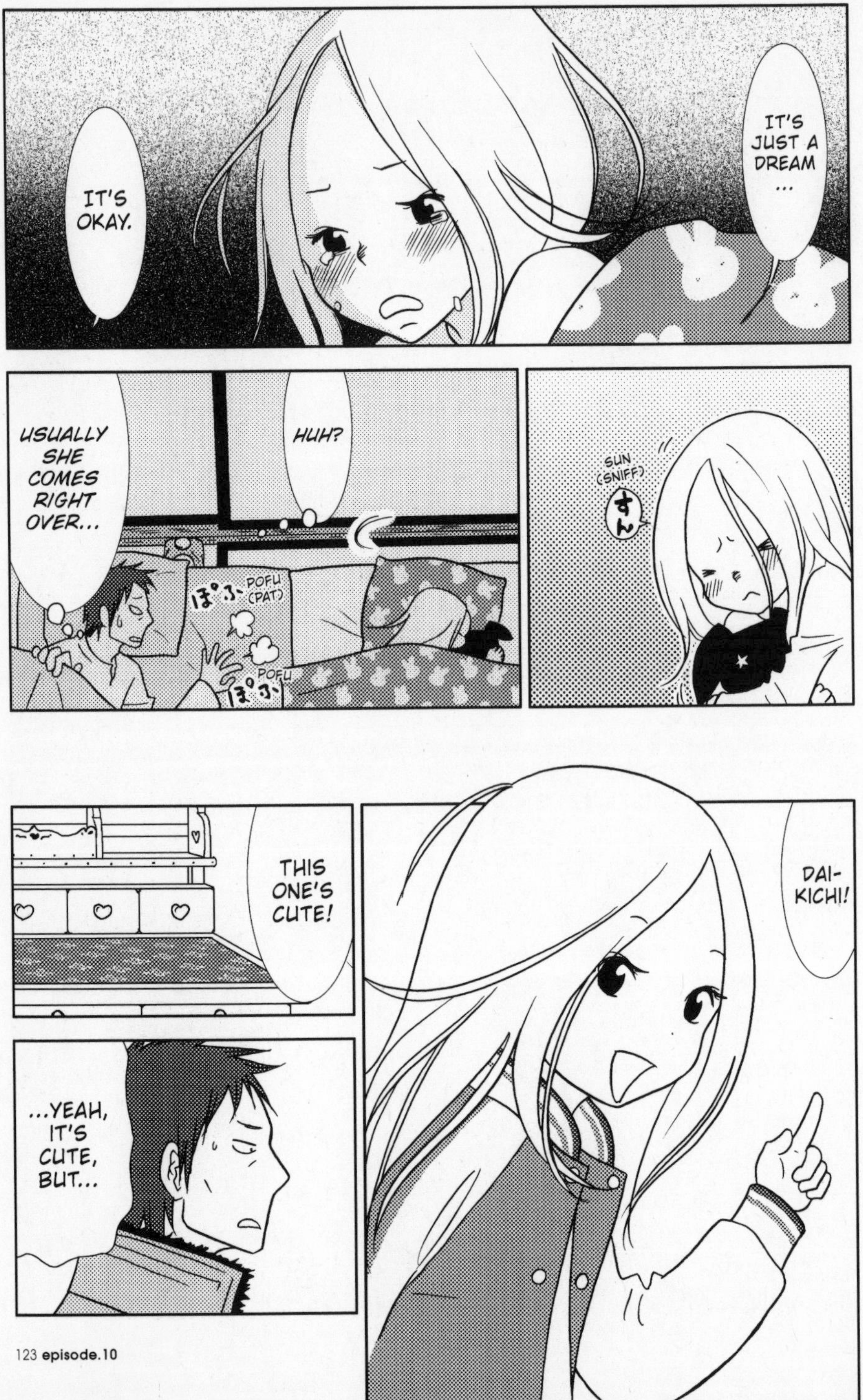
IT'S JUST A DREAM ...
IT'S OKAY.
SUN (SNIFF)
すん
HUH?
USUALLY SHE COMES RIGHT OVER...
POFU (PAT)
ぽふ
POFU
ぽふ
DAI-KICHI!
THIS ONE'S CUTE!
...YEAH, IT'S CUTE, BUT...

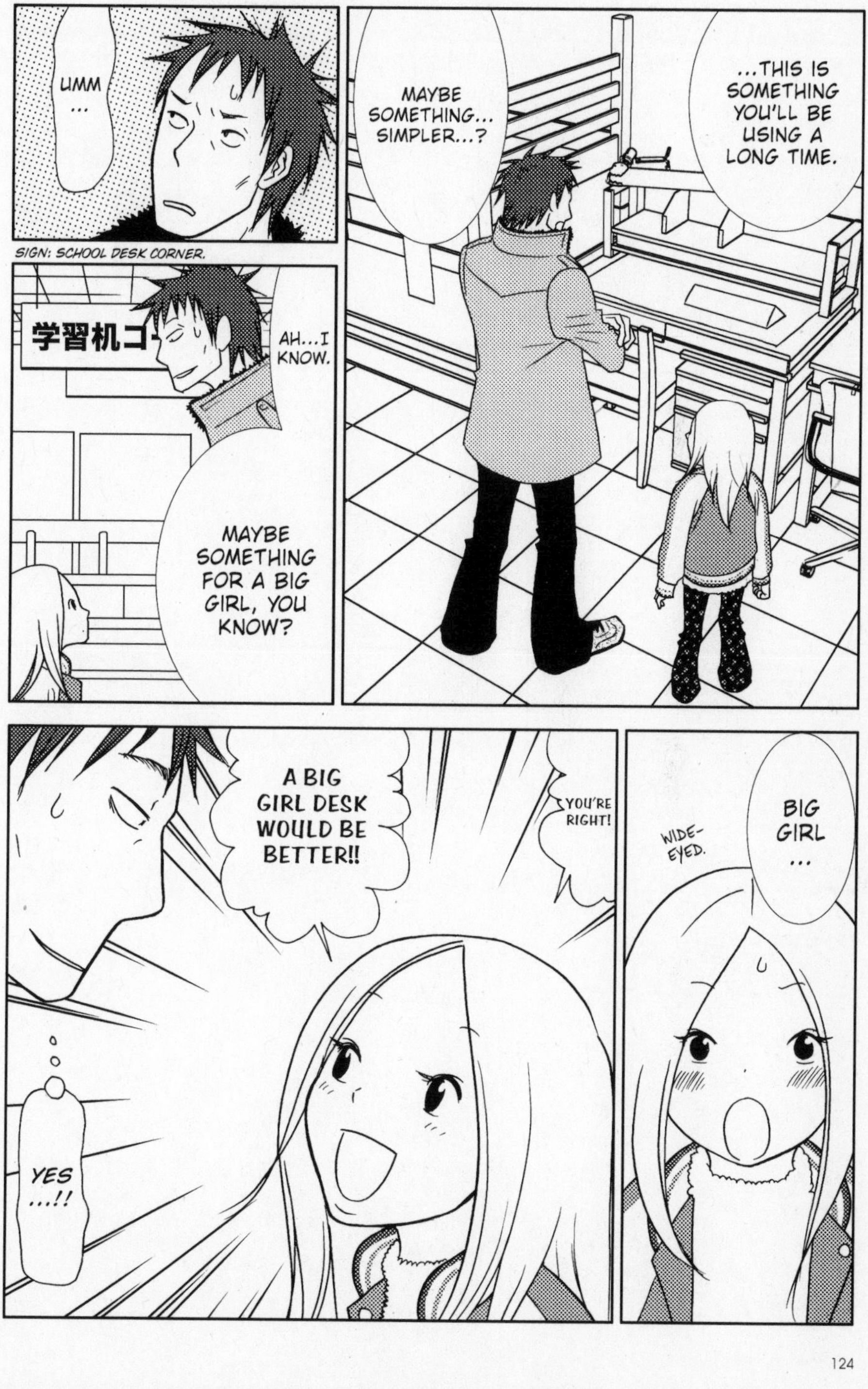
...THIS IS SOMETHING YOU'LL BE USING A LONG TIME.
MAYBE SOMETHING... SIMPLER...?
UMM ...
SIGN: SCHOOL DESK CORNER.
学習机コー
AH...I KNOW.
MAYBE SOMETHING FOR A BIG GIRL, YOU KNOW?
BIG GIRL ...
WIDE-EYED.
YOU'RE RIGHT!
A BIG GIRL DESK WOULD BE BETTER!!
YES ...!!

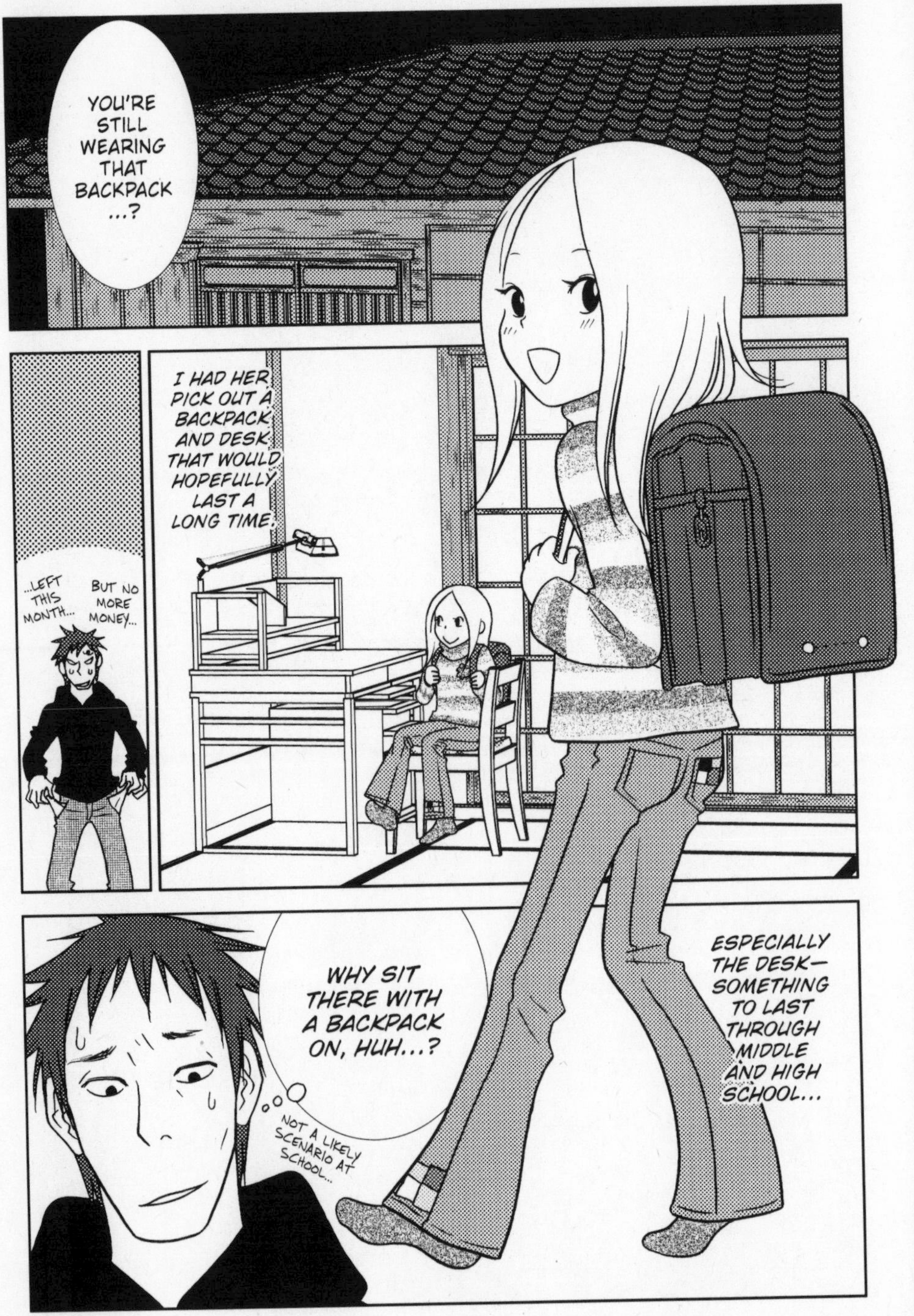
YOU'RE STILL WEARING THAT BACKPACK ...?
I HAD HER PICK OUT A BACKPACK AND DESK THAT WOULD HOPEFULLY LAST A LONG TIME.
BUT NO MORE MONEY...
...LEFT THIS MONTH...
ESPECIALLY THE DESK—SOMETHING TO LAST THROUGH MIDDLE AND HIGH SCHOOL...
WHY SIT THERE WITH A BACKPACK ON, HUH...?
NOT A LIKELY SCENARIO AT SCHOOL...

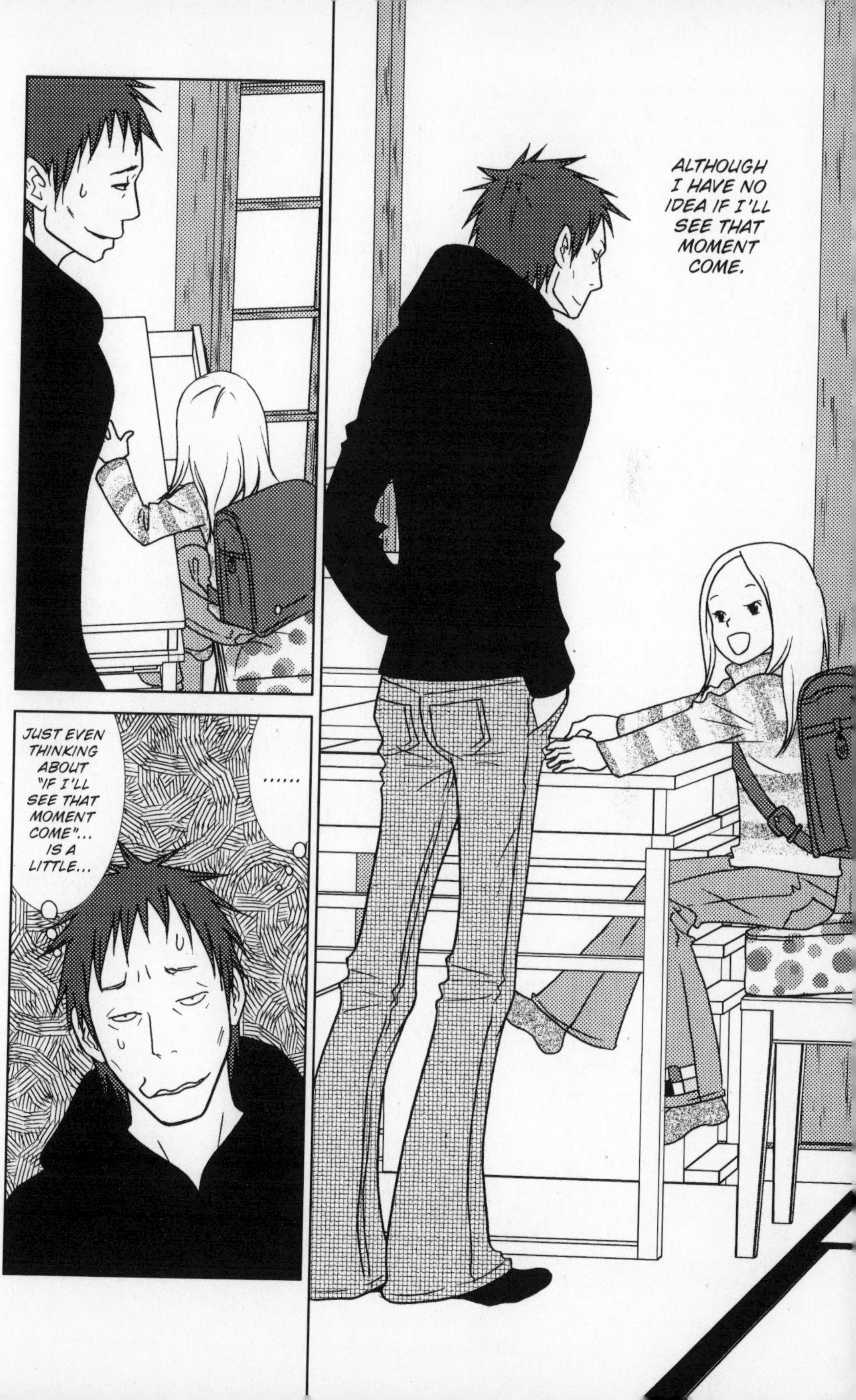
ALTHOUGH I HAVE NO IDEA IF I'LL SEE THAT MOMENT COME.
......
JUST EVEN THINKING ABOUT "IF I'LL SEE THAT MOMENT COME"... IS A LITTLE...

......
TODAY FOR SURE ...
...I'M GONNA CALL ...
ピッ
PI (BEEP)

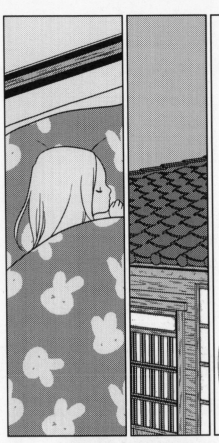

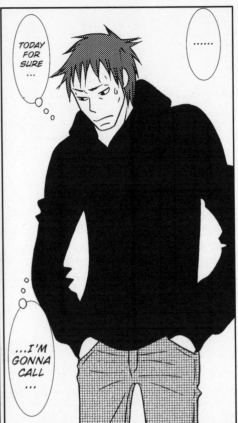

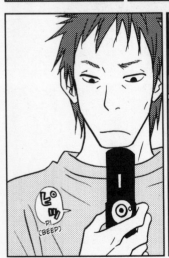

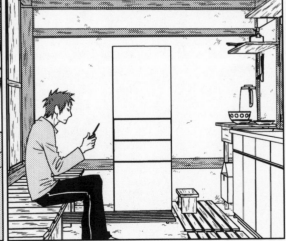

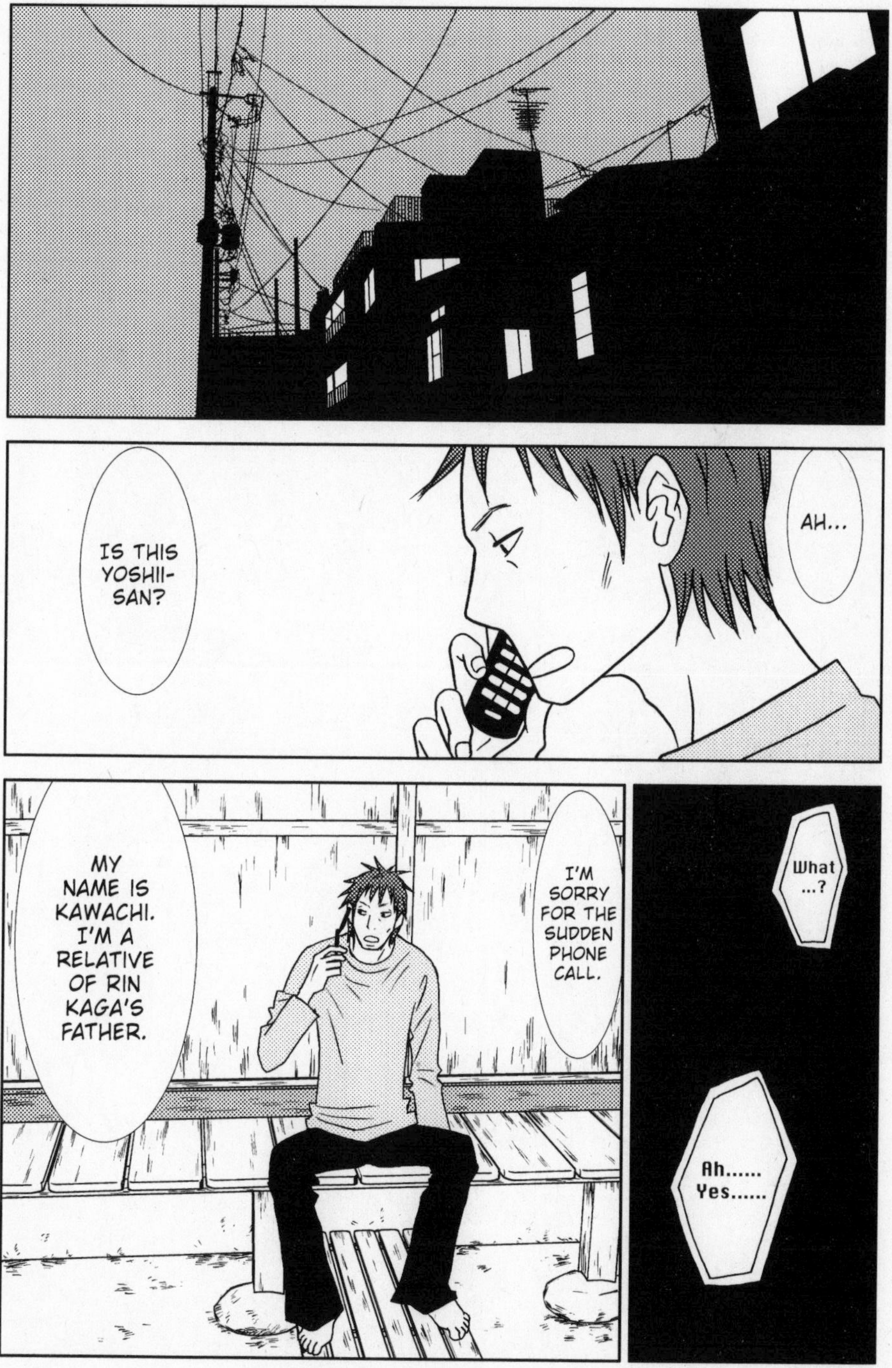
AH...
IS THIS YOSHII-SAN?
What ...?
Ah...... Yes......
I'M SORRY FOR THE SUDDEN PHONE CALL.
MY NAME IS KAWACHI. I'M A RELATIVE OF RIN KAGA'S FATHER.

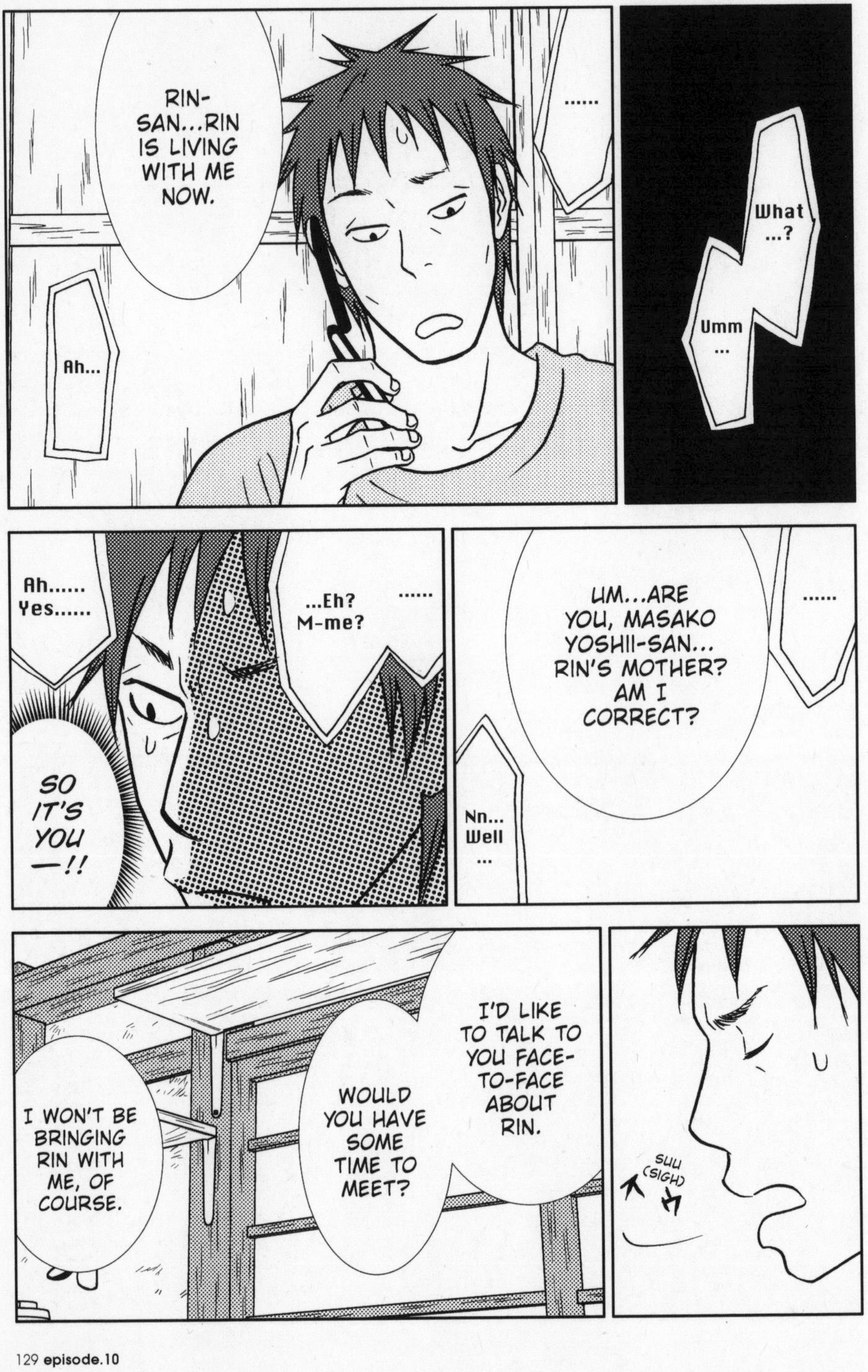

What ...?
Umm ...
......
RIN-SAN...RIN IS LIVING WITH ME NOW.
Ah...
......
UM...ARE YOU, MASAKO YOSHII-SAN... RIN'S MOTHER? AM I CORRECT?
Nn... Well ...
......
...Eh? M-me?
Ah...... Yes......
SO IT'S YOU—!!
SUU (SIGH)
I'D LIKE TO TALK TO YOU FACE-TO-FACE ABOUT RIN.
WOULD YOU HAVE SOME TIME TO MEET?
I WON'T BE BRINGING RIN WITH ME, OF COURSE.

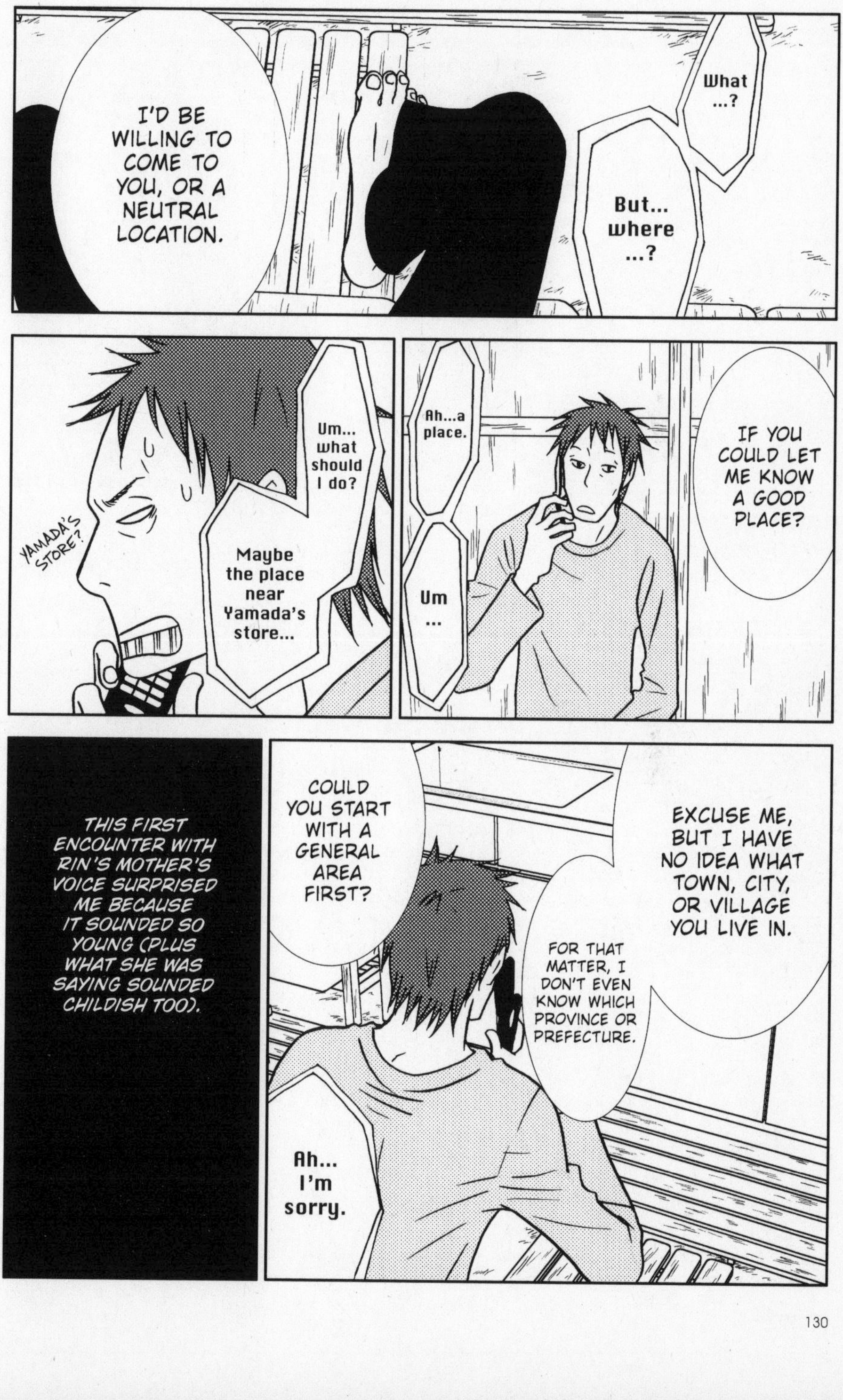
What ...?
But... where ...?
I'D BE WILLING TO COME TO YOU, OR A NEUTRAL LOCATION.
IF YOU COULD LET ME KNOW A GOOD PLACE?
Ah...a place.
Um ...
Um... what should I do?
Maybe the place near Yamada's store...
YAMADA'S STORE?
EXCUSE ME, BUT I HAVE NO IDEA WHAT TOWN, CITY, OR VILLAGE YOU LIVE IN.
FOR THAT MATTER, I DON'T EVEN KNOW WHICH PROVINCE OR PREFECTURE.
COULD YOU START WITH A GENERAL AREA FIRST?
Ah... I'm sorry.
THIS FIRST ENCOUNTER WITH RIN'S MOTHER'S VOICE SURPRISED ME BECAUSE IT SOUNDED SO YOUNG (PLUS WHAT SHE WAS SAYING SOUNDED CHILDISH TOO).

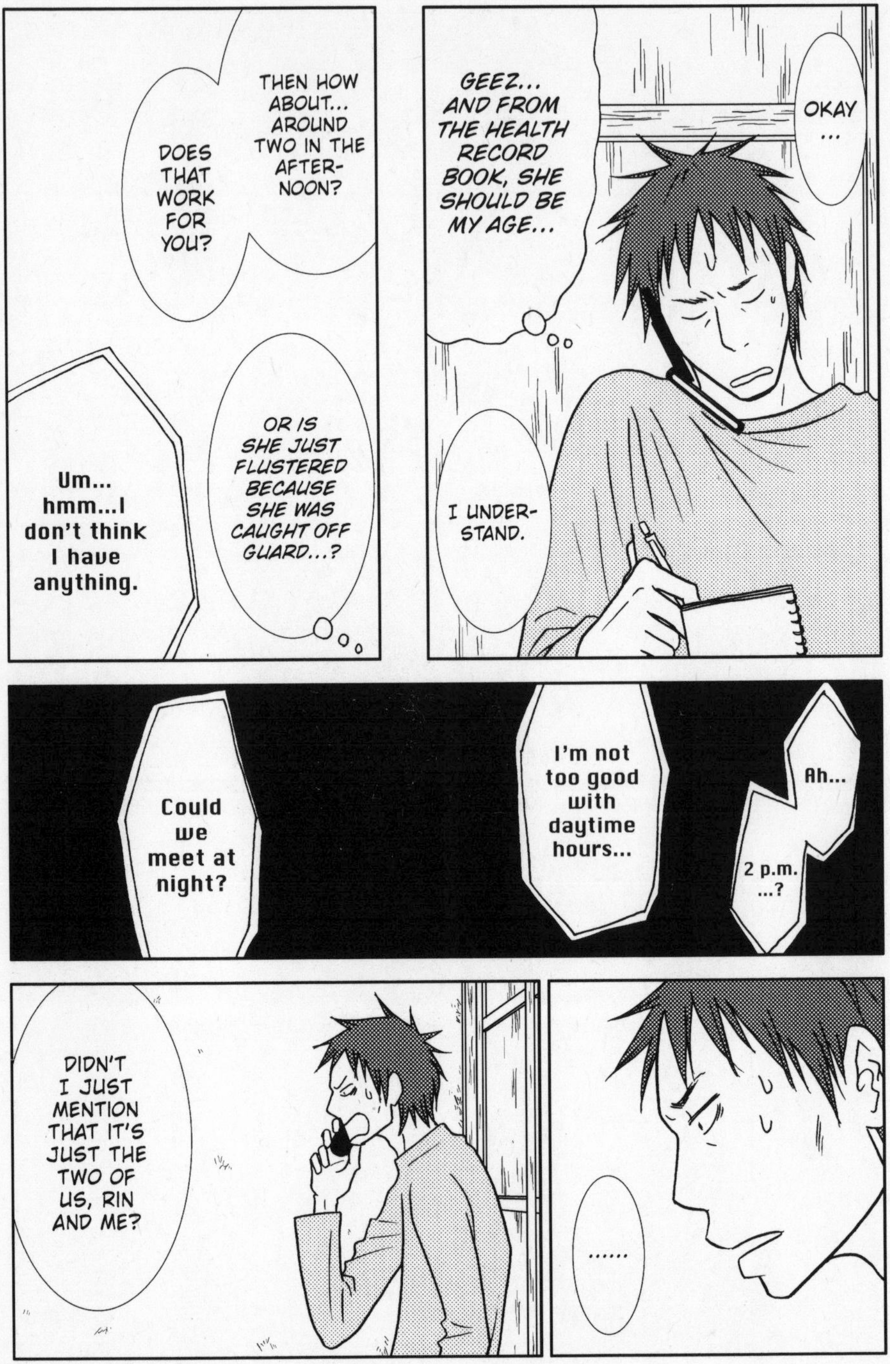
OKAY ...
GEEZ... AND FROM THE HEALTH RECORD BOOK, SHE SHOULD BE MY AGE...
I UNDER-STAND.
THEN HOW ABOUT... AROUND TWO IN THE AFTER-NOON?
DOES THAT WORK FOR YOU?
OR IS SHE JUST FLUSTERED BECAUSE SHE WAS CAUGHT OFF GUARD...?
Um... hmm...I don't think I have anything.
Ah... 2 p.m. ...?
I'm not too good with daytime hours...
Could we meet at night?
......
DIDN'T I JUST MENTION THAT IT'S JUST THE TWO OF US, RIN AND ME?

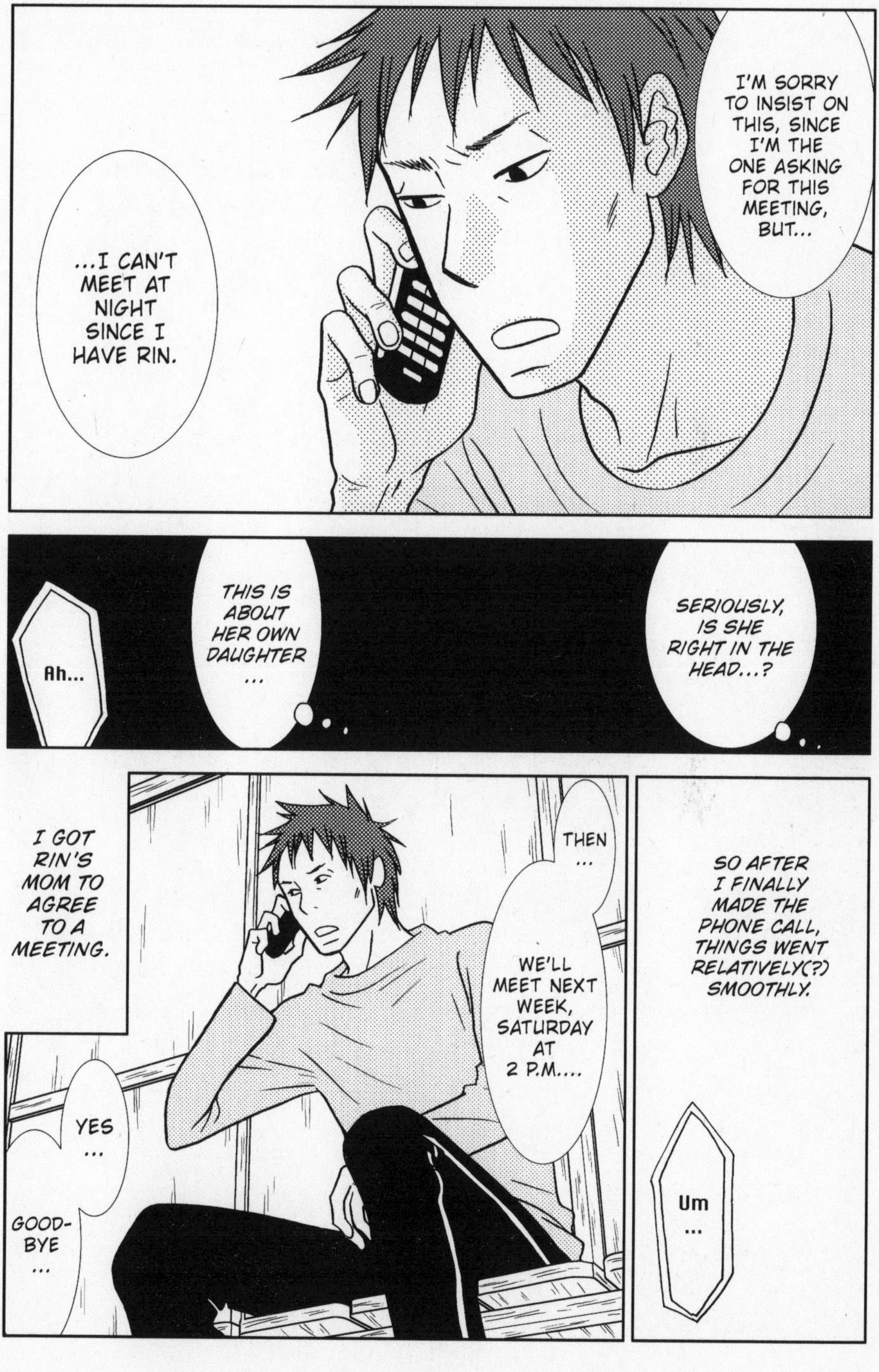
I'M SORRY TO INSIST ON THIS, SINCE I'M THE ONE ASKING FOR THIS MEETING, BUT...
...I CAN'T MEET AT NIGHT SINCE I HAVE RIN.
SERIOUSLY, IS SHE RIGHT IN THE HEAD...?
THIS IS ABOUT HER OWN DAUGHTER...
Ah...
SO AFTER I FINALLY MADE THE PHONE CALL, THINGS WENT RELATIVELY(?) SMOOTHLY.
Um...
THEN...
WE'LL MEET NEXT WEEK, SATURDAY AT 2 P.M....
I GOT RIN'S MOM TO AGREE TO A MEETING.
YES...
GOOD-BYE...

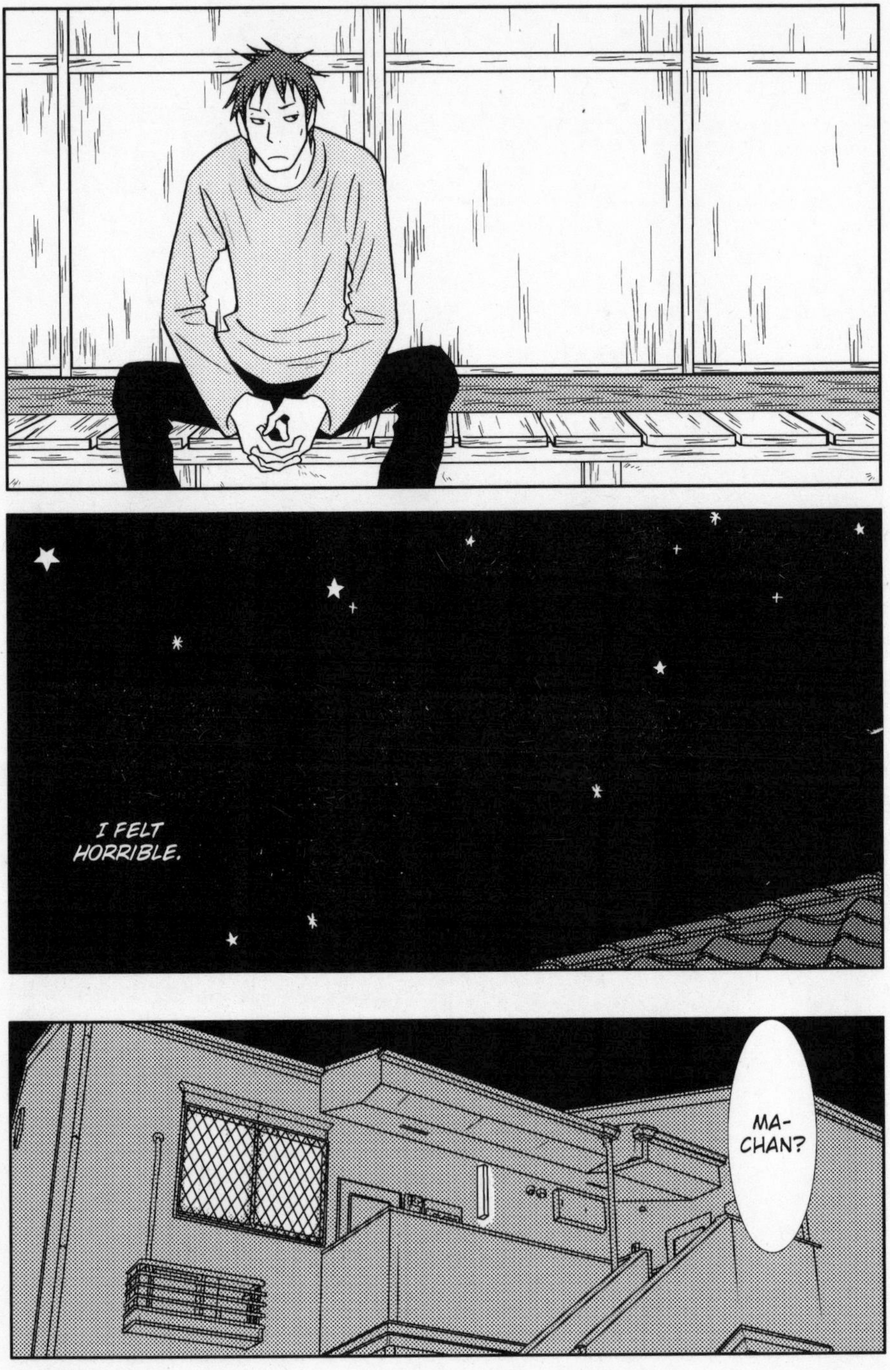
I FELT HORRIBLE.
MA-CHAN?

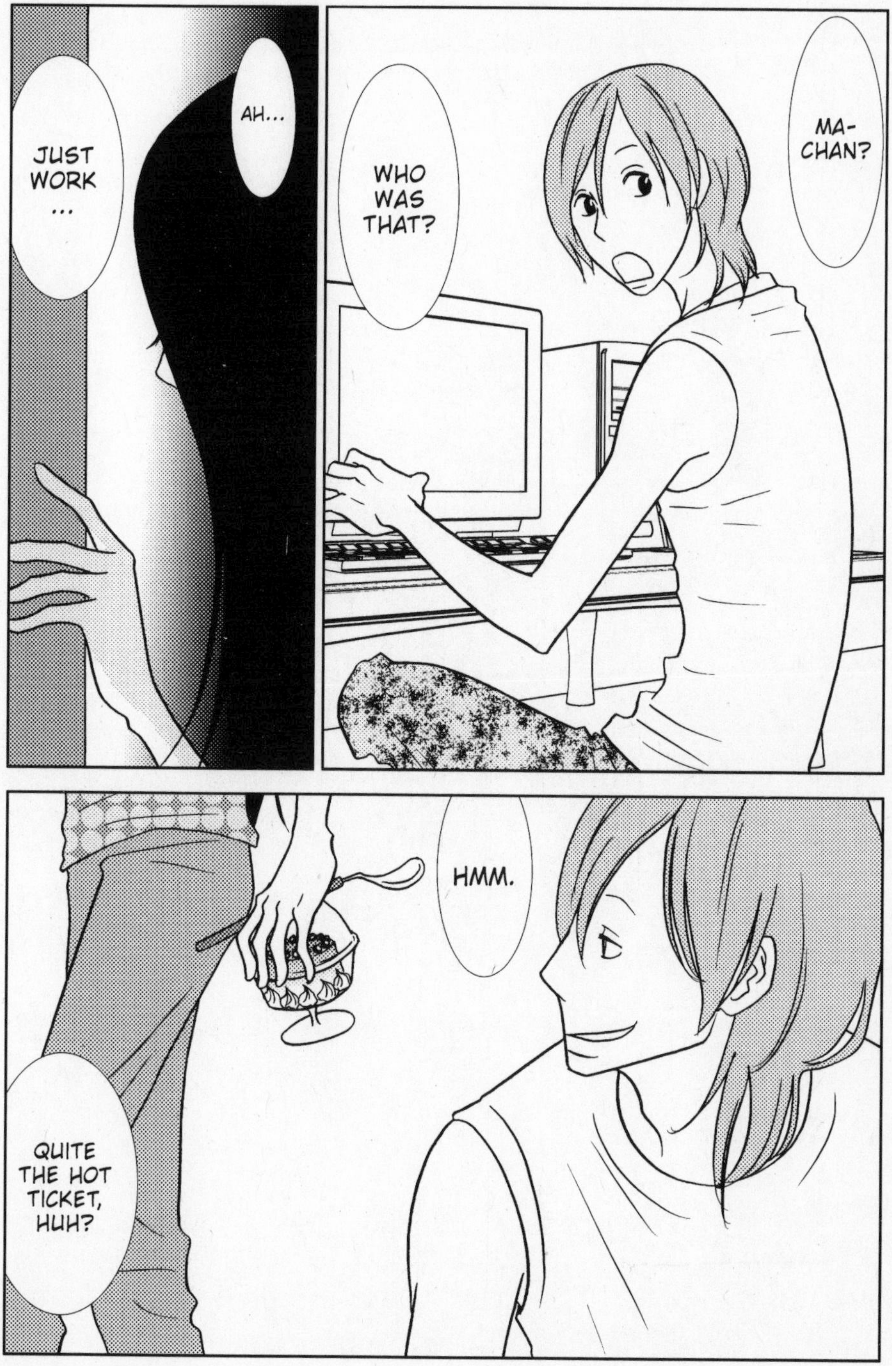
MA-CHAN?
WHO WAS THAT?
AH...
JUST WORK ...
HMM.
QUITE THE HOT TICKET, HUH?

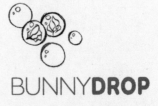

BUNNYDROP

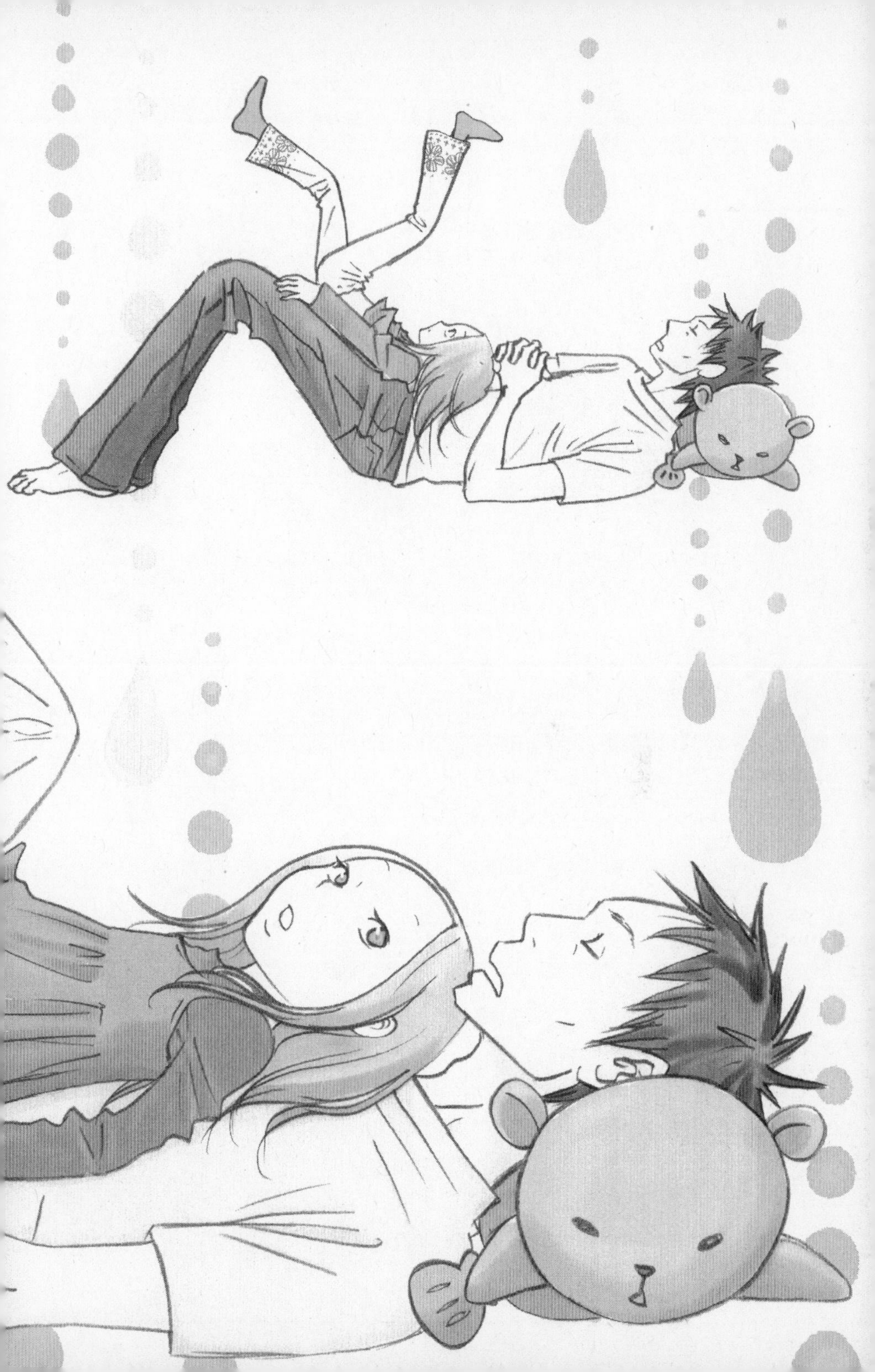

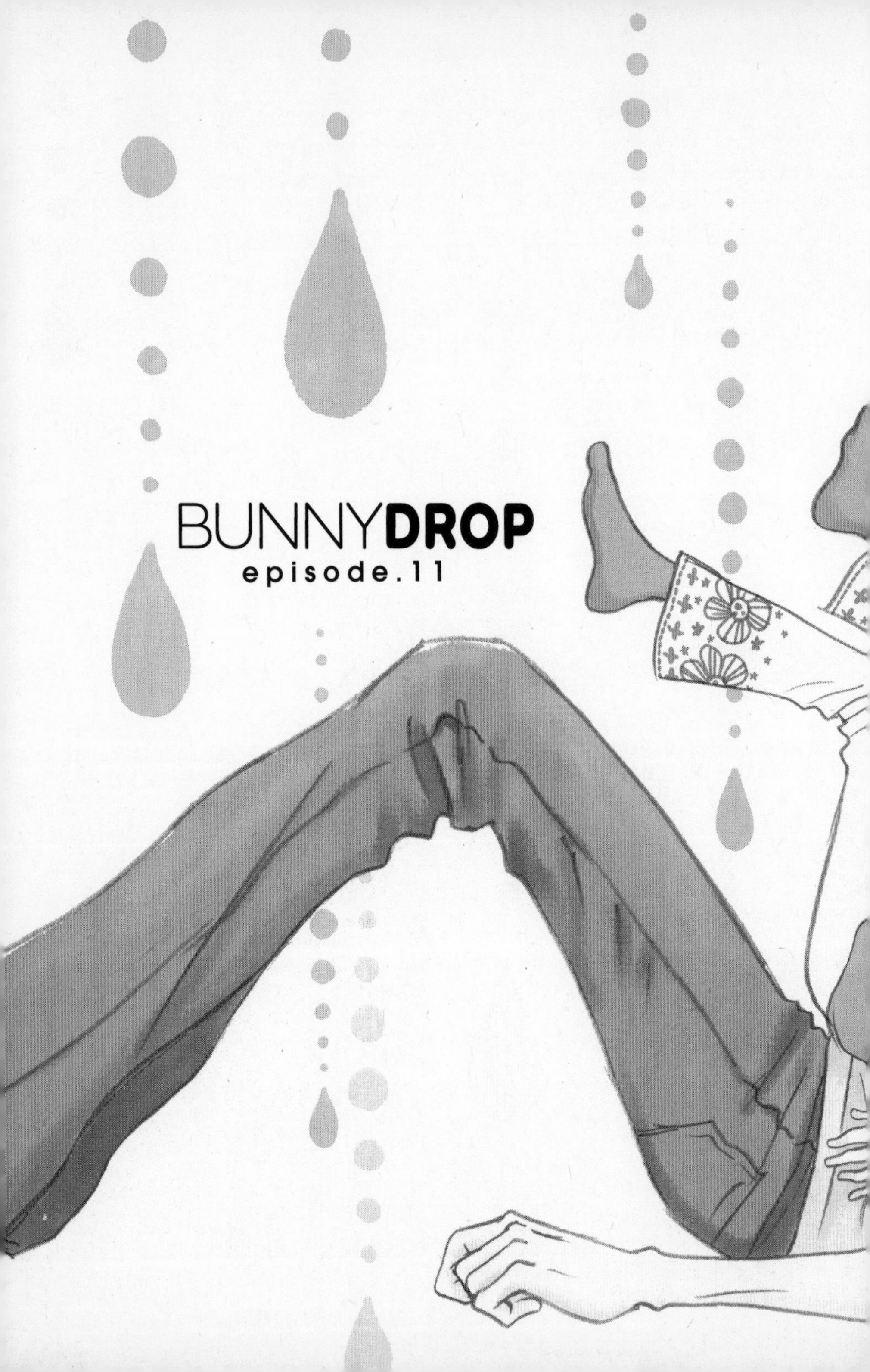
BUNNYDROP
episode.11

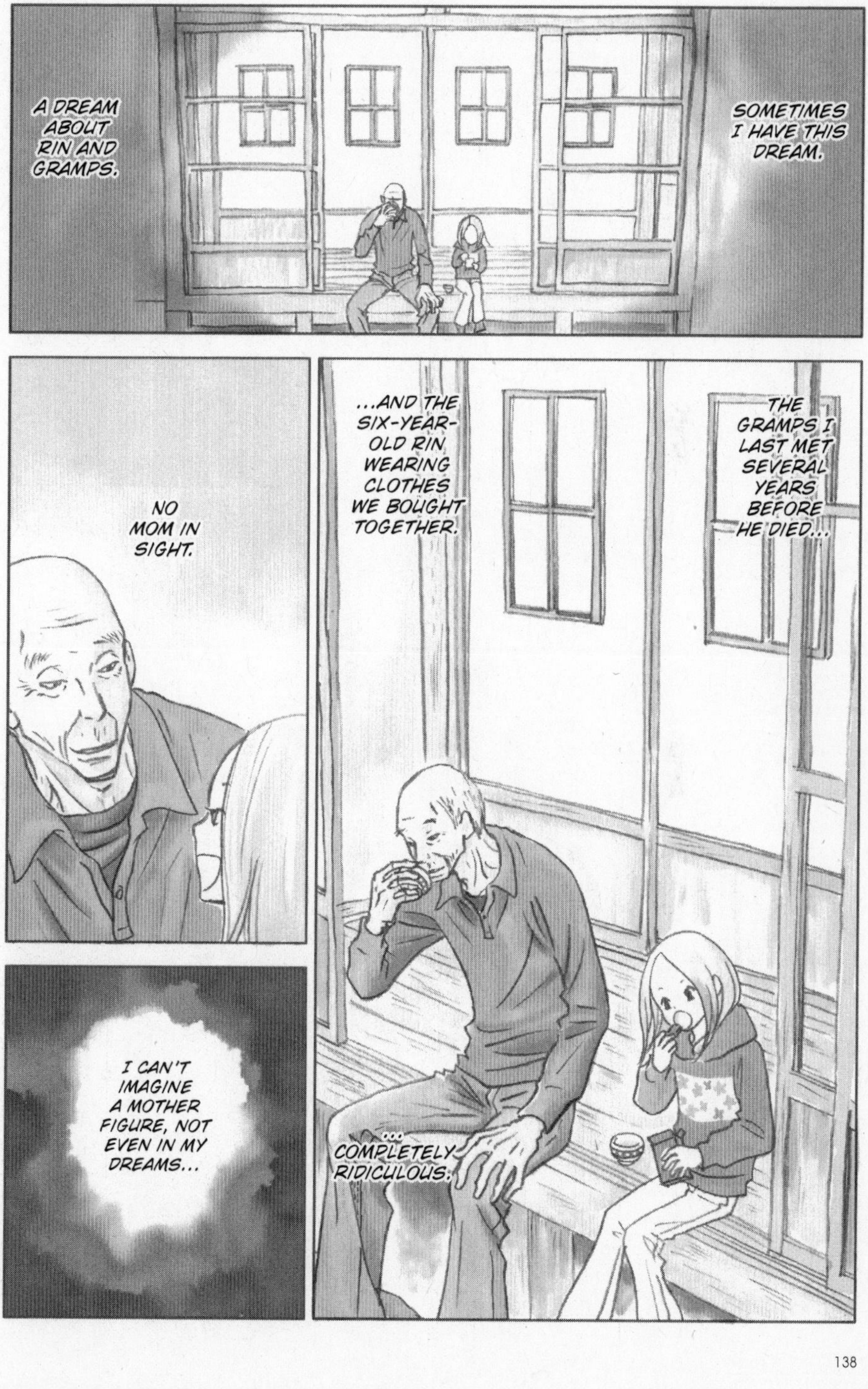
SOMETIMES I HAVE THIS DREAM.
A DREAM ABOUT RIN AND GRAMPS.
THE GRAMPS I LAST MET SEVERAL YEARS BEFORE HE DIED...
...AND THE SIX-YEAR-OLD RIN WEARING CLOTHES WE BOUGHT TOGETHER.
...COMPLETELY RIDICULOUS.
NO MOM IN SIGHT.
I CAN'T IMAGINE A MOTHER FIGURE, NOT EVEN IN MY DREAMS...

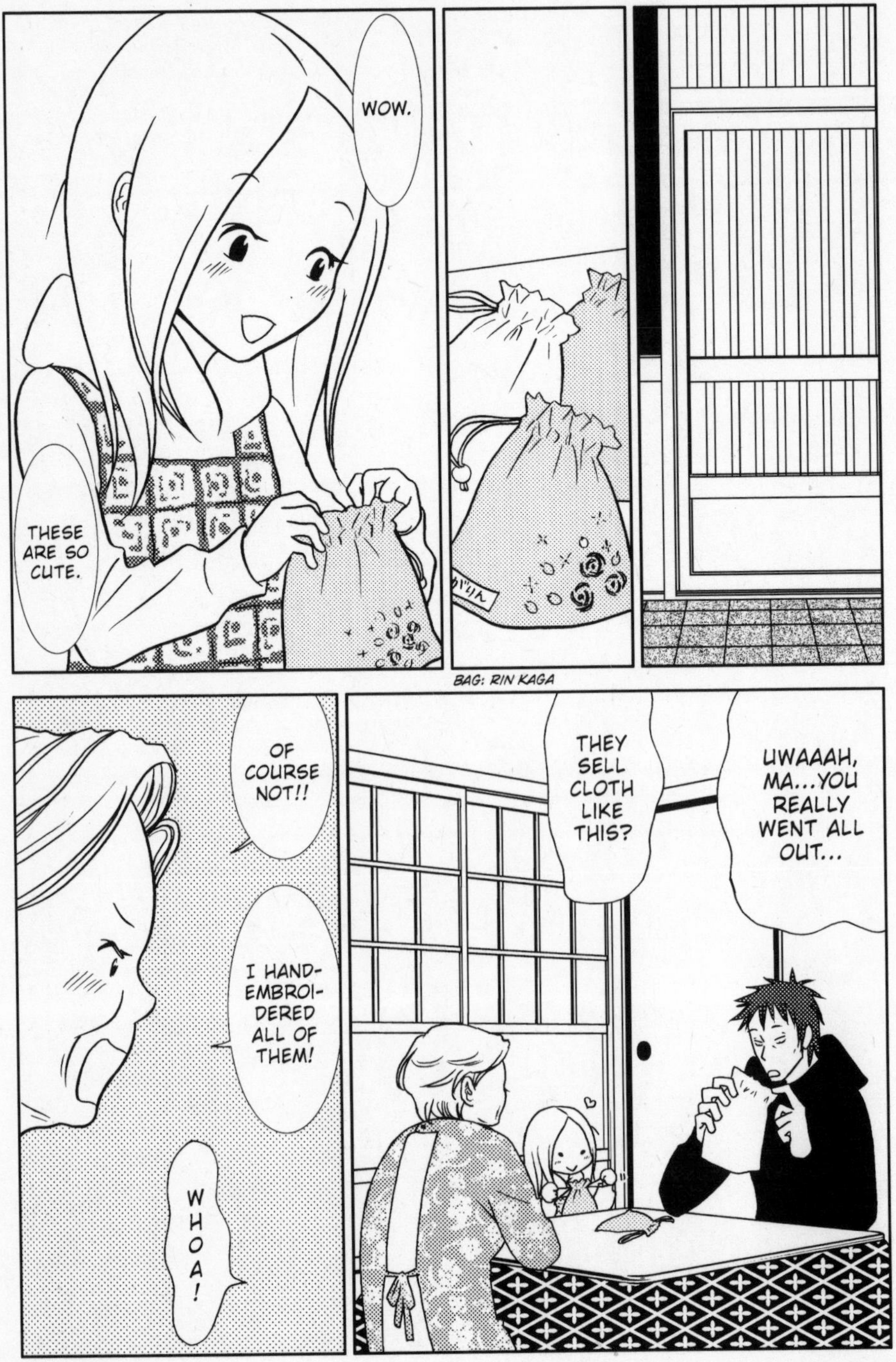
BAG: RIN KAGA
WOW.
THESE ARE SO CUTE.
UWAAAH, MA...YOU REALLY WENT ALL OUT...
THEY SELL CLOTH LIKE THIS?
OF COURSE NOT!!
I HAND-EMBROIDERED ALL OF THEM!
WHOA!

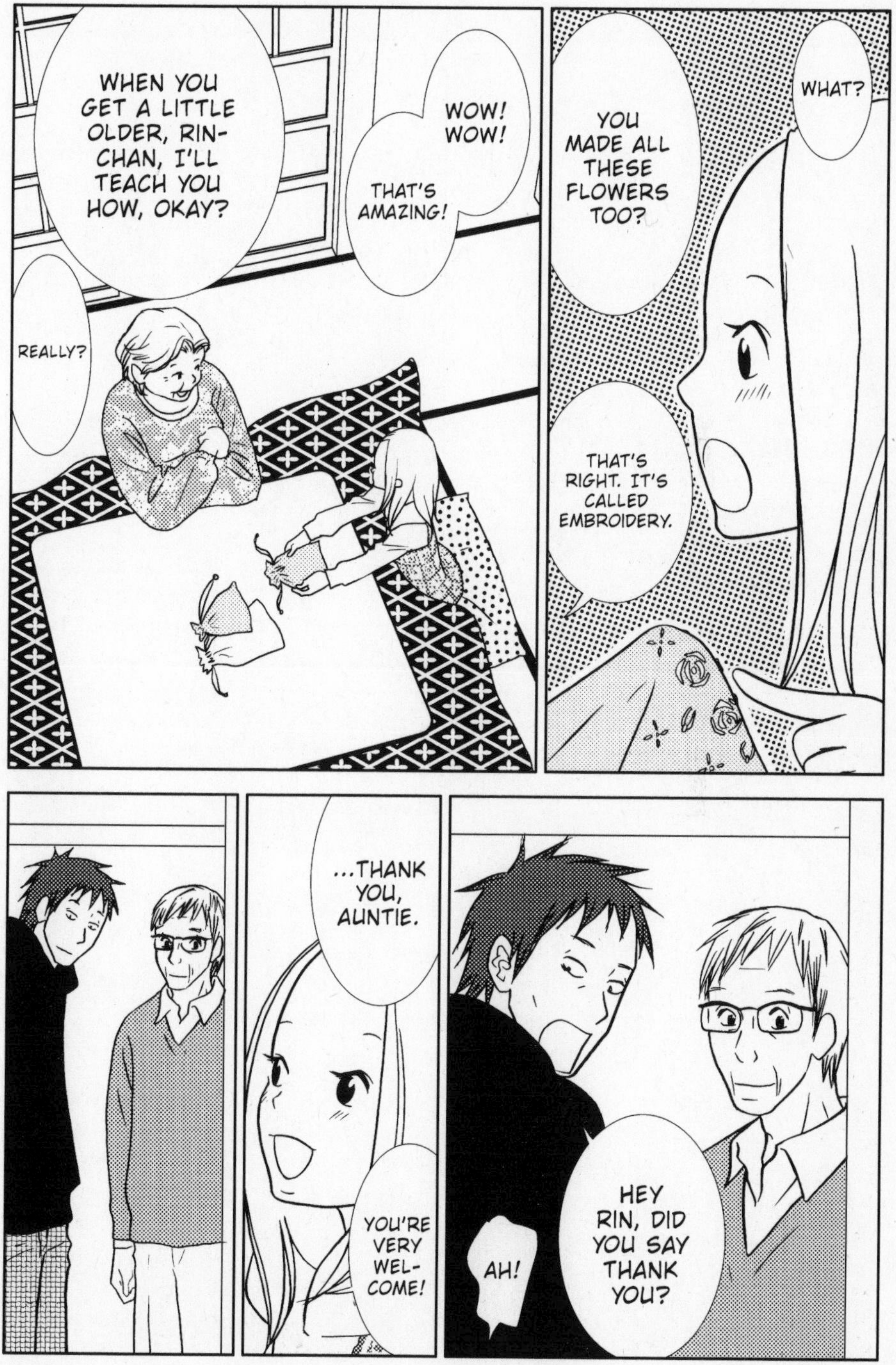
WHAT?
YOU MADE ALL THESE FLOWERS TOO?
THAT'S RIGHT. IT'S CALLED EMBROIDERY.
WOW! WOW!
THAT'S AMAZING!
WHEN YOU GET A LITTLE OLDER, RIN-CHAN, I'LL TEACH YOU HOW, OKAY?
REALLY?
HEY RIN, DID YOU SAY THANK YOU?
AH!
...THANK YOU, AUNTIE.
YOU'RE VERY WEL-COME!

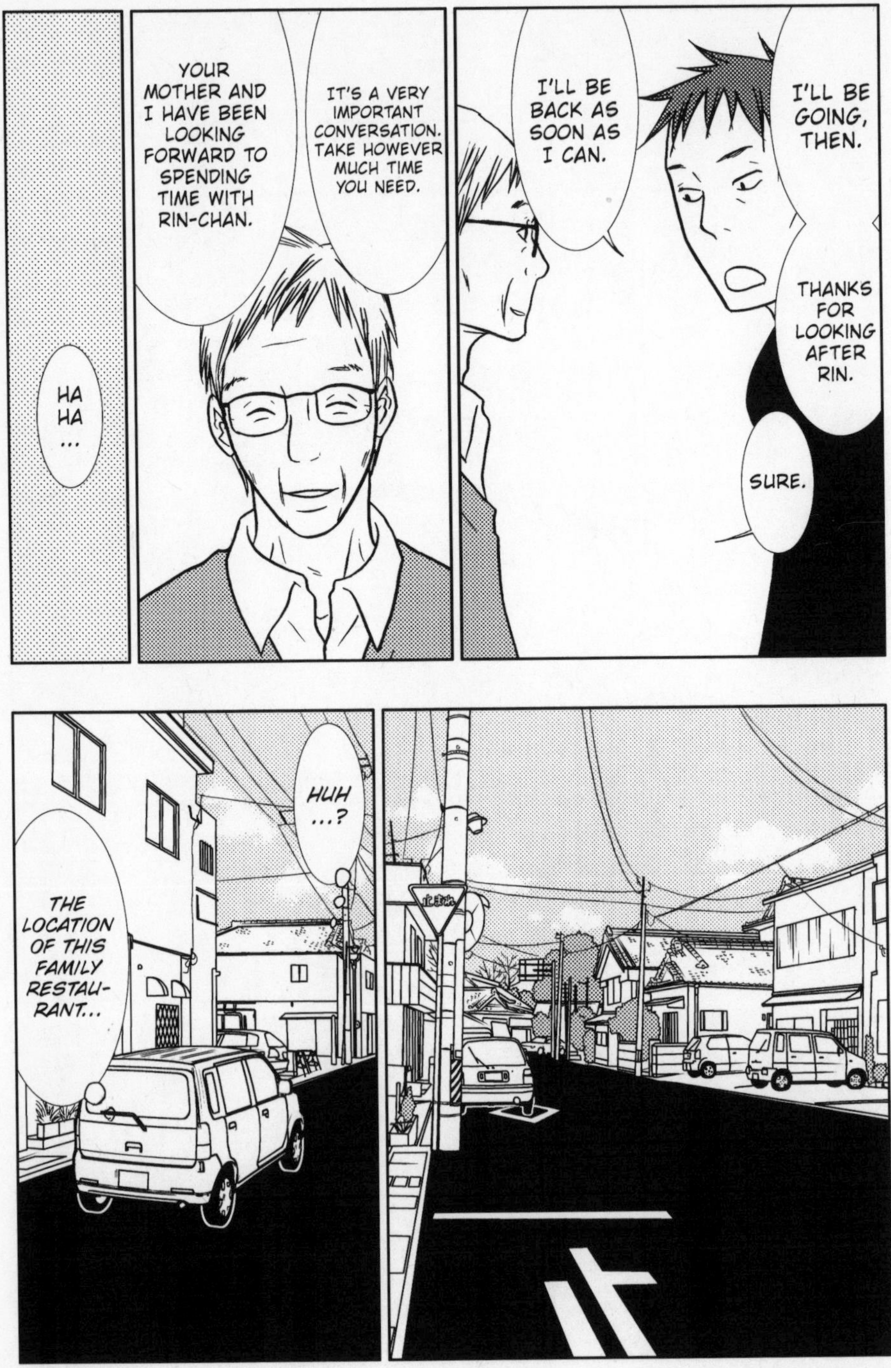
I'LL BE GOING, THEN.
I'LL BE BACK AS SOON AS I CAN.
THANKS FOR LOOKING AFTER RIN.
SURE.
IT'S A VERY IMPORTANT CONVERSATION. TAKE HOWEVER MUCH TIME YOU NEED.
YOUR MOTHER AND I HAVE BEEN LOOKING FORWARD TO SPENDING TIME WITH RIN-CHAN.
HA HA ...
HUH ...?
THE LOCATION OF THIS FAMILY RESTAU-RANT...

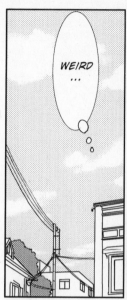

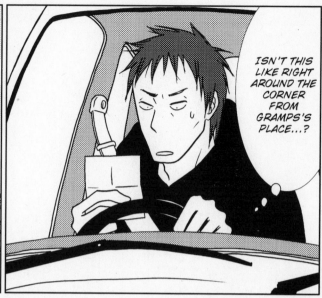

ISN'T THIS LIKE RIGHT AROUND THE CORNER FROM GRAMPS'S PLACE...?
WEIRD ...
SIGN: RESTAURANT CHOMP
WELCOME TO OUR RESTAURANT!
レストラン
RESTAURANT
ガブット
OPEN
9:00AM-5:00AM
SEATING FOR ONE?
THERE'LL BE SOMEONE JOINING ME.
RIGHT THIS WAY.
AH YES, I LIKE IT, SAIONJI-SENSEI!! GREAT IDEA!
THEN MAYBE IF YOU COULD GIVE EACH CHARACTER TWO TO THREE TRAUMA ISSUES...?
ISN'T THAT... A LOT?
AH! YOU'RE SPILLING IT!

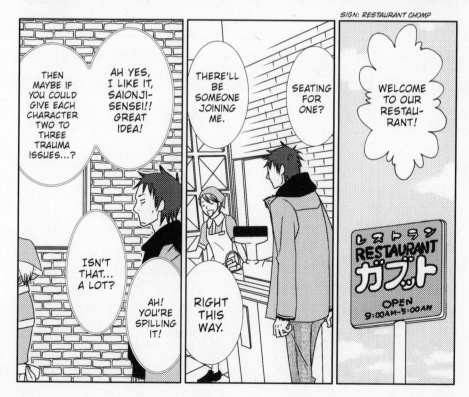

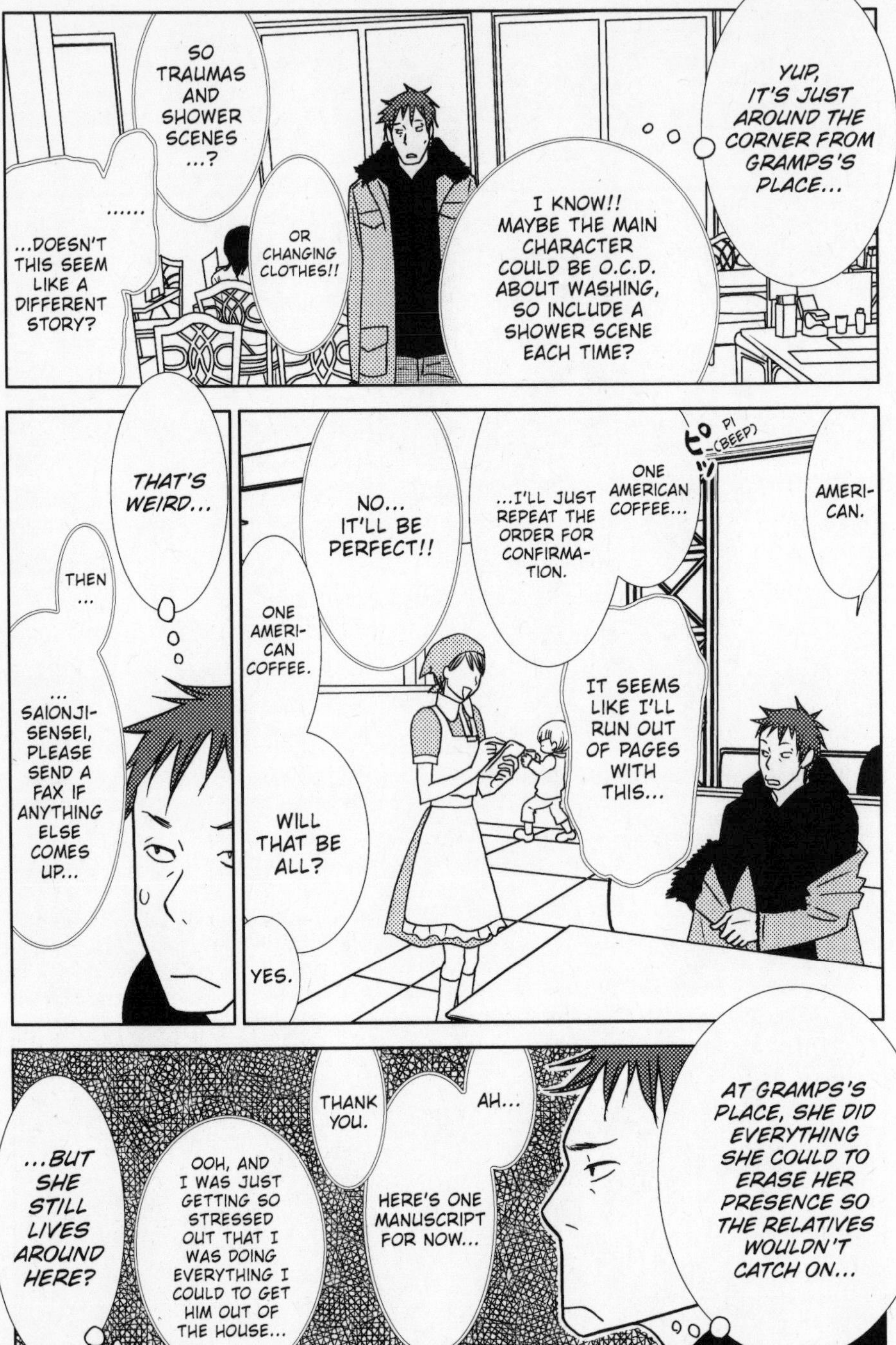
YUP, IT'S JUST AROUND THE CORNER FROM GRAMPS'S PLACE...
I KNOW!! MAYBE THE MAIN CHARACTER COULD BE O.C.D. ABOUT WASHING, SO INCLUDE A SHOWER SCENE EACH TIME?
SO TRAUMAS AND SHOWER SCENES ...?
OR CHANGING CLOTHES!!
......
...DOESN'T THIS SEEM LIKE A DIFFERENT STORY?
AMERI-CAN.
ピッ PI (BEEP)
ONE AMERICAN COFFEE...
...I'LL JUST REPEAT THE ORDER FOR CONFIRMATION.
NO... IT'LL BE PERFECT!!
IT SEEMS LIKE I'LL RUN OUT OF PAGES WITH THIS...
ONE AMERI-CAN COFFEE.
WILL THAT BE ALL?
YES.
THAT'S WEIRD...
THEN ...
... SAIONJI-SENSEI, PLEASE SEND A FAX IF ANYTHING ELSE COMES UP...
AT GRAMPS'S PLACE, SHE DID EVERYTHING SHE COULD TO ERASE HER PRESENCE SO THE RELATIVES WOULDN'T CATCH ON...
AH...
THANK YOU.
HERE'S ONE MANUSCRIPT FOR NOW...
OOH, AND I WAS JUST GETTING SO STRESSED OUT THAT I WAS DOING EVERYTHING I COULD TO GET HIM OUT OF THE HOUSE...
...BUT SHE STILL LIVES AROUND HERE?

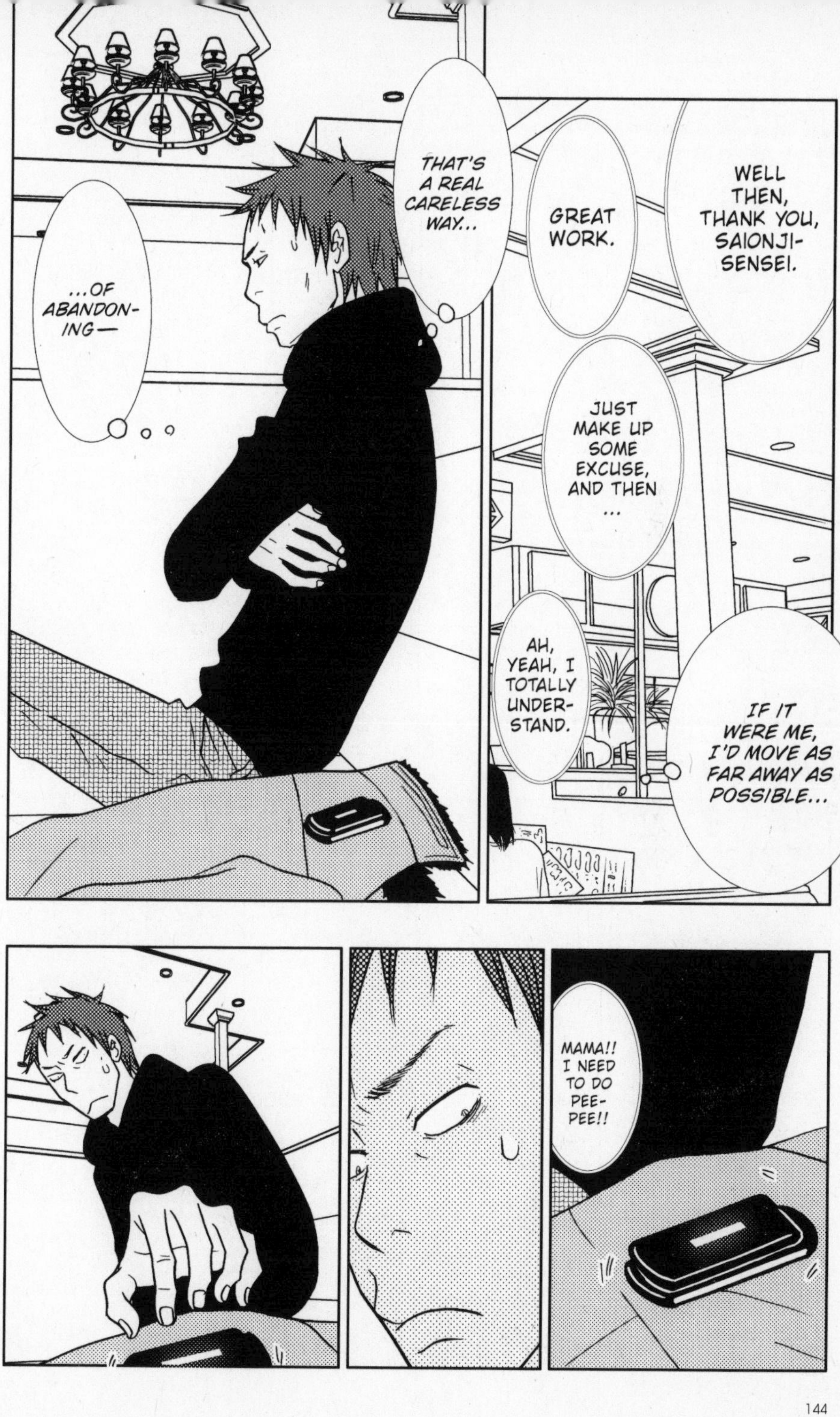
WELL THEN, THANK YOU, SAIONJI-SENSEI.
GREAT WORK.
JUST MAKE UP SOME EXCUSE, AND THEN ...
AH, YEAH, I TOTALLY UNDER-STAND.
IF IT WERE ME, I'D MOVE AS FAR AWAY AS POSSIBLE...
THAT'S A REAL CARELESS WAY...
...OF ABANDON-ING—
MAMA!! I NEED TO DO PEE-PEE!!

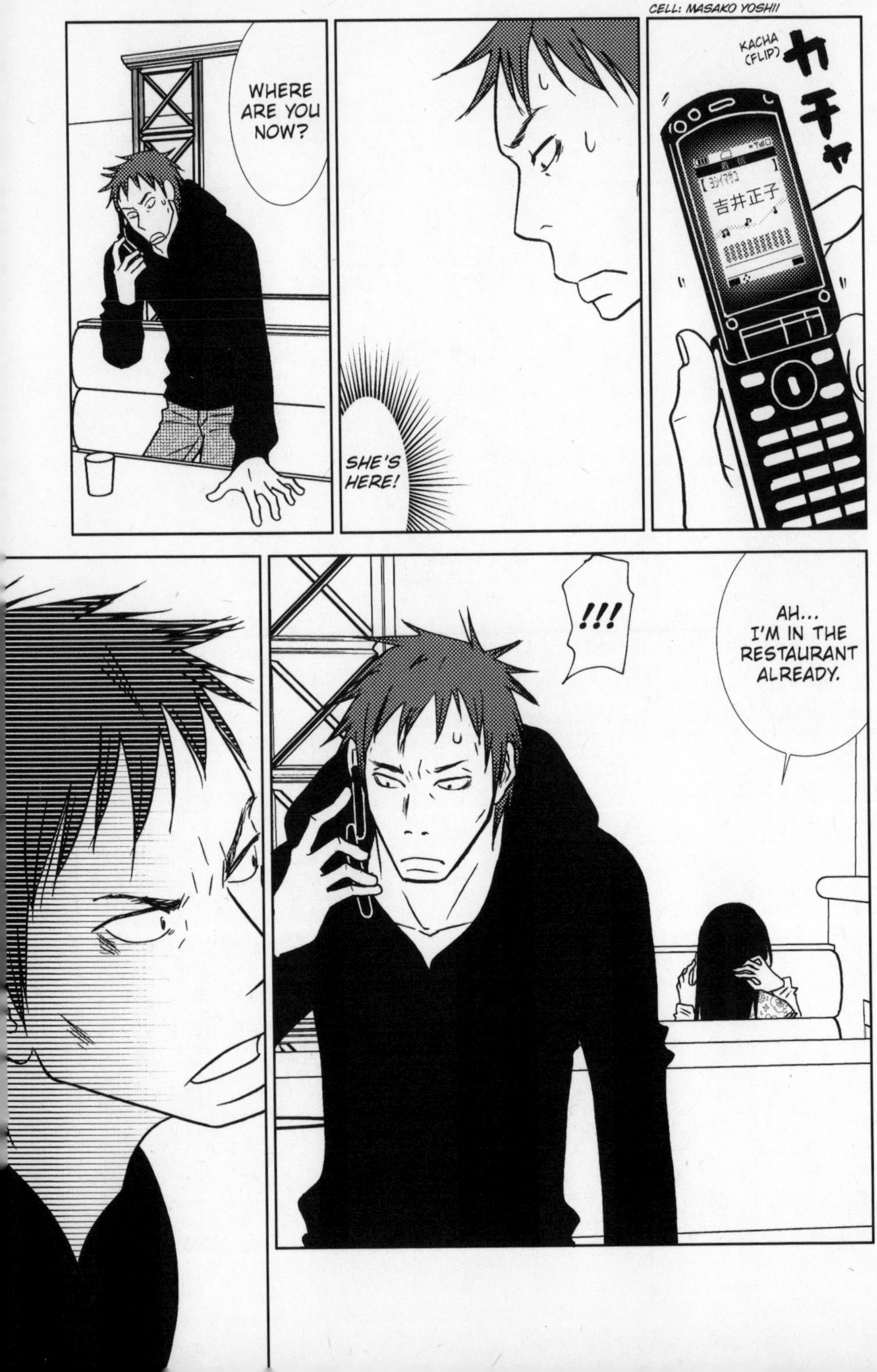
CELL: MASAKO YOSHII
KACHA (FLIP)
カチャ
吉井正子
SHE'S HERE!
WHERE ARE YOU NOW?
AH... I'M IN THE RESTAURANT ALREADY.
!!!

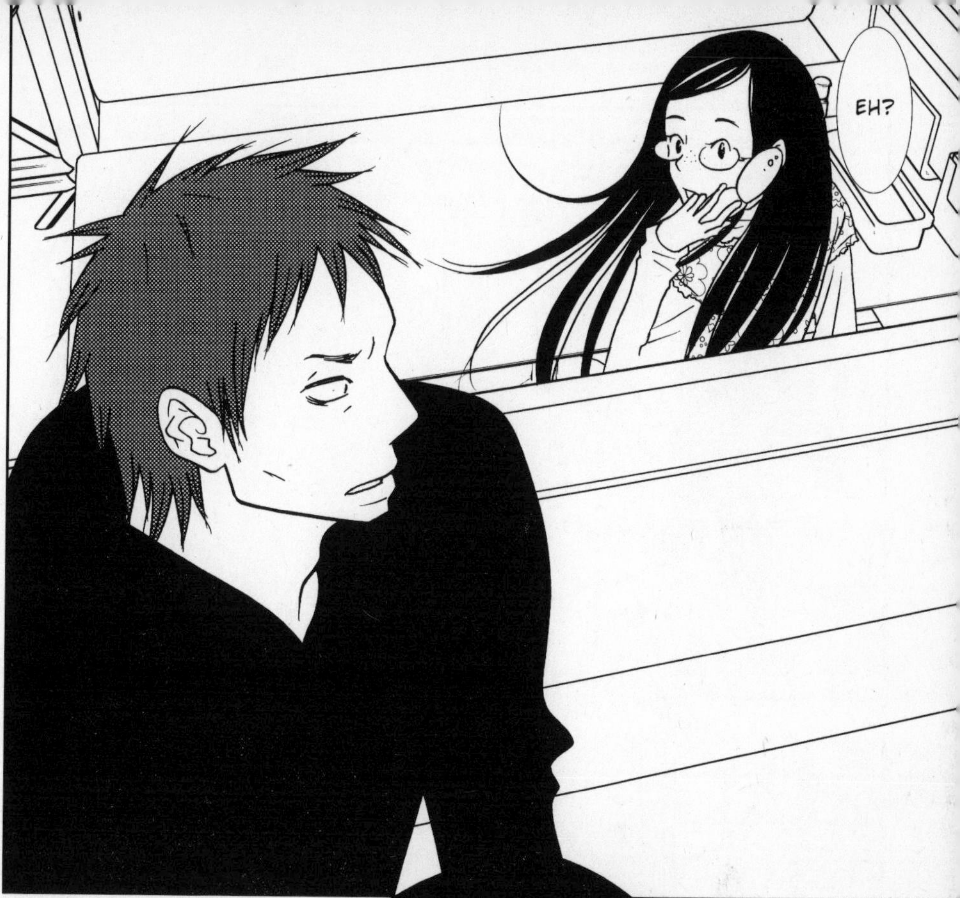
EH?
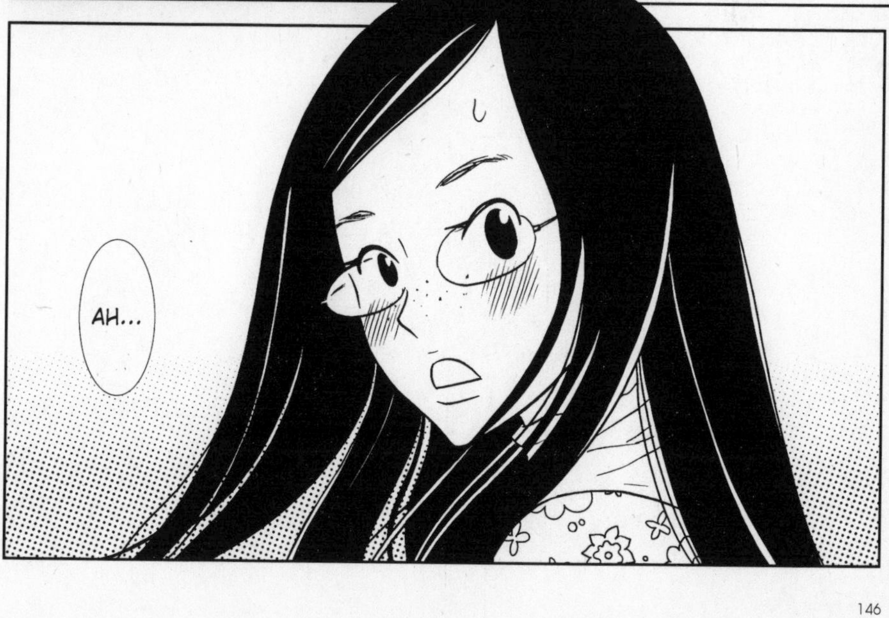
AH...

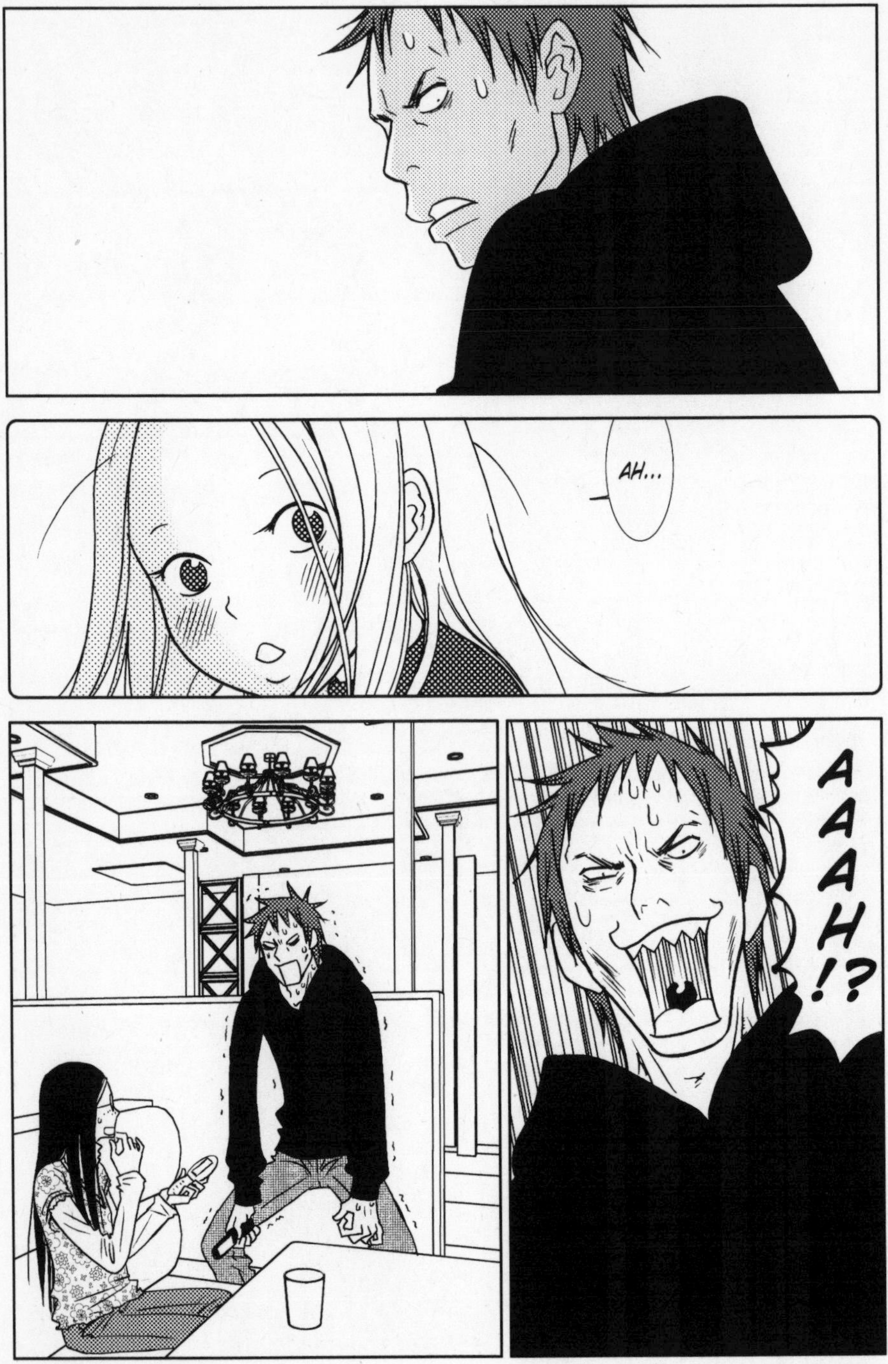
AH...
AAAAH!?

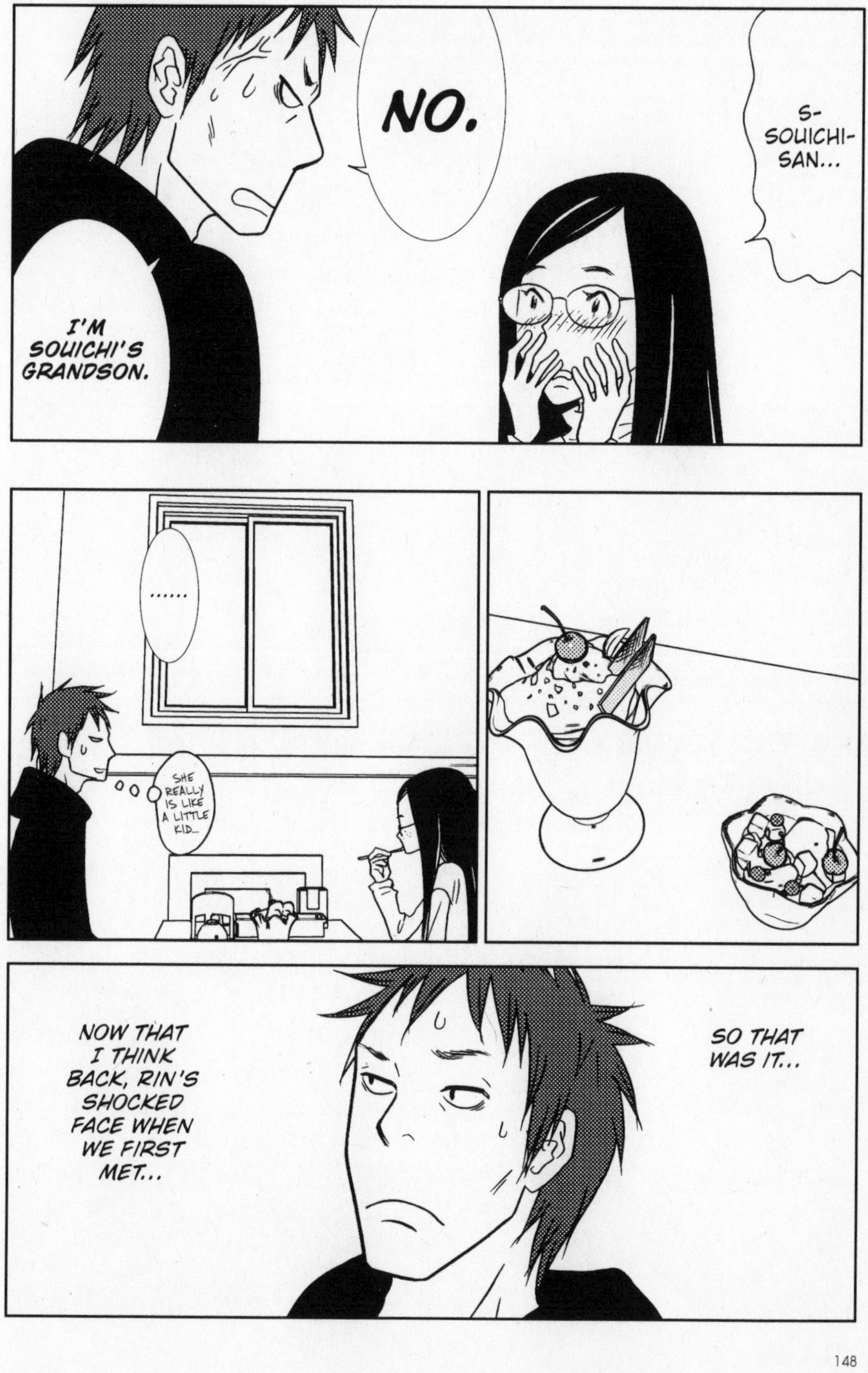
S-SOUICHI-SAN...
NO.
I'M SOUICHI'S GRANDSON.
......
SHE REALLY IS LIKE A LITTLE KID...
SO THAT WAS IT...
NOW THAT I THINK BACK, RIN'S SHOCKED FACE WHEN WE FIRST MET...

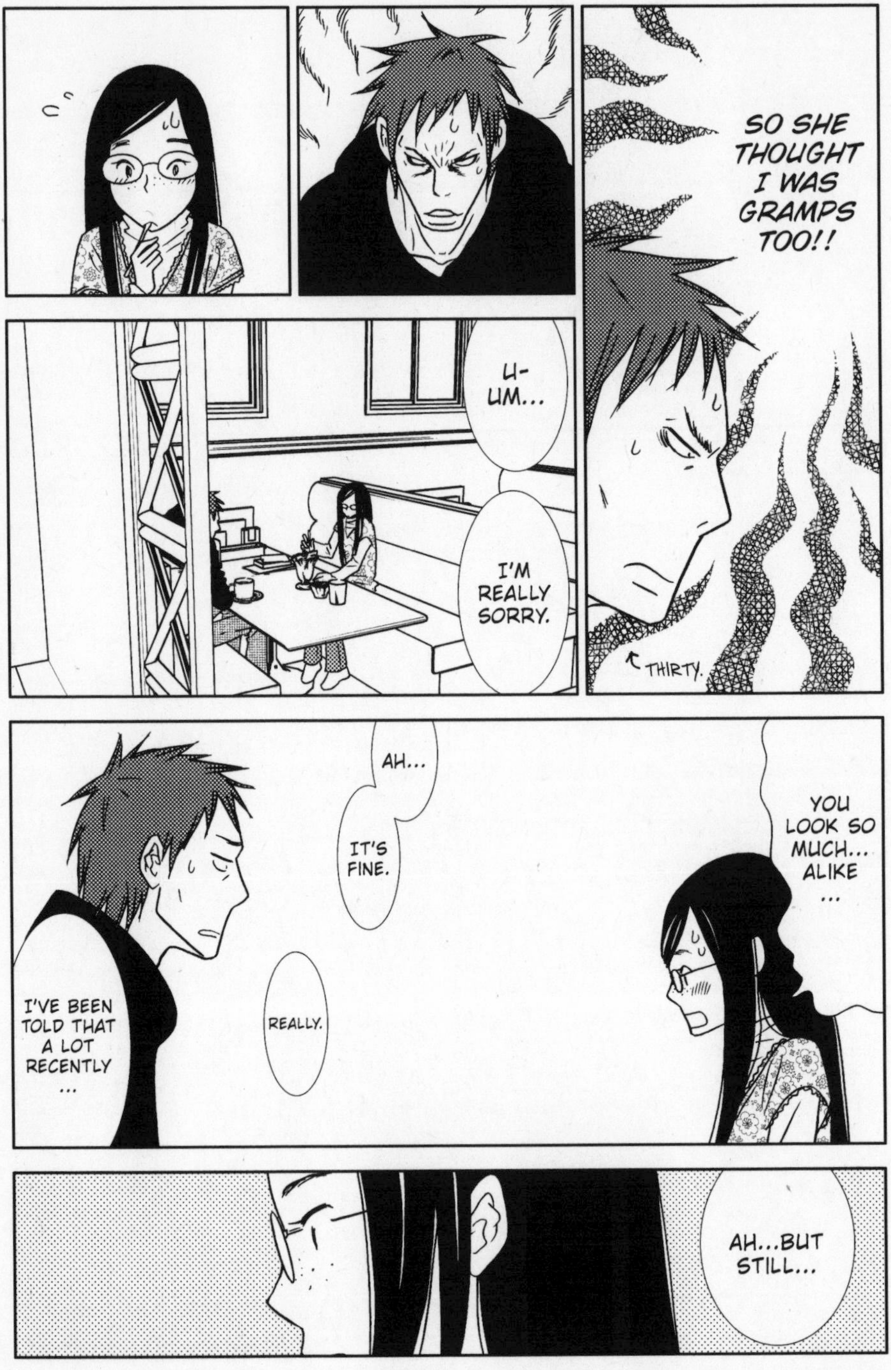
SO SHE THOUGHT I WAS GRAMPS TOO!!
THIRTY.
U-UM...
I'M REALLY SORRY.
YOU LOOK SO MUCH... ALIKE ...
AH...
IT'S FINE.
I'VE BEEN TOLD THAT A LOT RECENTLY ...
REALLY.
AH...BUT STILL...

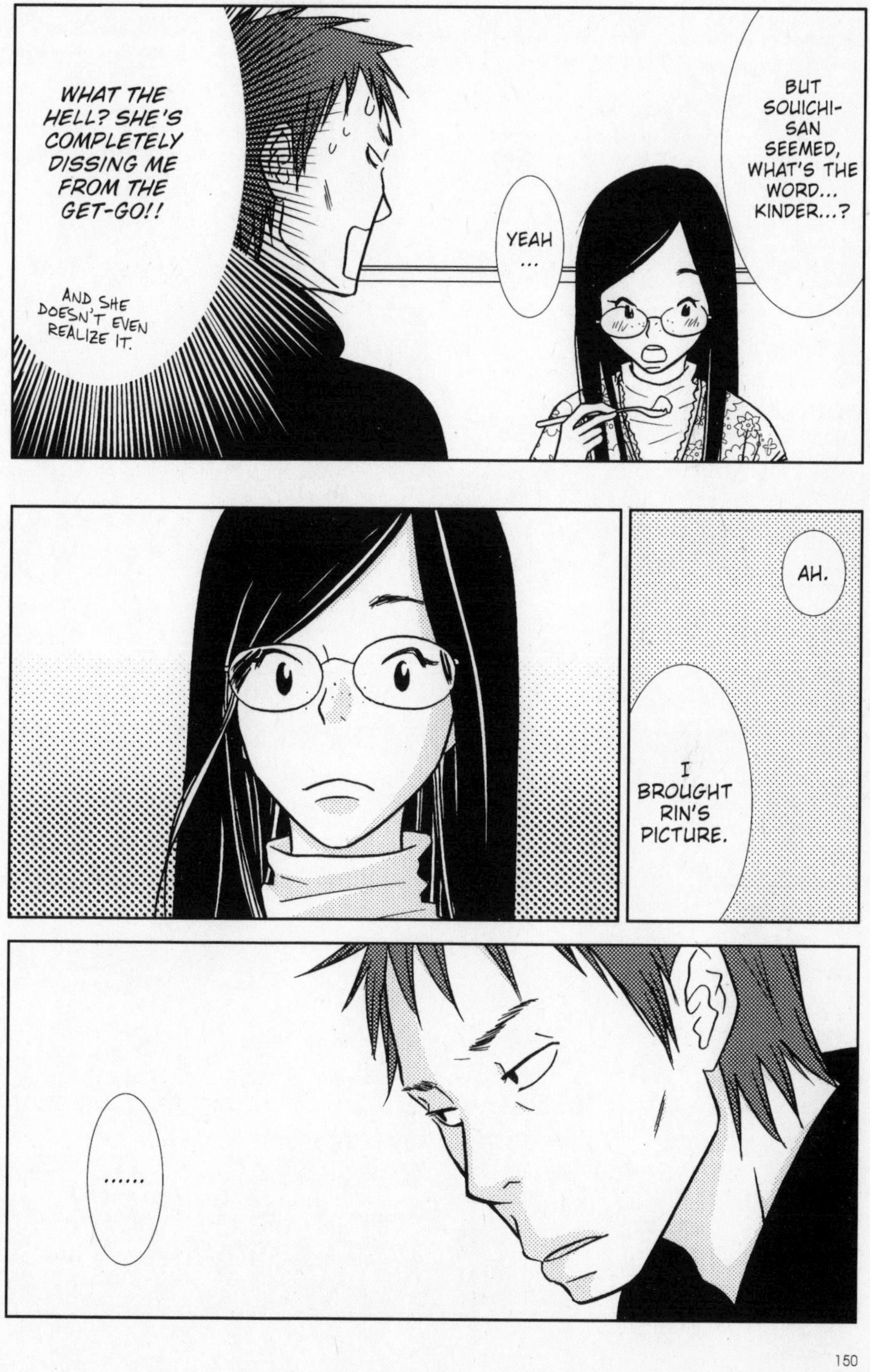
BUT SOUICHI-SAN SEEMED, WHAT'S THE WORD... KINDER...?
YEAH ...
WHAT THE HELL? SHE'S COMPLETELY DISSING ME FROM THE GET-GO!!
AND SHE DOESN'T EVEN REALIZE IT.
AH.
I BROUGHT RIN'S PICTURE.
......

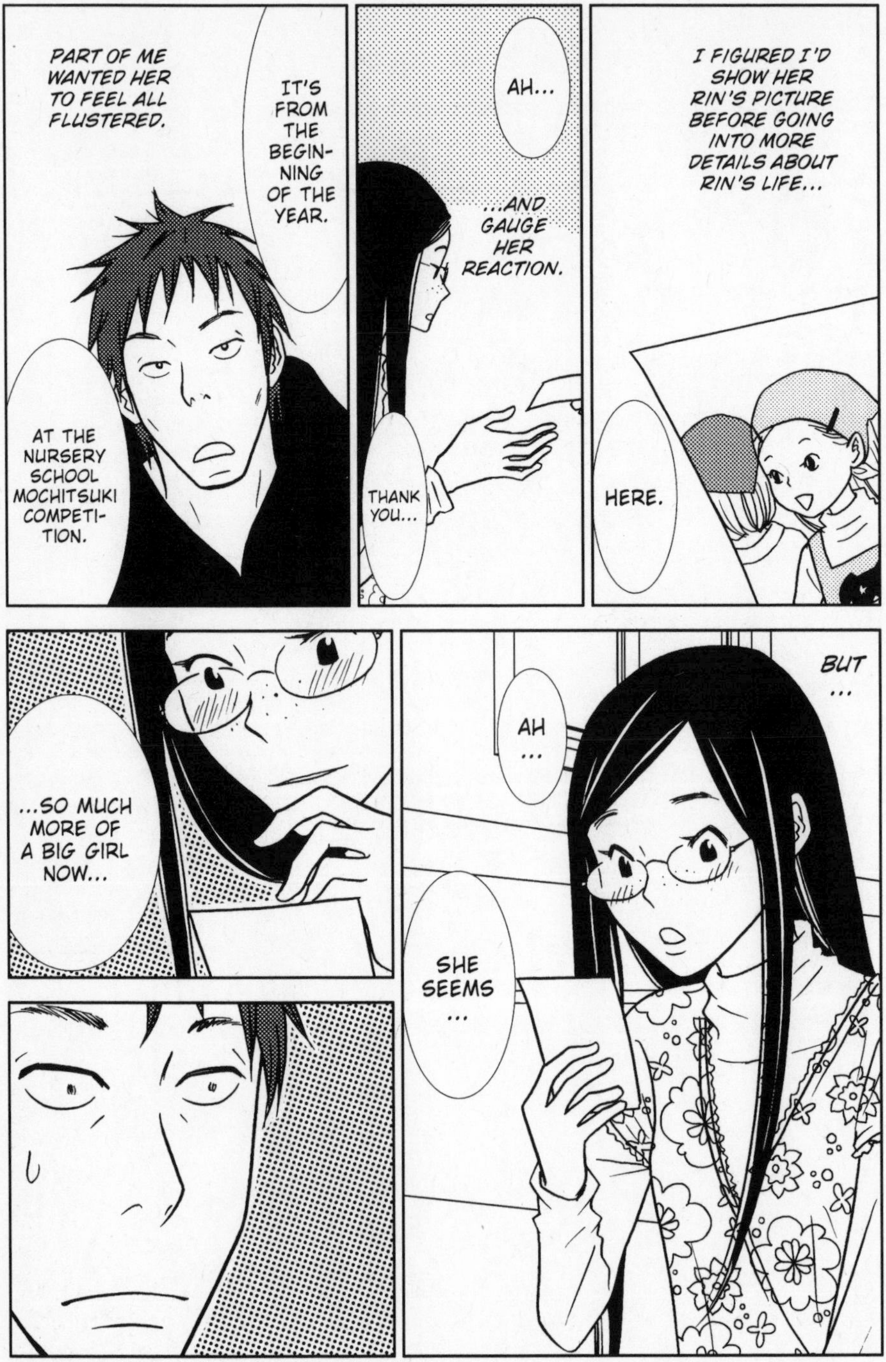

I FIGURED I'D SHOW HER RIN'S PICTURE BEFORE GOING INTO MORE DETAILS ABOUT RIN'S LIFE...
HERE.
AH...
...AND GAUGE HER REACTION.
THANK YOU...
IT'S FROM THE BEGIN-NING OF THE YEAR.
PART OF ME WANTED HER TO FEEL ALL FLUSTERED.
AT THE NURSERY SCHOOL MOCHITSUKI COMPETI-TION.
BUT ...
AH ...
SHE SEEMS ...
...SO MUCH MORE OF A BIG GIRL NOW...

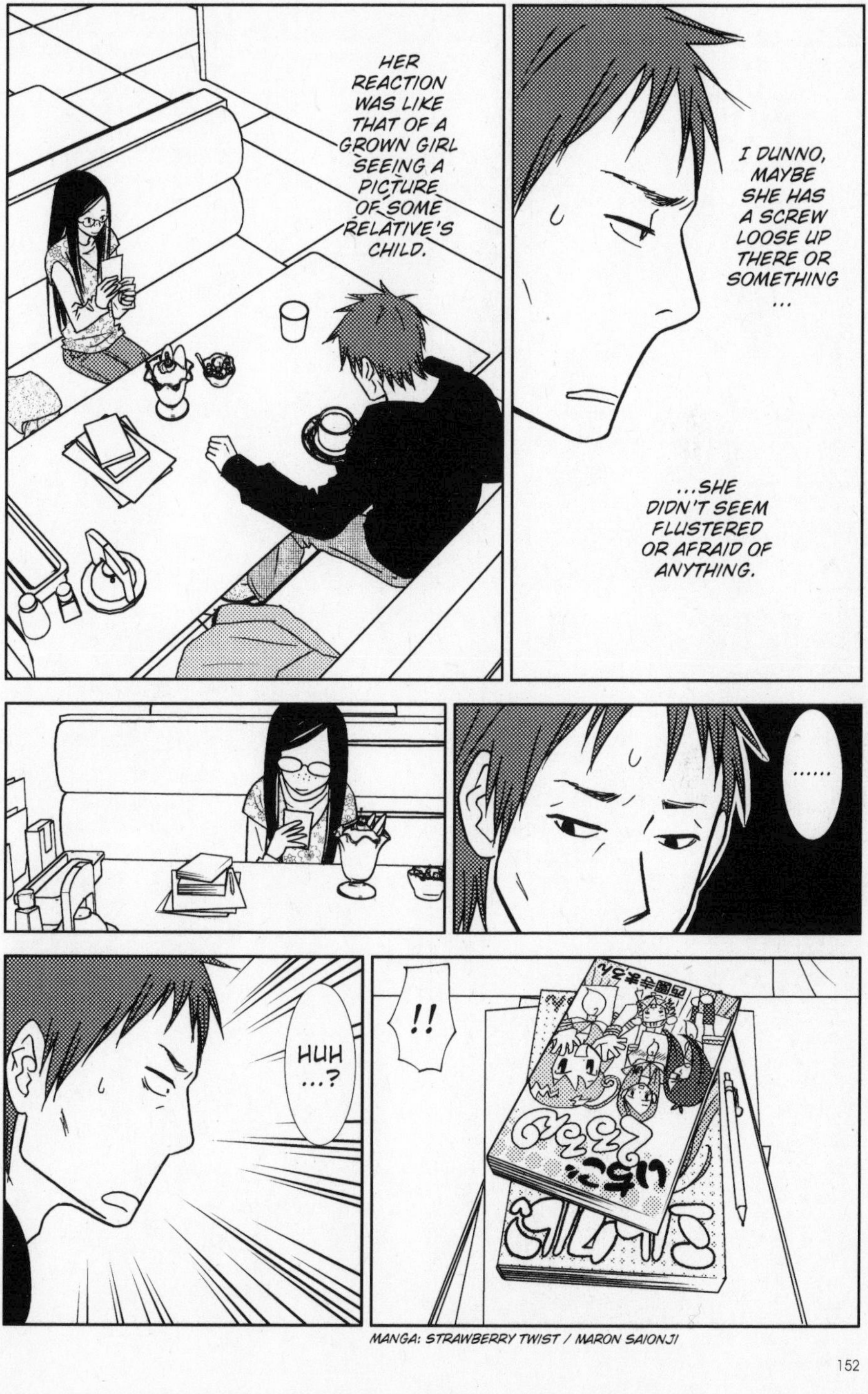
I DUNNO, MAYBE SHE HAS A SCREW LOOSE UP THERE OR SOMETHING ...
...SHE DIDN'T SEEM FLUSTERED OR AFRAID OF ANYTHING.
HER REACTION WAS LIKE THAT OF A GROWN GIRL SEEING A PICTURE OF SOME RELATIVE'S CHILD.
......
!!
HUH ...?
MANGA: STRAWBERRY TWIST / MARON SAIONJI

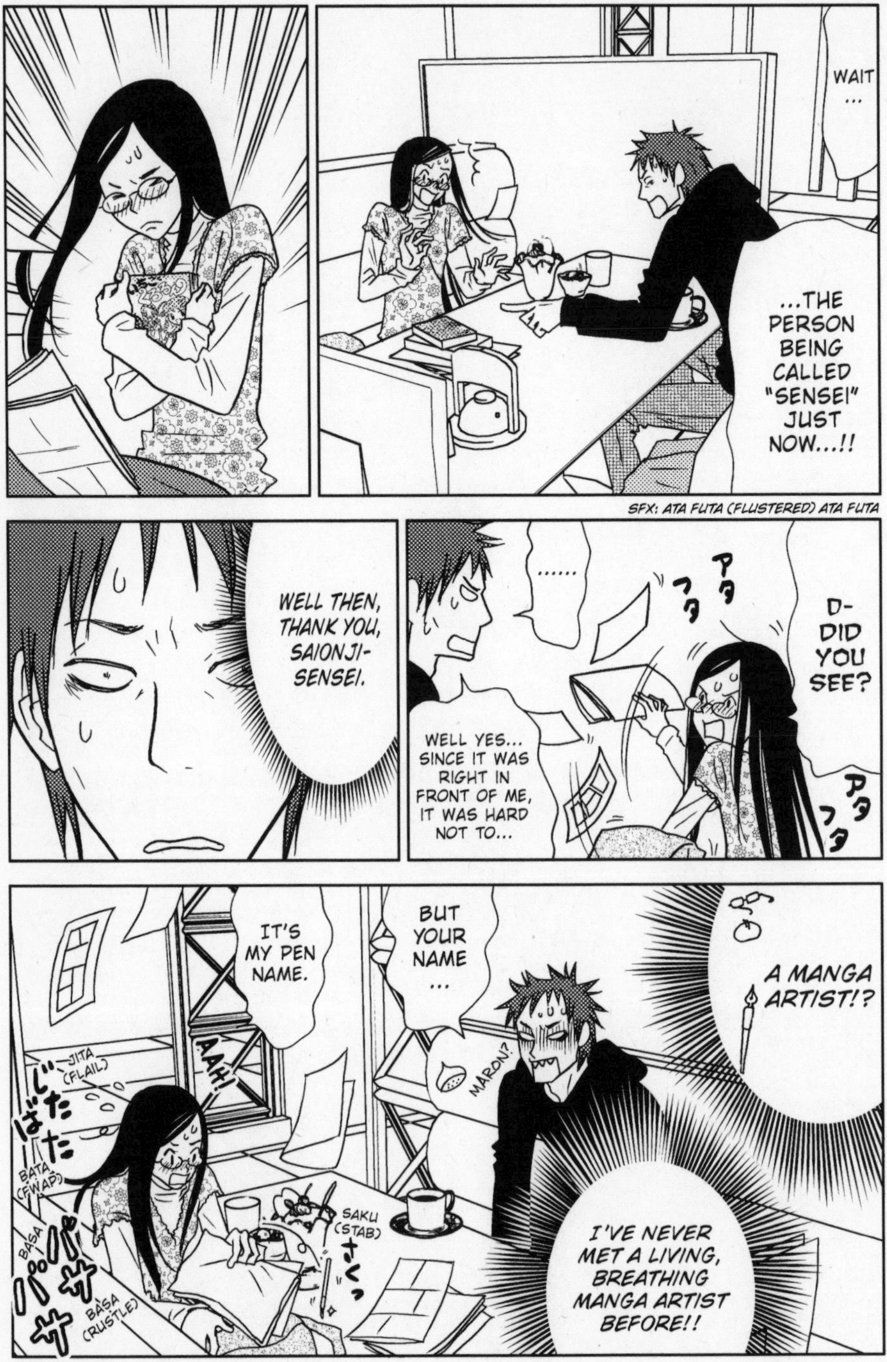
WAIT ...
...THE PERSON BEING CALLED "SENSEI" JUST NOW...!!
SFX: ATA FUTA (FLUSTERED) ATA FUTA
D-DID YOU SEE?
アタフタ
......
WELL YES... SINCE IT WAS RIGHT IN FRONT OF ME, IT WAS HARD NOT TO...
アタフタ
WELL THEN, THANK YOU, SAIONJI-SENSEI.
A MANGA ARTIST!?
BUT YOUR NAME ...
IT'S MY PEN NAME.
MARON?
AAH!
じたばた
JITA (FLAIL)
BATA (FWAP)
I'VE NEVER MET A LIVING, BREATHING MANGA ARTIST BEFORE!!
さくっ
SAKU (STAB)
パサ パサ
BASA
BASA (RUSTLE)

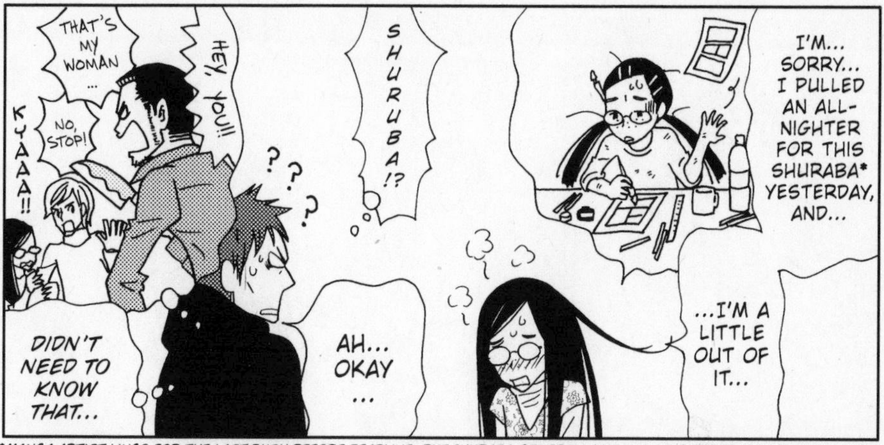
I'M... SORRY... I PULLED AN ALL-NIGHTER FOR THIS SHURABA* YESTERDAY, AND...
...I'M A LITTLE OUT OF IT...
SHURUBA!?
AH... OKAY...
HEY, YOU!!
THAT'S MY WOMAN...
NO, STOP!
KYAAA!!
DIDN'T NEED TO KNOW THAT...

*MANGA ARTIST LINGO FOR THE LAST PUSH BEFORE DEADLINE, BUT SHURABA GENERALLY MEANS A FIGHT BETWEEN RIVALS IN LOVE.

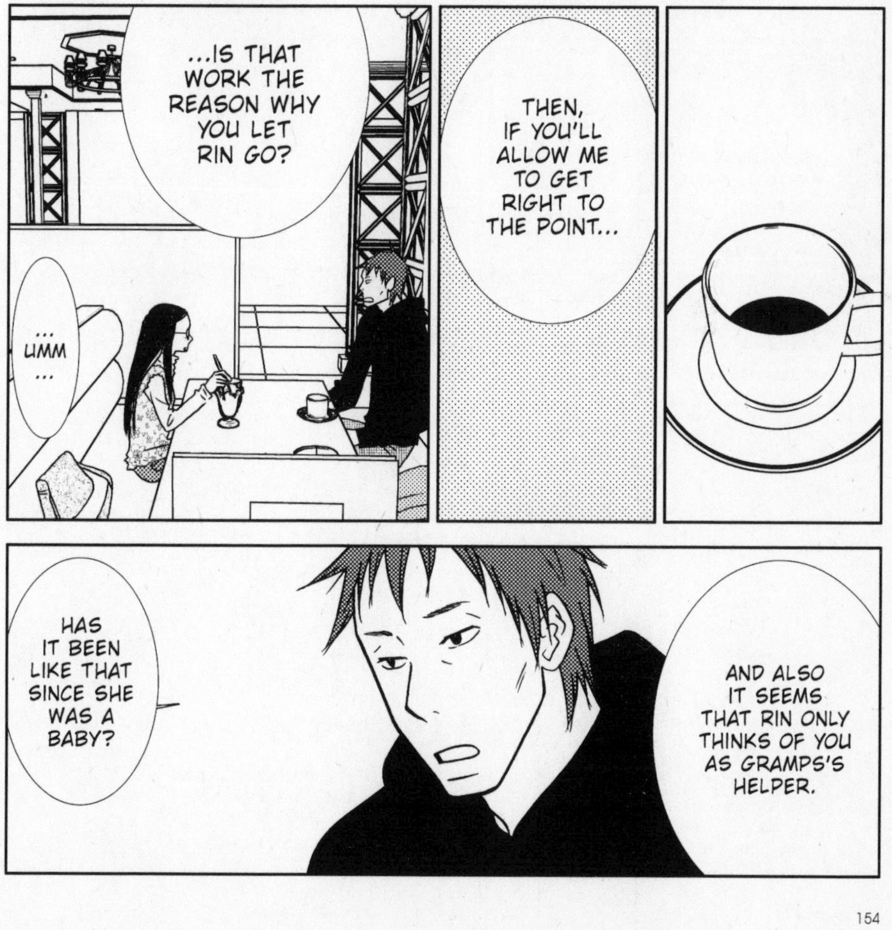
THEN, IF YOU'LL ALLOW ME TO GET RIGHT TO THE POINT...
...IS THAT WORK THE REASON WHY YOU LET RIN GO?
...UMM...
AND ALSO IT SEEMS THAT RIN ONLY THINKS OF YOU AS GRAMPS'S HELPER.
HAS IT BEEN LIKE THAT SINCE SHE WAS A BABY?

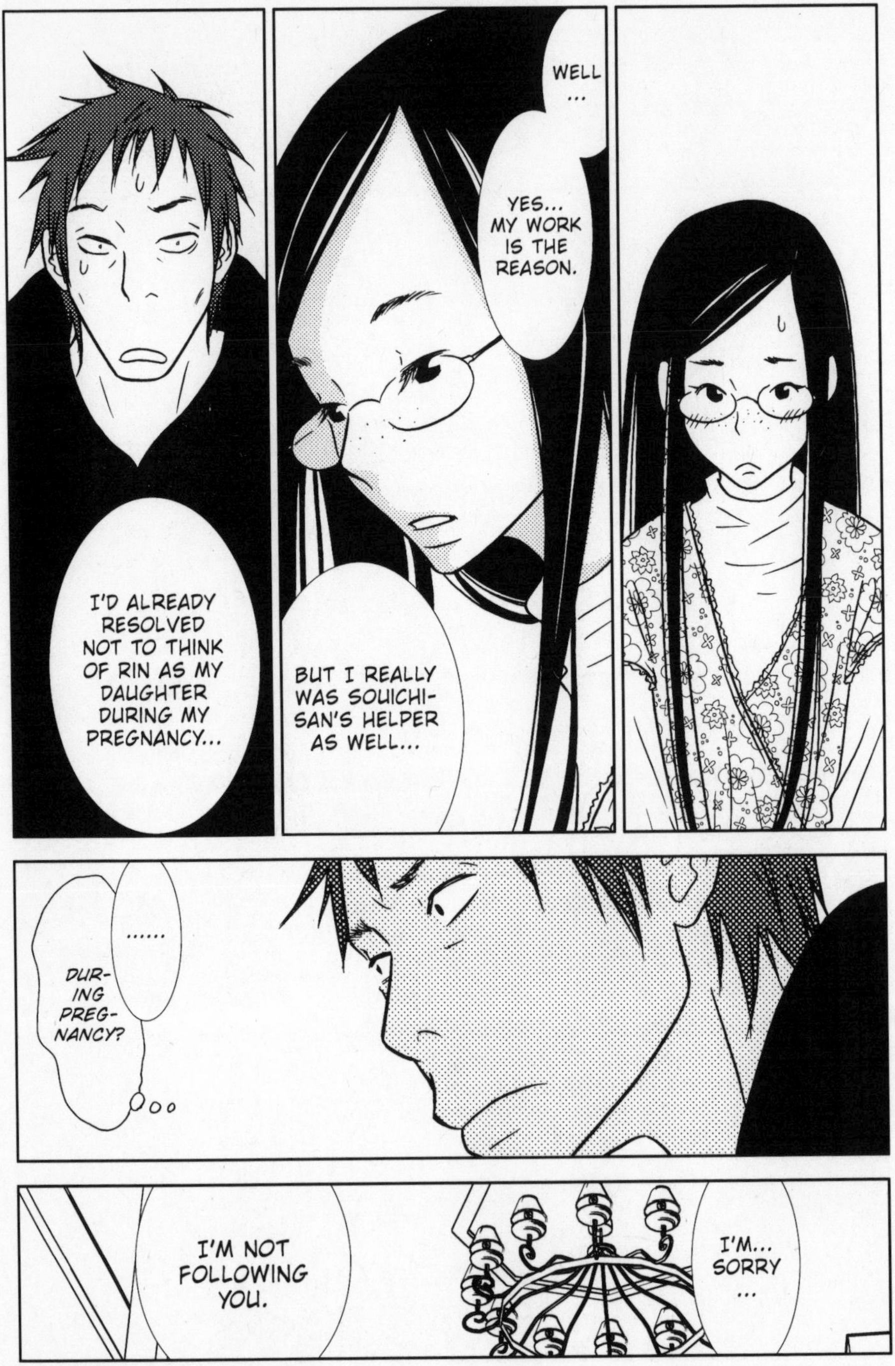
WELL...
YES... MY WORK IS THE REASON.
BUT I REALLY WAS SOUICHI-SAN'S HELPER AS WELL...
I'D ALREADY RESOLVED NOT TO THINK OF RIN AS MY DAUGHTER DURING MY PREGNANCY...
......
DURING PREGNANCY?
I'M... SORRY...
I'M NOT FOLLOWING YOU.

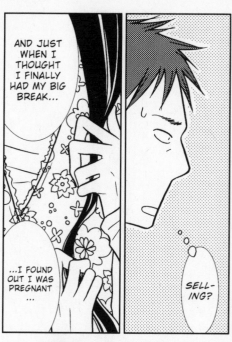

I WASN'T SELLING AT ALL...
...FOR THE LONGEST TIME.
SELL-ING?
AND JUST WHEN I THOUGHT I FINALLY HAD MY BIG BREAK...
...I FOUND OUT I WAS PREGNANT...
AH, SHE WAS TALKING ABOUT WORK...
I DIDN'T THINK IT WAS SOMETHING I COULD DO WHILE RAISING A CHILD... SO...
BUT SOUICHI-SAN REALLY PUSHED FOR ME TO HAVE THE CHILD...
HONESTLY, IT WAS REALLY DIFFICULT WHILE I CAME TO TERM.
THERE WERE EVEN TIMES WHEN I WAS ANGRY AT SOUICHI-SAN FOR MAKING ME GO THROUGH WITH IT.
AND I'D LASH OUT AT HIM...
DAY IN AND DAY OUT, I WAS EITHER WORKING OR SLEEPING, AND I KEPT GETTING BIGGER...

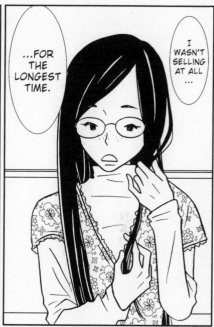

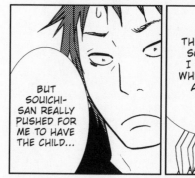

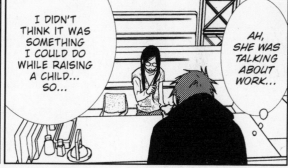

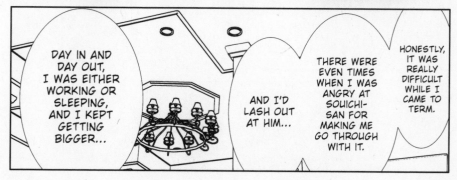

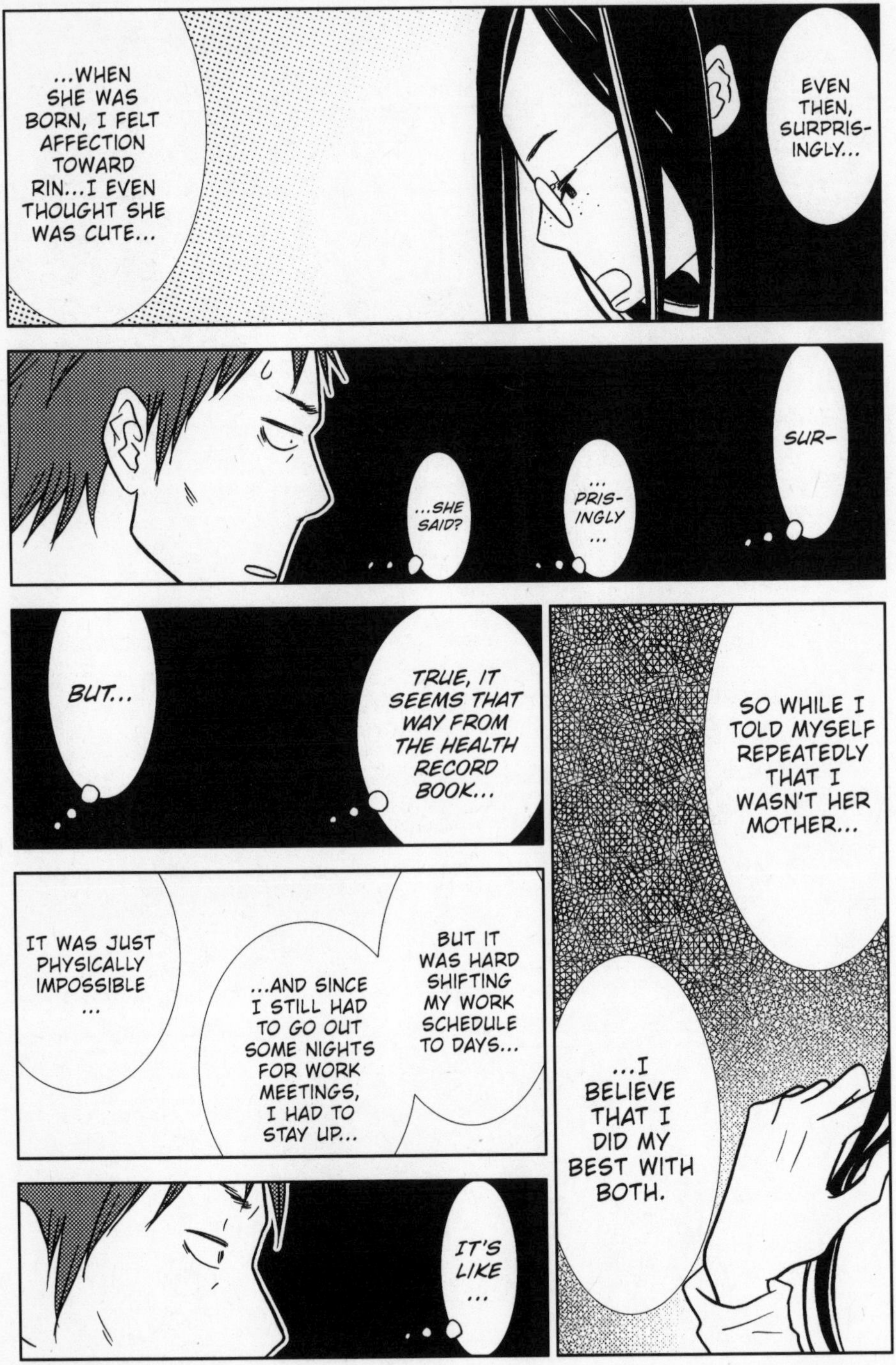
EVEN THEN, SURPRIS-INGLY...
...WHEN SHE WAS BORN, I FELT AFFECTION TOWARD RIN...I EVEN THOUGHT SHE WAS CUTE...
SUR-
...PRIS-INGLY...
...SHE SAID?
TRUE, IT SEEMS THAT WAY FROM THE HEALTH RECORD BOOK...
BUT...
BUT IT WAS HARD SHIFTING MY WORK SCHEDULE TO DAYS...
...AND SINCE I STILL HAD TO GO OUT SOME NIGHTS FOR WORK MEETINGS, I HAD TO STAY UP...
IT WAS JUST PHYSICALLY IMPOSSIBLE...
SO WHILE I TOLD MYSELF REPEATEDLY THAT I WASN'T HER MOTHER...
...I BELIEVE THAT I DID MY BEST WITH BOTH.
IT'S LIKE...

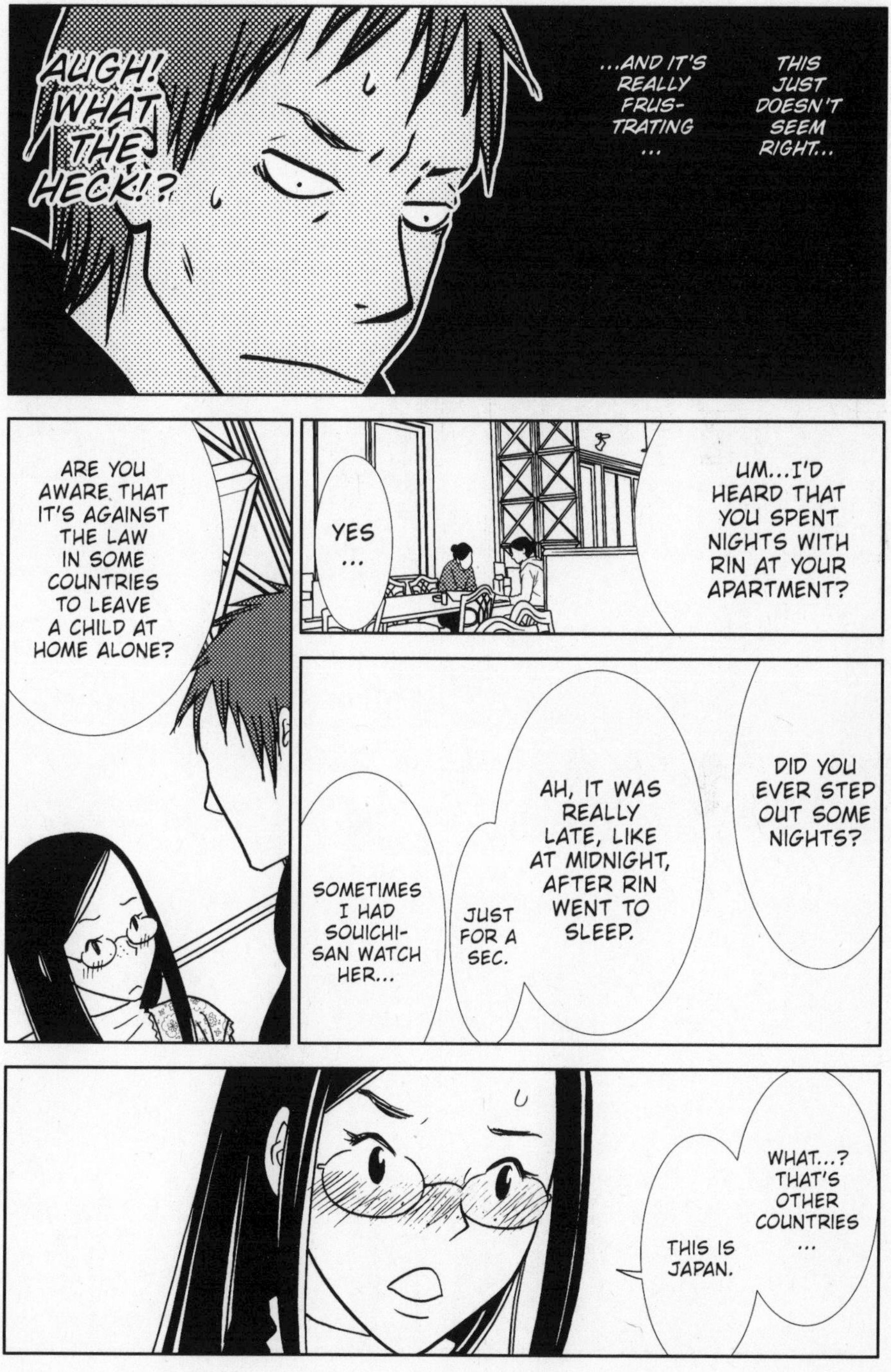
THIS JUST DOESN'T SEEM RIGHT...
...AND IT'S REALLY FRUS-TRATING...
AUGH! WHAT THE HECK!?
UM...I'D HEARD THAT YOU SPENT NIGHTS WITH RIN AT YOUR APARTMENT?
YES...
DID YOU EVER STEP OUT SOME NIGHTS?
AH, IT WAS REALLY LATE, LIKE AT MIDNIGHT, AFTER RIN WENT TO SLEEP.
JUST FOR A SEC.
SOMETIMES I HAD SOUICHI-SAN WATCH HER...
ARE YOU AWARE THAT IT'S AGAINST THE LAW IN SOME COUNTRIES TO LEAVE A CHILD AT HOME ALONE?
WHAT...? THAT'S OTHER COUNTRIES...
THIS IS JAPAN.

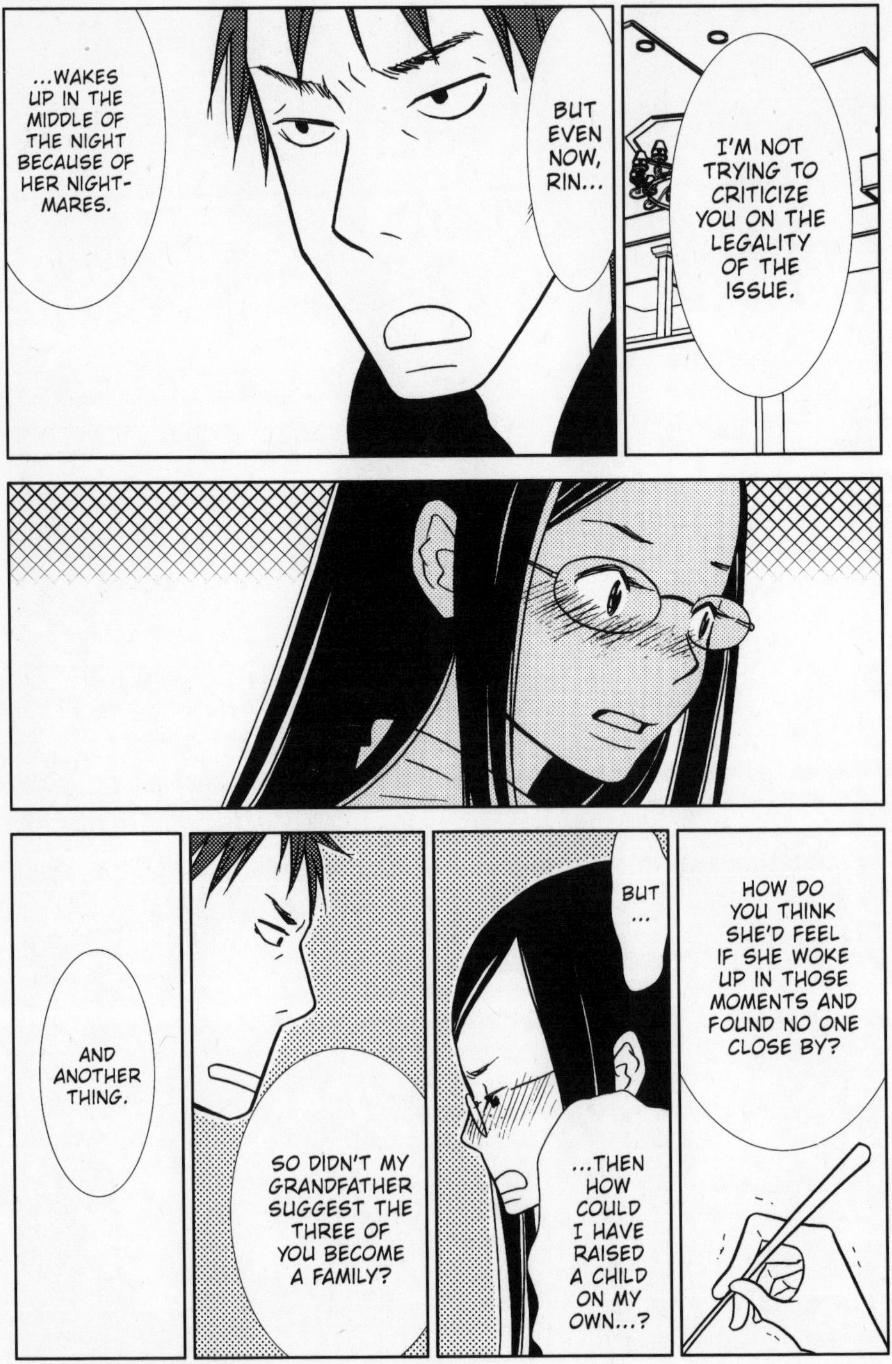
I'M NOT TRYING TO CRITICIZE YOU ON THE LEGALITY OF THE ISSUE.
BUT EVEN NOW, RIN...
...WAKES UP IN THE MIDDLE OF THE NIGHT BECAUSE OF HER NIGHT-MARES.
HOW DO YOU THINK SHE'D FEEL IF SHE WOKE UP IN THOSE MOMENTS AND FOUND NO ONE CLOSE BY?
BUT ...
...THEN HOW COULD I HAVE RAISED A CHILD ON MY OWN...?
SO DIDN'T MY GRANDFATHER SUGGEST THE THREE OF YOU BECOME A FAMILY?
AND ANOTHER THING.

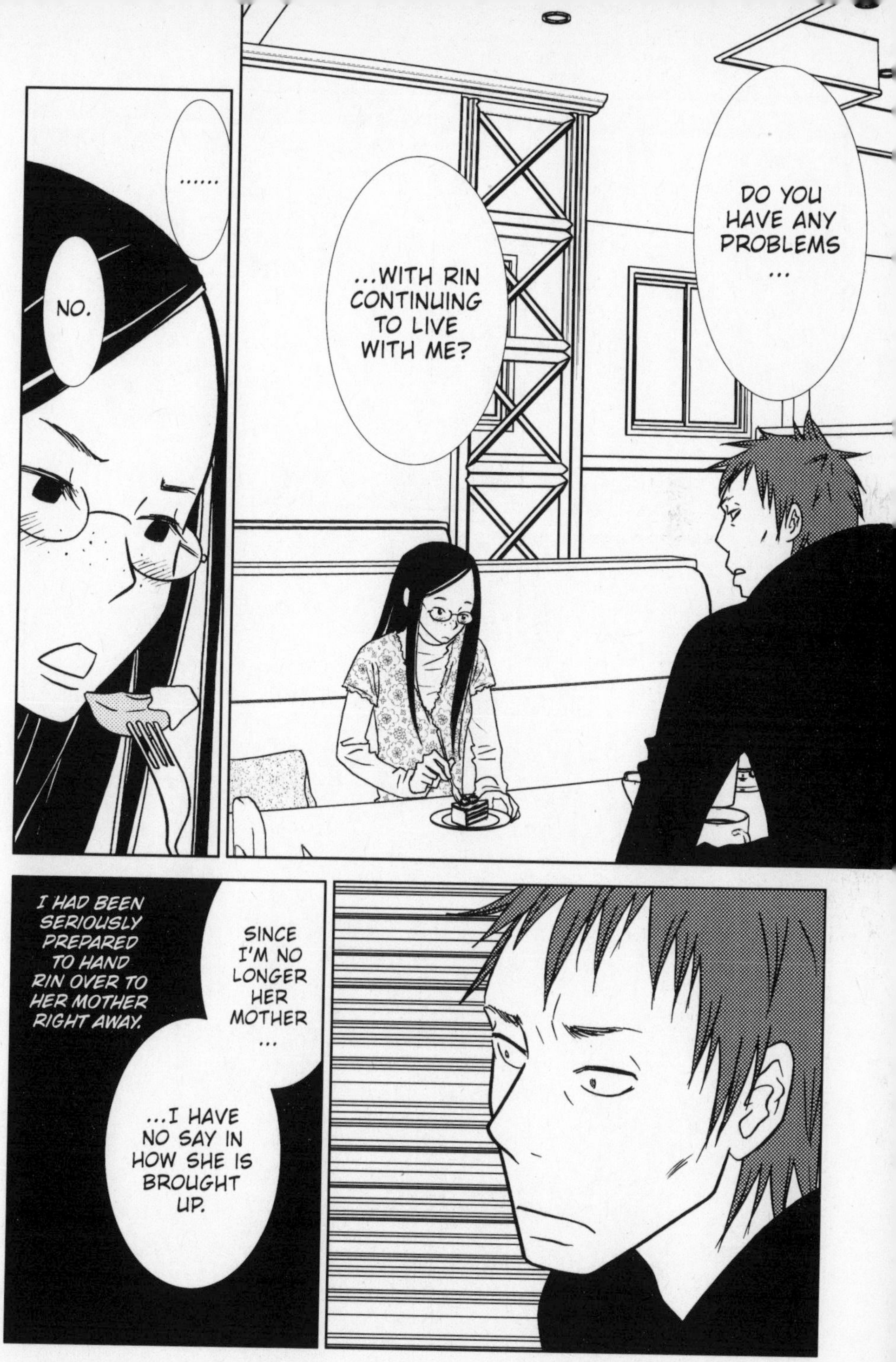
DO YOU HAVE ANY PROBLEMS ...
...WITH RIN CONTINUING TO LIVE WITH ME?
......
NO.
SINCE I'M NO LONGER HER MOTHER ...
...I HAVE NO SAY IN HOW SHE IS BROUGHT UP.
I HAD BEEN SERIOUSLY PREPARED TO HAND RIN OVER TO HER MOTHER RIGHT AWAY.

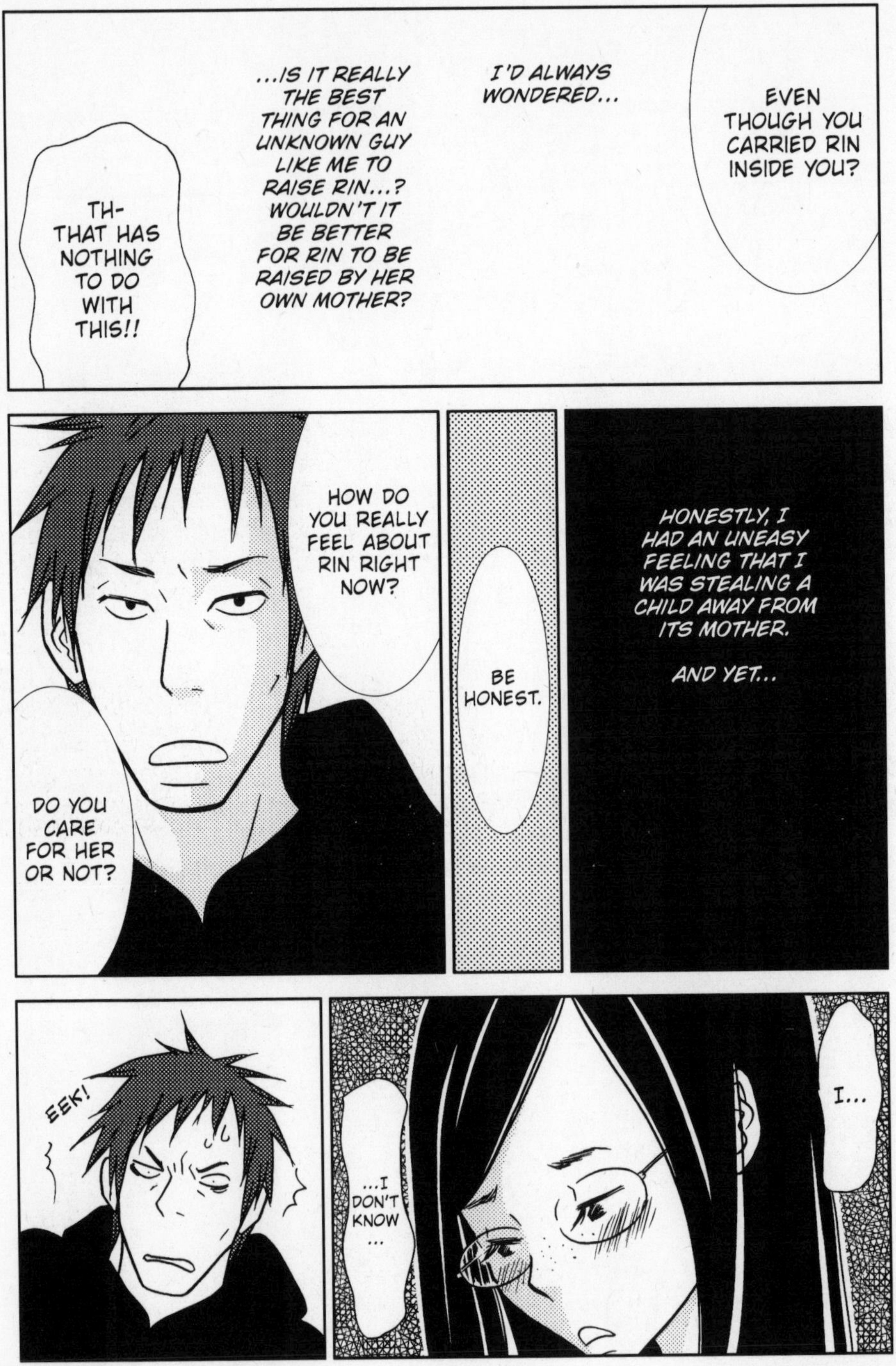
EVEN THOUGH YOU CARRIED RIN INSIDE YOU?
I'D ALWAYS WONDERED...
...IS IT REALLY THE BEST THING FOR AN UNKNOWN GUY LIKE ME TO RAISE RIN...? WOULDN'T IT BE BETTER FOR RIN TO BE RAISED BY HER OWN MOTHER?
TH- THAT HAS NOTHING TO DO WITH THIS!!
HONESTLY, I HAD AN UNEASY FEELING THAT I WAS STEALING A CHILD AWAY FROM ITS MOTHER.
AND YET...
BE HONEST.
HOW DO YOU REALLY FEEL ABOUT RIN RIGHT NOW?
DO YOU CARE FOR HER OR NOT?
I...
...I DON'T KNOW...
EEK!

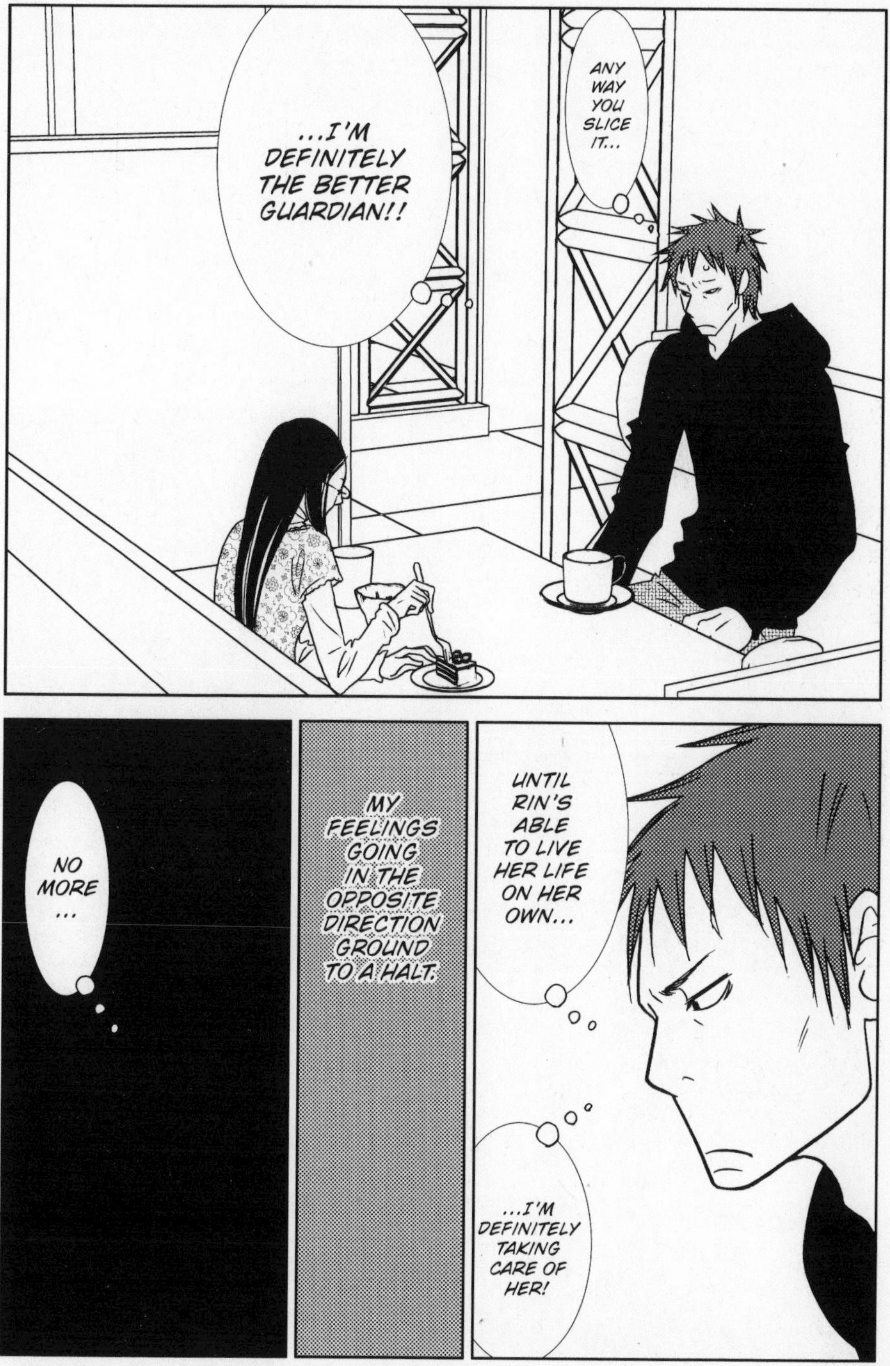
ANY WAY YOU SLICE IT...
...I'M DEFINITELY THE BETTER GUARDIAN!!
UNTIL RIN'S ABLE TO LIVE HER LIFE ON HER OWN...
...I'M DEFINITELY TAKING CARE OF HER!
MY FEELINGS GOING IN THE OPPOSITE DIRECTION GROUND TO A HALT.
NO MORE ...

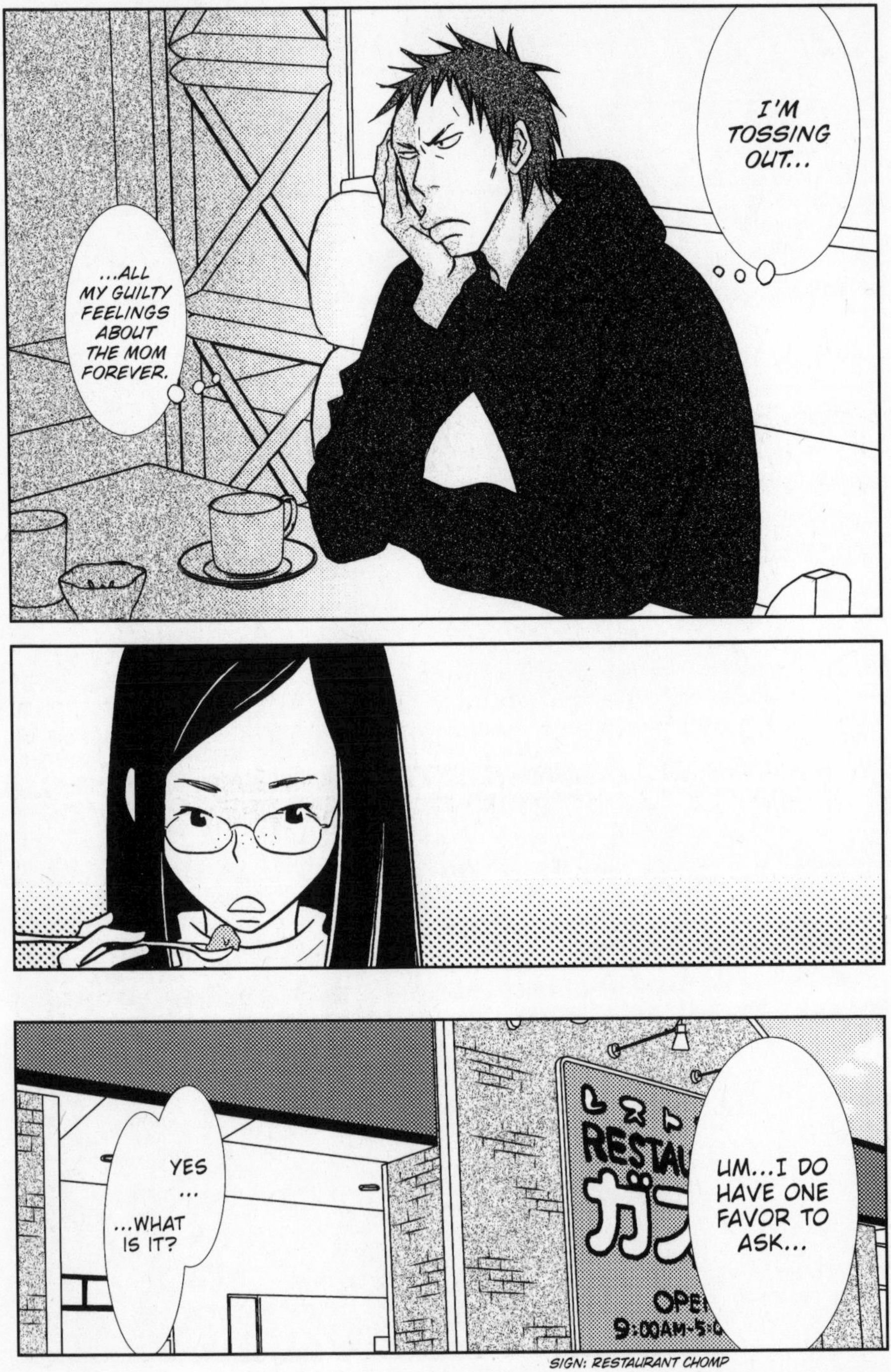
I'M TOSSING OUT...
...ALL MY GUILTY FEELINGS ABOUT THE MOM FOREVER.
UM...I DO HAVE ONE FAVOR TO ASK...
YES ... ...WHAT IS IT?

SIGN: RESTAURANT CHOMP

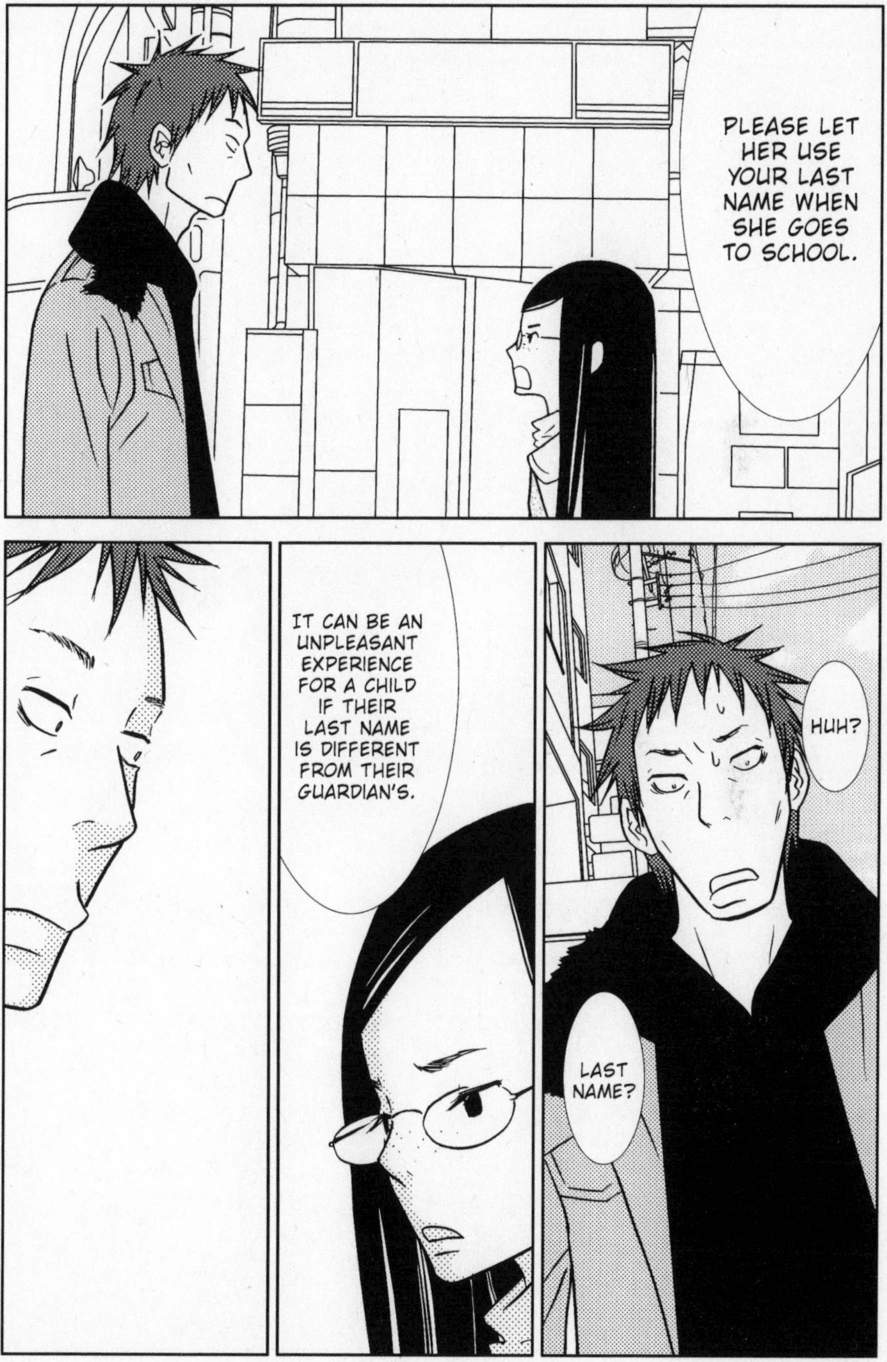
PLEASE LET HER USE YOUR LAST NAME WHEN SHE GOES TO SCHOOL.
HUH?
LAST NAME?
IT CAN BE AN UNPLEASANT EXPERIENCE FOR A CHILD IF THEIR LAST NAME IS DIFFERENT FROM THEIR GUARDIAN'S.

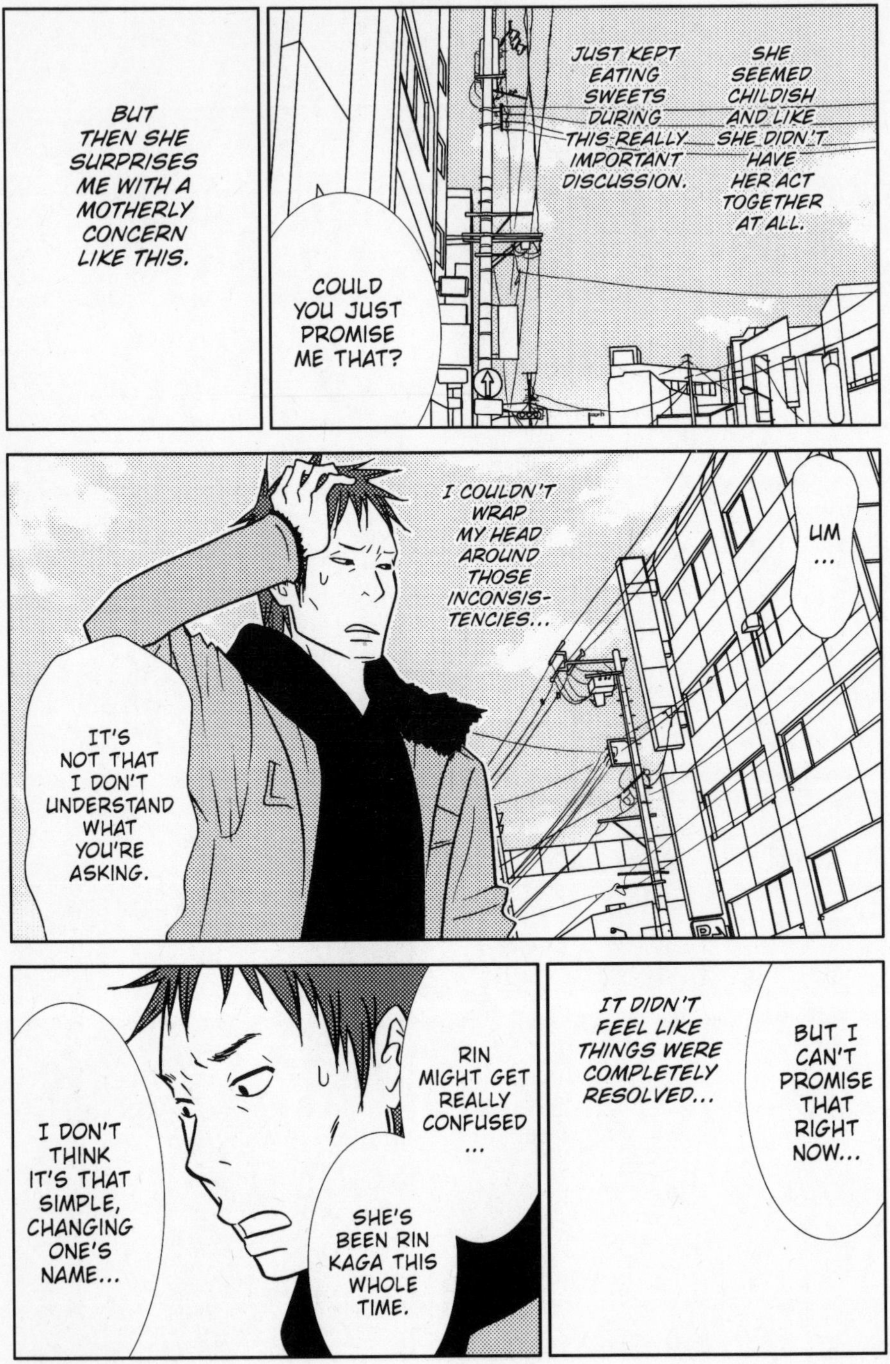

SHE SEEMED CHILDISH AND LIKE SHE DIDN'T HAVE HER ACT TOGETHER AT ALL.
JUST KEPT EATING SWEETS DURING THIS REALLY IMPORTANT DISCUSSION.
COULD YOU JUST PROMISE ME THAT?
BUT THEN SHE SURPRISES ME WITH A MOTHERLY CONCERN LIKE THIS.
UM ...
I COULDN'T WRAP MY HEAD AROUND THOSE INCONSIS-TENCIES...
IT'S NOT THAT I DON'T UNDERSTAND WHAT YOU'RE ASKING.
BUT I CAN'T PROMISE THAT RIGHT NOW...
IT DIDN'T FEEL LIKE THINGS WERE COMPLETELY RESOLVED...
RIN MIGHT GET REALLY CONFUSED ...
SHE'S BEEN RIN KAGA THIS WHOLE TIME.
I DON'T THINK IT'S THAT SIMPLE, CHANGING ONE'S NAME...

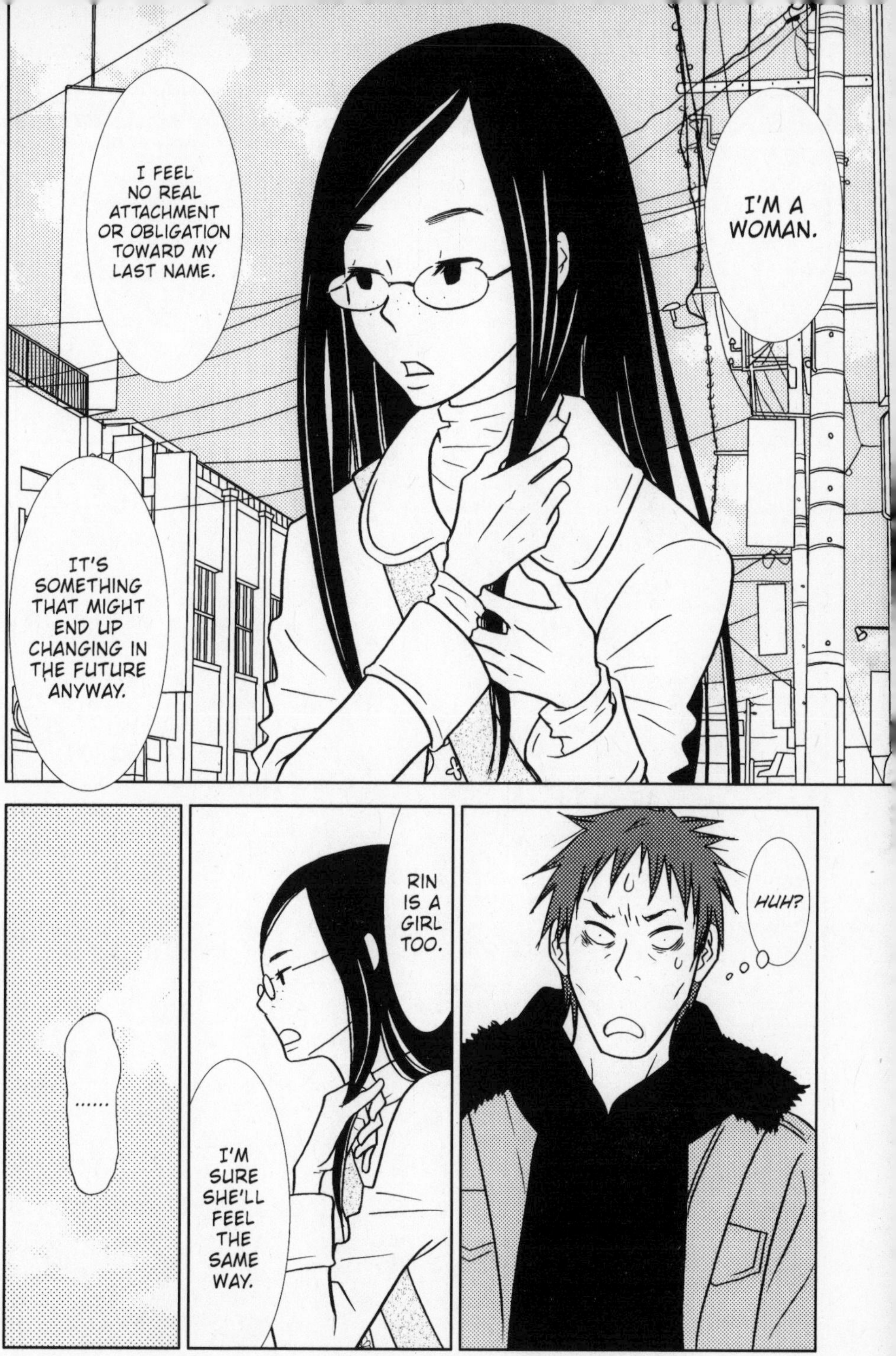
I'M A WOMAN.
I FEEL NO REAL ATTACHMENT OR OBLIGATION TOWARD MY LAST NAME.
IT'S SOMETHING THAT MIGHT END UP CHANGING IN THE FUTURE ANYWAY.
HUH?
RIN IS A GIRL TOO.
I'M SURE SHE'LL FEEL THE SAME WAY.
......

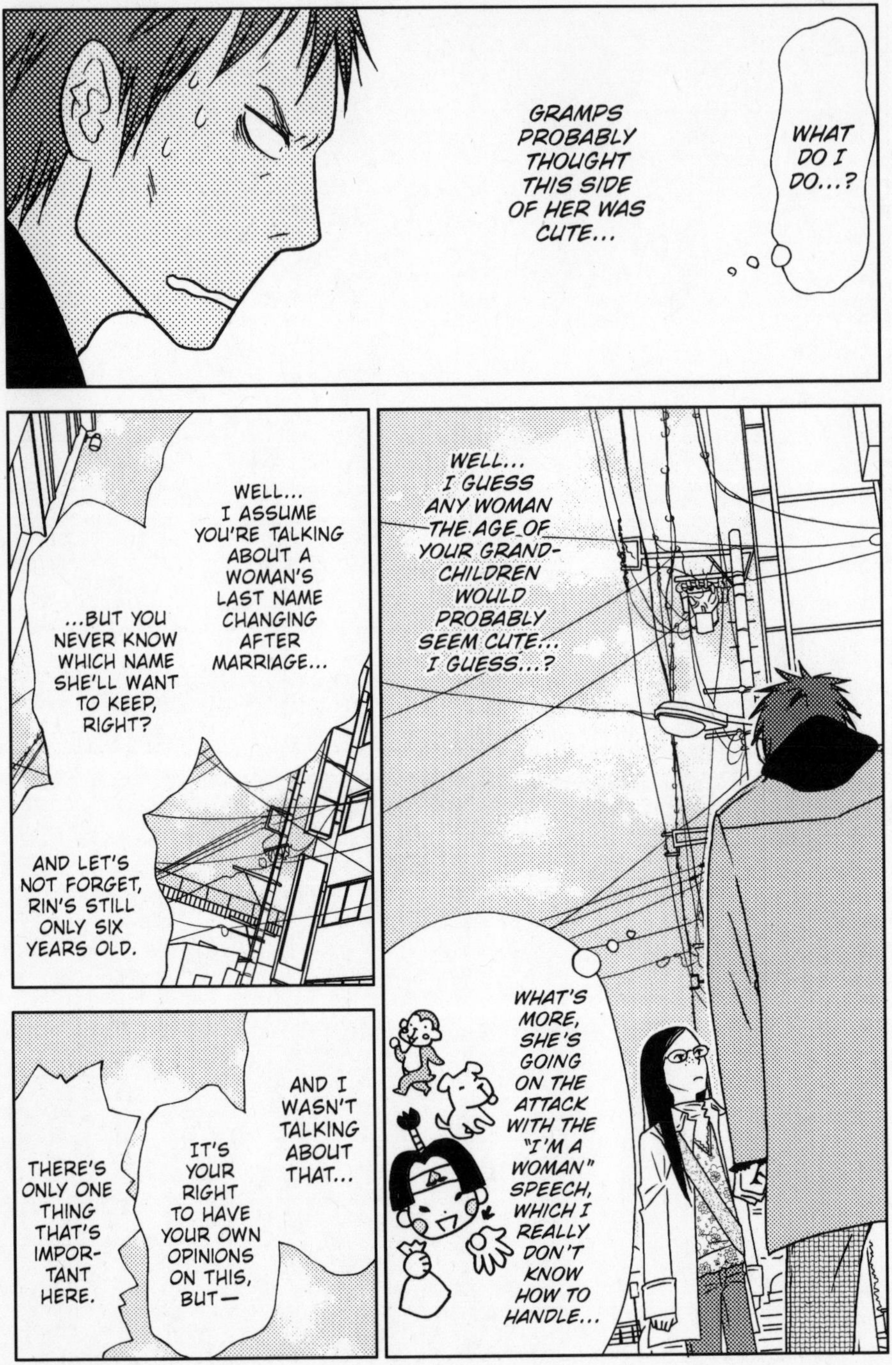
WHAT DO I DO...?
GRAMPS PROBABLY THOUGHT THIS SIDE OF HER WAS CUTE...
WELL... I GUESS ANY WOMAN THE AGE OF YOUR GRAND-CHILDREN WOULD PROBABLY SEEM CUTE... I GUESS...?
WHAT'S MORE, SHE'S GOING ON THE ATTACK WITH THE "I'M A WOMAN" SPEECH, WHICH I REALLY DON'T KNOW HOW TO HANDLE...
WELL... I ASSUME YOU'RE TALKING ABOUT A WOMAN'S LAST NAME CHANGING AFTER MARRIAGE...
...BUT YOU NEVER KNOW WHICH NAME SHE'LL WANT TO KEEP, RIGHT?
AND LET'S NOT FORGET, RIN'S STILL ONLY SIX YEARS OLD.
AND I WASN'T TALKING ABOUT THAT...
IT'S YOUR RIGHT TO HAVE YOUR OWN OPINIONS ON THIS, BUT—
THERE'S ONLY ONE THING THAT'S IMPOR-TANT HERE.

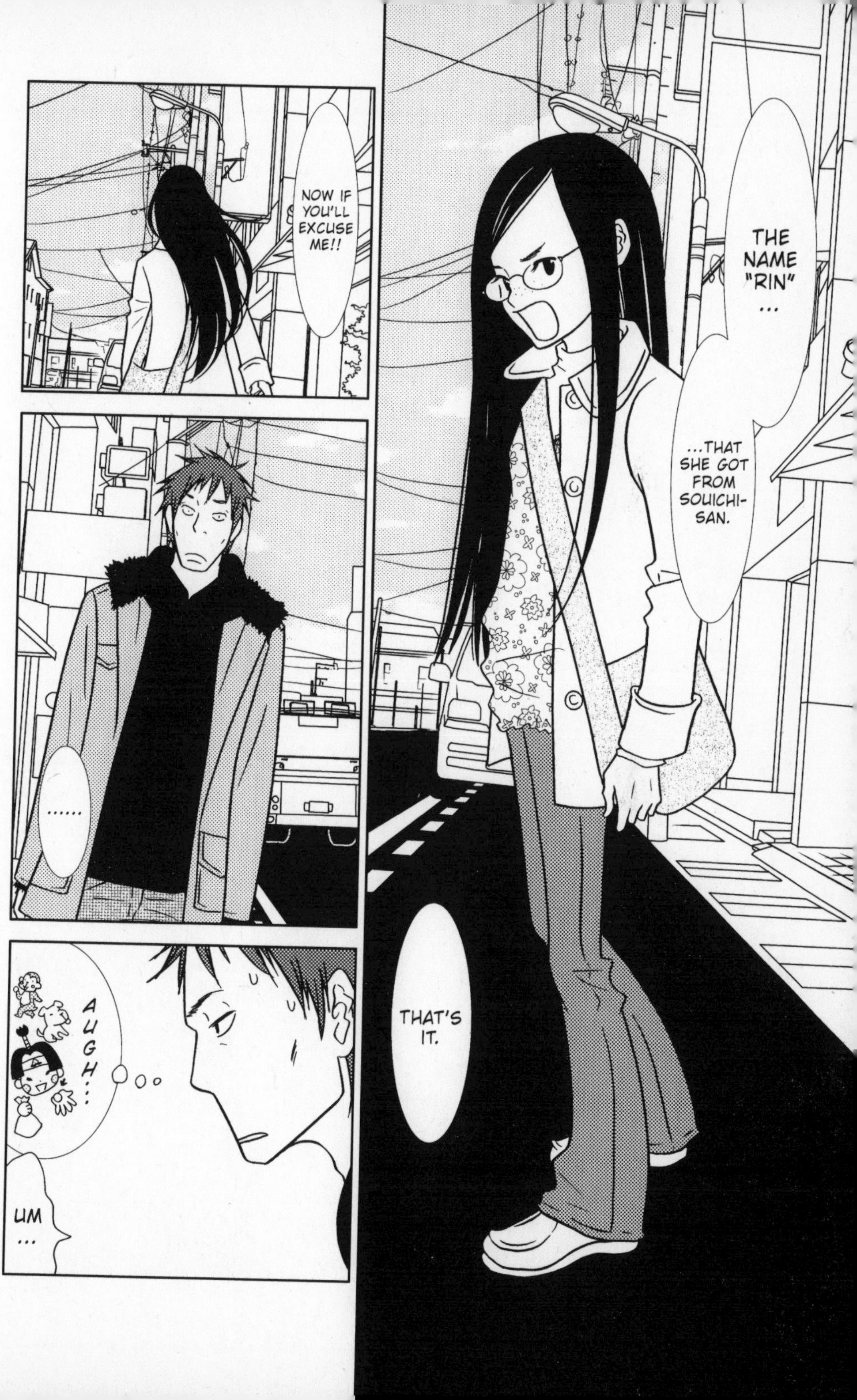
THE NAME "RIN"...
...THAT SHE GOT FROM SOUICHI-SAN.
THAT'S IT.
NOW IF YOU'LL EXCUSE ME!!
......
AUGH...
UM...

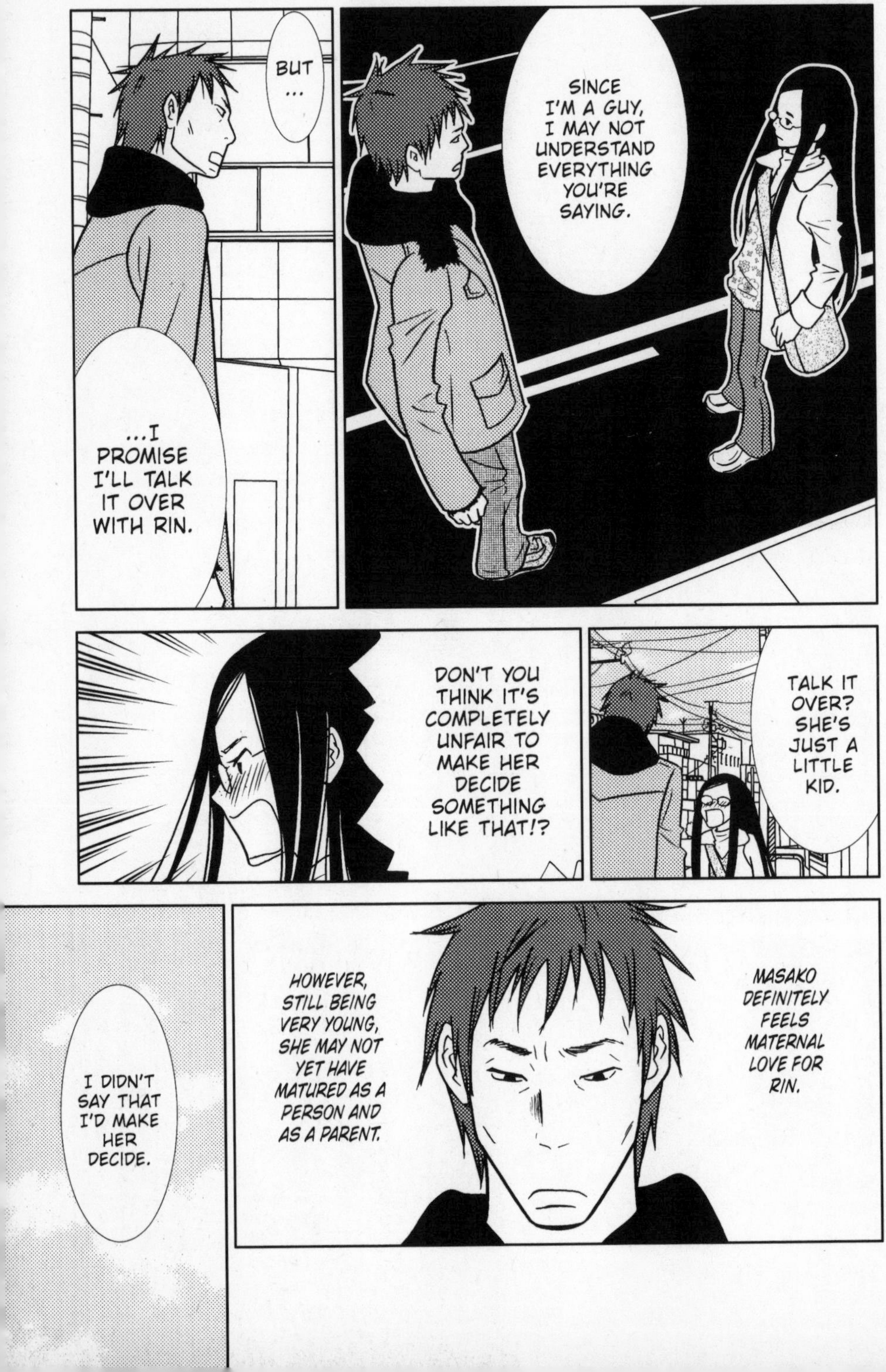
SINCE I'M A GUY, I MAY NOT UNDERSTAND EVERYTHING YOU'RE SAYING.
BUT ...
...I PROMISE I'LL TALK IT OVER WITH RIN.
TALK IT OVER? SHE'S JUST A LITTLE KID.
DON'T YOU THINK IT'S COMPLETELY UNFAIR TO MAKE HER DECIDE SOMETHING LIKE THAT!?
MASAKO DEFINITELY FEELS MATERNAL LOVE FOR RIN.
HOWEVER, STILL BEING VERY YOUNG, SHE MAY NOT YET HAVE MATURED AS A PERSON AND AS A PARENT.
I DIDN'T SAY THAT I'D MAKE HER DECIDE.

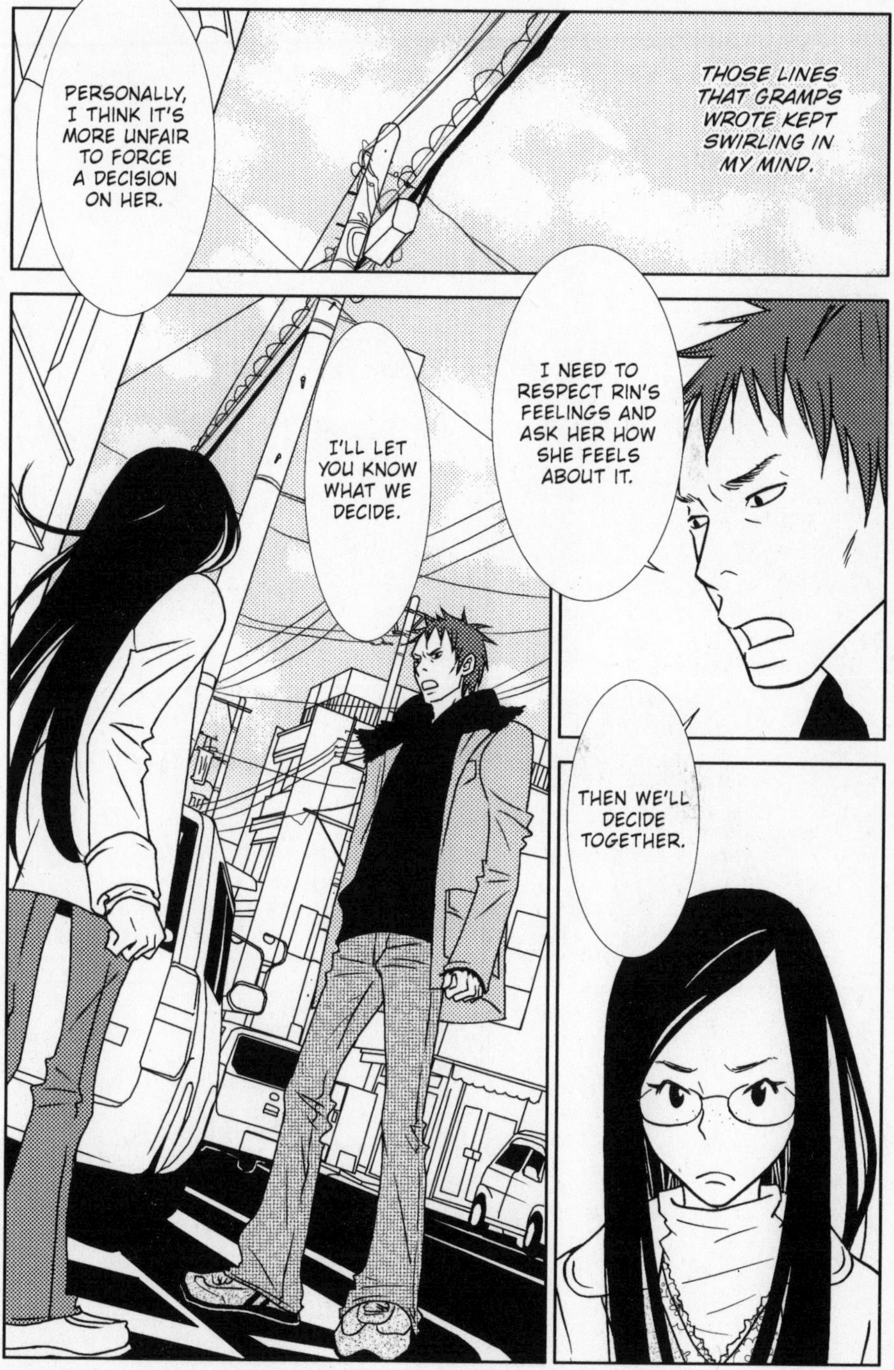
THOSE LINES THAT GRAMPS WROTE KEPT SWIRLING IN MY MIND.
PERSONALLY, I THINK IT'S MORE UNFAIR TO FORCE A DECISION ON HER.
I NEED TO RESPECT RIN'S FEELINGS AND ASK HER HOW SHE FEELS ABOUT IT.
I'LL LET YOU KNOW WHAT WE DECIDE.
THEN WE'LL DECIDE TOGETHER.

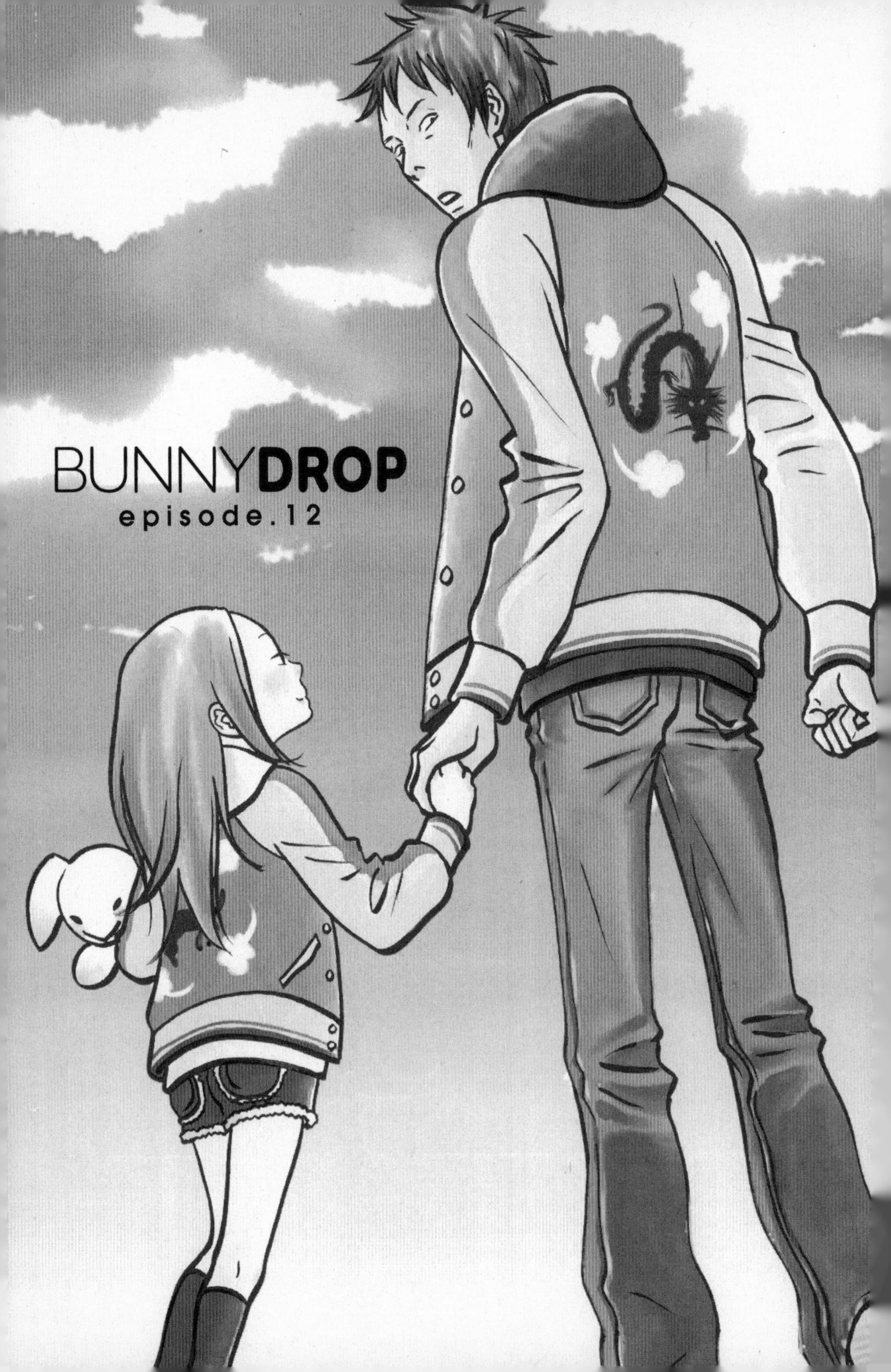
BUNNYDROP
episode.12

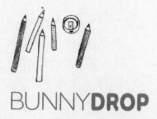

BUNNY**DROP**

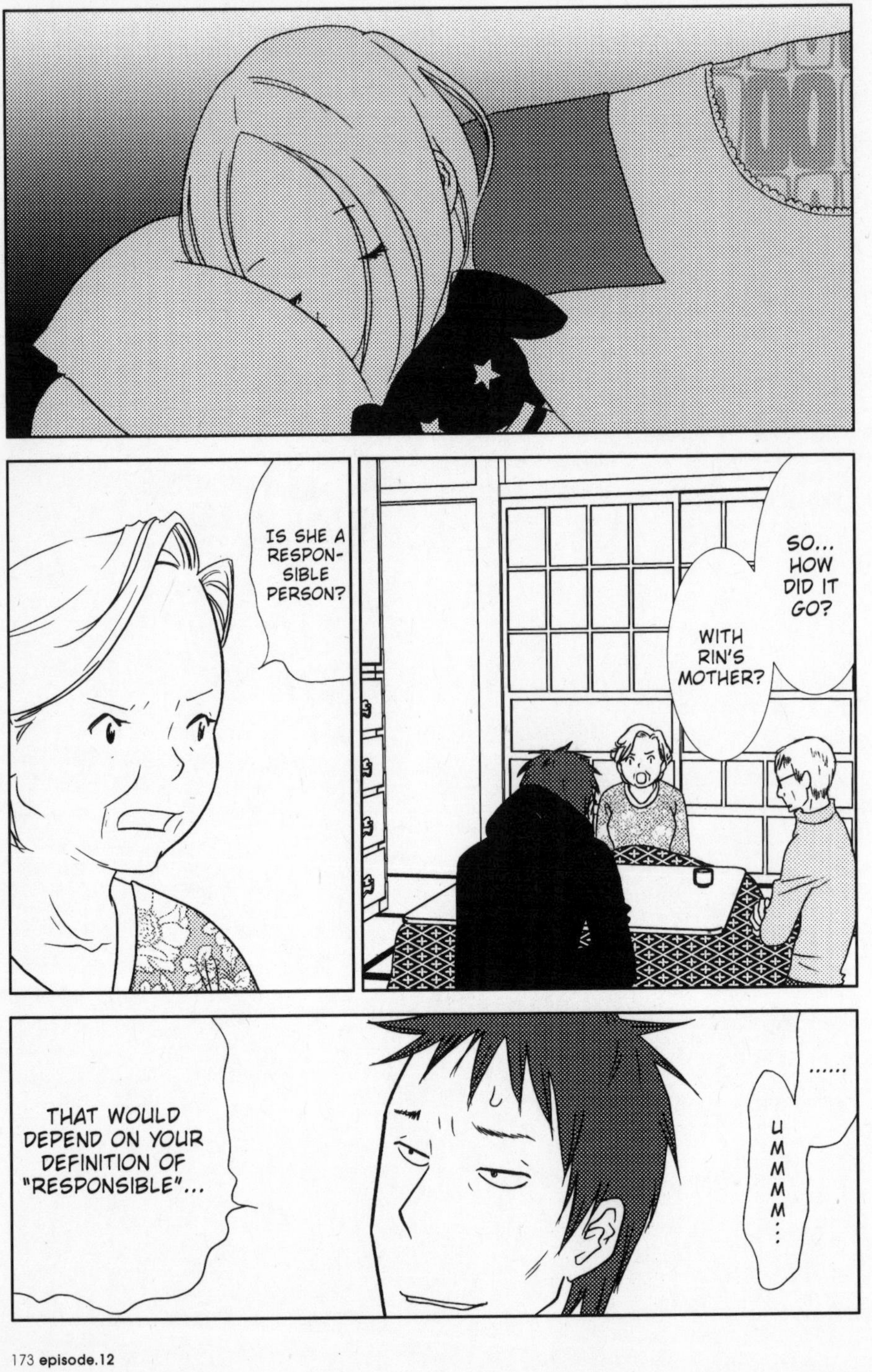
SO... HOW DID IT GO?
WITH RIN'S MOTHER?
IS SHE A RESPON-SIBLE PERSON?
...... UMMMM...
THAT WOULD DEPEND ON YOUR DEFINITION OF "RESPONSIBLE"...

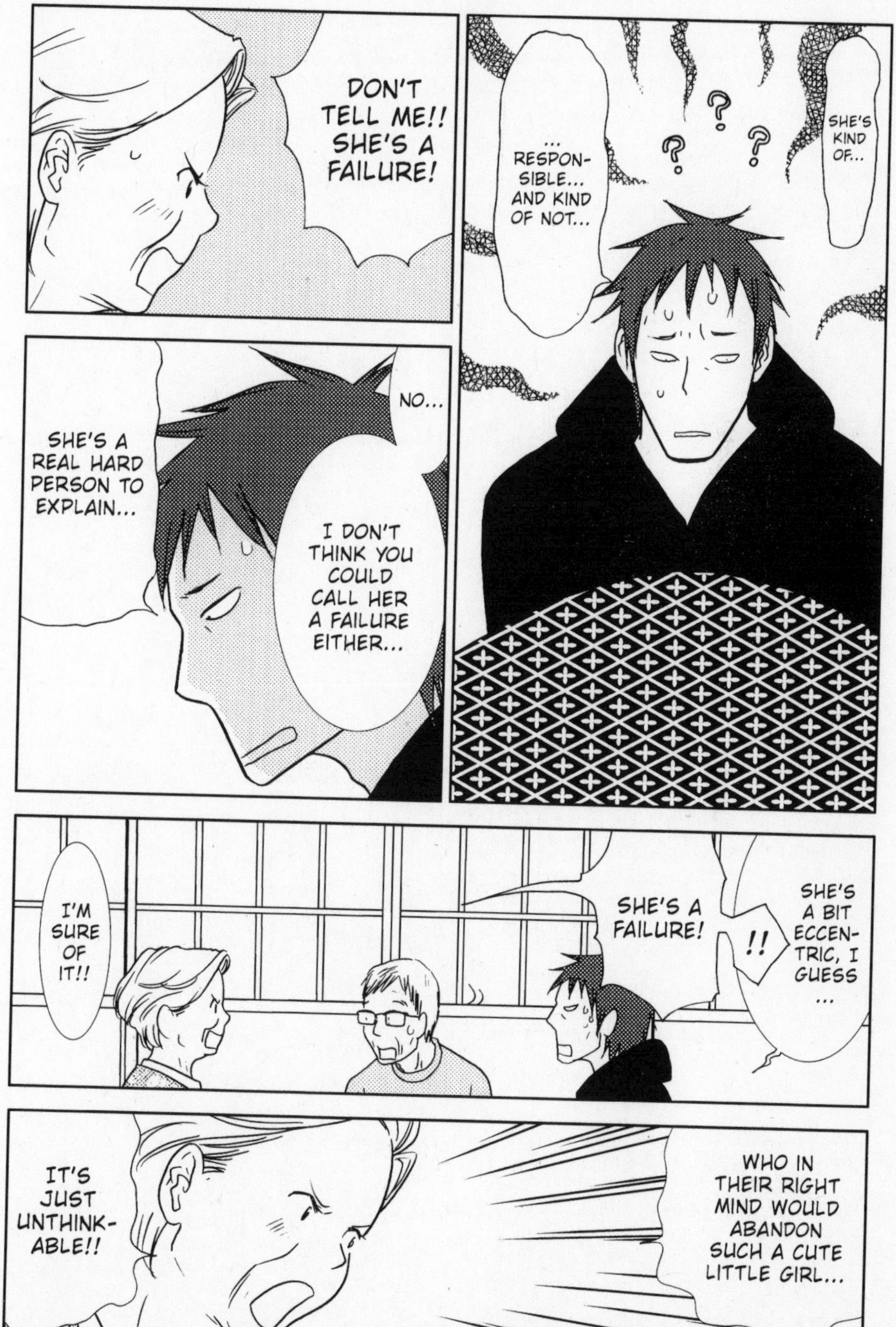
SHE'S KIND OF...
... RESPONSIBLE... AND KIND OF NOT...
DON'T TELL ME!! SHE'S A FAILURE!
NO...
I DON'T THINK YOU COULD CALL HER A FAILURE EITHER...
SHE'S A REAL HARD PERSON TO EXPLAIN...
SHE'S A BIT ECCENTRIC, I GUESS ...
!!
SHE'S A FAILURE!
I'M SURE OF IT!!
WHO IN THEIR RIGHT MIND WOULD ABANDON SUCH A CUTE LITTLE GIRL...
IT'S JUST UNTHINKABLE!!

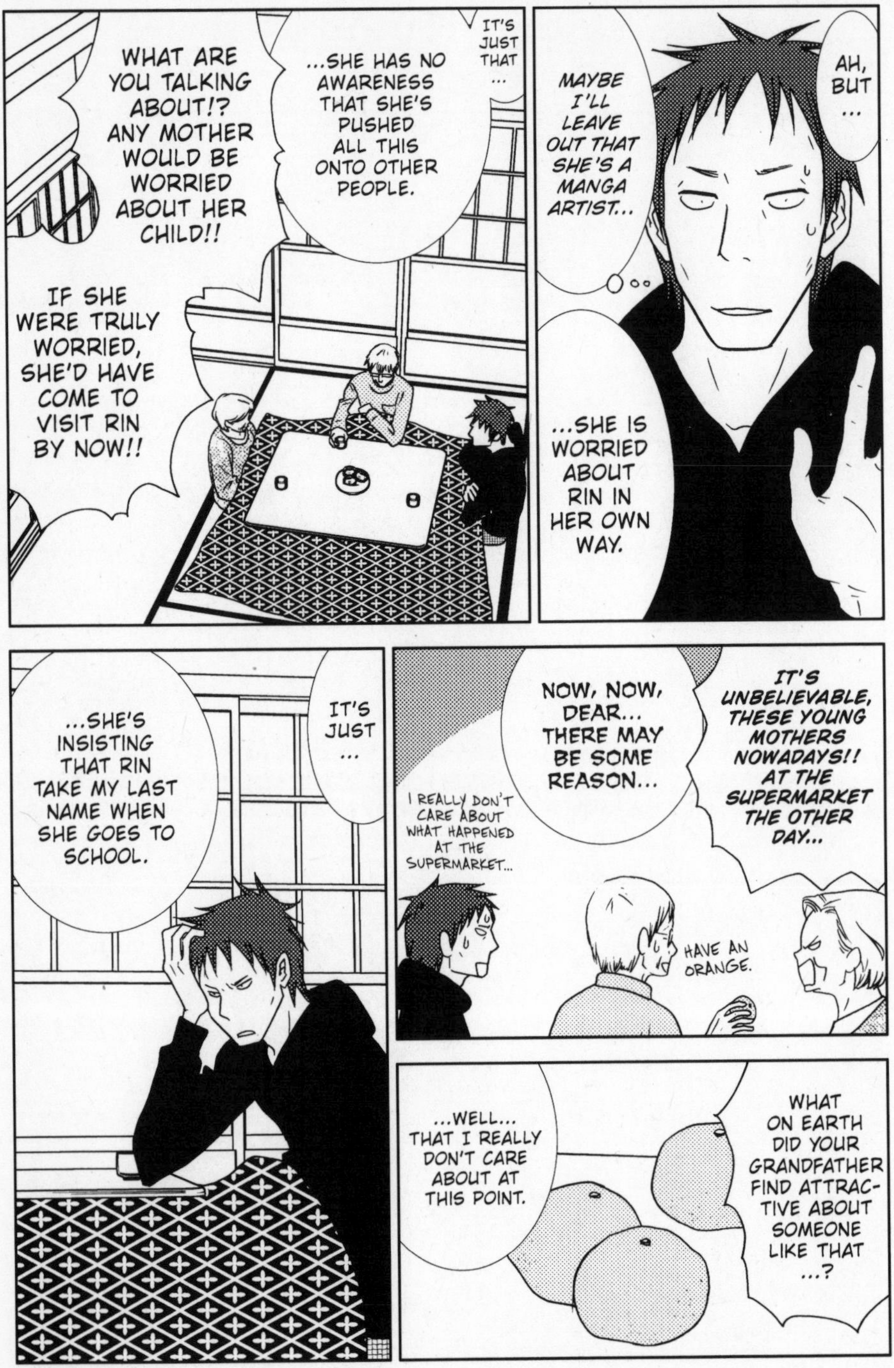
AH, BUT ...
MAYBE I'LL LEAVE OUT THAT SHE'S A MANGA ARTIST...
...SHE IS WORRIED ABOUT RIN IN HER OWN WAY.
IT'S JUST THAT ...
...SHE HAS NO AWARENESS THAT SHE'S PUSHED ALL THIS ONTO OTHER PEOPLE.
WHAT ARE YOU TALKING ABOUT!? ANY MOTHER WOULD BE WORRIED ABOUT HER CHILD!!
IF SHE WERE TRULY WORRIED, SHE'D HAVE COME TO VISIT RIN BY NOW!!
IT'S UNBELIEVABLE, THESE YOUNG MOTHERS NOWADAYS!! AT THE SUPERMARKET THE OTHER DAY...
NOW, NOW, DEAR... THERE MAY BE SOME REASON...
I REALLY DON'T CARE ABOUT WHAT HAPPENED AT THE SUPERMARKET...
HAVE AN ORANGE.
WHAT ON EARTH DID YOUR GRANDFATHER FIND ATTRACTIVE ABOUT SOMEONE LIKE THAT ...?
...WELL... THAT I REALLY DON'T CARE ABOUT AT THIS POINT.
IT'S JUST ...
...SHE'S INSISTING THAT RIN TAKE MY LAST NAME WHEN SHE GOES TO SCHOOL.

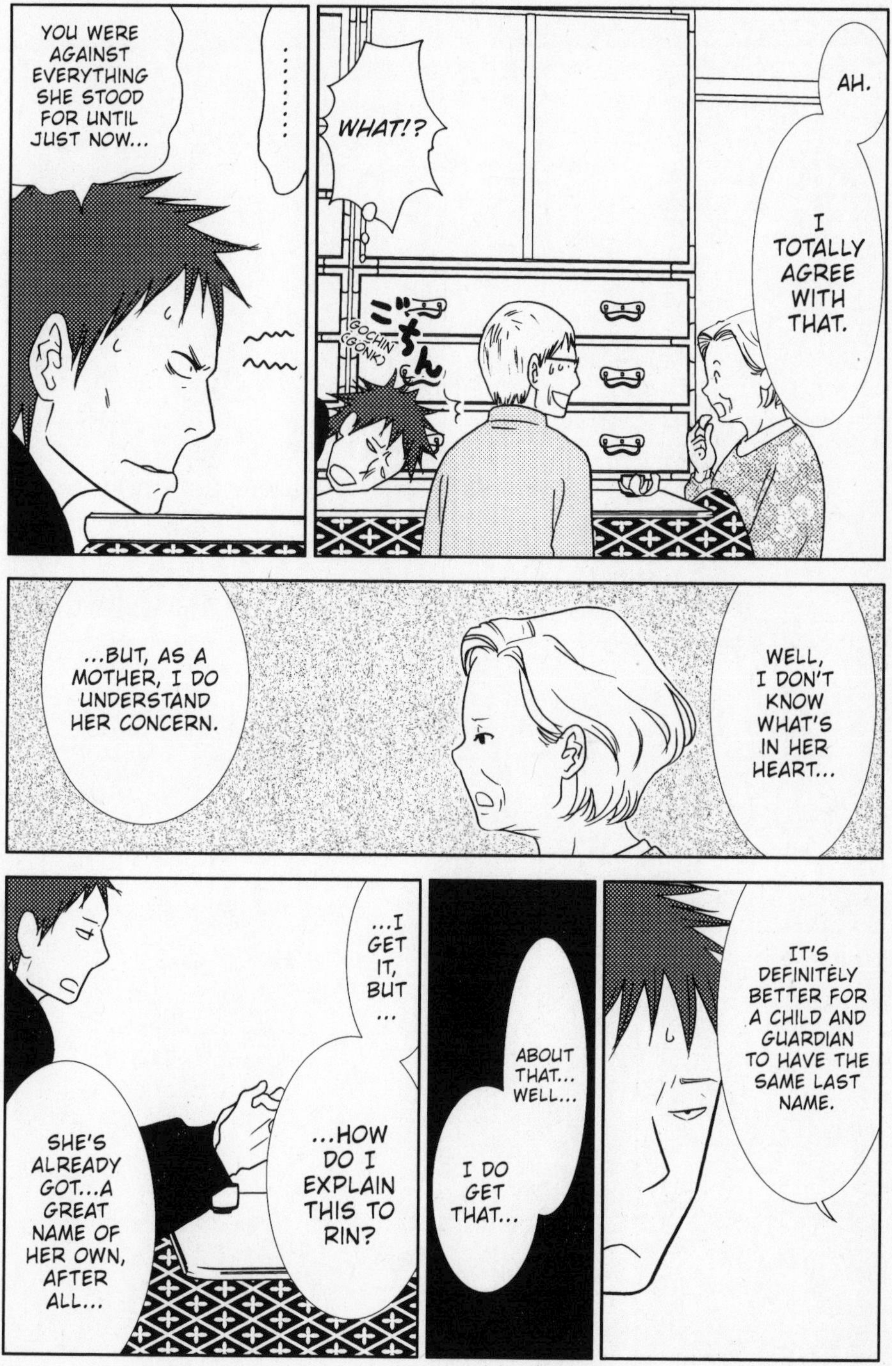
AH.
I TOTALLY AGREE WITH THAT.
WHAT!?
ごちん
GOCHIN (GONK)
YOU WERE AGAINST EVERYTHING SHE STOOD FOR UNTIL JUST NOW...
......
WELL, I DON'T KNOW WHAT'S IN HER HEART...
...BUT, AS A MOTHER, I DO UNDERSTAND HER CONCERN.
IT'S DEFINITELY BETTER FOR A CHILD AND GUARDIAN TO HAVE THE SAME LAST NAME.
ABOUT THAT... WELL...
I DO GET THAT...
...I GET IT, BUT ...
...HOW DO I EXPLAIN THIS TO RIN?
SHE'S ALREADY GOT...A GREAT NAME OF HER OWN, AFTER ALL...

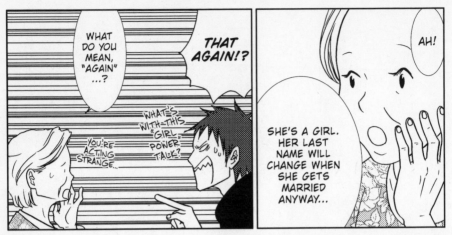

AH!
SHE'S A GIRL. HER LAST NAME WILL CHANGE WHEN SHE GETS MARRIED ANYWAY...
THAT AGAIN!?
WHAT DO YOU MEAN, "AGAIN" ...?
WHAT'S WITH THIS "GIRL POWER" TALK?
YOU'RE ACTING STRANGE...
IF SHE'S GOING TO GET TEASED OR BULLIED BECAUSE OF HER NAME...
...SHE'LL BE BETTER OFF USING OUR LAST NAME AT SCHOOL.
IS IT REALLY THAT EASY TO SWITCH LIKE THAT?
IF YOU DON'T, THERE'LL BE A LOT MORE ISSUES WHEN SHE GETS TO ELEMENTARY SCHOOL...
......
THAT'S JUST HOW THINGS ARE.

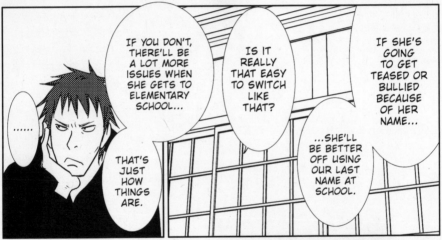

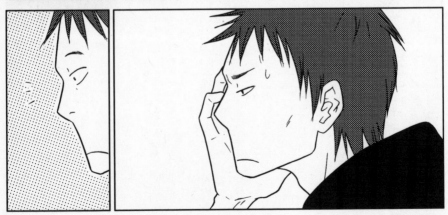

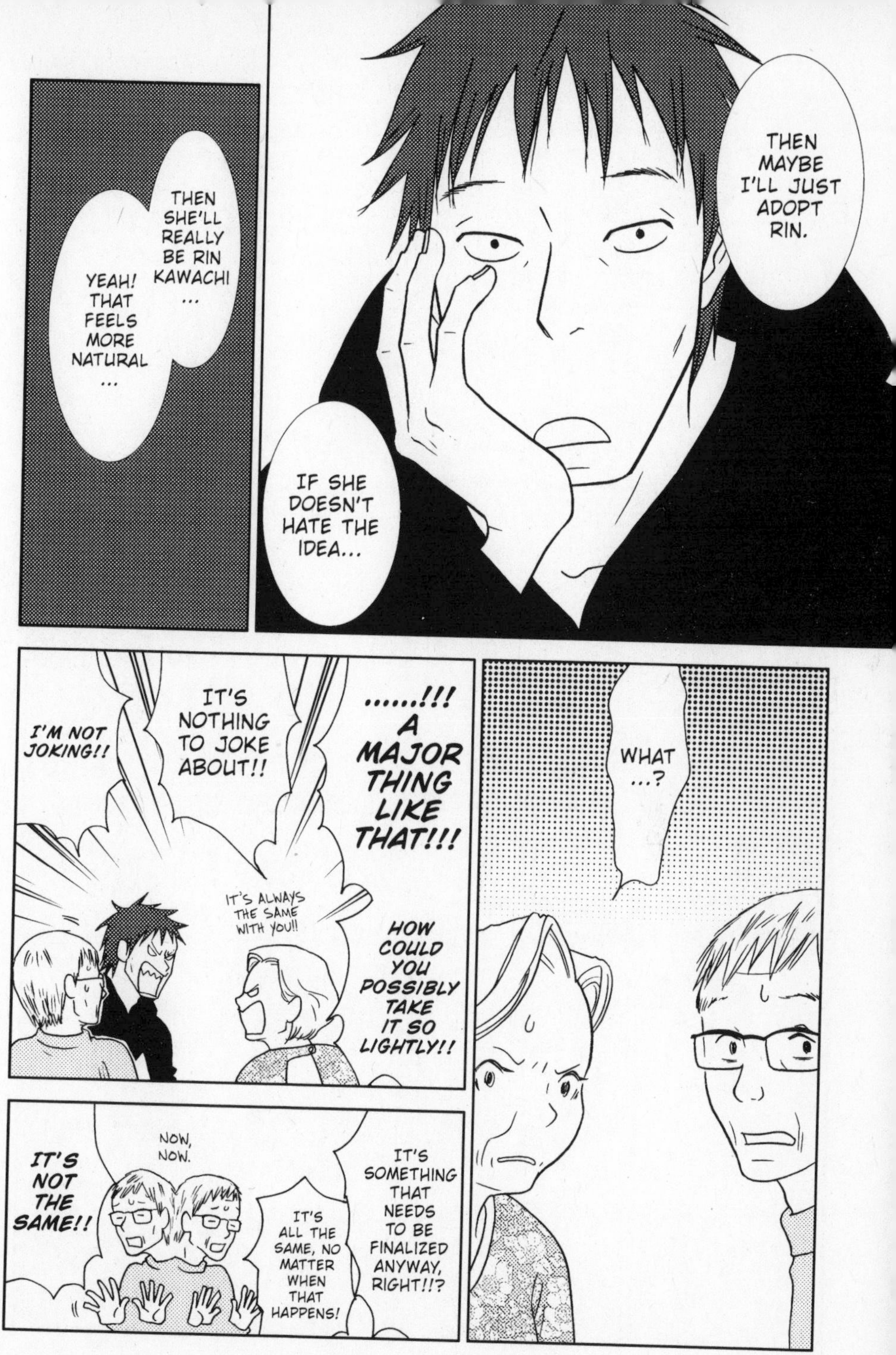
THEN MAYBE I'LL JUST ADOPT RIN.
IF SHE DOESN'T HATE THE IDEA...
THEN SHE'LL REALLY BE RIN KAWACHI ...
YEAH! THAT FEELS MORE NATURAL ...
WHAT ...?
......!!! A MAJOR THING LIKE THAT!!!
IT'S NOTHING TO JOKE ABOUT!!
I'M NOT JOKING!!
HOW COULD YOU POSSIBLY TAKE IT SO LIGHTLY!!
IT'S ALWAYS THE SAME WITH YOU!!
IT'S SOMETHING THAT NEEDS TO BE FINALIZED ANYWAY, RIGHT!!?
IT'S ALL THE SAME, NO MATTER WHEN THAT HAPPENS!
NOW, NOW.
IT'S NOT THE SAME!!

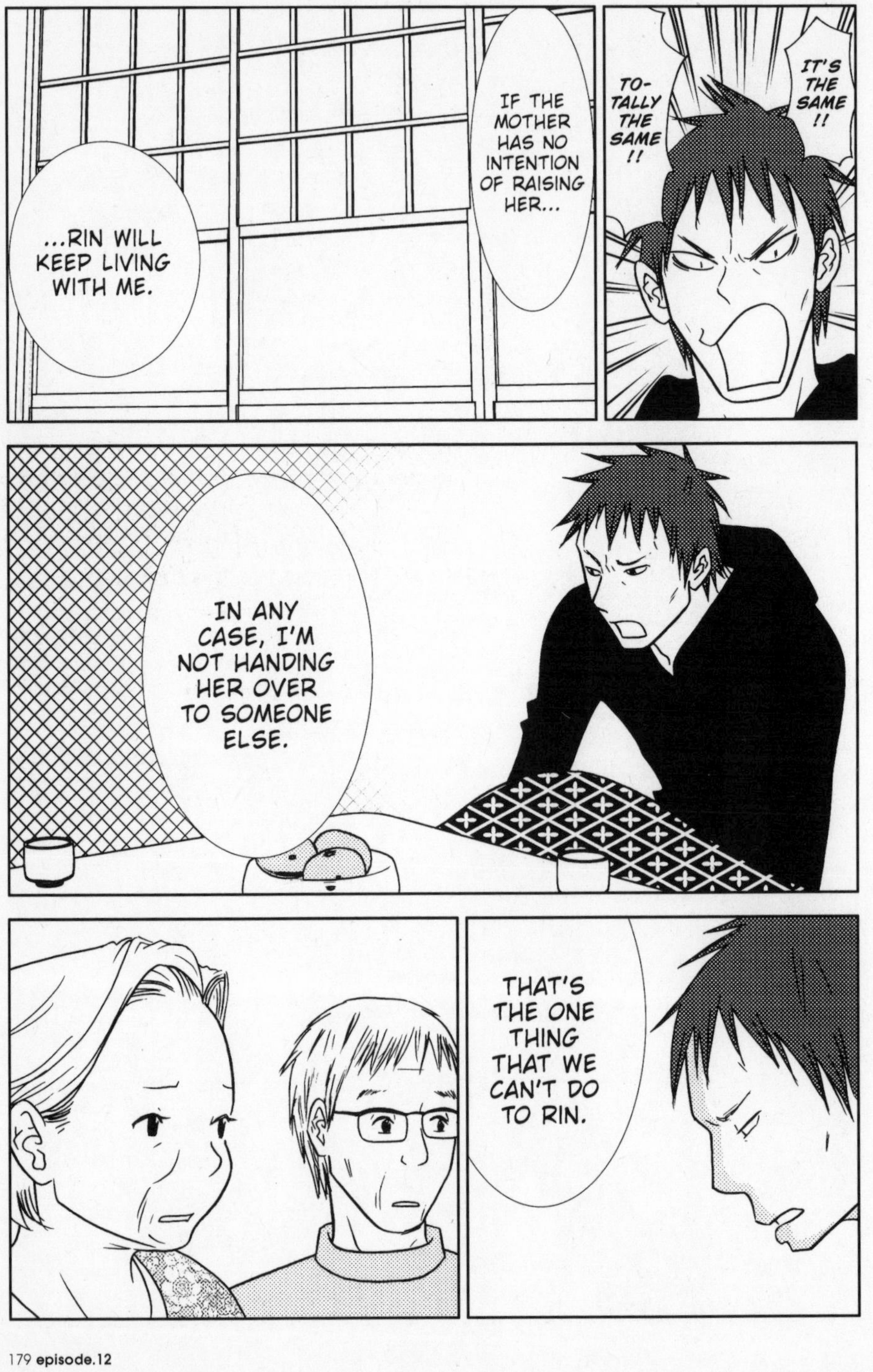
IT'S THE SAME !!
TO-TALLY THE SAME !!
IF THE MOTHER HAS NO INTENTION OF RAISING HER...
...RIN WILL KEEP LIVING WITH ME.
IN ANY CASE, I'M NOT HANDING HER OVER TO SOMEONE ELSE.
THAT'S THE ONE THING THAT WE CAN'T DO TO RIN.

I...
...CAN BUCKLE DOWN ON THIS, FOR RIN'S SAKE.
WITH THAT SAID...
SHAKA (BRUSH) シャカ
SHAKA シャカ
SHAKA しゃか
しゃか SHAKA

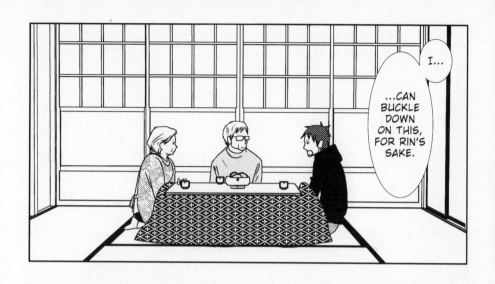

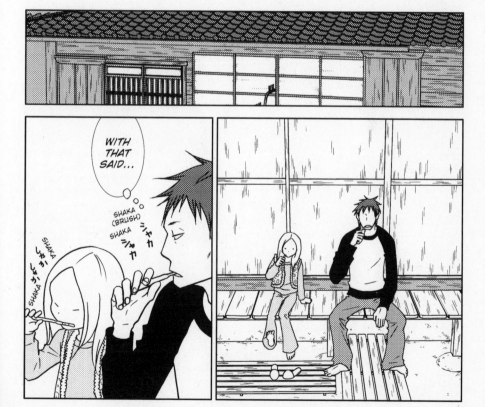

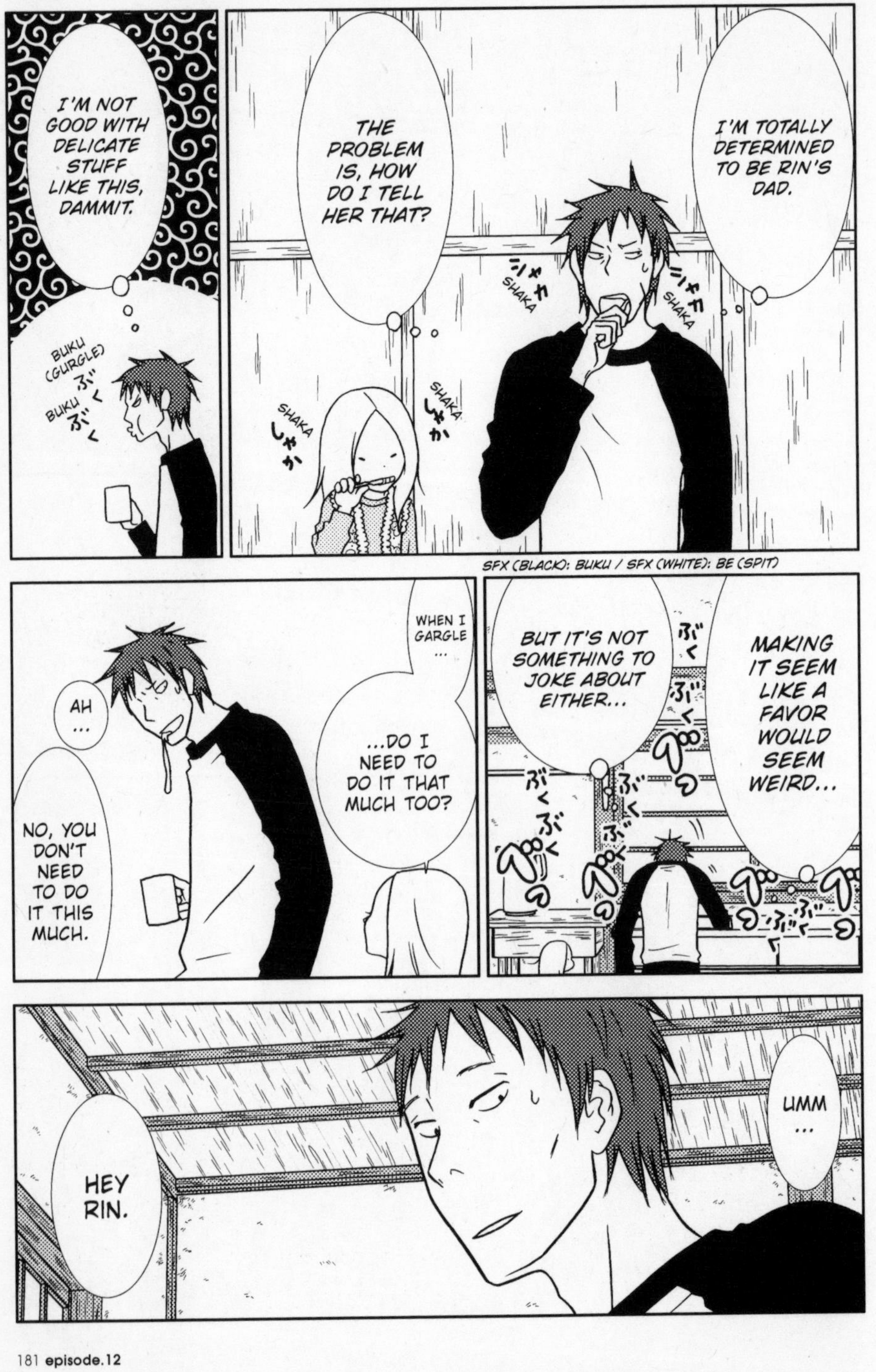
I'M TOTALLY DETERMINED TO BE RIN'S DAD.
シャカ SHAKA
シャカ SHAKA
THE PROBLEM IS, HOW DO I TELL HER THAT?
SHAKA しゃか
SHAKA しゃか
I'M NOT GOOD WITH DELICATE STUFF LIKE THIS, DAMMIT.
BUKU (GURGLE) ぶく
BUKU ぶく
SFX (BLACK): BUKU / SFX (WHITE): BE (SPIT)
MAKING IT SEEM LIKE A FAVOR WOULD SEEM WEIRD...
BUT IT'S NOT SOMETHING TO JOKE ABOUT EITHER...
WHEN I GARGLE ...
...DO I NEED TO DO IT THAT MUCH TOO?
AH ...
NO, YOU DON'T NEED TO DO IT THIS MUCH.
UMM ...
HEY RIN.

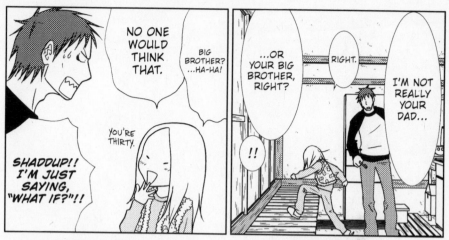

I'M NOT REALLY YOUR DAD...
RIGHT.
...OR YOUR BIG BROTHER, RIGHT?
!!
BIG BROTHER? ...HA-HA!
NO ONE WOULD THINK THAT.
YOU'RE THIRTY.
SHADDUP!! I'M JUST SAYING, "WHAT IF?"!!
MY POINT IS...SO WHAT AM I?
DAIKICHI!!
THAT'S MY NAME ...
......
LISTEN, THIS IS ONLY IF YOU WANNA, BUT...
WHAT I WANT TO SAY IS... WELL...
...I COULD ...

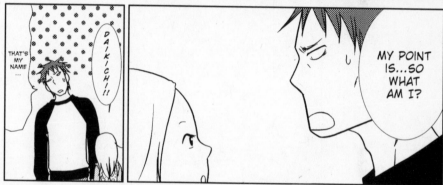

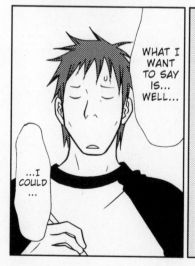

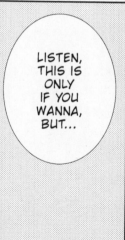

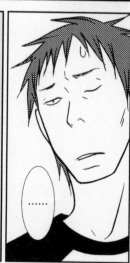

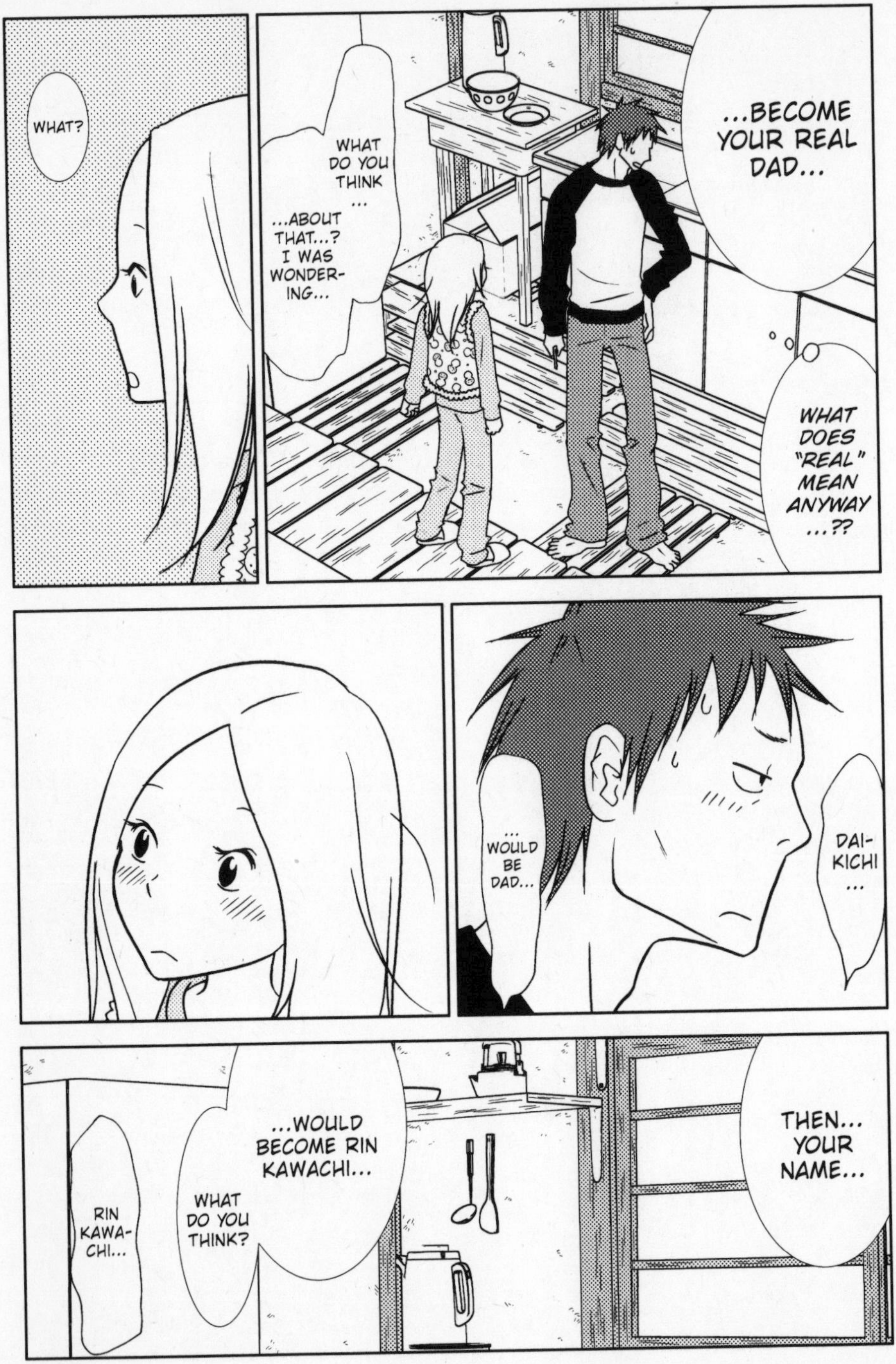
...BECOME YOUR REAL DAD...
WHAT DO YOU THINK ... ...ABOUT THAT...? I WAS WONDERING...
WHAT DOES "REAL" MEAN ANYWAY ...??
WHAT?
DAI-KICHI ...
... WOULD BE DAD...
THEN... YOUR NAME...
...WOULD BECOME RIN KAWACHI...
WHAT DO YOU THINK?
RIN KAWA-CHI...

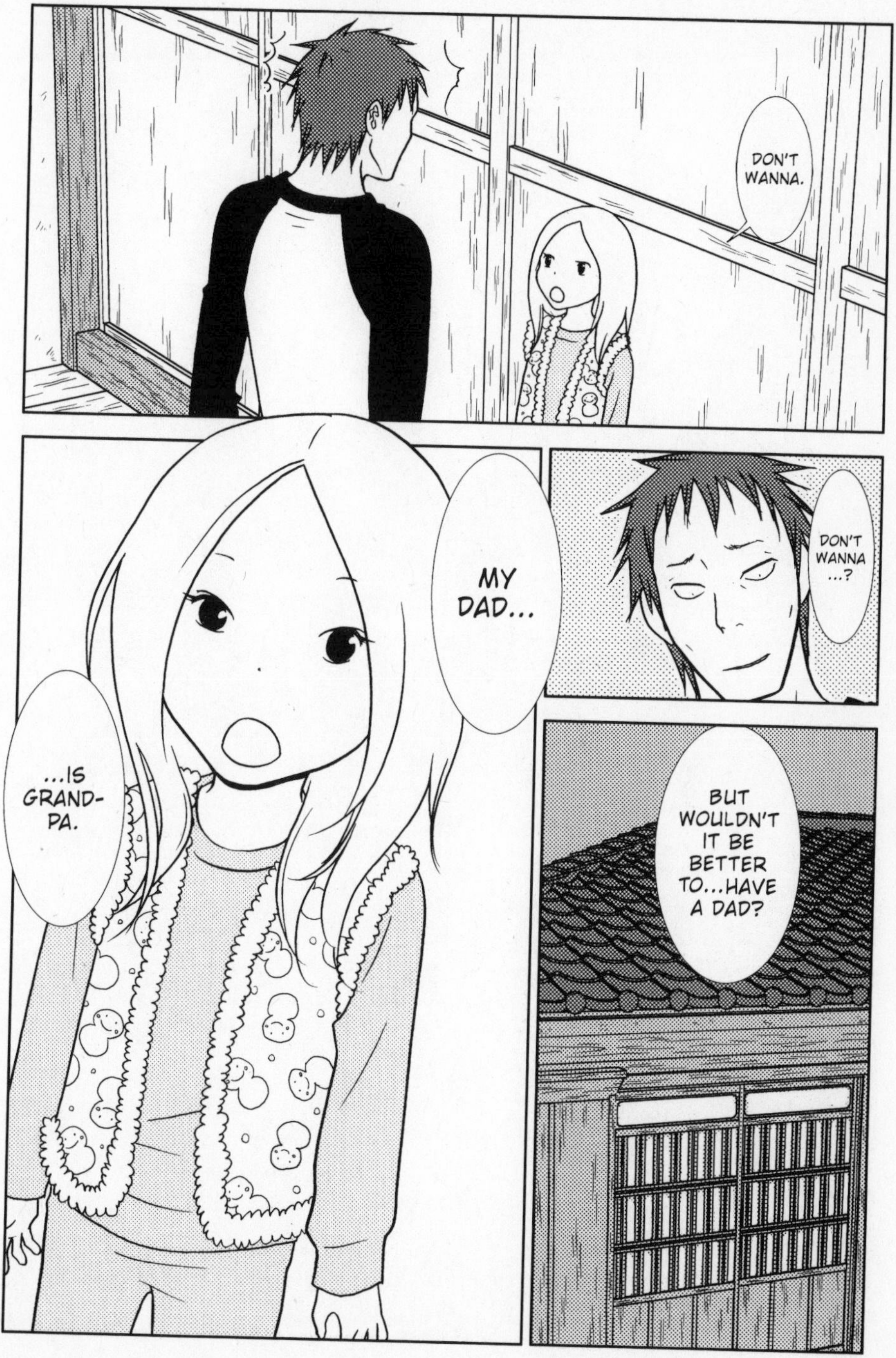
DON'T WANNA.
DON'T WANNA ...?
BUT WOULDN'T IT BE BETTER TO...HAVE A DAD?
MY DAD...
...IS GRAND-PA.

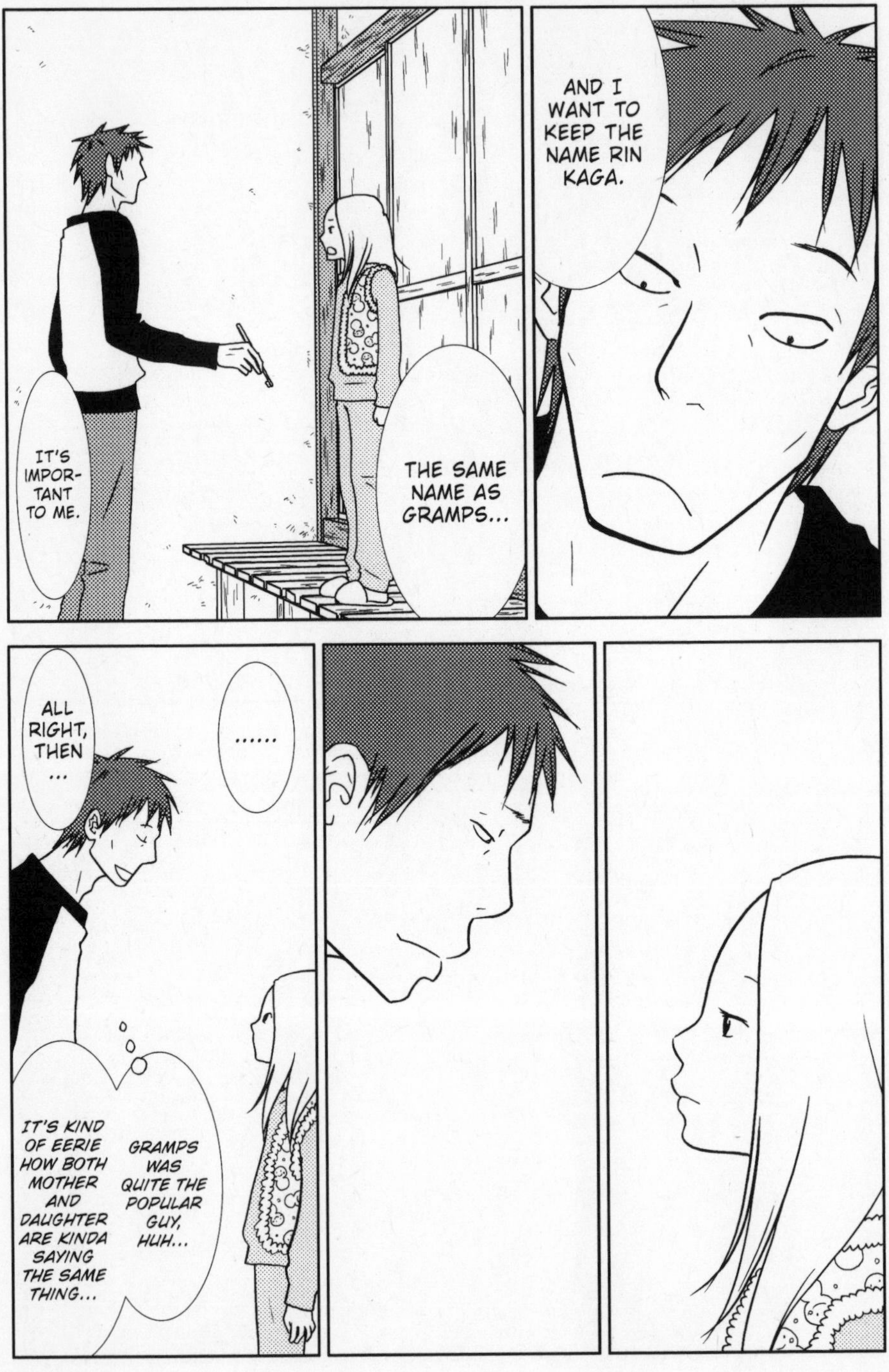
AND I WANT TO KEEP THE NAME RIN KAGA.
THE SAME NAME AS GRAMPS...
IT'S IMPOR-TANT TO ME.
......
ALL RIGHT, THEN ...
GRAMPS WAS QUITE THE POPULAR GUY, HUH...
IT'S KIND OF EERIE HOW BOTH MOTHER AND DAUGHTER ARE KINDA SAYING THE SAME THING...

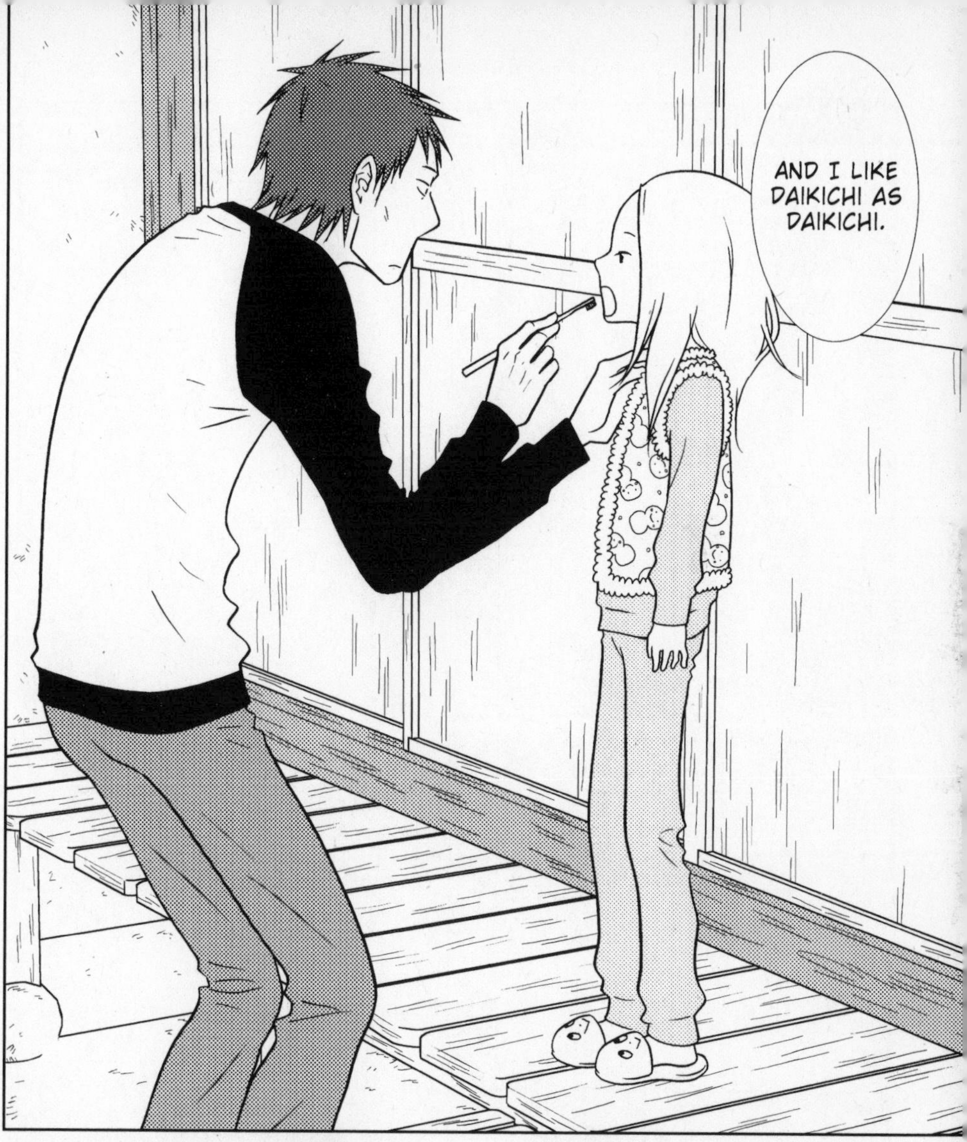
AND I LIKE DAIKICHI AS DAIKICHI.
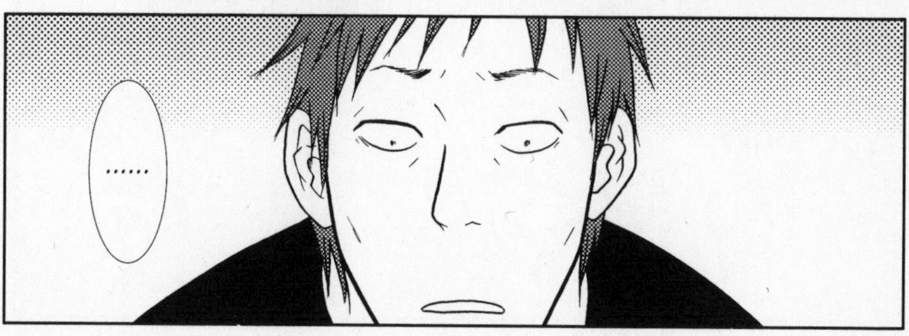
......

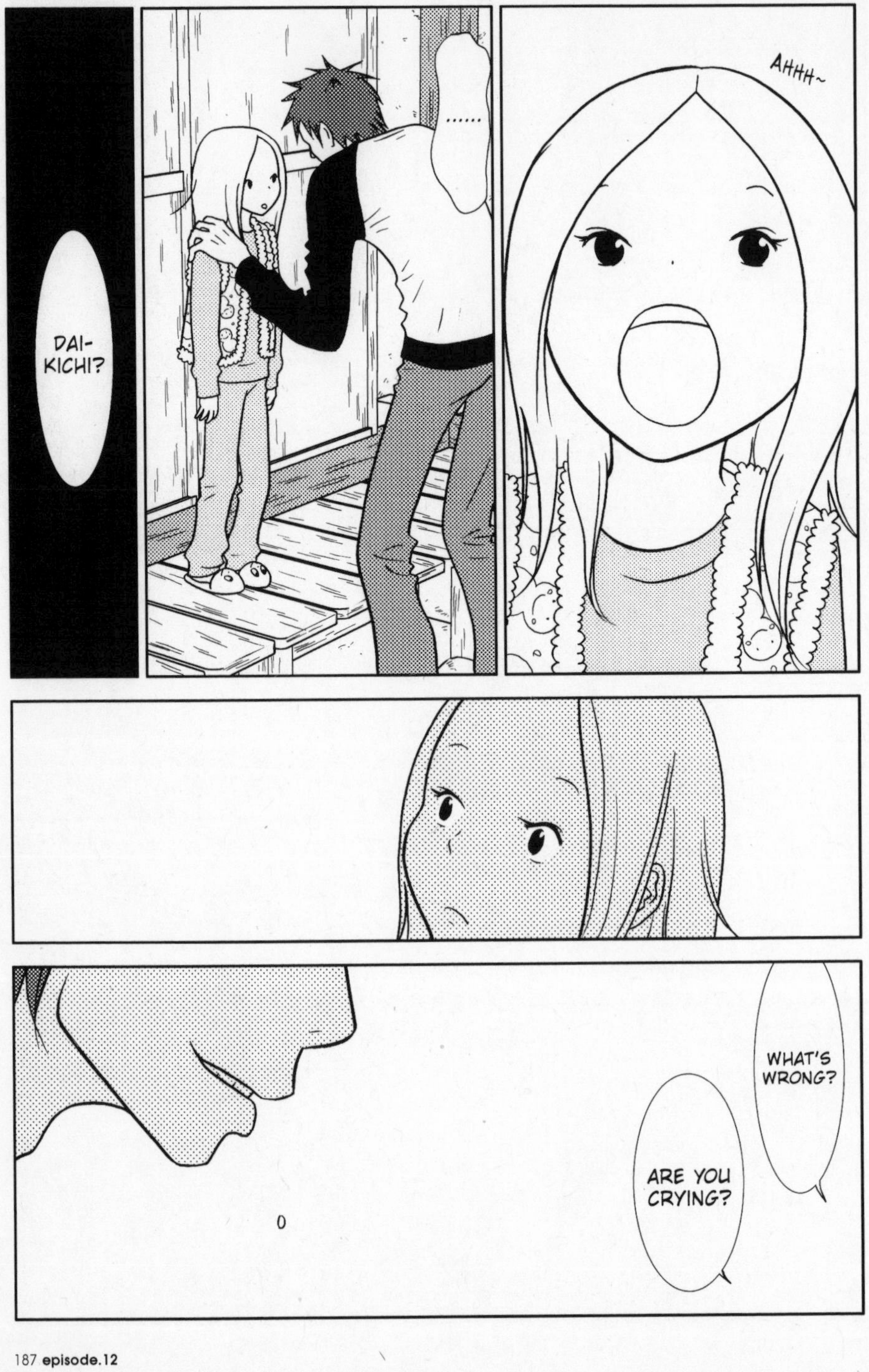
AHHH~
......
DAI-KICHI?
WHAT'S WRONG?
ARE YOU CRYING?

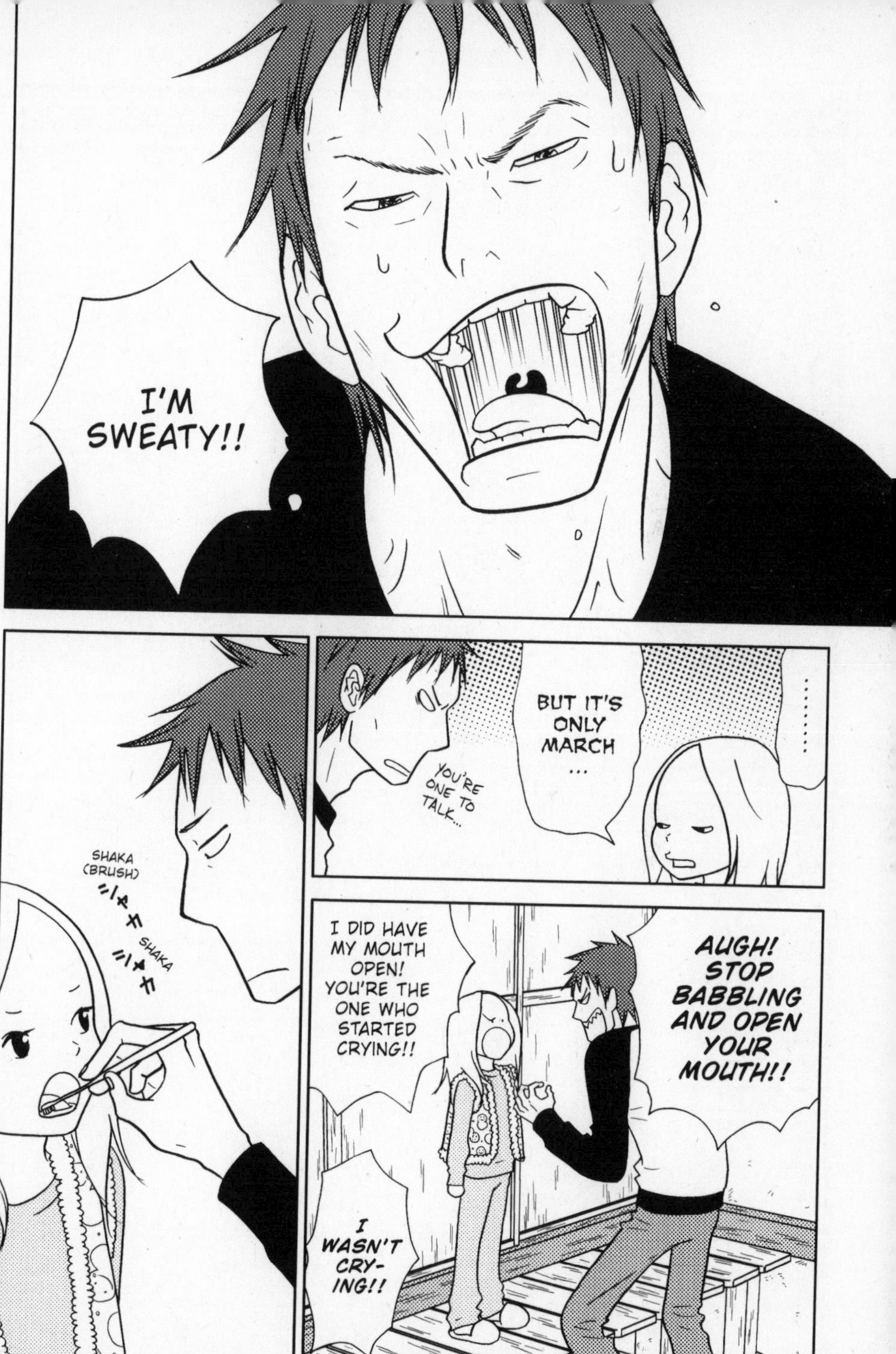
I'M SWEATY!!
......
BUT IT'S ONLY MARCH ...
YOU'RE ONE TO TALK...
AUGH! STOP BABBLING AND OPEN YOUR MOUTH!!
I DID HAVE MY MOUTH OPEN! YOU'RE THE ONE WHO STARTED CRYING!!
I WASN'T CRY-ING!!
SHAKA (BRUSH)
シャカ
SHAKA
シャカ

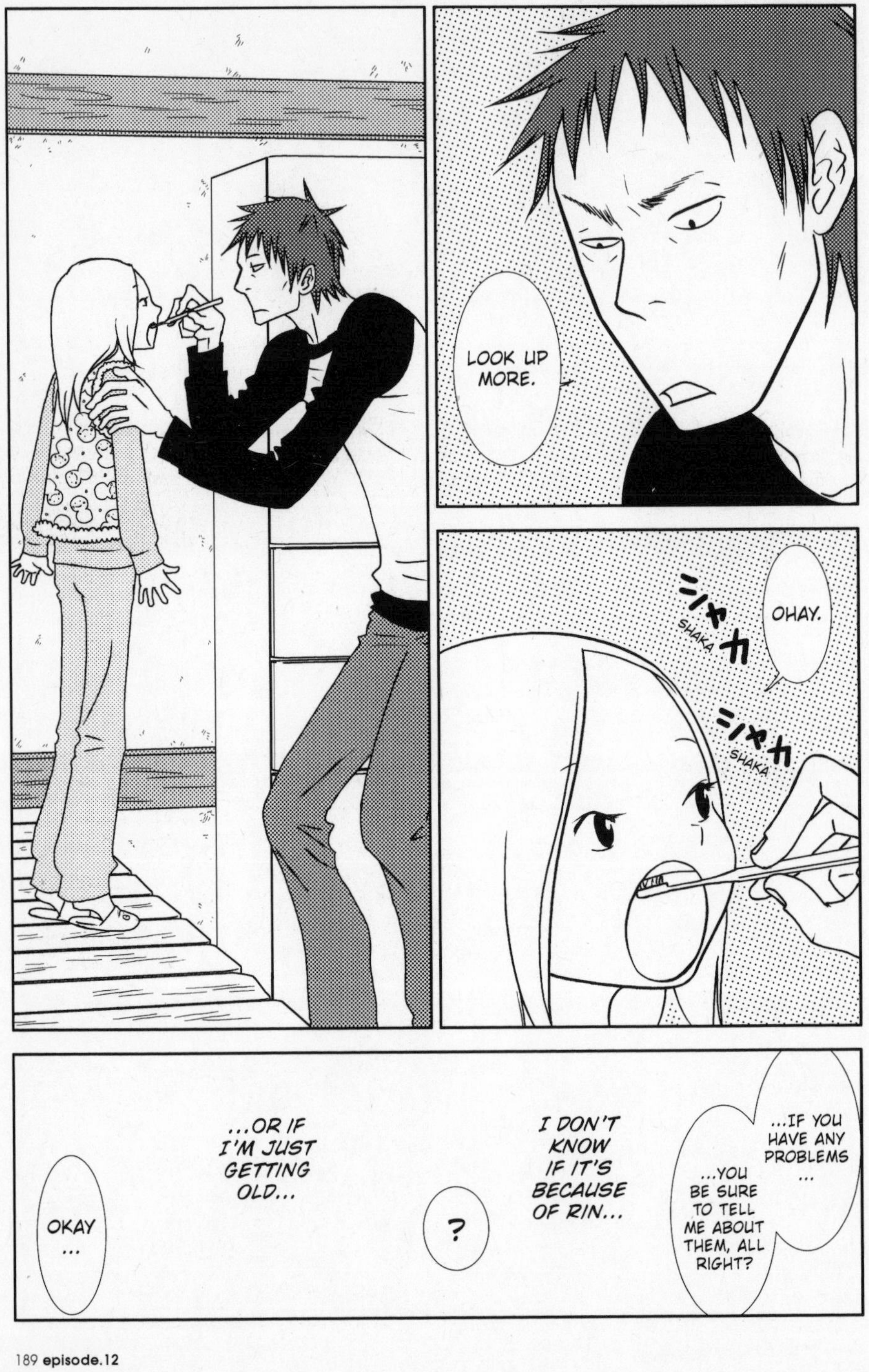
LOOK UP MORE.
シャカ SHAKA
OHAY.
シャカ SHAKA
...IF YOU HAVE ANY PROBLEMS ...
...YOU BE SURE TO TELL ME ABOUT THEM, ALL RIGHT?
I DON'T KNOW IF IT'S BECAUSE OF RIN...
?
...OR IF I'M JUST GETTING OLD...
OKAY ...

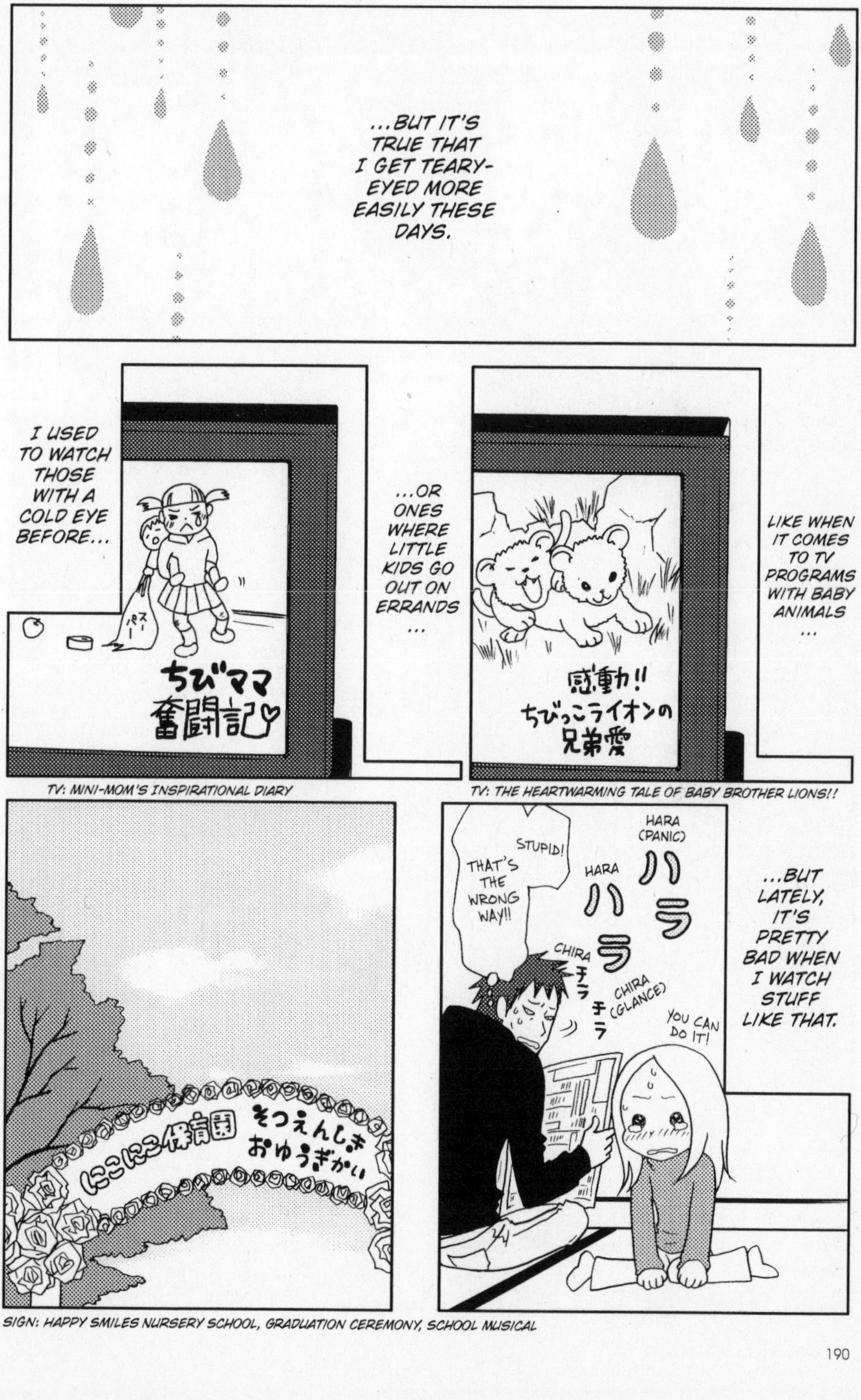
...BUT IT'S TRUE THAT I GET TEARY-EYED MORE EASILY THESE DAYS.
LIKE WHEN IT COMES TO TV PROGRAMS WITH BABY ANIMALS...
感動!! ちびっこライオンの兄弟愛
TV: THE HEARTWARMING TALE OF BABY BROTHER LIONS!!
...OR ONES WHERE LITTLE KIDS GO OUT ON ERRANDS...
I USED TO WATCH THOSE WITH A COLD EYE BEFORE...
ちびママ奮闘記
TV: MINI-MOM'S INSPIRATIONAL DIARY
...BUT LATELY, IT'S PRETTY BAD WHEN I WATCH STUFF LIKE THAT.
HARA (PANIC) ハラ
HARA ハラ
STUPID!
THAT'S THE WRONG WAY!!
CHIRA チラ
CHIRA (GLANCE) チラ
YOU CAN DO IT!
にこにこ保育園 そつえんしき おゆうぎかい
SIGN: HAPPY SMILES NURSERY SCHOOL, GRADUATION CEREMONY, SCHOOL MUSICAL

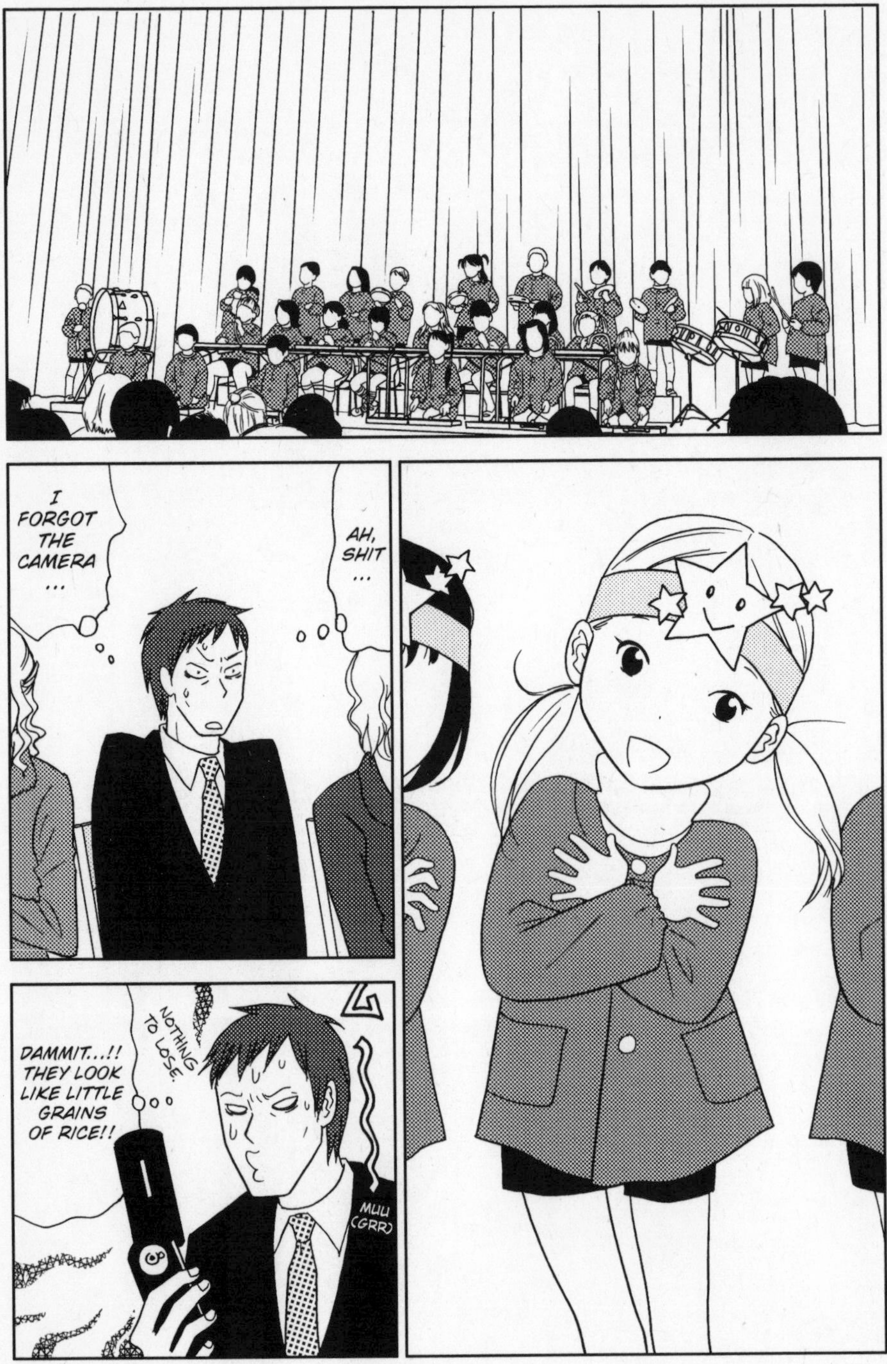
AH, SHIT ...
I FORGOT THE CAMERA ...
NOTHING TO LOSE.
DAMMIT...!! THEY LOOK LIKE LITTLE GRAINS OF RICE!!
MUU (GRR)

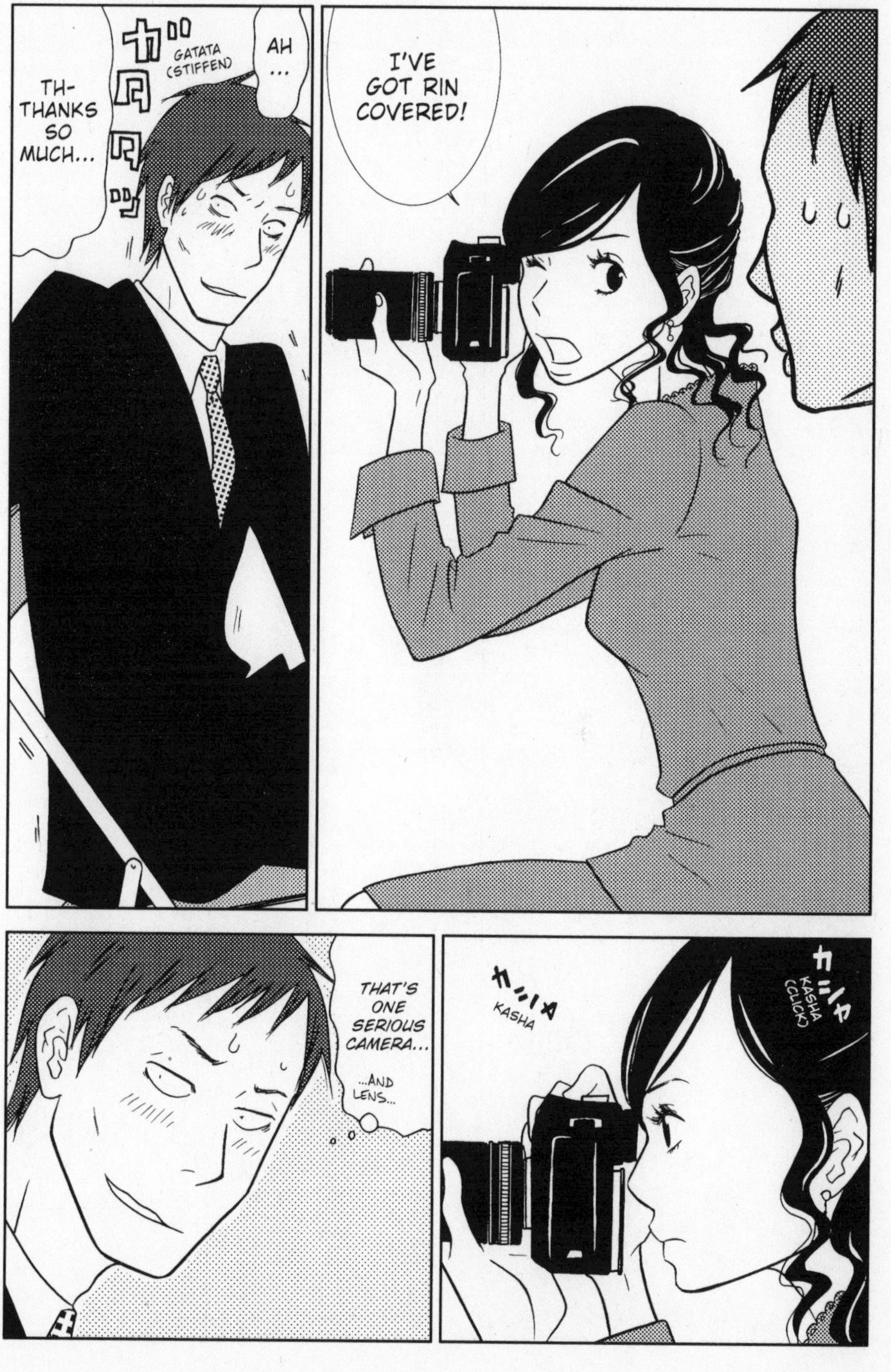
I'VE GOT RIN COVERED!
AH ...
GATATA (STIFFEN)
TH-THANKS SO MUCH...
KASHA (CLICK)
KASHA
THAT'S ONE SERIOUS CAMERA...
...AND LENS...

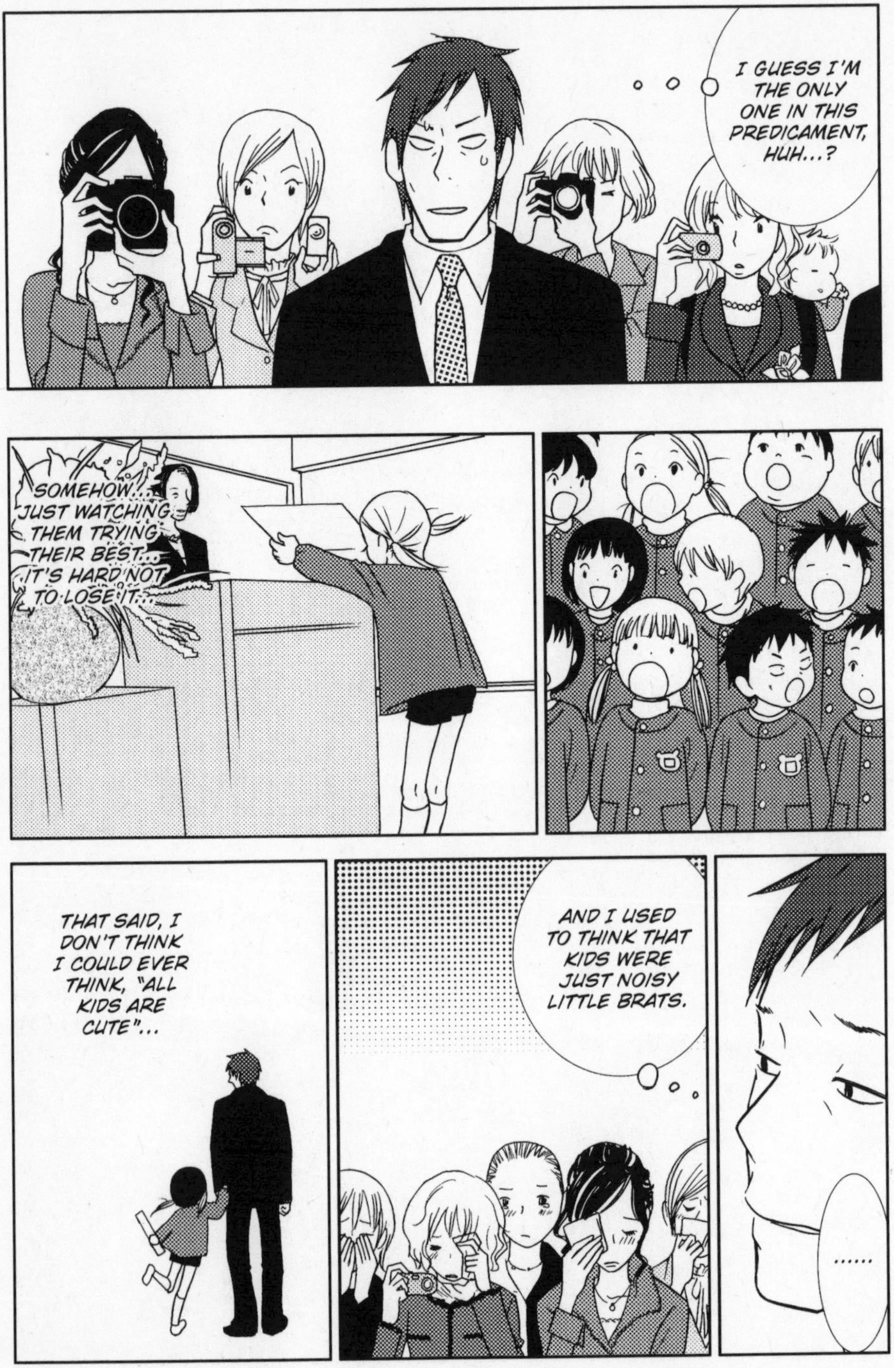
I GUESS I'M THE ONLY ONE IN THIS PREDICAMENT, HUH...?
SOMEHOW... JUST WATCHING THEM TRYING THEIR BEST... IT'S HARD NOT TO LOSE IT...
......
AND I USED TO THINK THAT KIDS WERE JUST NOISY LITTLE BRATS.
THAT SAID, I DON'T THINK I COULD EVER THINK, "ALL KIDS ARE CUTE"...

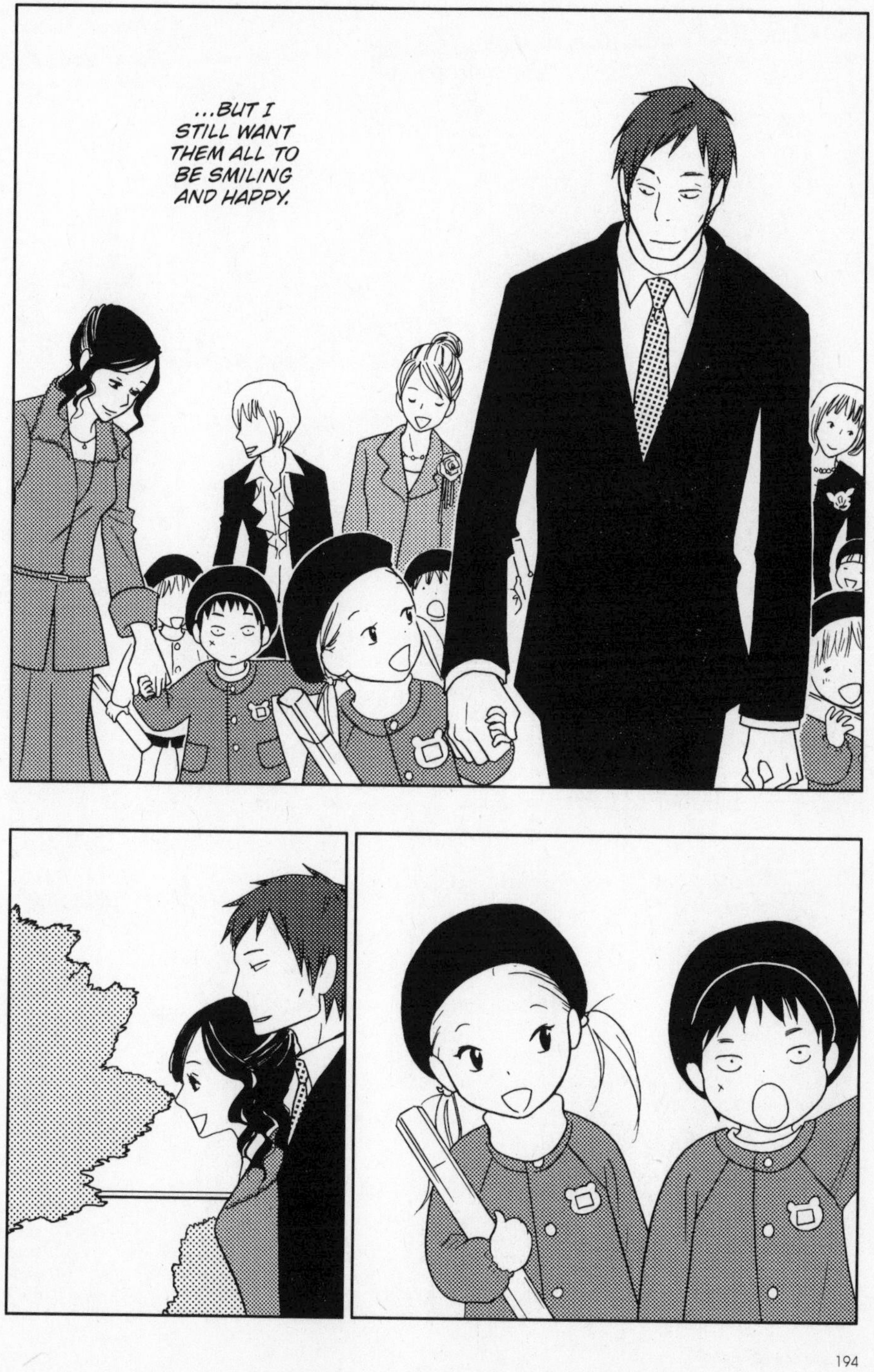
...BUT I STILL WANT THEM ALL TO BE SMILING AND HAPPY.

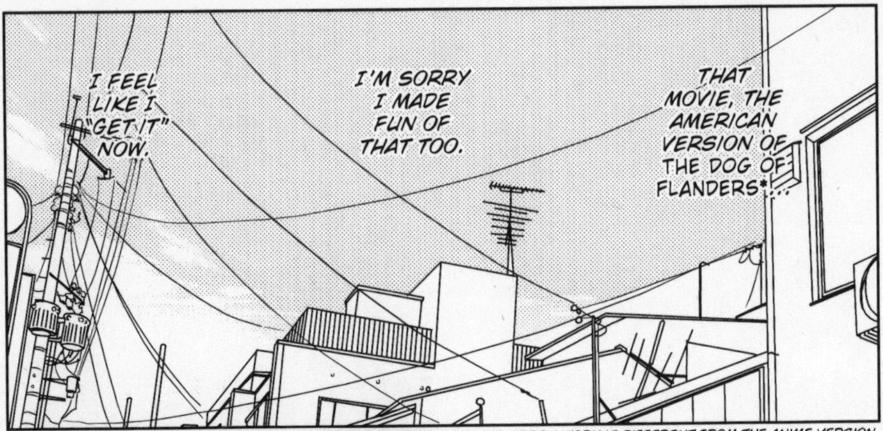
THAT MOVIE, THE AMERICAN VERSION OF THE DOG OF FLANDERS*...
I'M SORRY I MADE FUN OF THAT TOO.
I FEEL LIKE I "GET IT" NOW.

*THE ENDING TO THIS LIVE-ACTION WORK IS DIFFERENT FROM THE ANIME VERSION.

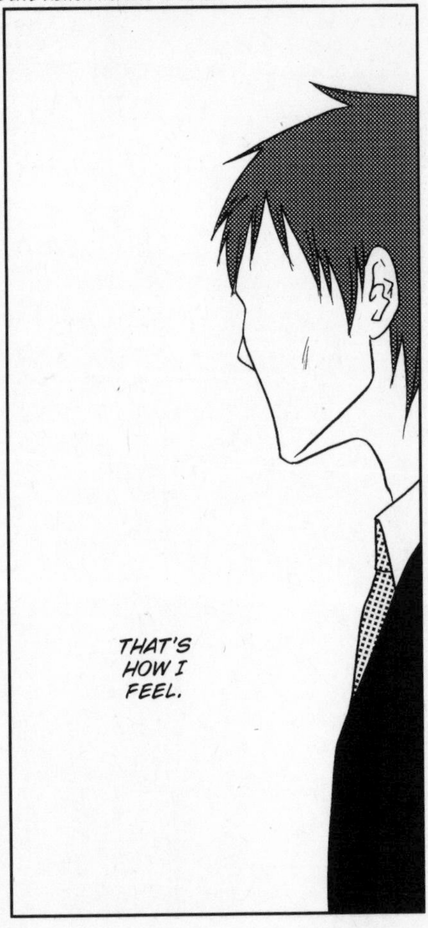
THAT'S HOW I FEEL.

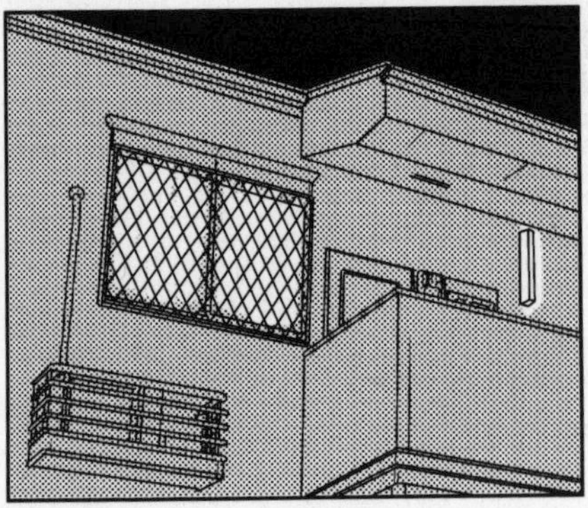

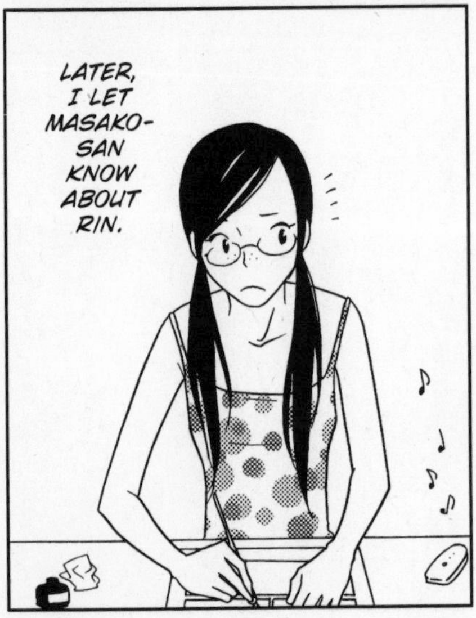
LATER, I LET MASAKO-SAN KNOW ABOUT RIN.

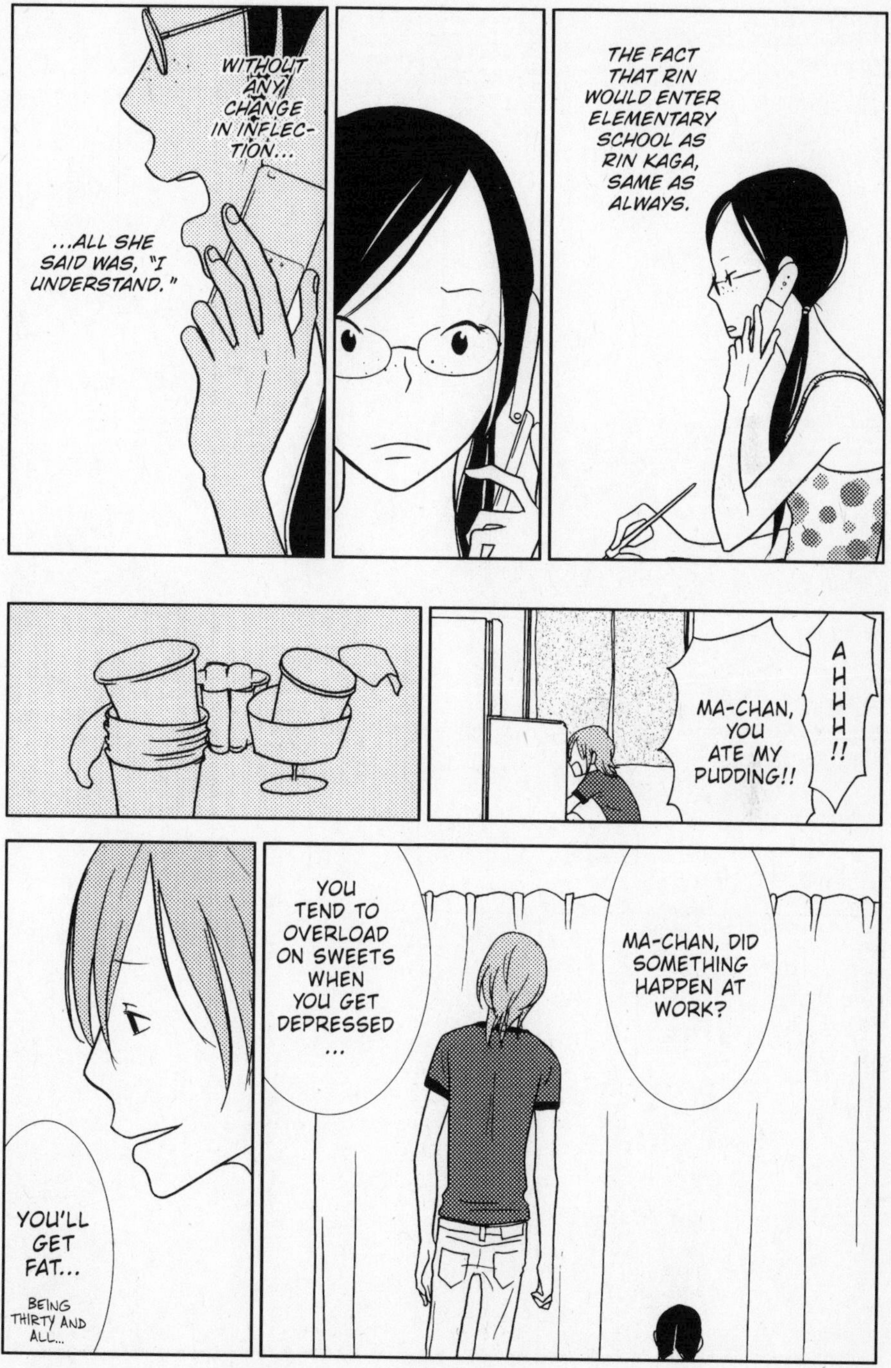
THE FACT THAT RIN WOULD ENTER ELEMENTARY SCHOOL AS RIN KAGA, SAME AS ALWAYS.
WITHOUT ANY CHANGE IN INFLECTION...
...ALL SHE SAID WAS, "I UNDERSTAND."
AHHH!!
MA-CHAN, YOU ATE MY PUDDING!!
MA-CHAN, DID SOMETHING HAPPEN AT WORK?
YOU TEND TO OVERLOAD ON SWEETS WHEN YOU GET DEPRESSED...
YOU'LL GET FAT...
BEING THIRTY AND ALL...

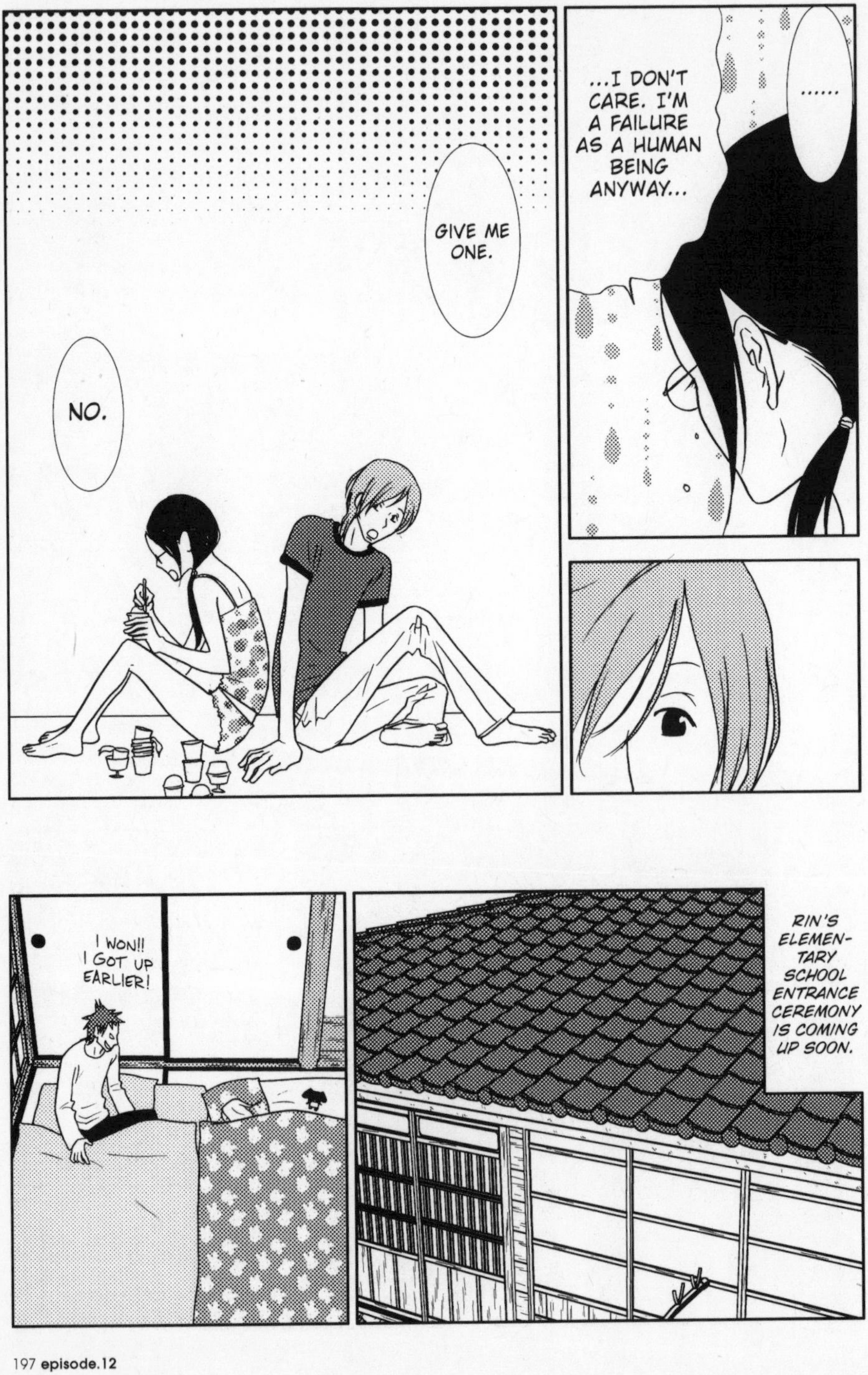
......
...I DON'T CARE. I'M A FAILURE AS A HUMAN BEING ANYWAY...
GIVE ME ONE.
NO.
RIN'S ELEMEN-TARY SCHOOL ENTRANCE CEREMONY IS COMING UP SOON.
I WON!! I GOT UP EARLIER!

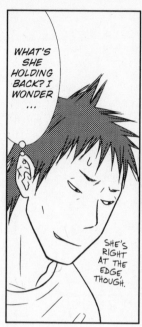

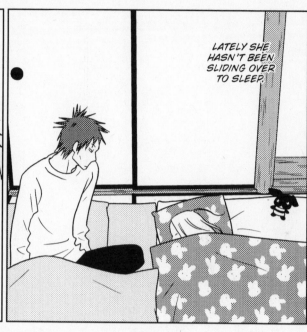

LATELY SHE HASN'T BEEN SLIDING OVER TO SLEEP.
WHAT'S SHE HOLDING BACK? I WONDER ...
SHE'S RIGHT AT THE EDGE, THOUGH.
WANT TO SIT WITH ME?
YUP.

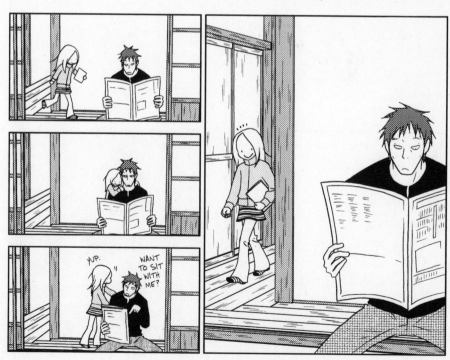

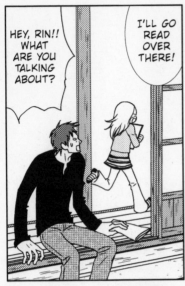

AH!
I CAN'T SIT ON LAPS EITHER!!
HUH!?
I'LL GO READ OVER THERE!
HEY, RIN!! WHAT ARE YOU TALKING ABOUT?
I'M A FIRST GRADER NOW!
SITTING IN LAPS IS AGAINST THE RULES!
... WHAT'S THAT ABOUT ...?
I GET IT...
THAT'S WHAT'S BEEN HOLDING HER BACK...
ALL MY FRIENDS SAY THAT TOO.
IT'S NOT EASY BECOMING A FIRST GRADER.
ONLY BABIES SIT IN LAPS.

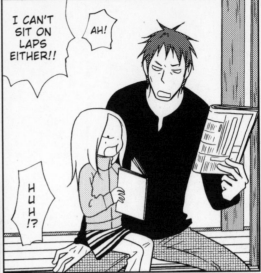

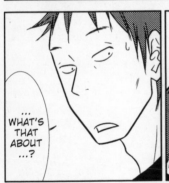

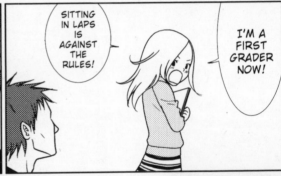

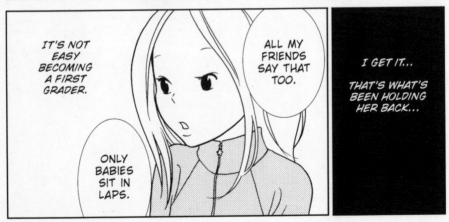

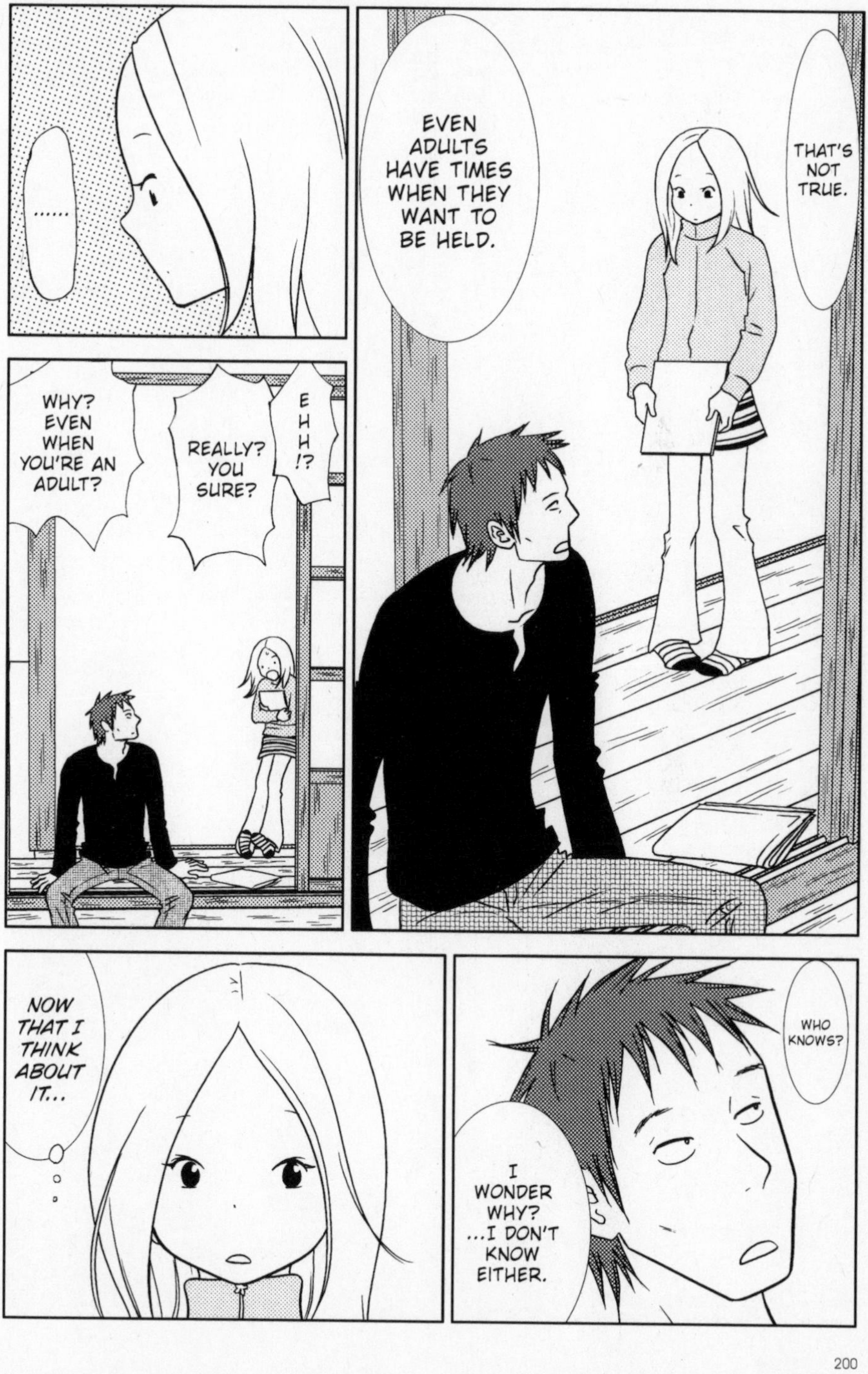
THAT'S NOT TRUE.
EVEN ADULTS HAVE TIMES WHEN THEY WANT TO BE HELD.
......
EHH!?
REALLY? YOU SURE?
WHY? EVEN WHEN YOU'RE AN ADULT?
WHO KNOWS?
I WONDER WHY? ...I DON'T KNOW EITHER.
NOW THAT I THINK ABOUT IT...

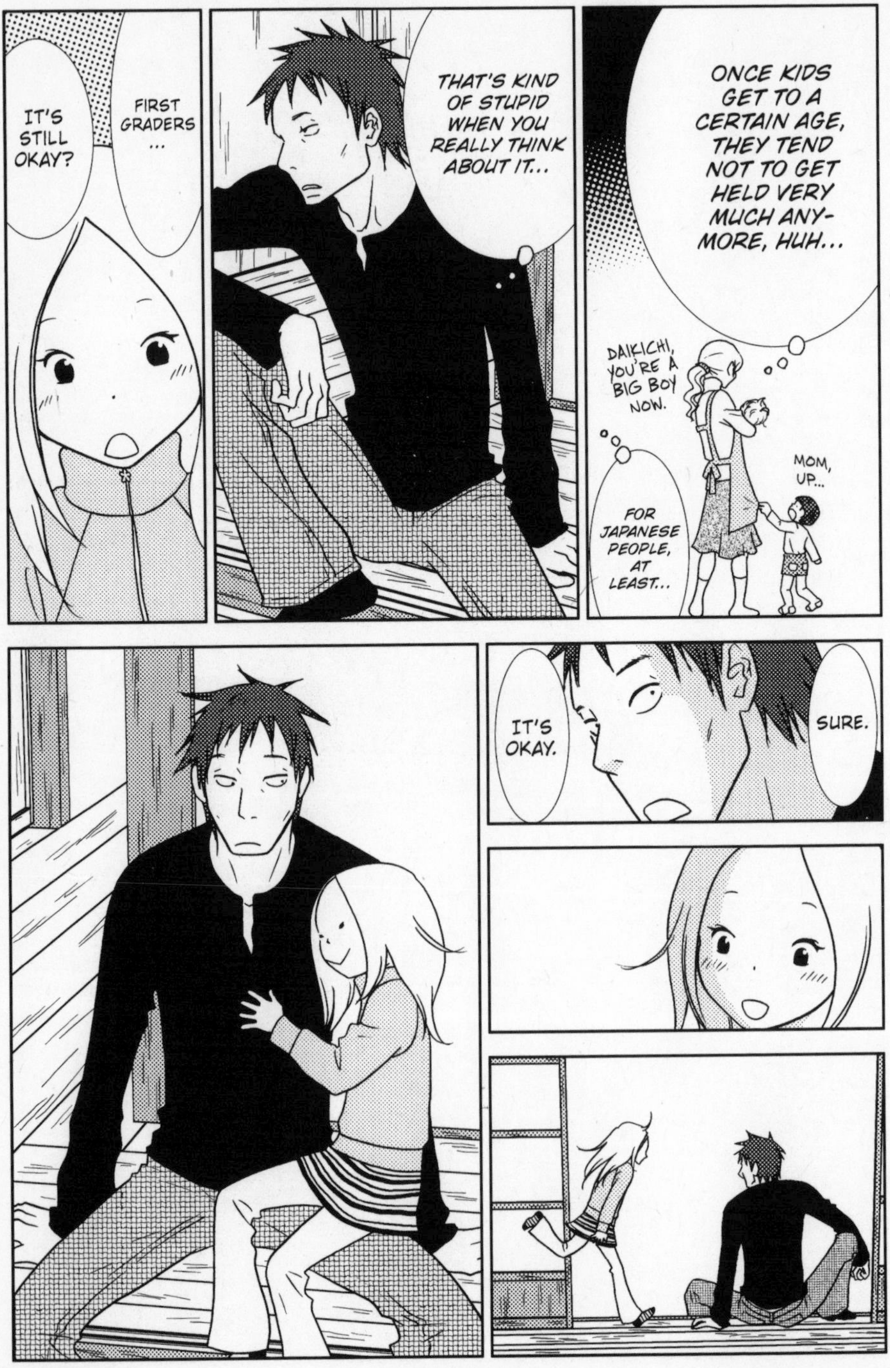
ONCE KIDS GET TO A CERTAIN AGE, THEY TEND NOT TO GET HELD VERY MUCH ANY-MORE, HUH...
DAIKICHI, YOU'RE A BIG BOY NOW.
MOM, UP...
FOR JAPANESE PEOPLE, AT LEAST...
THAT'S KIND OF STUPID WHEN YOU REALLY THINK ABOUT IT...
FIRST GRADERS ...
IT'S STILL OKAY?
SURE.
IT'S OKAY.

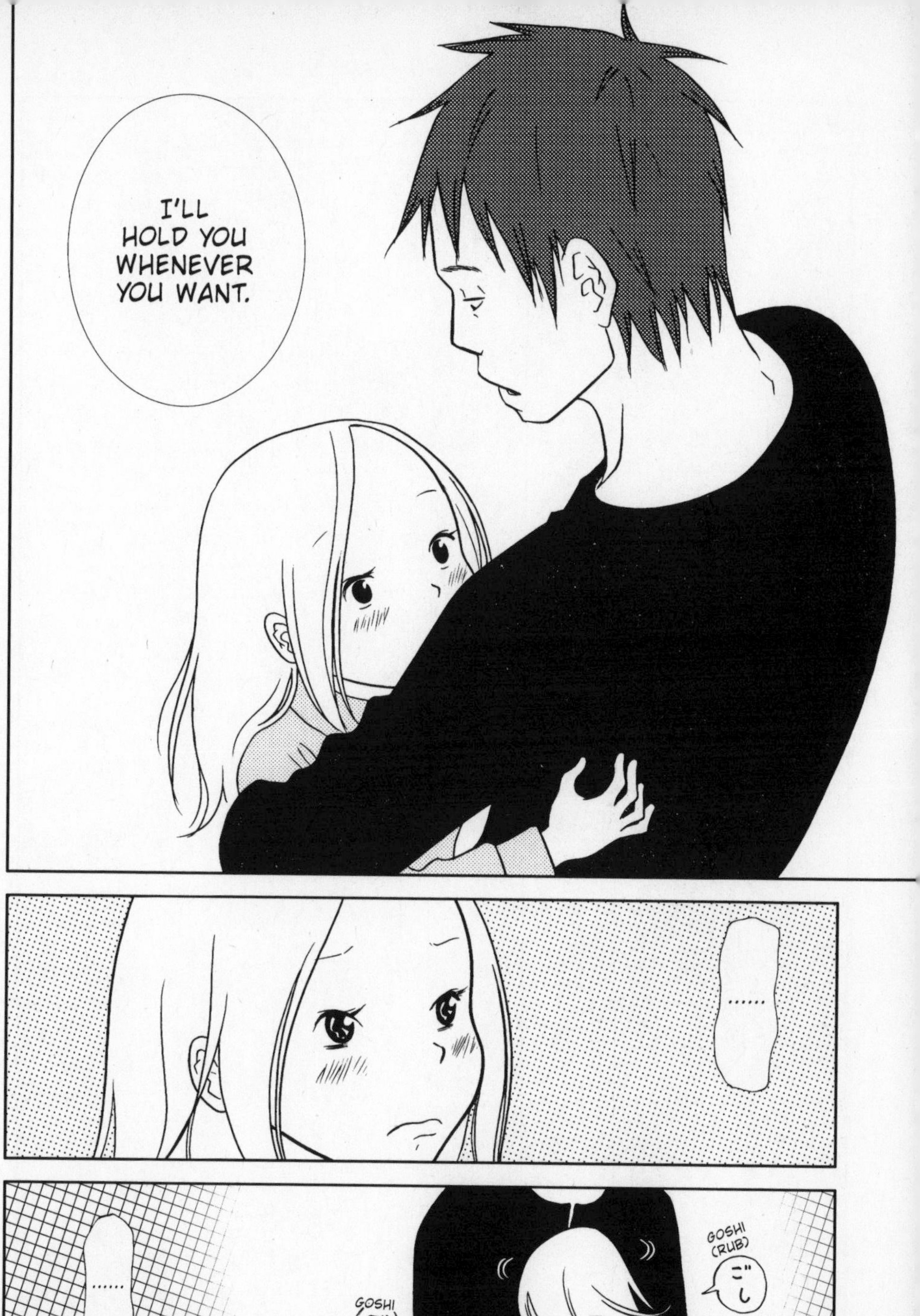
I'LL HOLD YOU WHENEVER YOU WANT.
......
GOSHI (RUB)
ごし
GOSHI
ごし
......

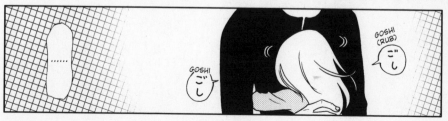

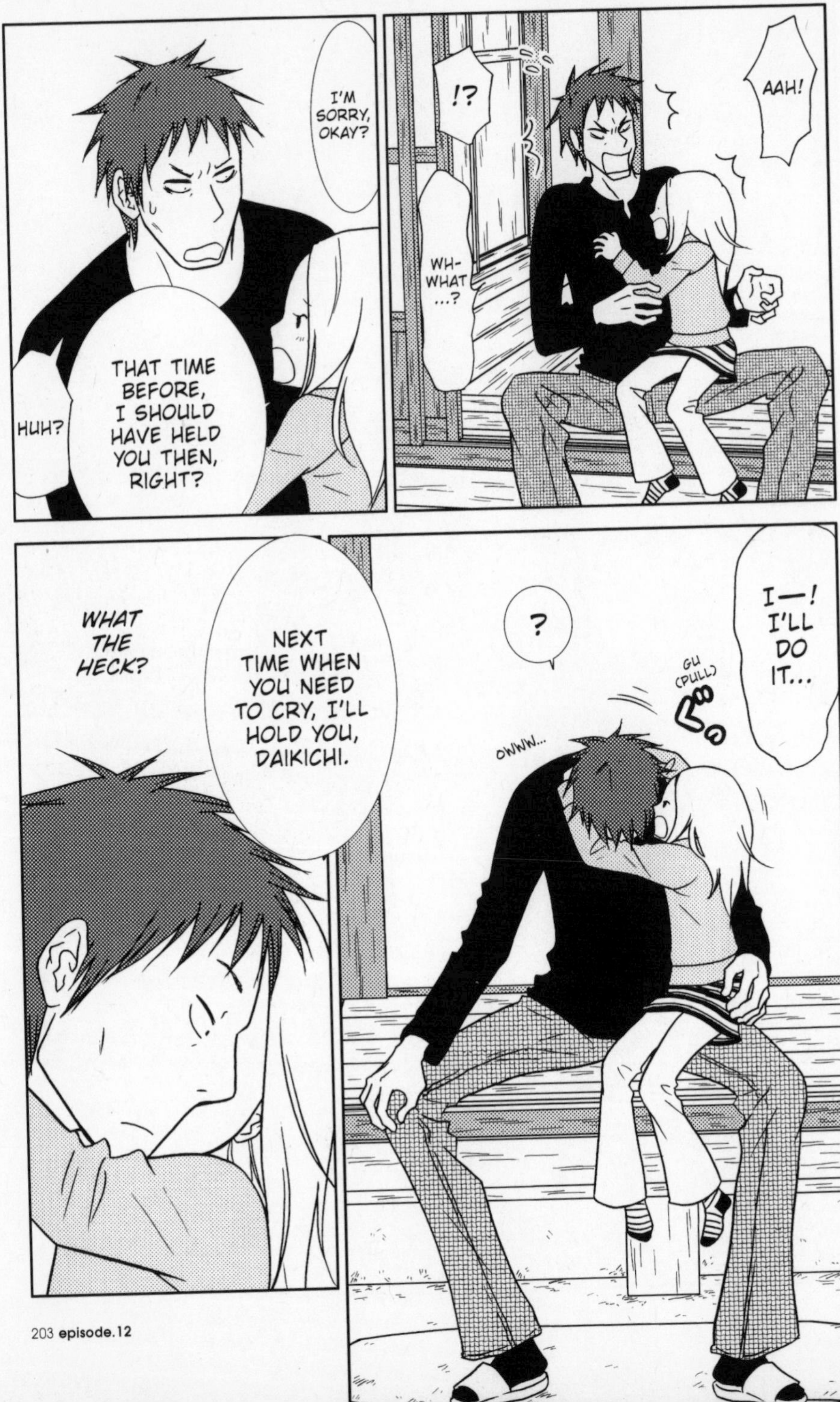
AAH!
!?
WH-WHAT...?
I'M SORRY, OKAY?
THAT TIME BEFORE, I SHOULD HAVE HELD YOU THEN, RIGHT?
HUH?
I—! I'LL DO IT...
GU (PULL)
?
OWWW...
NEXT TIME WHEN YOU NEED TO CRY, I'LL HOLD YOU, DAIKICHI.
WHAT THE HECK?

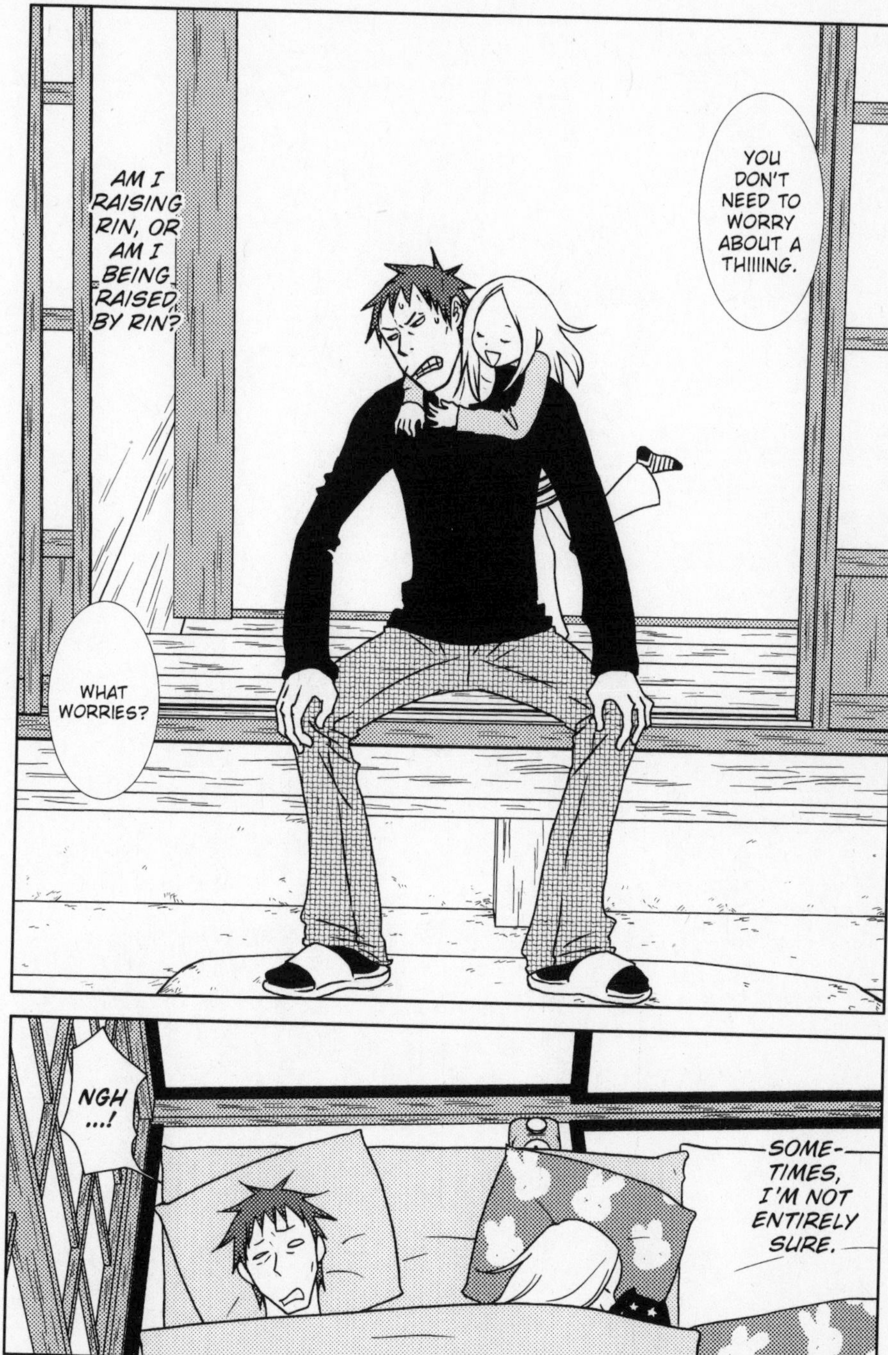
YOU DON'T NEED TO WORRY ABOUT A THIIIING.
AM I RAISING RIN, OR AM I BEING RAISED BY RIN?
WHAT WORRIES?
SOME-TIMES, I'M NOT ENTIRELY SURE.
NGH ...!

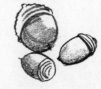

to be continued...

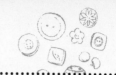
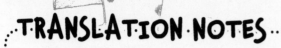

TRANSLATION NOTES

COMMON HONORIFICS

No honorific: Indicates familiarity or closeness; if used without permission or reason, addressing someone in this manner would constitute an insult.

-san: The Japanese equivalent of Mr./Mrs./Miss. If a situation calls for politeness, this is the fail-safe honorific.

-kun: Used most often when referring to boys (though it can be applied to girls as well), this indicates affection or familiarity. Occasionally used by older men among their peers, but it may also be used by anyone referring to a person of lower standing.

-chan: An affectionate honorific indicating familiarity used mostly in reference to girls; also used in reference to cute persons or animals of either gender.

Page 14
Showa: The period between approximately 1926 to 1989 during which Emperor Hirohito reigned in Japan.

Page 21
Japanese work etiquette: Although there are "standard work hours," it is usually frowned upon to follow these hours for work. Generally it is expected that workers arrive early and apologize if leaving earlier than a co-worker. It is considered improper to leave before the boss goes home.

Page 52
Going out drinking: Many workplaces and schools have a routine of participation in social parties where drinking is involved. Most often these are held in places such as restaurants, where the group can sit at one large table or use one section of the location. Employees are usually expected to participate to some extent, since it is considered a social aspect of work to strengthen the bond between coworkers. Drinking alcohol itself is not required, and all participants usually pay a set fee for all food, drink, and miscellaneous costs.

Page 56
Zashiki: Literally meaning a "room spread out for sitting," this is a room with floors completely laid out with *tatami*. There are workplace rules concerning seating.

Page 100
Taisho: The progressive period between approximately 1912 to 1926 during which Emperor Yoshihito reigned in Japan.

Page 116
"Sukeban-deka": A manga series that follows a girl gang member (*sukeban*) who is forced to play detective (*deka*) on behalf of the government. The hair of *sukeban* are generally wild and non-conformist.

Page 151
Mochitsuki: A traditional *mochi* (rice cake) pounding ceremony.

Page 152
Maron: Taken from the French *marron* which means "chestnut." Usually this flavor is used in sweets.

Page 153
Shuraba: Typically a fight, often between love rivals.

Page 167
Momotaro (picture of a child with a monkey and a dog): A Japanese folk tale in which a childless couple discovers a little boy inside a peach. The title character befriends a talking dog, monkey, and pheasant during his adventures.

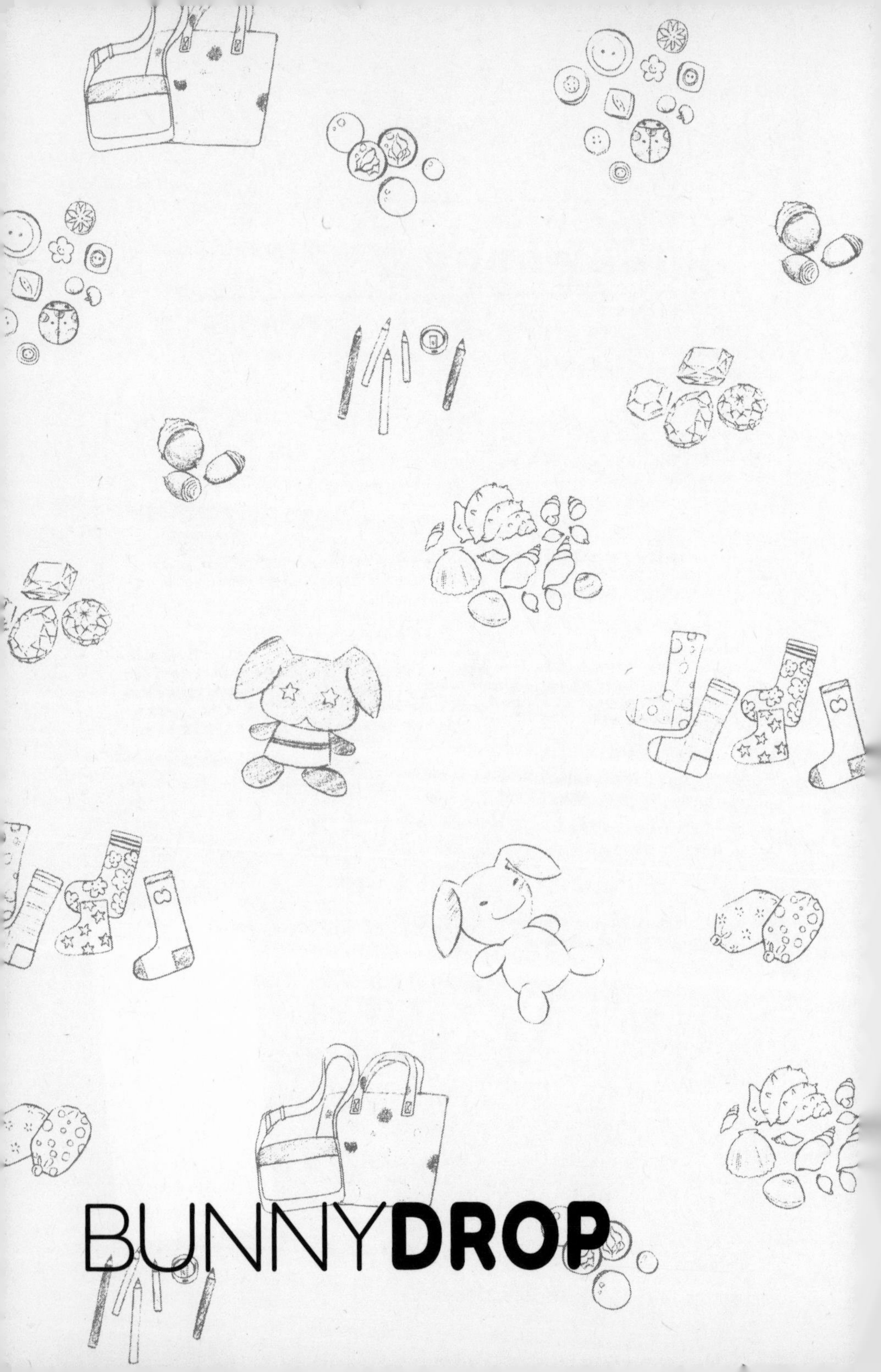

BUNNY DROP

BUNNY DROP ❷

YUMI UNITA

Translation: Kaori Inoue • Lettering: Alexis Eckerman

BUNNY DROP Vol. 2 © 2007 by Yumi Unita. All rights reserved. First published in Japan in 2007 by SHODENSHA PUBLISHING CO., LTD., Tokyo. English translation rights in USA, Canada, and UK arranged with SHODENSHA PUBLISHING CO., LTD. and Yen Press, LLC through Tuttle-Mori Agency, Inc., Tokyo.

English translation © 2010 by Yen Press, LLC

Yen Press
1290 Avenue of the Americas
New York, NY 10104

www.YenPress.com

Yen Press is an imprint of Yen Press, LLC. The Yen Press name and lo
trademarks of Yen Press, LLC.

First Yen Press Edition: September 2010

ISBN: 978-0-7595-3119-2

10 9 8

OPM

Printed in the United States of America